THE WILD GIRL
NATURAL MAN
AND THE MONSTER

D1714744

JULIA V. DOUTHWAITE

The Wild Girl Natural Man and the Monster

DANGEROUS EXPERIMENTS IN THE AGE OF ENLIGHTENMENT

THE UNIVERSITY OF CHICAGO PRESS
CHICAGO AND LONDON

JULIA V. DOUTHWAITE teaches French and comparative literature at the University of Notre Dame. She is author of *Exotic Women: Literary Heroines and Cultural Strategies in Ancien Régime France* (1992) and coeditor of the special issue of *EMF: Studies in Early Modern France* on cultural studies, vols. 6 and 7 (2000–2001, with David Lee Rubin).

The University of Chicago Press, Chicago 60637
The University of Chicago Press, Ltd., London
© 2002 by The University of Chicago
All rights reserved. Published 2002
Printed in the United States of America
11 10 09 08 07 06 05 04 03 02   1 2 3 4 5

ISBN: 0-226-16055-6 (cloth)
ISBN: 0-226-16056-4 (paper)

The University of Chicago Press gratefully acknowledges the support of the Institute for Scholarship in the Liberal Arts of the College of Arts and Letters of the University of Notre Dame in the publication of this book.

Library of Congress Cataloging-in-Publication Data

Douthwaite, Julia V.
The wild girl, natural man, and the monster : dangerous experiments in the Age of Enlightenment / Julia V. Douthwaite.
p. cm.
Includes bibliographical references and index.
ISBN 0-226-16055-6 (alk. paper)—ISBN 0-226-16056-4 (pbk. : alk. paper)
1. Philosophical anthropology—France—History—18th century. 2. French literature—18th century—History and criticism. 3. Philosophical anthropology—England—History—18th century. 4. English literature—18th century—History and criticism. I. Title.

BD450 .D665 2002
128′.09′033—dc21

2001008547

♾ The paper used in this publication meets the minimum requirements of the American National Standard for Information Sciences—Permanence of Paper for Printed Library Materials, ANSI Z39.48-1992.

This book is

dedicated to

Rich, Nicky, and Max,

my own "wild boys"

CONTENTS

ILLUSTRATIONS

ACKNOWLEDGMENTS

I am very glad to acknowledge the many people who have contributed to this book during the decade in which it came together, not only because my words may offer a tribute to their generosity but also because my acknowledgments in themselves are tied to the history of this undertaking. The idiosyncratic combination of materials analyzed in this book may make more sense to readers once they realize that I wrote it while raising two children from infancy to boyhood, in a historical moment that saw political and scientific developments of a most fascinating and unsettling nature. This era witnessed the failure of the Soviet experiment in social control and the consequent rise of troubled new nations in eastern Europe, as well as the success of genetic researches that have opened the door to the creation of strange new "Frankenfoods" and Dolly, the cloned sheep. Will cloning of human beings be far behind?

Along with the rapid changes in family structures and educational systems that also mark this epoch comes a sense of curious apprehension among early twenty-first-century Americans that recalls, in some ways, the mentality of late eighteenth-century Europeans. Now, as then, traditional social structures are giving way, and we are not quite sure what will take their place. Is it any wonder that now, as then, unprecedented numbers of readers turn to advice books for help with the most intimate aspects of their lives—childcare, procreation, and marriage? In the midst of all this turbulence—intellectual, scientific, political—not to mention the domestic turbulence of my own lively young household, I have turned to the following people and received sustenance and support for which I will always be grateful.

For research support, I thank the many students who have generously worked as my research assistants over the years, including Les Haygood, Dan Smith, Laura Winkiel, Maura Kenny, and Cecyll Seballos. This past year I was particularly fortunate to retain the services of L. M. Harteker, research assistant and editor extraordinaire, to whom I am very grateful for help in the final revision process. I would also like to thank Beth Bland for her administrative support during the past two years. Funding for various parts of this research was made possible by the National Endowment for the Humanities, the University of Notre Dame's Institute for Scholarship in the Liberal Arts, and Arizona State University's College of Liberal Arts and Sciences. Librarians are crucial to any long-distance research project; for their generous help with research and photography, I thank the Bibliothèque Nationale, the Musée de la Révolution Française, the British Library, the Mitchell Library in Glasgow, the National Library of Scotland, the Princeton University Library, and the Libraries of the University of Notre Dame. Special thanks go to Linda Gregory and the staff of the Interlibrary Loan Department at Notre Dame.

For mentoring along the way, I thank Chris Fox, J. Paul Hunter, Georges May, Bernadette Fort, and, as always, Joan DeJean. I would also like to thank colleagues at Notre Dame and other universities who were kind enough to read parts of the manuscript at various stages and to offer their constructive criticism and advice: Sue Lanser, Londa Schiebinger, John Waters, Ted Cachey, Kathy Biddick, Sandra Gustafson, Barbara Green, Christian Moevs, Glenn Hendler, Doris Bergen, Gail Bederman, Phil Sloan, Elizabeth Horan, Valerie Miner, and Joan McGregor. Many thanks to the editors and readers at the University of Chicago Press, as well, for their impeccable assistance in transforming the manuscript into a book.

A scholar does not succeed through research support alone; it is important to acknowledge the other kinds of life-enhancing aid I have received while writing this book: for their kindly care of my children, Eileen Byrne, Marian Appleton, Liz Appleton, and the staff of the Early Childhood Development Center at the University of Notre Dame. For friendship and fellowship over the years, Peaches Henry, Patty Chang, and Lesley Walker. For their unwavering belief that I could and would finish this project one day, my mother-in-law Regina Viglione and my mother, Mary Somerville. For his undying love, intellectual curiosity, and fine cuisine, my husband, Rich Viglione.

Some of the ideas in this book were earlier published in articles. Parts of chapter 1 appeared in "Rewriting the Savage: The Extraordinary Fictions of the Wild Girl of Champagne," *Eighteenth-Century Studies* 28, no. 2 (winter 1994–95): 163–92, published by Johns Hopkins University Press; and "*Homo ferus:* Between Monster and Model," *Eighteenth-Century Life* 20, no. 2 (May 1997):

176–202, published by Duke University Press. Some of the ideas in chapters 3, 4, and 5 are found in "Le Paradoxe de la féminité naturelle: Marie-Angélique, Sophie, et Nell" in *Sexualité, mariage, et famille au XVIIIe siècle,* ed. Olga Cragg and Rosena Davison (Québec: Presses de l'Université Laval, 1998), 159–72, and "Experimental Childrearing After Rousseau: Maria Edgeworth, *Practical Education,* and *Belinda,*" *Irish Journal of Feminist Studies* 2, no. 2 (December 1997): 35–56.

INTRODUCTION

In the eighteenth and early nineteenth centuries, science turned its attention to the nature of human beings. At the same time, a tremendous amount of literature kept a close eye on scientific inquiries into human nature and human potential. Although *Frankenstein* may be the first "science fiction," many earlier works build on an intimate knowledge of period science; their narratives are packed with explanations of scientific principles, accounts of apocryphal case studies, and experiments then in vogue—not to mention all the scientists, victims, and test subjects that went with them. Writers in all literary genres were very interested in the testing of human limits—both physical and moral—and they sought answers to questions about human nature and about the relation between mind and body. In their works one can see efforts to resolve perplexing questions about mankind's original state, the mind's independence from the body, and the process by which the body transforms nerve reactions into thought.[1] They argued whether morality is innate or acquired. If, as Locke professed, human nature is largely determined by environmental factors, how might one mold human beings? Is it possible to "perfect" mankind?

At the beginning of the eighteenth century, literary discourse was largely optimistic about science's ability to discover the truth about human nature. Although some writers expressed ambivalence about schemes to civilize or improve on "natural man"—whether found roving the woods, as in the case of feral children, or inhabiting faraway locales, as in the case of South Sea islanders—the general tendency was to assume that European society represented a paragon of intellectual and social progress that other peoples would do well to emulate. This pro-progress discourse culminated in the extravagant plans for social regeneration that were propounded by Jacobin legislators during the revolution and the terrifying "cleansing" of the Terror.

By the mid-1790s, literary opinion began to shift from optimism to apprehension. Many writers voiced concern that enthusiasm for social improvement might cloak private self-indulgence or veil a legislative arrogance that would create disappointing if not disastrous results. Long before the revolution, fault lines can be detected in the edifice of "progressive" thought. Through analysis of a variety of literary and scientific accounts of people attempting to tamper with, improve on, or perfect human beings, I will explore the ambivalences and contradictions of Enlightenment writing on perfecting mankind as it pertains to developments in science.

One of my goals is to track how literature reacted to developments in science and how various sites of sociability—parlor games, amateur experiments, fairground lectures—contributed to a new kind of popular science that itself was mirrored, debated, and ultimately condemned in literature. I study the discourse on improving mankind and explore it at key moments in Enlightenment history to see what this discourse wanted to achieve, what was at stake, and how its visions intimately linked literature and science.

I begin by discussing three famous "wild children" discovered in the eighteenth century as opportunities for contemporaries to learn (or fail to learn) about mankind's natural state. The texts and images that reported the discovery of Peter of Hanover (found in 1724), Marie-Angélique Leblanc (discovered in 1731), and Victor de l'Aveyron (captured in 1799) offer a privileged glimpse into period beliefs about mankind's difference from the beast and the means that might be used to civilize the uncivilized. Although all three children were deemed reparable and subjected to a variety of educational methods, especially language lessons, their mutism and proclivity for "savage" acts perplexed observers and raised doubts about their human status. Implicit in much of this material is a concern about having to admit the monstrous and a demonstrated resistance to doing so. Peter and Victor were visibly human (albeit somewhat uncouth), yet accounts of their lives seem unwilling to relocate the boundaries of civilization to include them. Marie-Angélique did become acculturated as a French woman, but her commentators prove unwilling to give up the attributes of monstrosity that defined her. All three cases were later considered failures because of the unscientific methods used to tame the children and the unsatisfactory results obtained.

The literary texts analyzed in this book present imaginative solutions to these unfortunate results insofar as they envision an analogous experiment, or part of an experiment, on a normative human subject in more controlled laboratory conditions. This material ranges from philosophical tales of animated statues and utopian schemes for "progressive" childrearing to Gothic tales of scientists gone berserk. Some carry the veneer of official science; others are explicitly products of the imagination. Although patently untrue, tales of animated statues, for instance, are woven into works of serious scholarship—Buffon's *Histoire naturelle* (1750), Condillac's *Traité des sensations* (1754) and Bonnet's *Essai analytique sur les facultés de l'âme* (1759)—and thus form a curious kind of documentary science fiction based on sensationist theories of the body's receptivity to the senses. Most intriguing is how these imaginary explorations into understanding human intelligence would inform ideas about social reform (or the undesirability of reform). As Adam Kuper has pointed out, "There are no neutral theories about human beings. Each carries a charge that can ignite a political program."[2] Whether it be related to the physical properties of sensibility or the potential for education, we find sensationist discourse guiding the thought of philosophers such as Helvétius, Condorcet, and Roussel in France and Hartley and Hume in Britain, taking on a very different ideological thrust in each, according to the writers' larger goals.

In its prescription of concrete means to draw the child's mind out of inertia into cognition, Rousseau's novel-treatise *Emile* (1762) provides the main point of departure for my literary discussions. Although drawing much from Locke's *Some Thoughts on Education* (1693) and the English Robinsonads (*Robinson Crusoe,* 1719, and Kirkby's *Automathes,* 1745), *Emile* exemplifies period ideas on human improvement and gives evidence for the close relations between literature and a variety of "scientific" sources, such as experiments on magnetism, tirades against charlatanism, and lessons borrowed from science books for children. The transition from the natural man's childhood to adulthood poses problems for Rousseau and other novelists, however, and suggests some of the ways progressive education could serve oppressive or abusive ends. The treatment of female "pupils of nature" is particularly interesting in this regard. By contrast to the moralistic tone of the British Robinsonads, the novels of Rousseau's followers Beaurieu (*L'Elève de la nature,* 1763) and Dulaurens (*Imirce ou la fille de la nature,* 1765) manifest a harsh materialism that presages Sade.

Alongside these literary readings, I explore real-life experiments applying Rousseauian methods to childrearing and the disastrous results that ensued. Through analysis of the correspondence, diaries, and memoirs of such famous parent-pedagogues as Richard Lovell Edgeworth, Manon Roland,

and Thomas Day, we see how people perceived children to have an essential nature that was pure—a nature that, if retained into adulthood, might somehow create a superior individual. In all three cases, however, the experiment ends in failure and prompts reflections on the dangers of progressive education and its unrealistic hopes for perfecting mankind. My discussion of real-life Rousseauian pedagogy ends with two works designed explicitly to supplement and correct the flaws in *Emile:* Genlis's fictional scheme of rational childrearing, *Adèle et Théodore* (1782), and the Edgeworths' weighty manual, *Practical Education* (1798), both of which are crammed with long lists of tools and materials for learning and advice for experimental educators.

The fault lines inherent in these texts of enlightened rationalism underwent a seismic shift in the revolutionary period, when the ideological tensions between natural rights and civil responsibilities—which run through all the discourse on perfecting mankind—suddenly created a schism between republican and loyalist groups. I explore the dialectical meanings of perfectibility in this era through imagery and metaphors of the revolutionary *homme régénéré* (regenerated man) and his female counterparts. After following the rise and fall of this imagery in republican and counterrevolutionary writings during the tumultuous years 1789–96, I explore literary works that pursue the troubling consequences of regeneration in the realm of pedagogy and scientific research. Franco-English antagonisms can be read in the "pedagogical" fictions of Edgeworth (*Belinda,* 1801) and Fenwick (*Secresy,* 1795), both of which depict French influences as a symptom of dangerous moral and political proclivities. The sinister implications of experimental method, which run through various other texts at hand, explode into full-fledged dystopias in the last works analyzed here, Révéroni Saint-Cyr's *Pauliska* (1798) and Sade's *Justine* (1791), *Juliette* (1797), and *Les 120 Journées de Sodome* (1785). *Frankenstein* (1818) forms the logical endpoint to this study. In the epilogue I consider *Frankenstein*'s relevance to period debates on mankind's potential for regeneration—or its mirror image, degeneration—and return to the issues of monstrosity raised early in my study to show the importance of aesthetics in efforts to define a normative human nature.

I contend that literature from the fin de siècle allows us to see just how far people's attitudes had fallen from the mid-century heyday of enlightened confidence. Unlike Barbara Stafford, who claims that there was no significant break between pre-revolutionary and postrevolutionary literature of experimentalism, I argue that something peculiar does emerge in the works of Fenwick, Edgeworth, Sade, Révéroni Saint-Cyr, and Shelley.[3] The literature of the 1790s and 1800s in England and France affords us a privileged glimpse into the breakdown of public confidence in the practices that purported to perfect mankind.

Any attempt to explore relations between experiments in fiction and in science must address the very broad meanings of "human science" in this period. In eighteenth-century usage, the "sciences of man" included what we know as the fields of biology, anthropology, sociology, psychology, comparative anatomy, medicine, and natural history, all of which would gradually be separated into specialized forms of study in the first decades of the nineteenth century. For the modern reader, issues of disciplinary nomenclature are further confused when one realizes that in the eighteenth century, writers such as Buffon, whom we now call a "naturalist," were commonly labeled "physicists" *(physiciens)* and when one considers that some of the fields listed above were also included under the aegis of "experimental physics" *(la physique expérimentale)*. This label was used to underline the experimental methods of "positive sciences" such as plant and animal anatomy and other "arts that produce considerable changes in natural beings," as a mid-century treatise put it.[4]

Our age comes at the end of a long process, which began in the 1700s, through which the sciences have become highly specialized and increasingly inaccessible to nonspecialists. In the first half of the eighteenth century, the distinction between scientists and amateurs (otherwise known as *curieux* or *virtuosi*) was unclear. In the early part of the period, this "human science" embraced all kinds of amateur contributions, including eyewitness accounts of natural history, reports of salon games, self-experimentation, and oddities displayed in the "market of curiosities." These contributions were gradually disowned as science developed into separate disciplines complete with their own specialized techniques, methodology, and theory, thus knowledge and authority. The boundaries dividing genres such as electrical demonstrations, lectures on chemistry, and public sessions at the Académie des Sciences were far from rigid, and people moved from one setting to another with ease. The historian Mary Terrall reminds us that practitioners of science "looked to the cultured nobility for approval and validation" and represented their work to the urban elite as "useful, amusing, and above all, difficult."[5]

Toward the end of the 1700s, however, the tenor of these interactions changed as the academy distanced itself from the display of curiosities tailored for polite consumption. Responding to the threat of charlatans such as Mesmer and Cagliostro, and to the increasing prestige of its members, the institution sought to strengthen its ties to the state and requested that its members use their authority to combat various perceived dangers, instead of sharing discoveries with the public. The revolution dealt a serious blow to any such distinctions, however, by dismantling the time-honored institutions of scientific learning and leveling all people to the status of *citoyen* (or *officiers de santé* for medical practitioners). The literature of distrust seen in Sade and Réveroni may well reflect this chaotic milieu, as well as the authors' apprehension of the move away from an accessible "salon science" toward a more professional kind of science that operated upon rhetorical and methodological conventions inaccessible to the uninitiated.

Nevertheless, the typical eighteenth-century scholar still believed that a good deal of weighing, measuring, and testing would likely reveal new facts about nature that would be serviceable to mankind,[6] and journals quickly printed reports from readers "especially these days, when one searches eagerly for everything connected with some discovery," as the *Journal de Bruxelles* wrote in 1784.[7] The *Encyclopédie* article "Experiment" approved this trend, declaring: "The practice of making *experiments* has been quite widespread in Europe for several years; as a result philosophical knowledge has grown and become better known."[8] Conversely, lack of curiosity was held to connote stupidity; the free-thinking doctor and botanist Erasmus Darwin joked with his friends at the progressive Lunar Society in Birmingham that a fool is "a man who never tried an experiment in his life."[9] As scientific societies grew in the capitals and provinces, and new publications flooded the market, popularizing science (or "natural philosophy") for amateurs, women, and children, experimentation became an accessible and popular pastime for many middle- and upper-class people in England and France.[10]

The discourse on perfecting mankind relies on this amateur scientism. To perfect something, one must first understand it, then adjust it to achieve an ideal standard or goal. The two efforts—to comprehend and to intervene in natural functions—are often intertwined, as in Dr. Charles Vandermonde's *Essai sur la manière de perfectionner l'espèce humaine* (1756). Vandermonde's ambitious treatise relies on the premise that humans, especially while young, are eminently perfectible. Children may be improved by a wide array of measures before birth and afterwards.[11] Although Vandermonde does not guarantee that better children will be produced through these techniques, implicit in his work and in that of many of his contemporaries is the effort to identify and control the variables that govern felicitous conception and development of children and thus to improve on the adult population. Indeed, Vandermonde's reasoning derived from successful breeding experiments, as he wrote: "Since one has succeeded in perfecting the race of horses, dogs, cats, chickens, [and] canaries, why would one not try to improve the human species?"[12] The human body was the site of much speculation and testing during this period. Although anatomists and surgeons had made important discoveries about human physiology as regards the function of the placenta and the ocular nerves, for instance, knowledge remained inadequate. Scientists may have agreed in principle with Boyle that human vivisection was a "violation of the laws, not only of divinity but humanity,"[13] but many nevertheless lamented that the great inroads being made into animal physiology could not be pursued—or were wilfully neglected—with human subjects.

Electrical experiments were particularly popular and often used the human body as a conductor. Although such work was not meant to decipher the secrets of physiology or to improve mankind as such, it is relevant for the cavalier attitude it reveals toward the human subject. Electrical trials, common parlor games in Parisian salons from the 1760s through the 1780s, often involved extensive human circuits. Le Monnier electrified 140 courtiers in the presence of the king on one occasion; never to be outdone, Nollet shocked 180 gendarmes in one human circuit and later performed the same feat on 200 Carthusians. "It is singular to see the multitude of different gestures, and to hear the instantaneous exclamation of those surprised by the shock," wrote one eyewitness.[14] Children were not exempt from such efforts; indeed, the apparatus known as the "electrified boy" (fig. 1) became a fixture in public performances. Devised by the lecturer Stephen Gray to increase the drama of his demonstrations, in this demonstration a boy—often a charity case—was suspended by silk cords and exposed to different electrical currents to attract leaf metal and other substances, which played the part of electrical receivers. The ostensible purpose of this demonstration was to prove that electricity could be communicated over distance and still produce known effects, which practitioners such as Gray and Nollet explained resulted from "effluvia" being stimulated across the air. But such experimentation brought risks; electrified subjects were known to suffer side effects ranging from headaches and blurred vision to death.[15] Nevertheless, most early to mid-eighteenth century writing on experimentation downplayed potential risks and embraced science for its transformative potential.

Drawing on the literary and cultural history of science in the eighteenth century, my book concentrates on a variety of discourses about human nature (how to know it and how to improve or perfect it) that were produced by writers who may have not been professional scientists but who certainly participated in science. This literary history includes in its discourse talk

FIGURE I

The Electrified Boy. Detail from Johann Gabriel Doppelmayr, *Neu-entdeckte Phaenomena von Bewunderns-würdigen Würckungen der Natur* . . . (Nuremberg: Johann Joseph Fleischmann, 1744), 89. Courtesy the Bancroft Library, University of California, Berkeley.

about science and what new things scientists were doing in this period. Central to both are the ways in which truth was constructed and how settings and tools were carefully orchestrated to create the image of performing science. The technology of *staging* scientific displays runs through many of the texts analyzed in this book, as does an interest in strategies of visualization. Common to both fictional and physical experiments was the desire to visualize new knowledge about living creatures and to make this knowledge accessible to the public. Just as contemporary scientists devised ingenious techniques of performing their discoveries in public experiments, in science books, or in machines such as the air pump, condensing engine, or electrical machine, so did novelists stage their pedagogical theories in carefully designed language, actions, and fictional apparatus.

The regulatory public eye is another concern shared by both scientific and literary writers. The public eye played a key role in experimental inquiry; it was a means of guaranteeing the scientist's veracity and of stimulating new discoveries. The image of a witness recurs in many literary experiments as well, as thematized in the tensions between public utility and private self-indulgence. It is important to understand what "experimentalism" meant, because people wrote about experiments and tried to shape them using words. They located meanings in such practices, criticized them, commended them, and projected them onto a variety of situations. The resulting discourse forms a kind of public participatory science.

Although historians of science such as Simon Schaffer, Jan Golinski, and Geoffrey Sutton and the art historian Barbara Stafford have recently published pioneering work revealing the diversity of practices, assumptions, and disciplinary conventions governing the widespread vogue of experimentalism in eighteenth-century France and Britain, their insights have had relatively few repercussions in literary history.[16] The reception history of G. S. Rousseau has shown that science texts held a prominent market share in eighteenth-century publishing and that readers of novels were likely well-versed in the scientific literature of their day.[17] That literature parodied science is well known, thanks to the work of Serge Soupel, who showed how English novelists mocked the obtuse vocabulary and pedantry found in works of natural history, astronomy, and especially medicine.[18] More recently, Anne Vila has demonstrated the intricate relations between works of eighteenth-century French fiction and medicine, including structural connections that are deeper than rhetoric. Vila's analysis is particularly acute to the diagnostic relation between patient and physician; she makes sense out of Diderot's novel *La Religieuse,* for instance, by revealing how the narrative simulates the patient-physician rapport advocated by Diderot's model, the famous doctor Bordeu.[19]

More important for my purposes, John Bender has addressed the epistemological similarities of literary and scientific texts during this period. Although later novels would lean more heavily toward the reader's identification, and later scientific texts would require documentary evidence in order to be taken as true, in the mid-eighteenth-century, Bender claims, both scientific and literary texts defined accuracy the same way. Contemporaries attributed "truth value" to any representation that "contextualized empirical sense-based 'facts' by arraying them in probable explanatory networks—be these experimental cases and reports or manifest fictional narratives."[20] This helps us understand why we find the same rhetorical strategies being used by literary and scientific authors to simulate plausible experiments and to defend their works against charges of implausibility or unfounded hypotheses. Some key facets of literature and science in the eighteenth century, then, have been explored, but connections between the literary texts and scientific practices of experimentalism have been largely neglected. And yet it is crucial to understand this history, for the discourse on experimentalism informs some of the most famous—and infamous—literary works produced in the eighteenth and early nineteenth centuries.

The Wild Girl, Natural Man, and the Monster is a literary history that seeks to show how Enlightenment writers conceptualized mankind as an infinitely malleable entity, for better or for worse. In both the Rousseauian experiments and the accounts of wild children, there is a great sense of irony and contradiction in that the "improvements" achieved with human subjects were, in the end, found to be unpalatable. For many writers, such schemes took on increasingly sinister overtones in the postrevolutionary years; indeed, the Jacobins' infamous attempts to "create a new people" incarnated the fears of a human science run amok. And as science grew more reliant on sophisticated apparatus and developed a disciplinary identity closed to nonspecialists, the representation of human experiments in literature became increasingly fraught with anxieties about the regulatory public eye and the dangers of meddling with nature. Although dreams of improving human beings did not entirely die out (witness the rise of eugenics in the later nineteenth century), the nightmarish visions of scientists scrutinizing and abusing human subjects seen in the fictions of Réveroni Saint-Cyr, Sade, and Shelley signaled the end of one strand of Enlightenment thought.

—CHAPTER ONE—

Wild Children

ESTABLISHING THE BOUNDARIES OF NATURE AND SCIENCE

Accounts of children found in the wild have long attracted the attention of storytellers and scholars. The mythological ancestry of such children goes back to ancient legends of children being raised by animals: Zeus (suckled by the she-goat Amalthea), Hippothoos (nursed by a mare), or the most celebrated, Romulus and Remus (nurtured by a she-wolf). Lucien Malson, in his much-contested study *Les Enfants sauvages* (1964), listed fifty-three reported cases of children abandoned in the wild dating from the fourteenth century to the twentieth, the most famous being Victor de l'Aveyron (discovered in 1797) and Kaspar Hauser (found in 1828).[1] These two cases alone have generated scores of scholarly works and retellings of the legends, many of which have achieved something like classic status.[2] Nevertheless, the focus of this scholarship has remained rather consistent.[3] What motivated me to revisit this well-trodden ground were my suspicions that some parts of this history—particularly as regards Marie-Angélique Leblanc—were missing and that a careful look at the cases from the eighteenth century would allow us to understand better what contemporaries meant when they proposed to define and improve on mankind.

For all the attention she received during her lifetime, it is surprising that Marie-Angélique Leblanc has been largely ignored by scholars of the eighteenth century. Although the French scholar Franck Tinland did much to prove the historical significance of her experience, he too has been neglected by English-language scholars.[4] Some simply dismiss Leblanc's case as a "bizarre episode" unworthy of analysis, and even in the many sources that include her in their lists of wild children, she is often dismissed as a hoax.[5] Wild children typically have been studied not by historians but by developmental psychologists whose main interest has been to answer questions regarding child development, language acquisition, humans' potential to bond with animals, and perhaps even more important, the power of science to overturn the effects of infantile trauma. Since Marie-Angélique never suffered total isolation or cohabited with wolves, and records of her early years and language learning are sketchy, her case holds little interest for such scholars. But for students of eighteenth-century literary and cultural history, this case is a treasure. My study seeks to analyze the history of Leblanc and, to a lesser extent, of her better-known contemporaries Peter of Hanover and Victor de l'Aveyron, because their experiences and the written accounts they inspired can afford us a privileged glimpse into some of the most important period debates regarding the limits and potentials of human malleability.

Accounts of wild children exemplify the great variety of conceptual devices that eighteenth-century Europe had for talking about savagery and civilization. These devices range from pseudoscientific inquiries into humanity's original nature and institutional schemes for improving society through control of undesirables to sensational tales of "surprising savages" and anthropomorphic apes. As period audiences likened these children to other monsters in the contemporary market of curiosities, so too period writers captured the children, so to speak, with familiar rhetorical strategies and narrative frames, with historically specific practices of interpretation and testimony. Children found in the wild posed wrenching questions about mankind's potential—both physical and moral. Some natural historians seized on the odd physiognomy and behavior of these children to fill in the links of taxonomies by inventing a new category, *Homines feri,* as an intermediary species between man and ape. Although the resultant narratives are descriptive rather than explanatory or prescriptive, they carried powerful moral implications by suggesting that the "great chain of being" might be ordered differently than once thought and by warning that mankind's superiority over the animal kingdom might not be absolute. Inspired by religious zeal, other writers used the children as evidence of mankind's postlapsarian propensity for evil and the hard work demanded for redemption. Whereas scientists claimed that the children existed on the boundaries between man and ape, moralists claimed that they inhabited an ambiguous limbo between man and his monstrous, violent ancestors.

Justified by such concerns, many writers celebrated the power of European culture to tame the wild children through speech and religious training, or, in the case of Victor, an experimental program of sensory and cognitive instruction. Alongside the celebratory visions of wild men leaving behind their simian origins to become fully civilized, however, we find anxious notes of caution for the subjects' well-being and suggestions that it would have been better just to leave them where they were. Implicit in this material are a concern about having to admit that monstrous tendencies inhabit all human beings, and a demonstrated resistance to doing so. Peter and Victor were visibly human (albeit somewhat uncouth), yet accounts of their lives seem unwilling to relocate the boundaries of civilization to include them. Marie-Angélique did become acculturated as a French woman, but her commentators prove somewhat unwilling to give up the attributes of monstrosity which defined her.

Nevertheless, the hopes and fears expressed in these accounts constitute one strand of the Enlightenment discourse on perfectibility. Paradoxically, these texts depict an epistemological shift that runs counter to the literary history of this period, which charts a story of decline. The history of wild children depicts an arc of rising ambitions. The reactions to the discovery of Peter, Marie-Angélique, and Victor reveal a shift from early apprehensions about mankind's place on the "great chain of being" and moral concerns about humanity's postlapsarian nature to a later stance of optimism about the powers of science to improve and even cure victims of isolation. This chiasmus effect is related to the changing status of science and fiction in the period. The writers I cite participated in science by having opinions and criticisms and by writing about its amateur application. The writers treated in chapters 2–5 were more closely aligned with philosophy or fiction than with science. As "human science" gradually moved out of the salon or coffeehouse into its new institutional homes, it moved out of the grasp of the educated gentry to become the special domain of the learned. It sprouted a number of discrete fields of study with increasingly costly and complicated apparatus, technical language, and techniques, and thus excluded the cultivated reader from engaging in serious science. This shift in scientific practice formed a chiasmus: whereas fictional texts increasingly depicted scientists as villains, scientific writings expressed ever greater optimism about technical mastery.

The main focus of this chapter is on theories of human nature and perfectibility as applied to the experience of three children found in the wild. Through analysis of a variety of texts, I aim to answer the following questions: How did people conceive of mankind's relation to beast? What constituted potential sites of improvement for the human mind and body? What measures were taken to realize such improvement? The natural history debates are the place to look for discourse speaking to these questions. Discourse on the wild children also shows how each got caught up in the widespread fascination with defining and improving on mankind, though with very different results.

DEFINING THE HUMAN

Although many eighteenth-century writers declared the "science of man" to be an enterprise of great importance, few agreed on the methods to use. Throughout the period self-proclaimed proponents of the empirical "new science"—many of them medical doctors[6]—attributed physical phenomena to moral causes and animated scientific taxonomies with creatures of myth. Comparative anatomy, used by such prominent figures as Tyson and La Mettrie, was one of the most important methods practiced in the eighteenth century, but it was often subsumed in speculative theories on human and primate morality or sensational suggestions of cross-species hybridization.[7]

In book 3 of his *Essay Concerning Human Understanding* (1690), John Locke pointed to one of the characteristic problems in early science. Describing the process by which scientists create taxonomies of human and animal species, Locke argued that "man" is an arbitrary label, given or withheld according to the observer's eye alone. Attempts at classification are made particularly difficult by creatures whose senses—and thus intellect—are impaired, such as wild children and deaf-mutes:

> There are creatures in the world that have shapes like ours, but are hairy, and want language and reason. There are naturals amongst us that have perfectly our shape, but want reason, and some of them language too. . . . If it be asked whether these be all *men* or no, all of human species? it is plain, the question refers only to the nominal essence: for those of them to whom the definition of the word man, or the complex idea signified by that name, agrees, are men, and the other not. But if the inquiry be made concerning the supposed real essence; and whether the internal constitution and frame of these several creatures be specifically different, it is wholly impossible for us to answer . . . only we have reason to think, that where the faculties or outward frame so much differs, the internal constitution is not exactly the same.[8]

Following Locke in trying to make the designation "human" less prone to nominal differences and social conventions, later thinkers pointed to a number of physical traits in order to distinguish mankind from animals and subhuman creatures: external signs such as fingers, upright posture, and bipedal locomotion and internal features such as skull measurements, the (human) intermaxillary bone, and the (orangutan) laryngial pouch.[9] But where Locke and later Diderot recognized the arbitrary basis of any such classification, others forgot this salutary caution in their zeal to systematize a *scala naturae* of living creatures.[10]

A case in point is the famous system of the Swedish naturalist Carl Linnaeus. Referring to himself as the "second Adam," who, by giving true names to God's creatures, would ensure a faithful representation of the natural order, Linnaeus argued that the task of natural history was to establish a hierarchy of species based on eternal, intrinsic characteristics. Confounded by the wild children's distance from normative humanity, Linnaeus classified them in a new subgenus of humankind. In the twelfth edition of his classic *Systema naturae* (1766), Linnaeus broke down the genus *Homo* into two subgenera: *Homo nocturnus* and *Homo diurnus. Homo nocturnus,* otherwise known as the "Troglodyte," refers to the chimpanzees, orangutans, and other anthropoids reportedly sighted by early explorers in Africa and Asia, such as the fantastic creatures represented in Figure 2.[11] *Homo diurnus* comprises three species: the normative *Homo sapiens,* distinguished by its characteristic skin, temperament, and location as European, American, Asian, or African, followed by the inferior *Homo monstrosus* and *Homo ferus. Homo monstrosus* embraces a number of hotly debated human anomalies, such as the Patagonian giant, the dwarf of the Alps, and the monorchid Hottentot. *Homo ferus,* or "feral man," on the other hand, covers a number of unfortunate individuals whose existence was well documented. Distinguished by bestial traits such as muteness, quadruped locomotion, and hairiness, the *Homines feri* listed by Linnaeus include the wolf-boy of Hesse *(Juvenis lupinus hessensis),* Peter of Hanover *(Juvenis hannoveranus),* and the wild girl of Champagne *(Puella campanica).* As befits the pared-down, technical style of this work—designed to demonstrate Linnaeus's innovative system of binominal nomenclature—these children are known only by artificial Latin names, with no mention of their peculiar histories or individual destinies aside from indicators of sex and place of origin. After all, the function of a taxonomy (what Foucault calls a "disciplinary space of natural beings") is to characterize (and thus reduce individual singularities) and constitute classes.[12] Details would clutter the table.

The history of Peter's and Marie-Angélique's inclusion in the *Systema naturae* is interesting in itself as a reflection on the uncertain authority of eighteenth-century scientific discourse. Although Linnaeus's work achieved lasting fame (some claim it is Sweden's greatest scientific achievement to date) and was one of the most widely cited sources on natural history in eighteenth-century Europe, the author's views were not always

FIGURE 2

Left to right: "Trogolodyte," "Lucifer," "Satyr," "Pygmee." From Carl Linnaeus, "Anthropomorpha," in *Amoenitates academicae,* vol. 6 (Stockholm: Laurentius Salvius, 1763), facing p. 76. Reproduced by permission of the Department of Special Collections, University Libraries, University of Notre Dame.

consistent. The first edition (1735), published when Linnaeus was twenty-eight, comprises only ten or so folio pages. In it, the young naturalist announced his mission to rid science of legend and superstition by demystifying the species *Paradoxa,* or monsters. For each of the extraordinary creatures on this list—including the Hydra, the Satyr, the Frog-Fish, and the Phoenix—Linnaeus gave a new Latin name and a simple scientific explanation. For example, the tailed Satyr, he explained, that creature who is "hairy, bearded, with a manlike body, gesticulating much, very fallacious, is a species of monkey, if ever one has been seen."[13] This edition created the genus *Anthropomorpha* as a catch-all category for human and human-seeming creatures, including *Homo* (man, described as European, American, Asiatic, African), *Simia* (apes, including the "Satyrus"), and *Bradypus* (sloths).

Twenty-three years later, in the tenth edition (1758), when, as Linnaeus's biographer Knut Hagberg writes, "the book had swollen to a vast catalogue of all the plant and animal species known to Linnaeus," readers found much that was new, such as additional human species and the terms *Mammalia, Primates,* and *Homo sapiens.*[14] *Homo nocturnus* (a kind of ape) here accompanies *Homo diurnus* (that is, *Homo sapiens, Homo monstrosus,* and *Homo ferus*), and six examples of "feral man" or wild children are given, including *Juvenis hannoveranus*. The list of feral children grew to nine in the twelfth edition (1766), this time including both Peter and Marie-Angélique *(Puella campanica)*. But in the thirteenth edition (1788), the individual cases of *Homines feri* disappeared, leaving only the generic classification and its normative description: "four-footed, mute, hairy." Clearly, the naturalist was working through his classifications over time, adding and correcting them as his ideas changed and his information grew.

The fixed subdivisions within *Homines feri* reveal the static character of Linnaean nomenclature. Linnaeus attached great importance to the notion that species were fixed, unchanged, and unalterable from the moment that God created the universe. "If we observe God's works," he wrote, "it becomes more than sufficiently evident to everybody, that each living being is propagated by an egg and that every egg produces an offspring closely resembling the parent. Hence no new species are produced nowadays."[15] The important issue was not that of possible links between species or between man and beast, but rather of correctly naming and classifying all creatures.[16] As H. W. Janson has pointed out, Linnaeus and other early modern naturalists were not working in a protoevolutionary mode; rather, they relied on habits of thought inherited from philology, with its emphasis on nomenclature.[17] The wild children had to inhabit a separate category because Linnaeus believed that "nature makes no leaps." The very existence of the *Homines feri*, the *Homo nocturnus*, and the *Homo monstrosus* proved that the chain of being held: they filled the gaps below man and above the apes and demonstrated the gradations in the hierarchical natural order.

Although Linnaeus had an immense impact on eighteenth-century natural history, some successors took him to task for devising a system whose criteria dealt a blow to mankind's dignity by allowing for *Homo sapiens* to be grouped alongside subhuman monsters and lesser primates. The prominent French naturalist Buffon, for example, rejected Linnaeus's emphasis on visible traits in favor of the intellect as the foremost proof of mankind's ascendancy over the animal.[18] In his *Histoire naturelle*, Buffon reiterated the Aristotelian premise that the essence of man resides in his rational mind and not in such "accidental" properties as the form of his body, asserting that "mind, reflection, and language, depend not on the figure nor on the organization of the body. They are endowments peculiar to man," and adding pointedly, "the orang-outang, though he neither thinks nor speaks, has a body, members, senses, a brain, and a tongue, perfectly similar to those of a man: he counterfeits every human movement; but he performs no action that is characteristic of man."[19]

For Buffon, language was the external sign of human thought. Locke and Descartes before him had already touched on this distinction, of course. Descartes cited the famous example of a talking parrot in his *Discours de la méthode* (1637) but argued that animals can only "proffer words," not communicate.[20] Like mankind, animals possess bodies—those material, ephemeral, mechanical, and unthinking machines of life. But they do not possess souls—those immaterial, immortal, conscious life forces that endow man and only man with the power to think. Locke reiterated this premise in his *Essay Concerning Human Understanding,* arguing that animals, no matter how articulate or seemingly intelligent, should never be confused with mankind. But Locke employed the distinction in the other sense as well, including in the category "man" any creature who shares the external human shape. As he wrote, "whoever should see a creature of his own shape or make, though it had no more reason all its life than a cat or a parrot, would call him still a *man;* or whoever should hear a cat or a parrot discourse, reason, and philosophize, would call or think it nothing but a *cat* or a *parrot;* and say, the one was a dull irrational man, and the other a very intelligent rational parrot" (*Essay,* 1:445–46). Locke thus placed mankind within a broad continuum of intellectual capabilities and argued that external form, not rational thought, dictated an individual's inclusion.

But many eighteenth-century thinkers were not so confident about these distinctions.[21] Prompted by the discovery of prehensile language organs in apes, by Linnaeus's subdivisions of *Homo* on the "great chain," and by travelers' reports of squalid savages in Africa and the Americas, people felt great unease about mankind's place in the natural world and in the divine order.[22] Arguments for and against the rationality (and thus the sanctity) of animals and other supposedly subhuman creatures emerged in many period writings.[23] Some adopted a radically pro-animal position; witness the French prelate, the Cardinal de Polignac, who reportedly dared a chimpanzee at the Jardin du Roi: "Speak, and I will baptise you."[24] Others defined the differences between mankind and beast not as a dichotomy but rather as a continuum. The English minister John Hildrop, for instance, challenged the traditional theological conception of man as quasi-divine but expressed doubt about the firm boundaries between mankind and beast because of the vast inequalities in human intelligence. In his *Free Thoughts upon the Brute Creation* (1743), he questioned Locke's definition of man, declaring, "Who can determine the lowest Degree of human Ignorance, and the highest Pitch of brutal Knowledge; who can say where one ends, and the other begins, or whether there be any other Difference betwixt them but in degree?"[25]

But Hildrop and virtually all other thinkers of this age agreed that speech made the man. As Hildrop wrote: "the Partition betwixt the lowest Degree of Human and the highest Degree of Brute Understanding, is so very slender, that it is hardly perceptible, and could not in any degree be distinguish'd but by a greater Fluency of Language; which . . . may be considered as an Advantage to our Species in general" (*Free Thoughts*, 73). The logical fallacy of this distinction—that only through speech could rational human thought be assured—comes out strikingly in accounts of wild children. Only through speech, people assumed, could the children learn to reason and to communicate their thoughts. Only through speech could they explain the mysteries of their feral past and move squarely into civilization.

Other writers rejected these static definitions of mankind for the exciting new evidence provided by theories of what we now call embryology.[26] They sought to define humanity through biological means and to demonstrate that anomalies were biologically reproduced and based not on similar appearances or similar traits but on real material connections. Wild children appear in this discourse as evidence of miscegenation between human and animal parents. Some speculated that feral children were products of incongruous couplings like those that produce mules, perhaps between women and bears or women and apes.[27] Although often discredited, accounts of animal-human interbreeding abound in eighteenth-century natural histories and reveal curiosity mixed with repulsion for hybrids of all kinds. In 1699 Edward Tyson presented an account of a man-pig to the Royal Society; in 1757 Delisle de Sales claimed to have seen a girl with the head and feet of a monkey and recorded the exhibit of a calf-child and a wolf-child in Lyon in the 1750s.[28] Such scientific displays exploited more common morphological anomalies, as well. The *kunsthammer* of Peter I held live exhibits such as a young hermaphrodite and Foma, a peasant with only two digits on each hand and foot. Foma's curiosity value continued well after his death, for Peter had him stuffed and displayed for years.[29] Like these morphological "monsters," children found in the wild played into key debates over mankind's malleability. Malleability was a crucial concept since many naturalists worked for or were themselves landowners who had an interest in the formation and disappearance of traits.[30] In the absence of breeding experiments on humans, full-fledged "monsters," it was thought, could reveal important insights into environment and heredity. Like the famous "Porcupine Man," who spawned a large family all sporting the same wartish growths (seen on the hand shown in fig. 23), such creatures were fascinating as grotesque carnival attractions and as clues to the mechanism of generation. They provided counterexamples to normal embryological development and fueled debates between advocates of preformationism and epigenesis.

These anomalies also raised the possibility that man's malleability might produce degraded instead of improved beings. Just as travelers had shocked readers with sordid descriptions of miserable Hottentots and abject Eskimos, news of quadruped, herbivorous children found in Europe challenged the European belief that civilization guaranteed an elevated standard of humanity. The French philosopher Delisle de Sales cogently pointed out that "we prefer to believe that bears give birth to humans, than to think a human capable of producing a quadruped."[31] De Sales posited that the bizarre appetites and conduct of the *Homines feri* may not be aberrations but rather may manifest mankind's primitive, original nature or its inevitable degradation in the absence of civilizing influences.

Worse yet, perhaps mankind's capacity for rational thought and intellectual growth was not a sign of potential genius but rather a symptom of innate weakness. Rousseau opted for the latter in the *Discours sur l'inégalité* (1755), where he explained imbecility as an emblem of human frailty: "Why is man alone subject to becoming an imbecile? Is it not that he thereby returns to his primitive state, and that . . . man, in losing through old age or other accidents all that his *perfectibility* has enabled him to acquire, thus falls even lower than the animal itself?"[32] The term *perfectibilité,* introduced by Rousseau in this *Discours,* was a commonplace by the 1760s; its quick acceptance is not surprising, since the term expressed a secular and historical view of man's moral development that many saw as a challenge to the orthodox Christian dogma of original sin. But whereas many writers used *perfectibility* to express their optimism for mankind, for Rousseau the term connoted man's potential for moral and political decline.[33] Diderot echoed a similarly pessimistic appraisal in his *Elements de physiologie* (1774–80), contrasting human thought to the strong senses of animals: "Man's perfectibility is borne of the weakness of his senses, none of which dominates the organ of reason. If [man] had a nose like a dog, he would sense odors all the time; if he had eyes like an eagle, he would be forever watchful; if he had the ears of a mole, he would be a listening creature. . . . The human species is thus no more than a hodgepodge of individuals who are more or less crippled, more or less ailing."[34] These ideas of inherent limited intellect and physical decline raised humbling questions about mankind's supposed nobility of soul and superiority over animals and undermined the notion that language is innate to humans. If the wild children were not anomalous individuals but exemplars of wild nature (understood as an inexorable physical force, indifferent to man), their experience would have to be read differently: as a cautionary or edifying tale. And such a perspective forced Enlightenment philosophers to rethink the distinctions between *le physique* and *le moral.*

PETER OF HANOVER: IDIOT OR IDOL?

The accounts of Peter's capture vary enormously, but most agree that when he was seized in a forest near Hamelen, Germany, in the summer of 1724, he was wearing the remains of a shirt and subsisting on acorns, berries, and tree bark.[35] His age was between eleven and fifteen. Some claim that he ran about on all fours, others that he walked upright. Although his sense of smell was acute, he was insensitive to noxious odors such as that of his own excrement. Alert and suspicious during his first days of captivity, he reportedly sat waiting by the door on all fours, as would a four-footed animal. He refused cooked food, preferring instead raw vegetables, grass, and the sap from raw wood. His senses of hearing and smell were said to be sharp, and he appeared to enjoy music.

By October 1725, fifteen months after capture, Peter was sent to Hanover and then to London in February 1726 as a "guest" of the royal house of Hanover, the recently appointed ruling family of Great Britain. Brought to court on the orders of Queen Caroline and King George I, Peter was soon thereafter entrusted to Dr. John Arbuthnot—a well-known socialite, fellow of the Royal Society, and friend of Pope and Swift—for the purpose of investigating the innate ideas of the wild boy. Although at first detainable only by force, he gradually accepted clothes and made several appearances in London society and at court. He disappointed expectations of "wild" virility with his general indifference to women. Arbuthnot abandoned his instruction after only two months; with a royal pension Peter was then placed with a chamber woman of the queen and later with a farmer in Hertfordshire, where he lived out his long life. He never learned to speak more than a few words, but he developed some sensitivity to sounds and mastered table manners and polite comportment. He is said to have passed his later years (he died a septuagenarian) happily enough. His curiosity value apparently continued well into his dotage; late in his sixties he was visited by such well-known intellectuals as the Scottish judge Lord Monboddo, the Anglo-Irish inventor Richard Lovell Edgeworth, and his novelist daughter, Maria Edgeworth. Looking back on their visits in the 1770s, the Edgeworths note that Peter received gifts from "curious strangers" and amassed a collection of coins thanks to the farmer's wife, who "collected the price of his daily exhibition."[36]

A sense of ambivalence about mankind's superiority to beasts comes out strongly in the literature on Peter of Hanover. In the flurry of pamphlets published during his heyday as a curiosity at the English court, Peter was most widely represented as a stupid and uncouth person. Instead of reinforcing mankind's power to reason, his presence—as an apparently incorrigible idiot—inspired a reappraisal of the God-given anthropocentric Nature of eighteenth-century natural history.[37] Citing his quadruped posture and predilection for roots, nuts, and berries, some claimed that he was raised by bears. He seemed to possess some bear-like talents; one observer claimed that with his "nails long and crooked . . . he would get uppon [*sic*] trees quicker than a cat could."[38] His inability to speak placed him outside humanity too; thus he was described as "a dumb creature" and "a poor animal."[39] Some believed he was bereft of the most rudimentary ability to think; as another witness claimed: "his memory is not as good as an animal's instinct. . . . his nature lacks humanness."[40] Despite his imbecility, Peter was held up as an example to contemporary Englishmen.

Of the half-dozen tracts featuring a character called "wild Peter," five are satires that used the wild man to lambaste the decadent lifestyle of the English court and aristocracy. These pamphlets, reportedly written by such notable polemicists as Jonathan Swift and Daniel Defoe, served the political function of challenging the Hanover court. In them the figure of Peter reveals the immorality of George I's entourage, protests the excessive freedoms of English women, and deflates the pretensions of doctors, savants, and vegetarians. The courtiers' reactions to Peter reveal their own foibles, not his deficiencies. The English ladies, for instance, are seen as coquettish and even libertine in their desire to be accosted by the young savage.[41] Although he may be stupid, and "behaveth like a dumb creature," as one text declares, he "is a Christian like one of us" (*It Cannot Rain,* 471). Moreover, Peter proves superior to the English, especially to the "modern Men of Mode, who would be thought wise" (*Mere Nature,* title page). Savagery and degradation are thus projected onto England instead of his feral past, the latter being depicted as a version of the Orson legend of a child raised in the wilderness with a kindly bear-mother.

Supporting Peter's role as a political foil, more than one work of fiction claimed that an education at the English court would corrupt, not improve, the boy. The 1726 poem "The Savage" warns that though Peter's friends at court are "Adorn'd with each politer Grace / Above the rest of human Race," the language that they speak—and the morality it implies—are "lustful," "lawless," and blinder to reason than the "brutish Converse" of his former life.[42] Whereas civilization harbors vice and deceit, the wilderness shelters innocence, as the poem concludes: "If you taint his spotless Heart: / Speechless send him back agen / To the Woods of Hamelen . . . Let him still a Rover be, / Still be innocent and free" (306). A similar reversal of the nature/culture dichotomy enlivens *The Manifesto of Lord Peter* (1726), allegedly written by Peter's philosopher father, who had "dedicate[d] his only Son to an Experiment . . . [to] convince the World, how much a nobler Creature a Wild Man was than a Tame one."[43] Peter achieves his final apotheosis as a teacher of humankind in *It Cannot Rain but It Pours.* Here the wild youth is seen inventing an ironic natural language (a young lady is a "peacock"; old women are "magpies"; a heap of gold is a "turd"), conversing with beasts and birds, and teaching a "new sect of herb-eaters" about the virtues of a vegetarian regime.[44]

One text rejects the satirist's humor for a serious lesson on the necessity of education. Part sermon, part cautionary tale, *Mere Nature Delineated: or a Body without a Soul* (1726; attributed to Defoe) uses Peter to challenge the notion that animals are inferior to men yet retains hope for his eventual improvement. It describes Peter arriving in London as the long-awaited natural man who would prove or disprove theories on language-learning: "He seems to be the very Creature which the learned World have, for many Years past, pretended to wish for, *viz.*, one that being kept entirely from human Society, so as never to have heard any one speak, must therefore either not speak at all, or, if he did form any Speech to himself, then they should know what Language Nature would first form for Mankind" (17). Much to everyone's disappointment, however, Peter was mute and apparently unteachable. Nevertheless, the author defends Peter's humanity (à la Locke) by citing his physical attributes and thus his soul: "we see him . . . in a State of MERE NATURE, acting below the Brutes, and yet we must grant him a Soul: He has a Body, in its Shape Human, the Organick Parts Anatomically, we believe, the same as Human" (23). Religious concerns inform the call for continued instruction and cast education as a curious combination of divine and monarchical regeneration: "[I]f his uncultivated Soul may be recover'd to Action, and being improv'd, may be brought to the Use of its ordinary Powers, his Majesty will have the Glory to give one of God's lost Creatures to the World, in a kind of new Creation" (26). Ultimately, Peter's novelty disappears and he becomes instead a metaphor for the humble character of everyman. As the author concludes: "Such a plain coarse Piece of Work is a Man in the mere Condition he is born in, just coming out of Nature's Hand: And, by Consequence, the Improvement of the Soul by Instruction, which we call Educating, is of the highest Importance" (68). By watching Peter struggle with language and complex ideas, "modern men of

Mode" are taught a humbling lesson about humanity's origins as well as the value of true wisdom: the long, arduous process by which "mere Nature" receives the "help of Art to bring it to perfection of living" (61).

This concept of perfectibility informed much of eighteenth-century philosophy. Whether the writer speculated on the history of an entire people or compared different forms of society around the globe, it was widely believed that the English and French cultures of the time—thanks to their cultivation of the arts, sciences, and diverse forms of industry—had achieved the apogee of cultural perfection. It was not until a century later that this notion of progress would be adopted by biologists and give rise to the concept of interspecies evolution. But already in the 1770s, one amateur naturalist, the Scottish judge Lord Monboddo, was trying to reconcile the difference of people like Peter with the static boundaries that distinguished mankind from beast. Monboddo visited Peter and Marie-Angélique and observed their behavior at length before theorizing on their place in the natural order. (Such careful methods, however, did not save Monboddo from ridicule. He was widely considered an eccentric, and his interest in apes prompted images of the savant as a wizard with a chimpanzee for a familiar.) In *Antient Metaphysics* (1779–99), Monboddo conflated the histories of Peter, Marie-Angélique, and the orangutan into a theory of universal human progress. Peter exemplifies the infantine stage, being unable to walk erect or speak articulate language until the age of fifteen; the orangutan represents the second stage, being bipedal and possessing some virtues and social arts; Marie-Angélique represents the third stage because of her skillful swimming, use of weapons, and acquisition of language.[45] Note that the potential to cross boundaries lay not in individual initiatives such as education but rather in a vaguely delineated, atemporal change in species. Because of his quadrupedal locomotion and lack of speech, Peter thus represented the origin of the species and of each life cycle—eternal childhood. We will return to Monboddo below, for his most in-depth discussion of the wild children revolved around Marie-Angélique, whom he saw as a truly middling species between ape and human.

Other observers advanced similarly specious claims about Peter's evolution from beast to man. The rumor of his former life as an adoptive bear cub prompted startling images of his progress through time. One of the 1726 brochures concerning Peter (fig. 3) displays a triptych of his steps toward civilization that rivals Linnaeus's "Anthropomorpha" (fig. 2) for scientific mystification. On the left we see his past as a cub, on the right his condition at capture as a tree-climbing anthropoid, and in the center a vision of his future as a well-dressed young gentleman who, while holding a symbol from his past (an oak branch), is prophesied to achieve "Great Feats" in London society. Although the text does not explain how Peter achieves this radical transformation, the iconography is interesting in that it traces his life as a trajectory ascending through the biological and social hierarchy of the scala naturae: from a member of an animal family, to a lone anthropoid, to mankind's finest product: a gentleman with a necktie and waistcoat.

Clearly there was great confusion over the boundaries between mankind and beast, although education seemed to offer some clues to human superiority. Rousseau claimed that mankind's perfectibility lay in his innate disposition to learning—which for Rousseau was both a blessing and a curse, as we saw above. Unlike beasts, who were incapable of learning, mankind seemed to possess innate imitative tendencies that allowed him to adopt—or aspire to adopt—a variety of skills. Rousseau thus cited Peter's quadrupedal locomotion as proof of the boy's capacity to learn and, by extension, his humanity. Peter walked on all fours by necessity—he copied his animal hosts.[46] Other writers seized on this same imitative ability to explain Peter's mutism. Wild children were not subhuman, claimed Rousseau's disciple Manon Roland, they were simply victims of isolation. If abandoned in the forest without human contact, any child would probably become an idiot, "like that savage of Hanover and that little girl found in the woods of Champagne: without language, signs, and likely without ideas."[47] Human contact and education were far more important than any innate superiority.

The case of Peter of Hanover proved Locke's claim about mankind's innate yet variable levels of intelligence and prompted people to rethink the criteria of language and perfectibility. Instead of assuming that lack of speech implied lack of thought, some tried to show that Peter did think, but in a different way. In their progressive manual of childrearing, *Practical Education* (1798), Maria and Richard Lovell Edgeworth describe performing psychological experiments on Peter as one of their many efforts to make education an "experimental science" (1:v–vi). Having for several years observed Peter as a neighbor, they report that he "had all his senses in remarkable perfection" but could only articulate "imperfectly a few words, in particular *King George,* which words he always accompanied with an imitation of the bells, which rang at the coronation of George the Second" (1:64). His intelligence seemed to consist in a "few automatic habits of rationality and industry" (1:63). In order to see if Peter could be prodded into independent thought, they devised the following scheme: according to a daily plan, after Peter fetched water, the Edgeworth children would dump

An ENQUIRY
HOW THE
Wild Youth,

Lately taken in the Woods near *Hanover*, (and now brought over to *England*) could be there left, and by what Creature he could be ſuckled, nurſed, and brought up.

That of this Youth the famous Aſtrologer Mr. *William Lilly* 100 Years ago propheſied, appears by the four other Things which are come to paſs, *viz.* —1ſt. The *Pope*'s going to *Benevento*. 2*ly*. *Spain*'s breaking the *Aſſiento* Treaty. 3*ly*. The Emperor's ſending the *Oſtend* Company to *China*. 4*ly*. The Quality's admiring the new *Italian* Singing Woman lately come over, and really named Signiora *Fauſtina*.

And 5*ly*. This *Wild Youth*, in his following famous Prophecy.

When Rome ſhall wend (i. e. go) to Benevento,
And Spaniards break the Aſſiento:
When Spread Eagle flies to China,
And Chriſtian Folks adore Fauſtina:
Then ſhall the Woods be Brought to Bed,
Of Creature neither taught nor fed,
Great Feats ſhall he atchieve——

WILD YOUTH

Given Gratis Up One Pair of Stairs at the Sign of the Celebrated *Anodyne Necklace* Recommended by Dr. *Chamberlen* for Children's Teeth over againſt *Devreux-Court*, without *Temple-Bar*. And by the Author's Servant *R. Bradſhaw* at the *Golden Key* between *Church-Street* and *Great-Ruſſel-Street End*, St. *Giles*'s in the Fields, *London*.

London: Printed by *H. Parker* in *Jewin-ſtreet*. 1726.

FIGURE 3

Title page of anonymous brochure, *An Enquiry How the Wild Youth*, . . . (London: H. Parker, 1726). Reproduced by permission of the British Library, G14679.

it out and put a shilling in the bucket. This practice seemed to go unnoticed by the old man, apart from his stolid persistence in performing the chore again. When the maid finally took the water buckets from Peter, however, he carefully extracted the shilling and put it with his other treasures (1:64). It seems clear that he did register the intervention and valued the reward gained therein, though he used no words to say so.

Most significant are the implications drawn from this encounter between the experimentalists and their subject. Instead of reaffirming his idiocy or expressing frustration over his plodding movements, the authors follow this experiment with a meditation on the variable value of words. "Words without correspondent ideas are worse than useless, they are counterfeit coin," they assert, "but words which really represent ideas, are . . . of sterling value." As if appreciating the real, albeit rudimentary, intelligence exhibited by Peter, they then offer some pragmatic advice for suiting language to the pupil's ability: "It is a nice and difficult thing in education to proportion a child's vocabulary exactly to his knowledge, dispositions, or conformation; our management must vary; some will acquire words too quickly, others too slowly" (1:64). The Edgeworths thus stress the variable nature rather than the qualitative value of mankind's "perfectibility" and suggest that it may be attained by any number of techniques. By applying new methods of relieving eye fatigue to other kinds of mental phenomena, for instance, the authors suggest: "Might we not hope to cultivate the general power of attention to a degree of perfection hitherto unknown?" (1:112). Although his stubborn mutism and rote movements made Peter appear more automaton than man, the Edgeworths did not question his humanity; they merely saw him inhabiting a low level on the developmental continuum.

For Buffon, however, the wild boy was rife with human potential—symbol of mankind's "natural" propensity to sociability and attraction to the opposite sex. In a text as mixed with myth and hearsay as Linnaeus's, Buffon claims at one point in his *Histoire naturelle* that one could know mankind's "natural" state by observing "an absolute savage" ("un sauvage absolument sauvage") such as the wild children found in Europe[48] and asserts in another volume: "Thus the state of pure nature is a known state."[49] To prove his theory that mankind is naturally a sociable, language-using animal, Buffon advances a romantic scenario linking the destinies of Marie-Angélique Leblanc and Peter of Hanover. This passage, remarkable for its lyricism, Epicurean undercurrents, and primitivist philosophy, merits complete citation:

> Thus the state of pure nature is a known state: it is that of the savage living in the desert, but living in a family, knowing his children, and being known by them, using words, and making himself understood. The savage girl picked up in the woods of Champagne, and the man found in the forests of Hanover, are not exceptions to this doctrine. They had lived in absolute solitude; and could not, therefore, have any idea of society, or of the use of words: but if they had ever met, the propensity of Nature would have constrained, and pleasure united them. Attached to each other, they would soon have made themselves understood; they would have first learned the language of love, and then of tenderness for their offspring.[50]

In Buffon's natural history the wild couple incarnates the vision of the solitary savage that Rousseau would immortalize in the *Discours sur l'inégalité,* but with a dash of romance. They are a spectacle for philosophical inquiry; their wild bodies are reinterpreted as the healthy, sensual bodies of young lovers and devoted parents—in their union we see the origins of the nuclear family. Buffon speculated on the origins and destiny of the Peter and Marie-Angélique in an abstract manner, as if they lived long ago in some atemporal utopia. Just as Linnaeus glossed over the differences between *Juvenis hannoveranus* and *Puella campanica* in order to fill in the gaps of his taxonomy, Buffon cited their names as heuristic tools for his normative theories of social development.

Later commentators, however, would reject this rhetorical strategy on the grounds of the wild children's inherent abnormality. Instead of being depicted more or less sympathetically as a "wonderful wild man"or a "Ship without a rudder," Peter would later be considered a "freak" or a "very old child" whose experience exemplified the "defects and imbecilities" that may be produced by physical anomalies and social isolation.[51] Some scientists claimed that Peter's mutism was not due to "Non-use" but rather to a physical pathology, for example, a deformed throat.[52] The observers' very terms of analysis shifted from moral to physical evidence, from efforts to define and improve on nature to efforts to cure the ill. In his *Lectures* (delivered 1816–18), William Lawrence summed up the new attitude of savants toward *Homines feri:* "they are merely instances of defective organization; malformed animals, incapable of speech, and exhibiting few and imperfect mental phenomena; pathological specimens, therefore, rather than examples of human perfection. Nothing can be conceived as more widely removed from the natural condition of man, than these half-witted beings."[53] But since they were not naturally bereft, perhaps one might cure them?

MARIE-ANGÉLIQUE LEBLANC: MONSTROUS FEMININITY

There are thus no Monsters in the physical order, but there are many in the moral.

—Delisle de Sales, *De la Philosophie de la nature*

Like Peter, Marie-Angélique has a history shot through with contradictory claims, but the basic facts of her life story may be summarized as follows.[54] Research suggests that she may have been born a Sioux from the Wisconsin region, bought by a French woman, and transported with her to Labrador then France.[55] In September 1731 the girl was sighted in an orchard near the village of Songi, where she was stealing apples from a tree. Her feet were bare and she wore only rags and skins on her small black body, but she was armed with a short club. The villagers set a bulldog on her, which she killed with one blow before scaling the tree and swinging, branch to branch, back into the woods. The village nobleman, Monsieur d'Epinay, ordered that she be caught; a townswoman succeeded by tempting her down from a tree with a pail of water and an eel. Once confined on the d'Epinay estate, the girl (who appeared to be anywhere from ten to eighteen years old, depending on sources) amazed her captors by skinning and eating a rabbit uncooked and devouring a chicken in the same way. After several washings, her skin became white. Her huge thumbs and long, tough fingernails were a source of astonishment, as were her sharp, piercing cries. She escaped several times and surprised the villagers with her unusual flying run, strong swimming, and imperviousness to the cold.

To avoid further escapades, d'Epinay, in cooperation with the bishop of Châlons and the intendant of Champagne (the provincial governor), placed the wild girl in the municipal Hôpital St-Maur (near Châlons) in October 1731. Proof of her baptism is found in the records of the nearby parish church of St Sulpice from June 16, 1732. Called the "shepherd's beast" *(la bête du berger)* on the d'Epinay estate, she was henceforth named Marie-Angélique Memmie Leblanc. Her predilection for tree climbing and swimming, like her fondness for raw frogs and rabbit blood, was immediately discouraged. Forced to eat the institutional fare, she soon lost her teeth, which together with her fingernails were preserved as curiosities. More serious consequences followed: her once-robust health, weakened by the diet of cooked food and the sedentary lifestyle at the Hôpital (and later at convents in Châlons and Paris), was permanently damaged. Under the nuns' care, however, Marie-Angélique was gradually "humanized": she learned the French language and Catholic dogma along with needlework and domestic tasks. Once she became fluent enough to answer questions, her interrogators were able to piece together part of her past. She apparently had been roaming the Champenois countryside in the company of another girl, living off raw fish, frogs, rabbits, and roots and taking shelter in trees. They communicated using gestures, grunts, and whistles. After a dispute over a trinket (some claim it was a rosary), Marie-Angélique wounded her companion with her club. She had run off to fend for herself when she was discovered in the apple orchard near Songi.

Thanks to articles in the *Mercure de France* and contemporary interest in anthropological exotica, word of this prodigy quickly spread to the capital and beyond—to England, Scotland, even Sweden.[56] Numerous visitors descended on Châlons to see the marvel: in 1737 the queen of Poland paid her respects and wrote a letter on behalf of Marie-Angélique to her daughter, the queen of France. The powerful duc d'Orléans took Marie-Angélique permanently under his protection in 1744 and graced her with a generous pension (600 livres per year—not a bad sum, considering that female domestics earned about 200 livres per year).[57] She then moved to the capital and began preparations for taking the veil. Thus we find her mentioned in the 1750 *Journal de la Communauté des Nouvelles Catholiques* as a twenty-three-year-old pensioner who was "born savage" *(née sauvage)* and lived in the convent from April 23, 1750, to January 20, 1751, at which time she entered the convent of Ste Perrine at Chaillot as a postulant. She remained at Ste Perrine until 1752, when her benefactor died, her financial support temporarily vanished, and she was forced to move into cheaper quarters.

Judging from reports of her existence in later years, her solitude was regularly broken by the visits of curiosity-seekers, including the poet Louis Racine, the scientist Charles-Marie de La Condamine, her purported biographer, Mme Hecquet, and the Scottish philosopher Lord Monboddo. She suffered some difficult years after the death of the duc d'Orléans forced her to leave Ste Perrine, but she later settled in central Paris with a comfortable pension.[58] She must have been rather well connected in Parisian high society because one night in September 1755 we find her at the home of Mme de Luynes, where she enjoyed a one-hour audience with the queen, who made her a gift of three or four louis. According to the duc de Luynes, her pension had at this point already been restored by the new duc d'Orléans, but only at a rate of 200 livres a year. Unable to afford convent life, she was apparently living with a Mme Meyra (wife of the president of the Chambre des comptes) (de Luynes, 3:72). In later years, she surfaces anew on lists of people receiving royal pensions *(Rentes viagères—emprunts du roi)* allocated by the Hôtel de Ville in the years 1758, 1761, 1762, 1773, and 1775. In her last years, this woman seems to have entertained visitors regularly, as witnessed by the twenty chairs inventoried in her apartment at the end of her life. Judging from the *inventaire après décès,* she was relatively wealthy at her death on December 15, 1775, and favored garments of black silk and velvet.[59] Mystery continued to shroud Leblanc's legacy into the next century and continues still today. In the imperial archives of papers seized during the revolution, we read the notes of a certain Procureur Guichard, who expressed frustration over his inability to uncover more than twenty or so documents left behind by Leblanc, who apparently left a great many valuable papers at her death.[60] Although she never married, this woman clearly made a life for herself and wielded a certain influence in Parisian society.

The wild girl's metamorphosis from an avid carnivore and unsociable forest dweller into a toothless, meek novitiate intrigued more than one author. But her other, less sensational changes—from inarticulate to French-speaking, from free-willed to docile, from nameless to named—are equally significant, suggesting the various means used to absorb this abnormal child into the norm. Although she may have already had the name Marie-Angélique before the baptism, it is still striking to see how her name's rhetoric of familiarity (based on Christianity, local legend, and common usage) could have reduced her threatening difference.[61] The name Marie-Angélique Memmie Leblanc, with its triple signifiers of female virtue, belies an almost hyperbolic desire to place the wild within the confines of the civilized. *Marie* recalls the Christian epitome of womanhood, the Virgin Mary, with her connotations of female sacrifice and humility; *Angélique* denotes a saintly, devout character; and *Leblanc* (the white) signifies unsullied pureness, as well as ordinary Frenchness (Leblanc was then and still is a common French name). *Memmie* provided the orphan with a paternal heritage, being the name of her godfather (the administrator of the Hôpital Général) as well as that of the patron saint of Châlons, where she was baptized.

The kind of re-education imposed on Leblanc in the convent reflects the typical mode of female socialization during her day. Silence, immobility, physical constraint, and social surveillance formed the guiding principles in female pedagogy. Conveying a profound mistrust of children, especially young girls, who were seen either as carriers of original sin or as potential victims, the texts of convent educators prescribed a regimen of the most rigorous material and moral subordination. "Every aspect of school life," writes the historian Martine Sonnet, "suggests a molding *(modelage),* whether it is the issue of the hours the girls must spend seated on their benches or their rare opportunities for movement. In all circumstances, the girls must display modesty and decency, their most glorious attributes."[62] Profoundly negative, female education focused on preventing evil rather than on inspiring good: as Sonnet explains, "the regulations of convent schools organize the pedagogical space and time just as they mold the student's body, so that nothing can happen."[63] The body was viewed as a spectacle of sin; one convent manual demanded: "When they get dressed they will do so in such a manner that no one can see them nude, nor will they look at themselves."[64] Movement was equally restrained by a rhetoric of bodily impropriety: "the students will beware that it is very indecent to lean against the wall or against the back of one's chair, . . . to spread out one's arms and legs, to show one's feet, to bite one's nails with one's teeth and other similar things."[65] Hence when contemporary observers celebrated the wild girl's "progress," they were commemorating the achievement of a quiet, controlled, still body and an uneventful domestic existence.

This pedagogical practice of immobilizing the body and narrowing the thoughts, so common in female education of the time, was enforced to a different degree in the education of boys. Discipline and punishment were central to the program, but some physical exercise and intellectual curiosity were encouraged. The histories of wild children raise interesting questions concerning the conflicting relations between norms of gendered behavior and human nature. Whereas Marie-Angélique was confined to a series of convents, urged to convert and spend her life in penitence for her one-time savagery, the wild boys encountered a rather different re-education process. After his capture in 1724, Peter of Hanover was entrusted to a well-known scientist, John Arbuthnot, for an albeit short-lived program of study and teaching. Victor de l'Aveyron (first captured in 1798) was initially analyzed by the prominent physician Philippe Pinel, who then placed him in the care of Jean Itard, an up-and-coming physician from the Institution Nationale des Sourds-Muets, who undertook a six-year program of instruction with the boy. Given the notoriety of Marie-Angélique's discovery and capture, and her evident intellectual abilities, it is surprising that she did not enjoy the same kind of attention as the males, for she seemed to incarnate the same kind of raw "nature." Although La Condamine and Monboddo did visit her, she spent a great deal of her life sequestered in convents.[66] Could it be that because of her sex a feral girl was considered unfit for scientific experimentation or intellectual cultivation? As Londa Schiebinger has noted with regard to the eighteenth-century treatment of female apes—another group of "subhumans": "No one *denied* that female apes were capable of such accomplishments; the question did not arise. Europeans simply assumed that active, cultured individuals were male. The question of the humanity and rights of apes was intimately tied to the question of rights for women."[67]

The conceptual leap from ape to feral human was not wide; in fact, the destinies of these two figures became intertwined in contemporary iconography. In the literature on natural history, perfectibility was located in the ability to wield arms or bear tools. Just as chapbook illustrations showed Leblanc holding her cudgel, period illustrations of apes often depicted them as females wielding a stick (as in figs. 4 and 2). But the meanings of such images vary: the stick can be read as evidence of their less-than-human status, symbolizing the extra help they need to remain erect, or as proof of their proximity to man, symbolizing their capacity for self-defense. By extension, the stick suggests both creatures' potential threat to humankind, as in the iconography of club-wielding medieval wild man seen in figure 5. All three connotations (less than human, human, and threatening) mark the imagery of Marie-Angélique Leblanc.

The first accounts of Leblanc evince great confusion over her human status. The two articles in the December 1731 *Mercure de France* stressed the girl's exoticism in order to justify her bizarre behavior. Before offering any details of her capture, the author refuted one theory of her nationality and launched immediately into another:

> she is not from Norway (as some have said); we believe rather that she was born in the Antilles Islands of America, which belong to the French, such as Guadeloupe, Martinique, St. Christopher, St. Domingue, etc. because [when] a gentleman from Châlons, who had been to Guadeloupe, showed her a cassave or manioc [root,] which is a bread eaten by the savages of the Antilles, she cried for joy, and taking a morsel, she ate it with great appetite.[68]

The proof of her Antillaise identity comes from a food preference. Food and eating act as metaphorical barometers of civilization and savagery in much contemporary ethnography and fiction, with the cannibal, who feeds on his own kind, inhabiting the lowest degree of humanity. By imagining her as a native of the French Antilles, France's most beloved and lucrative colonial possession, this author naturalized her as a French speaker and a colonial subject, member of a conquered, compliant people.

The question of the wild girl's original language, arising in a time when theories of universal languages, linguistic geneaologies, and the possibilities of animal speech occupied Europe's leading savants, gave rise to detailed explanations in the *Mercure* as well.[69] Because he conceived of

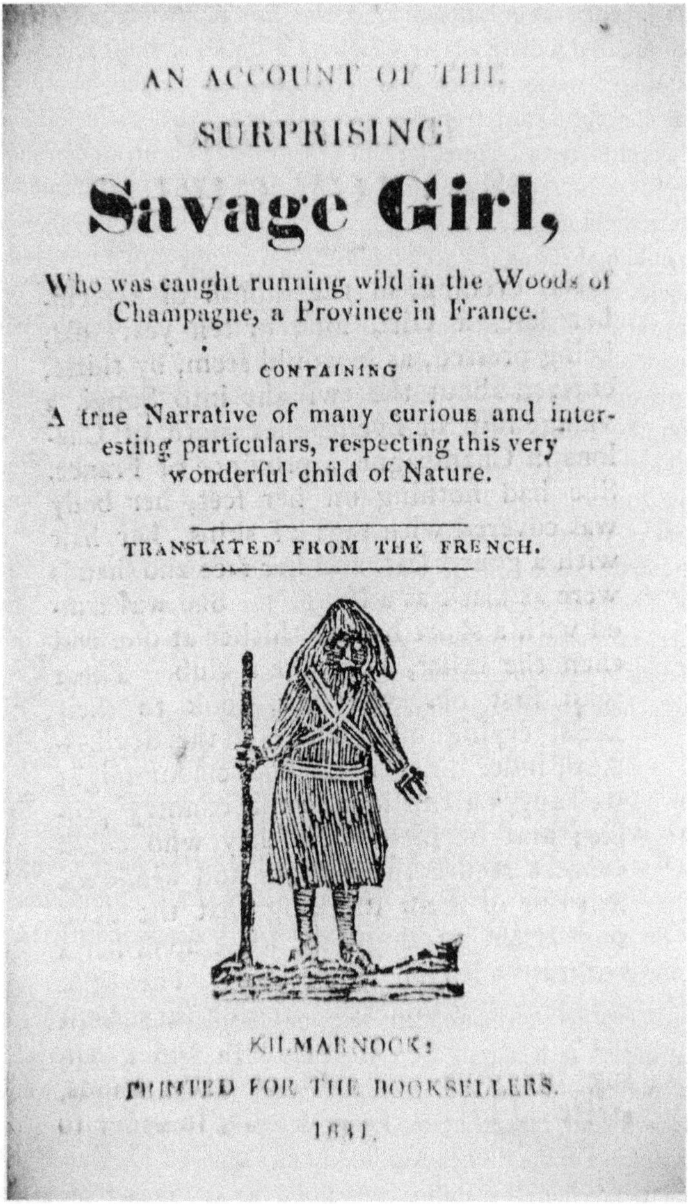
AN ACCOUNT OF THE

SURPRISING

Savage Girl,

Who was caught running wild in the Woods of Champagne, a Province in France.

CONTAINING

A true Narrative of many curious and interesting particulars, respecting this very wonderful child of Nature.

TRANSLATED FROM THE FRENCH.

KILMARNOCK:

PRINTED FOR THE BOOKSELLERS.

1831.

FIGURE 4

Title page of anonymous chapbook, *An Account of the Surprising Savage Girl* (Kilmarnock: printed for the bookseller, 1831). Reproduced by permission of the Mitchell Library, Glasgow.

FIGURE 5

Wild man with club and coat of arms. Martin Shongauer. German, fifteenth century.

Marie-Angélique as an exotic foreigner, one writer interpreted her primitive attempts to communicate as traces of her indigenous tongue: "she calls a net 'debily,' in the patois of her country; to say 'hello girl' ['bonjour fille'] one says, according to her, 'Yas yas fioul,' adding that when one called her one said 'Riam riam fioul': this is what makes us realize that she is beginning to understand the meaning of French terms, interpreting them with terms of her own land."[70] By valorizing her sounds, this sympathetic witness suggested that the girl's strangeness resulted from cultural, not physical, difference and gave evidence of her aptitude for socialization.

But the line between the human and the animal breaks down repeatedly in these narratives. Indeed, what strikes me most in the *Mercure* letters is the desire to capitalize on the semibestial aspect of the wild girl's appearance and to underscore her value as a cultural phenomenon or spectacle, a kind of exotic, ill-behaved zoo specimen. Both accounts spotlight her physical eccentricities—her abhorrence of being touched, her swift run, shifty eyes, and ability to hunt and fish with her bare hands—as visual proof of her wildness, performed on demand. The surprise and shock felt by "civilized" observers while witnessing Marie-Angélique's "savage" habits, especially her food preferences and table manners, emerge vividly and form a leitmotif in these and other wild girl stories. Hence the first writer notes: "We noticed that everything she ate, she ate raw. . . . As for water, her ordinary drink, she drinks it from a pail, lapping it up like a cow, on all fours,"[71] and the second relates the amazement and disgust felt by observers watching her perform her savage tricks: "We saw that day, with a feeling of horror, the girl eat more than a pound and a half of raw beef, without chewing it a bit, and then saw her pounce with a kind of fury on a hare that one put before her, which she skinned in a wink with the facility that comes of habit, and then devoured in an instant without removing the entrails."[72]

In both *Mercure* letters, the girl's attraction—and value as a news item—lay in her potential to shock, to disturb the norms of female physicality and polite behavior in a society that prided itself on cleanliness and refined manners.[73] Her diet itself constituted a threat to reigning views of proper female conduct. According to the influential doctors Cheyne and Tissot, as well as Rousseau, overly fancy food was a temptation to be fought: the peasant diet of grains, fruits, and water was proposed as the dietary equivalent of good morals. One might have thought that such theorists would have touted Leblanc's active lifestyle as a model for their sedentary readers; after all, Cheyne declared in 1733, "When Mankind was simple, plain, honest, and frugal, there were few or no diseases. Temperance, Exercise, Hunting, Labour, and Industry kept the Juices Sweet and the Solids brac'd."[74] But her penchant for raw meat set Leblanc squarely on the side of vice in this medico-moralistic equation. Her preference for the raw was tantamount to a violation of fundamental taboos of civilized life: it transgressed the boundaries between human and animal and, symbolically at least, threatened to rip asunder the social order and reveal man's basest instincts. As Claude Lévi-Strauss has written, "Between the social person and his or her own body, in which nature is unleashed, between the body and the biological and physical universe," food taboos and table and toilet etiquette "moderate our exchanges with the external world, and superimpose on them a domesticated, more peaceful and more sober rhythm."[75] For the self-consciously refined, *propre* (or at least elegant) readers of the *Mercure,* Marie-Angélique's alimentary transgression into the wild was at once repulsive and titillating, amusing if kept under control.[76]

Given its importance in both *Mercure* letters, this juxtaposition of untamed bestiality and socialized femininity seems to have been precisely what intrigued contemporary audiences in the wild girl's story. As proof of the powerful urges hiding in man, her bizarre eating habits thrilled readers at the same time that her successful re-education as a demure religious demonstrated the triumph of order over chaos, that is, the power of a well-run institution to reform and humanize a savage. As Foucault and historians of the *Annales* school have shown, in the eighteenth century unprecedented numbers of civic facilities were designed to contain society's outcasts and remove them from the public eye.[77] The insane asylums, prisons, schools, and foundling homes built during this time were a source of no little civic pride and popular interest. One writer described the Hôpital St-Maur in typically appreciative terms as the key to Marie-Angélique's survival in French society, touting the institution's multiple functions as a charity home, a vocational school, and a place of moral redemption:

> the Bishop [of Châlons] has since taken care to have her placed in the Hôpital Général of that city, where the poor children are sheltered and fed until the age of fifteen or sixteen, when they are taught a trade. It is there that one tries to humanize her completely and to educate her. . . . The Superior of the Hôpital says that she knows how to embroider very well . . . they teach her Christian religion as well, she says she wants to be baptised in the "Terrestrial Paradise," the term she uses for our churches.[78]

Redemption forms the central theme of the Jansenist Louis Racine's "Epître II sur l'homme" of 1747, an impassioned lament on the violence and vices that plague the human condition. Racine brings up the wild girl in an early stanza on primitive man, the distant ancestor of contemporary Europeans, identifying her as "this surprising girl, a sad example of what we would be without education and society."[79] So as to reinforce a Hobbesian conception of man's vicious and immoral nature, his portrait of Marie-Angélique capitalizes on her violent past, her lack of language, her bestial—almost cannibalistic—eating habits, and the rumored murder of her companion:

> And what were then our savage forefathers,
> A girl in our day reveals to the eye,
> It was not words her mouth articulated:
> Only one sound came out, a piercing, wild cry.

With living animals that she ripped apart by hand,
Palpitating morsels assuaged her hunger.
From early childhood she wandered from mountain to mountain,
And sullied the deserts with the blood of her companion.
Why did she immolate her [companion] to rage?
What desire was so great that it separated two hearts
United by the forest, their youth, and their shared misery?
Let us admit, those were the ways of our forefathers.[80]

Reading the wild girl's past as a moral flaw, a vestige of original sin, Racine suggests that her savagery could be remedied only by religious instruction and rigorous discipline, if not punishment. For only through punitive measures and repressive tactics can man's natural propensity for violence be controlled and society maintained, as the poet affirms: "Chains, prisons, gallows and tortures, / Such were the foundations of society."[81] In a later stanza he casts his net wider yet and, surveying human history from tyrants of antiquity to the Cyclops and new-found cannibals, he pronounces a dire prognosis: "What do I conclude from these awful monsters? / The penchant where guilty nature leads us. / Whoever gives free reins to his anger / Can, when left free, *easily become a monster.*"[82] Like the Roman monsters Nero and Caligula, the wild girl was a specimen from this instinct-driven state who signals humankind's true essence: she *demonstrates* that the monster is within.

Like the *Mercure* letters, Racine's epistle and his "Eclaircissement sur la fille sauvage" (c. 1756) reveal an obvious fascination with the girl's animality. Comparing her spiritual struggle to refrain from thinking evil thoughts with her physical efforts to refrain from eating raw meat, Racine suggests that the believer's battle against doubt is on a par with the savage's battle against instinct. For Racine, savagery translated as wickedness: the girl's notorious fondness for animal blood was no mere infraction of human law but was a violation of God's own commandments as recorded in the Old Testament. He declares: "The blood of animals, so forbidden to man ever since the flood, was her nectar."[83] Like a repentant sinner who was sorely tempted by the pleasures of the flesh, the wild girl lived in constant threat of relapse, her thirst for blood making a travesty of the Eucharist:

> the most violent of her temptations was to drink the blood of a living animal. She herself confessed to me that when she saw a child, she was tormented by this desire. When she told me that, my daughter, who was still small, was with me; [Marie-Angélique] noticed the emotion on [my daughter's] face at the confession of such a temptation and, laughing, she

> told her, "Do not worry about a thing, Mademoiselle, God has changed me very much."[84]

The threat of relapse haunts the girl's character even in the biographical note to the "Epître," where Racine remarks, "After all the pains one has taken to soften her ferocity, she conserves some vestiges in her eyes and her manners: she doesn't like our food or society, she only stays out of obedience to God. The religion she has been taught prevents her, she says, from returning to the woods."[85] Exaggerating her moral ambivalence and cannibalistic tastes, Racine rewrote the wild girl as a monstrous example of the tortured sinner seeking redemption. Here her extraordinary *péripéties* became a cautionary tale about the misery of man without God and the hard work that salvation requires.

Accounts of Leblanc's sexuality are cloaked in suspicions of monstrosity. It appears that Marie-Angélique dreaded being touched, especially by the opposite sex: she reportedly emitted piercing screams when men came too close. On one occasion she responded to unwanted contact by striking and temporarily blinding a man with a piece of raw beef; on another she nearly strangled an overly friendly soldier.[86] Equally horrific were the rumors of her bloodlust. Racine claimed that the very sight of a child tormented Leblanc, since her longing to drink warm blood was so great.[87] These legends of abnormal sexuality and vampire passions culminate in a bizarre episode related in Buirette de Verrière's 1788 history of Châlons-sur-Marne. Apparently, an extremely fat young woman visited Châlons one day and asked to see Leblanc. Marie-Angélique arrived as requested and found the woman devouring a chicken: "Our savage considers her, stares at her with avid eyes, her face changes: Mlle de Net——thinks she covets her chicken. *'No,'* [Marie-Angélique] says, clenching her fists as hard as she can, *'I do not hunger for your chicken, but for you. . . . How I would . . . you!'* We barely had time to take her away."[88] In Racine's work, as in this text, such fearsome anecdotes substantiated the benefits of civilization for man and, perhaps more important, for woman.

Images of woman's unruly appetites were widespread in eighteenth-century texts; in medical writings woman was associated with her "insatiable" womb and her tendency (especially marked among spinsters and nuns) to succumb to hysteria and the vapors, which were attributed to excess "female sperm."[89] Links between sexuality and eating habits are found in myriad eighteenth-century texts, from the medical writings of Cheyne and Tissot to Buffon's *Histoire naturelle,* the *Encyclopédie,* and Rousseau's *Emile,* which lists among Sophie's "feminine" attributes her fondness for milk and sweets and her distaste for meat.[90] As Michèle LeDoeuff has shown, these myths were further reinforced by Roussel's influential *Système physique et moral de la femme* (1775). In a striking conflation of *le moral* and *le physique,* the physician Roussel conferred the status of physiological fact on what in Rousseau was merely an ideal, and thereby reinforced the distinction of woman's body and temperament from the normative temperaments of man.[91] Little wonder that the experience of Marie-Angélique became distorted and seemed monstrous in such a milieu.

This materialist discourse had a long history by the 1770s and clear connections to the case of Mlle Leblanc through the work of the philosopher La Mettrie. Despite the fact that La Mettrie, like Diderot, argued that there is nothing unnatural in nature, he thoroughly vilified Leblanc in his work: he cited her first as a creature of questionable humanity, then as a criminal. These judgments follow the progression in his thought toward a thorough materialism. In the *Traité de l'âme* (1745), La Mettrie notes that Marie-Angélique "ate her sister," but he does not discuss the implications of this cannibalism until *L'Homme machine* (1748), in which the girl reappears as a mentally deranged murderess—living proof of the intellect's dependence on physiology.[92] In his effort to free human psychology from the restrictive reins of morality, La Mettrie claimed that criminal activity must be understood as a physical reaction to adverse stimuli (such as climate, illness, sleep, food, or passions—in this case "depraved desires"). Being dependent on the body, the mind changes in tandem: both sleep or become agitated at the same time; a sick body makes for a sick mind.

In his discussion of deviant psychology, La Mettrie ventured beyond *le physique* into *le moral* and posited that all creatures possess an innate sense of natural law that manifests itself as remorse in the conscience of the guilty. To forestall critics who would cite mankind's moral superiority to animals, La Mettrie gave examples of animals showing "human" feelings and humans committing cruelties rivaling any horrors of the animal kingdom. Leblanc figures on this list as a murderess who killed and allegedly ate her sister alongside other known female criminals: a woman who became obsessed with stealing during pregnancy and whose children inherited the vice; another pregnant woman who ate her husband; and a mother who disemboweled her children, cured their bodies, and ate the flesh like ham.[93] Thieves, cannibals, and bulimics all were victims of involuntary appetites and vices: powerful physical conditions that could easily deprave the human mind. La Mettrie concluded, "If reason is enslaved by a depraved or mad desire, how can it control the desire?"[94] Such examples proved that man's mind does not reign supreme. Although Leblanc's rationality was never questioned, La Mettrie debunked the mind's supposed control over the body and reduced all human actions to laws of mechanical cause and effect.

Leblanc's purported biography, *L'Histoire d'une jeune fille sauvage trouvée dans les bois à l'âge de dix ans,* seems expressly designed to combat such negative portrayals of her character and to elicit interest if not empathy from the reader.[95] Indeed, La Condamine and Lord Monboddo both claimed that *L'Histoire d'une jeune fille sauvage* was published to promote public interest in the wild girl and to allow her to earn some money from the book's profits, with Monboddo going so far as to offer her address to the curious who may care to visit.[96] The very circumstances of publication performed a publicity function: attributed to a certain Mme H——t on the title page, and afterward to the scientist La Condamine, this text's origins pique the reader's curiosity. La Condamine set the stage when, publicly refuting authorship of *L'Histoire d'une jeune fille sauvage* in a letter to M. de Boissy of the Académie française, he evoked a fiction of female community. Alluding to a friendship between the wild girl and a lady known only as Mme Hecquet, "a widow, who lives near St. Marceau," he claimed that the widow was so moved by Leblanc's plight that she recorded the girl's story for posterity.[97]

As if to reinforce this image of a female community between the author/benefactor and the subject/victim, the author of *L'Histoire d'une jeune fille sauvage* deploys textual strategies reminiscent of another "primitive" story, Mme de Graffigny's best-selling novel, *Lettres d'une Péruvienne* (1747). Like *L'Histoire d'une jeune fille sauvage,* Graffigny's fiction relies on the premise that an unnamed female "editor" has come into contact with a beleaguered woman from the New World and has agreed to relay this foreigner's story to her contemporaries in order to alert them to the injustices of European schemes for civilizing or colonizing savages. Both texts use ethnographic data (foreign terms and details of dress, hygiene, and social rituals) to render the fiction more plausible and give it the veneer of a scientific document.[98] Whereas Graffigny used information about the Incas' magnificent empire to naturalize the mores of her primitive heroine, Hecquet tried to make the habits and actions of the wild girl more comprehensible to French readers by labeling her an Eskimo—a race popularly known as the "eaters of raw meat," notorious for their cannibalism, hostility to Europeans, and disgusting personal habits.[99]

These contradictory images of the wild girl in *L'Histoire d'une jeune fille sauvage*—the needy human being versus the savage Eskimo—grew out of the two representational strategies informing Hecquet's (and Graffigny's) narratives. Stressing the wild girl's human qualities—her suffering and vulnerability—allowed the author to criticize indirectly the French and the supposed superiority of the civilized over the primitive; emphasizing the girl's primitive past and remarkable travels allowed the author to reinscribe her tale as an exotic romance, a genre well-known and loved by eighteenth-century audiences. As I argued in *Exotic Women,* tales of exotic and savage women in eighteenth-century France gave a colorful cast and distinct ideological accent to scenarios of gendered dominance and resistance. One might read *L'Histoire d'une jeune fille sauvage*'s literary premise—the penitent wild girl/sinner tells her story to a benevolent widow, who publishes it as a document of public interest under the aegis of a noted male scientist—as a mirror of the powerful paternal authority and religious forces that initially caught the wild girl and had her tamed for French society.

L'Histoire d'une jeune fille sauvage begins with a vivid image reminiscent of medieval tradition—of the uncouth, strong, and threatening forest dweller who inhabits the edges of the civilized world. After seeing the dirty, disheveled girl in an apple tree, the villagers, according to Hecquet, cried out, "There is the devil," locked themselves in their homes, and set upon her a bull dog with a spiked collar. The description of her ensuing conduct embodies the supernatural strength and vicious glee of a medieval wild man, as the narrator announces: "The little savage perceiving [the mastiff] advancing furiously toward her, kept her ground without flinching, grasping her little club with both hands. . . . Perceiving the dog within her reach, she struck him so violently on his head as laid him breathless at her feet. Elated with her victory, she jumped several times over the dead carcass of the dog."[100] Her skillful handling of the club is significant. According to medieval historian Richard Bernheimer, one could always identify a wild man by certain totemic signs: his furry body, bare feet, and the heavy club or tree trunk that he carried.[101] Figure 5 shows such a wild man, hairy and crowned with leaves, wielding the talismanic club in one hand and a coat of arms in the other, as imagined by a fifteenth-century German engraver. Figure 4, from an 1831 chapbook on Leblanc, shows her holding a stick but in a less menacing posture.

Once captured, the heroine becomes less threatening, and her wild conduct looks more like the antics of an undisciplined child. Instead of describing her as a phenomenon worthy of scientific investigation or as a warning about godlessness, the author cites the girl's youth, suffering, and lack of education as the causes of her uncivilized appearance. Of the wild girl's early attempts to speak French, Hecquet writes that "her voice, though weak, was sharp, shrill, and piercing; and her words were short and confused, like those of a child, at a loss for terms to express its meaning" (21). As for the evening when she threw live frogs on the plates of d'Epinay's dinner guests, this author chuckles: "The little savage, quite amazed at the small value they seem'd to set on her delicate fare, carefully gathered up the scattered frogs, and threw them back again on the plates and table" (43).

Echoing Rousseau's pessimistic appraisal of society's power to perfect mankind in the *Discours sur l'origine de l'inégalité* (published the same year as *L'Histoire d'une jeune fille sauvage*),[102] Hecquet emphasizes the pathos of Marie-Angélique's taming by embellishing her narrative with strategies to garner the reader's sympathy. Instead of describing the girl's former physical exploits with shock or disgust, the author sadly remarks on the girl's reduced capacity at present: "I myself have seen some instances of the ease and swiftness with which she ran, than which nothing could be more amazing; and yet what I saw was but the remains of her former agility, which long sickness, and the want of practice for many years, have very much impaired" (19). The girl's body has suffered from the slow coercion toward civilization. In a passage that recalls the warnings of Cheyne and Tissot against the ailments that befall overly civilized bodies, Hecquet explains how, when Leblanc was forced to forgo her customary regimen of "raw bloody flesh, and the leaves, branches and roots of trees," for a civilized diet of cooked meats, bread, salt, and wine, she contracted health problems that proved incurable by civilized methods. "From one dangerous disorder, she immediately fell into another. . . . These pains frequently produced an universal spasm over her whole body, and weaknesses irreparable by all the arts of cookery" (44–45). The wild body remains a compelling object of the reader's gaze, but now the visual interest derives from the display of violent suffering and uncontrollable illness, a tragic spectacle of human frailty. The sickly woman's longing for animal blood is thus recast as an understandable desire for a proven cure, which, the girl claimed, "penetrated every part of her body, softened the acrimony of her throat, and brought back her strength" (48). Moreover, Hecquet asserts that Leblanc was finally so completely humanized (and physically broken) that when the author interviewed her, twenty years after her capture, she abhorred raw flesh.

Once she began to digest the dogma taught by her Catholic "tamers," the girl discovered new moral sensations as well: shame and self-loathing. The tableau depicted in *L'Histoire d'une jeune fille sauvage* of Leblanc's desperate situation after the death of the duc d'Orléans underlines her vulnerability in an uncaring, profit-oriented society: "LeBlanc found herself in a manner totally neglected. I shall leave the reader to imagine the melancholy reflections of this unhappy girl, on being, by the death of her noble patron, left weak and languishing, without either relation or friend to take care of her among these religious [sisters], who, by that event, saw all their [financial] expectations blasted" (57). Yet when the author asked how she planned to survive in the big city with neither financial nor medical aid, Marie-Angélique reportedly replied, "For what purpose . . . has God brought me from among wild beasts and made me a Christian? not surely, afterwards to abandon, and suffer me to perish for hunger, that is impossible" (59–60). After this the author piously concludes, "The pleasure with which I set down this answer, repays, with usury, the pains I have taken to compose the preceding relation" (60).

But the book does not end here. Instead, the author abruptly changes registers and advertises her tantalizing second half to the reader: "I shall subjoin the conjectures I have already promised about her native country, and the accidents which may have brought her into France, and given occasion to the very singular circumstance of her discovery and capture" (60–61). The tragic present is over, the past adventure begins. The second half of *L'Histoire d'une jeune fille sauvage* relates the search for the wild girl's lost origins. In spite of the author's claims to the contrary ("here it is by no means our province or intention to compose a romance, or to devise imaginary adventures," 89), the structure of this part is typical of the voyage literature that enjoyed great popularity in the eighteenth century. Based on interviews conducted partly by means of gestures, which supposedly brought out vague recollections of the girl's homeland and two maritime voyages, Hecquet reconstructs her life as follows.

Given the girl's propensity to swim in the coldest weather, her white skin, and her taste for raw fish, Hecquet deduces she was born an Eskimo. To explain the girl's familiarity with manioc root, Hecquet imagines Marie-Angélique (and her companion) kidnapped from their native Labrador by a ruthless European trader and taken to the Antilles to be sold. This same ship captain, "either through a frolic, or with a fraudulent intention," painted the girls black, trying to pass them for Africans. After crossing the Atlantic on his ship and being given away or sold, the girls escaped, and "perhaps their master or mistress being tired of them, and having despaired of being able to tame them, were very well pleased to get rid of them." As for their route, Hecquet projects an itinerary from "some part of the Zuyder Sea" through the woody country of the lowlands down into the Ardennes, whence they arrived in Champagne. "In this manner the adventures of Leblanc may be easily accounted for," the narrator asserts (92–99).

All the elements of romance are present in this narrative: kidnapping, disguise, perilous voyages, encounter with exotic peoples, and closure. The author adroitly uses the plot to achieve sensationalism and containment, for it captures the native interest through marvelous *péripéties*, only to order everything at the end. Once the girl is labeled an Eskimo (more precisely, a native of slightly less ferocious Labrador), her strangeness dissipates and her assimilation takes on greater value. But the generic indeterminacy of this work leaves many questions unanswered. The many authorial asides, with their claims of veracity and eyewitness evidence, remind one of the text's historical moment (formulas for simulating truth value were legion in the eighteenth-century novel) and paradoxically reinforce the fictional resonance of *L'Histoire d'une jeune fille sauvage.* Is this a novel or a travel tale? Or is it a public service? The narrative ends with a call for help in solving this mystery: "Perhaps it may not be too late still; and the publication of this relation may procure new light in this very curious and dark affair; which is one of the chief motives that have made me compose it" (101–2). By the end of the biography, one's sense of the author's desire to help Leblanc has changed. The protective observer/biographer becomes a novelist/detective, hot on the trail of a tantalizing mystery.

But for all its problems of generic impurity and *invraisemblance,* this work is remarkable in its unquestioning acceptance of the girl's humanity. Hecquet seems dubious about society's self-interested intentions toward Marie-Angélique. She eschews the notions of wonder and optimism about acculturating a "wild" person and instead represents Leblanc's habits as the documented, appropriate customs of a foreign people notoriously resistant to *and* vulnerable to captivity. The girl's physical and mental decline suggests that re-education is an arbitrary act of noble prerogative and forced female socialization, rather than the necessary "taming" of a wild beast. Denouncing the fickleness of noble patronage and the financially motivated Catholic sisters assigned to care for the wild girl, the author caustically remarks, "That Prince has undoubtedly received the reward of his charity in the other world; but in this [one] the unhappy Leblanc received very little advantage from his good intentions" (56–57).

Such moral considerations governed much of the discourse on Leblanc, although not in the purportedly scientific texts we saw above by Linnaeus and Buffon or in the work of Lord Monboddo. Loosely modeled on Rousseau's *Discours sur l'origine de l'inégalité* (1755), Monboddo's *Of the Origin and Progress of Language* (published anonymously, one volume at a time, from 1773 to 1792) posited that humans in the natural state are inarticulate, solitary, nomadic creatures who are preoccupied by their physical needs. Indolence and lack of opportunity, claims Monboddo, are the sole factors that hinder supposedly inferior species from practicing human speech and enjoying other benefits of civilization: "They [orang-utans and solitary savages caught in Europe] want therefore nothing in order to speak, but instruction or example, which the savages who invented the first languages likewise wanted."[103] Language, then, was not an innately human practice or sign of spiritual privilege but a fundamentally social institution, at once a by-product and a founding principle of society.

Eliminating all divine connotations from linguistic practices, Monboddo went on to declare that even in the natural state humans could communicate, if they would imitate the languages of animals. Monboddo cites Leblanc as an example, because "she herself could once have imitated the notes of any bird" (1:208). If the girl's pre-captivity lifestyle resembles Rousseau's theoretical first society (subsistence, nomadism, communication by gesture, cry, and song, use of primitive weapons), her taming resembles a journey through evolutionary time—an evolution that is not physical but social. Although discovered in a "natural" state of brutish egotism, her progressive acquisition of language and socialization brought her from the prehistory of primitive ignorance into the modern world of rational eighteenth-century existence. But the transformation brought losses as well as gains: once she learned to act in a civilized manner and speak French, the wild girl lost her ability to imitate birdcalls.

For Monboddo, Marie-Angélique's experience was not only fascinating as a glimpse of man's evolution, but also provided evidence for his theories on human and primate perfectibility. By stressing the parallel between the wild girl's bestial traits and the orangutan's human traits, Monboddo revealed the permeability of the classifications "man" and "beast." To suggest that Marie-Angélique came from a primitive, half-man/half-beast society such as the legendary Ethiopian "wood eaters" (thought to be early ancestors of the orangutan), Monboddo interrupts his description of the wood eaters with a note: "The wild girl . . . must have been of a race of people very like this mentioned by Diodorus: For she climbed trees like a squirrel, and leapt from one branch to another, upon all-four, with wonderful agility. . . . And she still retained, when I saw her, a mark of the use of her hands as feet in leaping; for her thumbs were of an unusual breadth." She changes from a symbol of the primitive to a symbol of the fluidity and transformation possible between human and animal. Monboddo's vision of her acculturation is singularly optimistic; as he confidently declares: "I am persuaded, it is with wild men, as with wild fruits, which we know will not lose their savage nature at the first remove, but can only be tamed by continued culture for a succession of generations" (1:242–43, 300).

Monboddo's confident claims about interspecies transformation were clearly based on an idiosyncratic vision of period science. More typical is the ambivalent mix of science and morality we find in other accounts from the 1770s. In Gaspard Guillard de Beaurieu's *Cours d'histoire naturelle* (1770), one discovers a classificatory system that embraces creatures as bizarre and unlikely as those listed in Linnaeus's *Paradoxa*. The naturalist classifies "savage man" alongside "merman" *(l'homme marin)*, arguing that the two share the indignity of being called ordinary animals because they have no speech or perfectibility. Beaurieu's work sounds a note of sympathy for animals and especially one of optimism toward the value and power of (French) culture to improve the lives of all creatures. In a passage that echoes the dogmatism of his *Elève*, Beaurieu declares: "What a conquest, what true glory, if we could succeed in making animals that have hitherto been only brutish and nasty as capable as and better than ourselves!"[104] But on arriving at the case of Leblanc, Beaurieu seems to lose this enthusiasm. Describing her as a tragic example of forced socialization, the author concludes with a nostalgic image of peasant simplicity: "Did she not regret the woods one took her from . . . [?] When, after emerging from the hands of nature, one sees our manners, our injustices, etc. if one [cannot] go back into the forest, at least one should be able to lead the life of a good and honest peasant."[105] These calls for respect for animals and a return to a simpler life recall the intellectual climate of Beaurieu's day, in the wake of Rousseau's best-selling *La Nouvelle Héloïse* (1761) and the Physiocratic theories of Morelly, d'Argenson, and Mably, which idealized physical labor and agriculture as the remedy to the moral and economic ills of worldly society.[106] But they also strike a political note, questioning the moral viability of civilizing savages without allowing them any rights as citizens (not even the "natural right" of choosing one's own abode) and criticizing the injustices inherent in French society.

Contrasting with this idealism, a vigorously anti-speculative discourse emerged in the work of late eighteenth-century natural historians, who transformed the wild girl from an exemplar of nature into a pathological case. As we saw above, the story of Peter of Hanover underwent a similar shift in focus. Eberhard von Zimmermann's *Zoologie géographique* (1777) is a prime example. Citing Buffon as his source of information about humanity's natural state, von Zimmermann advances the time-worn theory that man's faculty of speech marks his superiority over beasts. What is interesting in von Zimmermann, however, is his rhetoric of disease. Denouncing the unscientific theories of earlier natural historians, he writes: "Let no one cite the young savage from Hanover, the girl of the forest from Songi or other individuals who have been abandoned. They lived in isolation, and their example . . . teaches us absolutely nothing about man's natural state, since they were never in it. That would be like studying physiology through the observation of a man attacked by the most violent of diseases."[107]

As the positivist spirit gradually began to assert itself, the scientists' appraisal of Leblanc's wildness read sickness (and perhaps a cure?) where people once saw natural essence; they diagnosed a pathological case of isolation where people earlier imagined exotic origins, picaresque adventures, and simian similarities. But the negative resonance of such reasoning was not entirely new; already in *Emile* Rousseau had laid the foundations for this attitude by warning educators against wasting their efforts on sickly or disabled children.[108] Since the senses were the only route to the intellect, any individual whose senses were disabled posed an insurmountable obstacle to education. This logic is symptomatic of what Margaret Doody has labeled the "fascism" lurking in Enlightenment philosophy, which appreciated individuals only insofar as they were capable of having value added or of performing some function in the *polis*.[109]

But we must not assume that this new wave of empiricism put to rest the popular fascination with novelties and curios. In fact, the exhibition of anthropological anomalies and exotica reached its apogee in the nineteenth century when institutional settings were permanently in place to show them. The display of the wild girl in the *Mercure* articles, with their sensational scenes of eating, was part of the genealogy of world-as-exhibit. Such journalistic shows gradually became regularized in the new institutional structures (world fairs, exhibit halls), and eventually they were cut off entirely from the real world in museums. Although Leblanc faded from the collective memory, she lives on today in regional lore. Near the chateau of the vicomte d'Epinoy at Châlons, there is still a place called "Ile de la Fille sauvage."[110] More important, her story continued to fascinate British readers for years after she was forgotten in France.

In the dozen or so British chapbooks and broadsides on Leblanc, one finds a combination of sensationalism, religious didacticism, and optimism about the girl's acculturation. These publications—which all carry more or less the same title *(The Surprising Savage Girl, Caught Wild in the Woods)* and text (an abridged version of Hecquet's biography)—are doubly curious by reason of their national origin and historical moment: their dates range from 1795 to 1831. Leblanc was first discovered near the site of the foremost publisher of chapbook literature in France (Troyes, home of the *Bibliothèque bleue*), yet it appears her story was never taken up in that genre. Why was she so intriguing to British audiences decades after the French had forgotten her? How did an incident in a French province in the 1730s, publicized in a biography of 1755, become so compelling half a century later?

The pious sentiments attributed to Leblanc in *L'Histoire d'une jeune fille sauvage* likely have much to do with her popularity among British publishers. The 1755 biography presented her as something of a Christian martyr, quoting her stoic acceptance of God's will as a lesson to us all and appending a record of her baptism to the text, but such clues were buried within the romance of exotic travels and ethnographic speculation. In the popular genre of the chapbook, the uplifting potential of this tale would be highlighted. The years 1795–1830 in Britain gave rise to a series of intense initiatives on the part of Methodists and evangelical Anglicans to improve working-class morality. Led by the pioneering efforts of Hannah More's Cheap Repository Tract Society, millions of religious tracts resembling chapbooks were published and distributed during this time.[111] Although Leblanc was not explicitly appropriated in this literature, some chapbook publishers cashed in on the trend by emphasizing her new-found religion. Note the subtitle to an 1820 edition: *La Belle Sauvage: The True and Surprising History of a Savage Girl, Found Wild in the Woods of Champagne,* "Containing an Account of the Manner of her first being discovered—Her Battle with her Companion, in which she was victorious—Her passage to England in a Danish ship, to the Captain of which she gave an Account of her former situation in Life, and her Conversion to Christianity."[112] Note also the illustration attached to this edition, which shows the initial moment of taming when Marie-Angélique ventured down from the tree to seize the villagers' offerings (fig. 6). Instead of conjuring up adventure, wildness here connotes that which we leave behind in becoming civilized: the uncouth and unwanted brute Nature.

The chapbooks on Leblanc allow us to see how multiple genres and conventions run through pseudoscientific discourse. The "invented tradition" visible in this corpus manipulates historical records in surprising ways and exhibits a singular disregard for empirical truth. The concept of reinventing tradition, originally coined by Hobsbawm to explain how pervasive imagery can create an illusion of national unity, applies more literally to chapbooks that, to create an illusion of timeliness and wonder, retold the same story again and again with subtle revisions in chronology.[113] Of the eleven chapbook versions of Leblanc's life, seven correctly date the girl's capture (1731) but misdate the certificate of baptism as 1750 (instead of 1732). The four others take great liberties with the dates, claiming that her saga began in 1816, in 1761, in 1755, or "one evening in the month of September last." This chronological license often leads to laughable incongruities, as in the

THE SAVAGE GIRL.
The Manner in which the Savage Girl was taken
Vide Page 4

FIGURE 6

"The Manner in which the Savage Girl was taken." Frontispiece of anonymous chapbook, *La Belle Sauvage: The True and Surprising Story of a Savage Girl, Found Wild in the Woods of Champagne* (London: J. Bailey, 1820?). Reproduced by permission of the British Library, 10601.aa.32.(6).

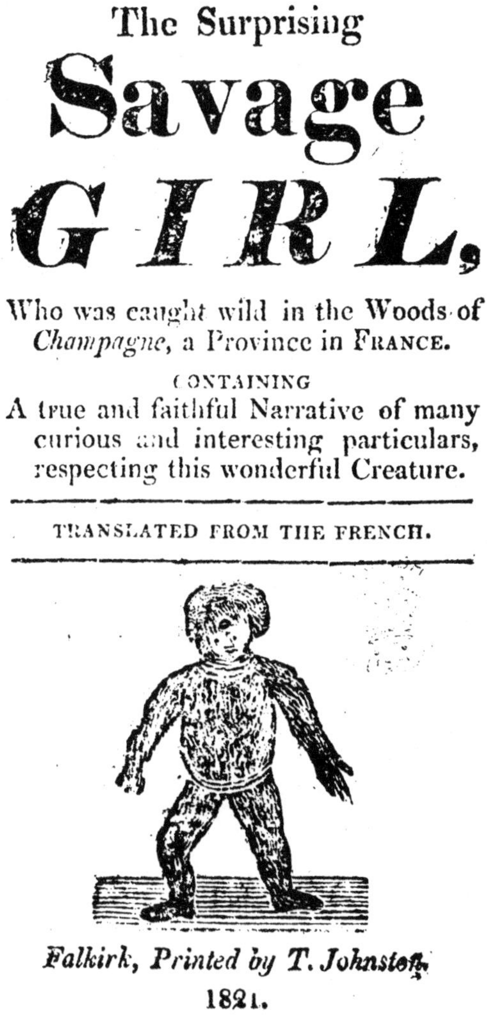

The Surprising
Savage
GIRL,

Who was caught wild in the Woods of *Champagne*, a Province in FRANCE.

CONTAINING

A true and faithful Narrative of many curious and interesting particulars, respecting this wonderful Creature.

TRANSLATED FROM THE FRENCH.

Falkirk, Printed by T. Johnston,
1821.

FIGURE 7

Title page of anonymous chapbook, *The Surprising Savage Girl* (Falkirk: T. Johnston, 1821). Reproduced by permission of the British Library, 12230.cc.42(3).

edition which claims that the girl's baptism took place in 1772 yet dates the certificate of baptism to 1750. The portraits affixed to these texts constitute another invented tradition that suggests hope for the girl's eventual civilization. Her persona runs the gamut from a brute beast (fig. 7) or a primitive wielding a stick (fig. 4) to a beautiful, well-groomed demoiselle (fig. 8).

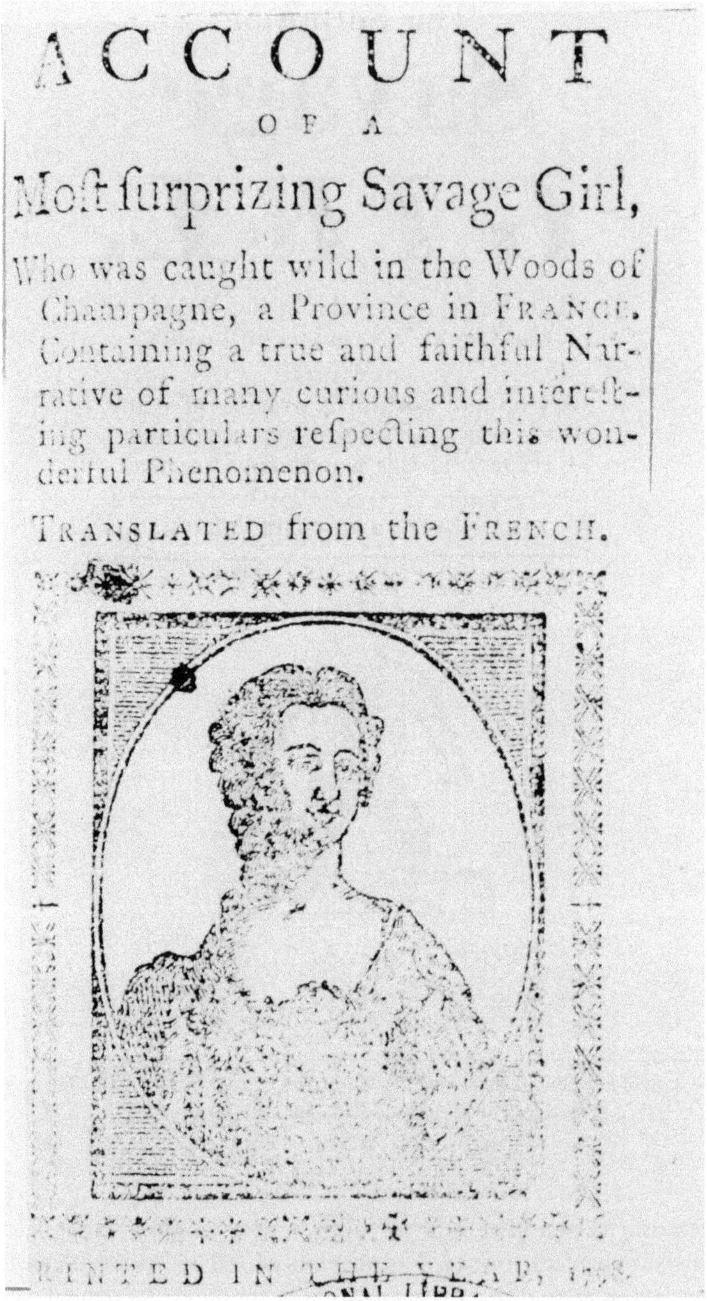

ACCOUNT

OF A

Moſt ſurprizing Savage Girl,

Who was caught wild in the Woods of Champagne, a Province in FRANCE. Containing a true and faithful Narrative of many curious and intereſting particulars reſpecting this wonderful Phenomenon.

TRANSLATED from the FRENCH.

PRINTED IN THE YEAR, 1798.

FIGURE 8

Title page of anonymous chapbook, *Account of a Most Surprizing Savage Girl* (n.p., 1798). Reproduced by permission of the Trustees of the National Library of Scotland.

Taken together, these crude woodcuts and engravings retrace a tale of perfectibility that recalls the triptych of Peter's life shown in figure 3. That these portraits offer unreliable standards for truth in representation becomes glaringly evident when we note that the woodcut image attached to a late seventeenth-century English broadside ballad about a pretty farmer's daughter (fig. 9) bears an uncanny resemblance to the portrait of Leblanc in an 1821 Scottish chapbook (fig. 10)![114] Clearly, this popular literature drew on the same stock imagery and plot lines, reinventing the news and reshaping women's wildness in response to audience demand. Or lack thereof. After 1831, the "surprising savage girl" disappeared from chapbook literature, just as the chapbooks themselves would soon disappear from the literary landscape.

VICTOR DE L'AVEYRON: THE LAST NATURAL MAN

The locals of Lacaune (*département* of Tarn) rival their neighbors in the Aveyron for claims of Victor's origins. Long before his first capture in the spring of 1798, people in nearby villages had caught glimpses of a wild boy running on all fours in the rugged forest and mountains of the Tarn. When at last he was caught and brought to Lacaune, observers recorded, "Everyone wanted to look upon this man of the woods; to satisfy the curiosity of the crowd, he was exhibited publicly on official order, in the middle of the town square."[115] His curiosity value quickly wore off, however, and after a few days in captivity, the guards let him escape back into the forest. Fifteen months later, in June 1799, he was captured forcefully by hunters and confined in Lacaune again, where they dressed him and taught him how to roast the potatoes and root vegetables he liked so much, but he escaped after a week. This time he stayed relatively nearby, and although he hid in the mountains and woods by night, he often ventured into neighboring farms in search of food. The peasants of the region gave him potatoes and called him Joseph (likely in honor of the saint on whose feast day they met him). He passed the whole winter this way, wandering the forest and mountains in the cold, wearing nothing but the rags of a shirt. Finally, in January 1800, he was captured for good and taken to the Hospice de Saint-Affrique, then to the town of Rodez in the Aveyron *département* (hence his nickname), where after biting a few people who got too close, he was confined in the Ecole centrale under close surveillance.[116] The commissioner demanded his transfer to the municipality for two reasons: as "a police measure" and because of his "great interest for observers and naturalists."[117] These two axes of interest—the suspicion of Victor's potential danger to society and

In this Purse, sweet Soul, said I,
twenty pound lies fairly,
Seek no farther one to buy,
for I'se take all thy Barley:
Twenty more shall purchase delight,
thy Person I love so dearly,
If thou wilt lig by me all night,
and gang home in the morning early.

If Forty pound would buy the Globe,
this thing I'de not do Sir,
Or were my Friends as poor as *Job*,
I'd never raise 'em so Sir:
For shou'd you prove to night my Friend,
we'se get a young Kid together,
And you'd be gone e'er nine Months end,
and where shall I find the Father?

Pray what would my Parents say,
if I should be so silly,
To give my Maidenhead away,
and lose my true Love *Billy*?

Oh, this would bring me to Disgrace,
and therefore I say you nay, Sir;
And if that you would me Embrace,
first Marry, and then you may Sir.

I told her I had Wedded been,
fourteen years and longer,
Else I'd chuse her for my Queen,
and tye the Knot yet stronger.
She bid me then no farther rome,
but manage my Wedlock fairly,
And keep my Purse for poor Spouse at home
for some other should have her Barley.

Then as swift as any Roe,
she rode away and left me;
After her I could not go,
of Joy she quite bereft me:
Thus I my self did disappoint,
for she did leave me fairly,
My words knock'd all things out of joint
I lost both the maid and barley.

Printed for *P. Brooksby*, *J. Deacon*, *J. Blare*. *J. Back*.

FIGURE 9

Anonymous broadside, *The Northern Ditty: or the Scotch-man Out-witted by the Country Damsel*, in *The Euing Collection of English Broadside Ballads in the Library of the University of Glasgow*, ed. John Holloway (Glasgow: University of Glasgow Publications, 1971), 422. Reproduced by permission of the Glasgow University Library, Department of Special Collections.

the desire to record and classify Victor's existence for science—would continue to dominate the boy until his death.

For several months, the boy remained at Rodez under the care of the eminent naturalist Pierre-Joseph Bonnaterre (formerly a contributor to the zoology section of the *Encyclopédie;* now a professor of natural history at the Ecole centrale of Aveyron). The early accounts of this boy describe him

THE SURPRISING
SAVAGE GIRL,
Who was caught wild in the Woods of Champagne, a Province in France. Containing a true and faithful Narrative of many curious and interesting particulars respecting this wonderful Phenomenon.

TRANSLATED FROM THE FRENCH.

GLASGOW:
Published and Sold, Wholesale and Retail, by ROBERT HUTCHISON, *Bookseller,* No. 19, *Saltmarket.*

1821.

FIGURE 10

Title page of anonymous chapbook, *The Surprising Savage Girl* (Glasgow: Robert Hutchison, 1821). Reproduced by permission of the British Library, 1078.k5(23).

in terms similar to those we've seen in the accounts of Peter and Marie-Angélique: he reportedly drank from streams and climbed trees "with a surprising agility," and he ran very fast, sometimes on all fours "like a quadruped." But observers give evidence of the somewhat romantic sensibility one finds in Itard, too; listening to the wind, the boy would "turn his head toward the south, laughing out loud and gazing at the sky. He seemed to listen to the aerial symphonies and let his thoughts wander among the clouds. An ironic smile would cross his lips, but we never knew what feelings filled his soul at such times."[118]

It is from this period that his story caught the interest of savants and politicians in Paris. On a request from the minister of the interior, Lucien Bonaparte, he was brought to Paris by Bonnaterre and entrusted to Abbé Sicard at the Institution Nationale des Sourds-Muets in the late autumn of 1800. (By a fortunate coincidence, Itard, who had not yet finished his medical studies, encountered Sicard at this time and was named by him officier de santé for the institution.) Reports from this period describe the wild boy as aged at about twelve, subject to sudden fits of anger, fond of fires, and incorrigible in his efforts to escape. His preferred diet consisted of berries, roots, and raw chestnuts, although he also liked roasted potatoes and would throw them on the fire and retrieve them with his bare hands. Like Marie-Angélique, he disliked sleeping in a bed and was able to tolerate intense cold and damp. His body was covered with scars, notably a long suture crossing his throat—presumably caused by a knife wound. He never spoke, but he expressed his needs through signs, grunts, and cries. Indifferent to all sounds save the cracking of a nut (his favorite food), he appeared a true idiot (from the Greek meaning "a private person" sufficient unto himself).

In the months before he arrived in Paris, the boy became the subject of much public curiosity. A vaudeville act loosely based on his story, *Le Sauvage du département de l'Aveyron ou Il ne faut jurer de rien,* which debuted in March 1800 to great acclaim, offers us a glimpse of how contemporaries perceived the wild boy. Although the play is based on the age-old conceit of mistaken identities (a love-lorn Cossack disguises himself as the savage in order to gain the love of a misanthropic noblewoman), this work inscribes the story of a wild man in a context specific to Napoleonic France. It expresses disgust toward the strong-arm tactics of the new government, for instance, and apprehension toward the ambitions of contemporary science. Audiences particularly applauded songs that satirized the way the state handled this child, as when the mayor declares him a "vagabond non domicilié" (homeless vagrant) and orders him to be locked up in the name of his "rights" and "freedom."[119] Once trapped in a cage exhibit, this "curious rarity" becomes a profit-making spectacle, like other oddities on the market of curiosities. He draws in all manner of curiosity-seekers from the area, most notably a doctor who scares the savage by plotting to do anatomical experiments on him.[120] All ends well, with the Cossack winning his ladylove and adopting the savage (who never actually appears on stage). The final song reinforces the awesome powers of contemporary science, though its reference to a dummy aligns this work with showmanship rather than serious research. Citing the "invisible woman" (an anatomical wax model of the female body) and other popular phenomena, the song acclaims the creation of marvels unknown by the ancients and suggests that one "never can tell" what the French genius will come up with next.[121]

Even more famous was the melodrama *Victor ou l'enfant de la forêt,* which was also running in Paris at this time (in its second year). A conventional tale of forbidden love between an "unfortunate child found in a forest" and the daughter of the baron who adopted him, this play holds little interest except for the hero's name. Notwithstanding Itard's claim of having named Victor after the *o* sound, which was the first sound to attract his attention, legend has it that the "wild boy of Aveyron" was actually named Victor because of this popular fiction.[122]

In these and other works, the legend of a mild-mannered, eminently teachable wild boy spread to the French public.[123] Six months later, when he finally arrived in Paris, the boy was a so-called nine-day wonder drawing huge crowds and igniting a debate in the Parisian newspapers over his authenticity.[124] But those who ventured to see him were sorely disappointed when they found a dirty, scarred, inarticulate creature who trotted and grunted like a beast, ate with apparent pleasure the most filthy refuse, was apparently incapable of even elementary perceptions such as heat or cold, and spent his time apathetically rocking himself backwards and forwards like the animals at the zoo.[125] After the novelty wore off, he spent his days alone, apathetic and unsociable, often masturbating frenetically in the gardens of the institution.

Yet the boy had his admirers. Most notable was Julien-Joseph Virey, a prominent naturalist and member of the progressive Société des Observateurs de l'Homme, who included in his *Histoire naturelle du genre humain* (1800) a long panegyric on the savage of Aveyron. Virey does not gloss over the facts: he offers detailed descriptions of the boy's all-consuming appetite, squalid apathy, and indifference to human contact, cleanliness, and decency. Ultimately, however, this long list of lacks becomes in Virey's primitivist rhetoric a long list of virtues. The boy's self-centered existence suggests his independent spirit; as Virey writes, "Thus his ignorant and savage soul is simple; it is known at first sight; exempt from hypocrisy . . . it is limited, gross; vulgar, egotistical, but it is one unto itself, pure and candid."[126] The boy's idiocy becomes a symbol of his integrity. Citing his habit of defecating in public, Virey claims: "A king before him would be no different than the lowest of mortals; like a new Diogenes, he would tell a modern-day Alexander to move out of his sunshine."[127]

In a passage that seems very naive in retrospect, Virey speculates on what happy mysteries this earthy creature will discover when he enters puberty, and "new sources of life will gush forth from all sides, flooding his soul with new pleasures" (243). The "natural man" (still named Joseph) receives his final apotheosis at the work's end, when Virey equates him with the unfortunate peasant of Rousseau's second *Discours,* who with the advent of agriculture saw his existence transformed from a state of solitary, primitive subsistence to a state of eternal misery and injustice at the hands of other men:

> Go, young unfortunate, venture into this unhappy land, leave behind your primitive and simple ruggedness for the ties of civil life. . . . How you will lose your absolute independence in the shackles of society, in our civil institutions! How many tears you will cry! . . . oh, may you live happily in the midst of your compatriots! May you, simple man, inspire the sublime virtues of generous souls, and transmit to future generations [your] honorable example, as an eternal proof of what a student of innocent Nature might be.[128]

This apostrophe is striking in its simplistic primitivism—a mode of thought one might have assumed would be obsolete in the 1800s, the heyday of positivism. But it is also instructive, since it reveals how eighteenth-century habits of mind lived on after the revolution—despite many claims, and efforts, to the contrary.

When the boy was brought before a group of doctors, however, he elicited no such enthusiasm for brute nature but rather reactions of ambivalence and suspicions of mental pathology. His existence demanded a medical response, if not a cure. Hopes of a cure were not unrealistic at the time. Buoyed by recent innovations in medicine, many contemporaries expressed optimism about physical and mental rehabilitation of supposedly incurable "monsters" such as deaf-mutes. "[A]ll the infirmities that affect humanity have found new help," declared Gudin de la Brenellerie in 1776, citing successful new methods in physical therapy, osteotomy, and especially speech therapy (teaching the quasi-bestial deaf to speak) as "fabulous" inventions that must be witnessed to be believed.[129] The English scientist Thomas

Beddoes echoed this optimism toward medicine in 1793, writing to the naturalist Erasmus Darwin that "a great revolution in this art is at hand. . . . And if you do not, as I am almost sure you do not, think it absurd to suppose the organization of man equally susceptible of improvement from culture with that of various animals and vegetables, you will agree with me in entertaining hopes not only of a beneficial change in the practice of medicine, but in the constitution of human nature itself."[130]

Medicine was thus believed to supply the cornerstone for an entire philosophy of man in which improved public health would be indivisible from enlightened morality and from political reform. But, as David Morris has explained, such hopes relied on a change in practice; reformers demanded that physicians renounce their traditional reliance on "hypothetical explanations" and "imaginary systems" in favor of scientific experiments and clinical observations.[131] Philippe Pinel led this reform and made remarkable innovations in psychology and psychiatry. Before the 1790s, attitudes toward mental abnormalities in France were primarily determined by morality rather than physiology; Pinel was one of the first physicians to maintain that lunatics could be cured, and one of the first to realize the social and medical conditions necessary for recovery (in the therapeutics of "moral medecine").[132] Like his colleagues Cabanis and Alibert, who sought to understand the mind's power over specific bodily conditions, Pinel tried to reveal correlations between the physiological abnormalities of his mental patients and the passions that tortured them.[133] The chasm separating practical applications of medicine from the philosophical study of human intelligence was apparently growing smaller; Itard exclaimed in 1801: "Lighted by the torch of analysis and lending each other a mutual support, these two sciences have in our day laid aside their old errors and made immense progress."[134] But many diseases remained incurable, and medical methods remained rooted in the mixture of moral and physical concerns noted above. Reflecting the tensions of this era are the reports on the "savage" by Pinel, who observed him soon after his arrival in Paris in 1800, and by Itard, who tried to teach him from 1800 to 1806.

In spite of his humanitarian hopes for the boy, Pinel's 1800 report offered a grim prognosis for his future. Whereas other savants—including members of the Société des Observateurs de l'Homme—had hoped the boy would resolve age-old controversies over man's original character and innate ideas, Pinel focused on the resolutely clinical, basing his work strictly on observations of the boy's psycho-motor development and behavior. Pinel vehemently rejected analogies linking the boy to earlier cases of wild children and compared him instead with his patients at the mental asylums of Bicêtre and Salpêtrière. Some of his patients' afflictions, he wrote, derive from physical pathologies (epilepsy, deformed speech organs, deafness), others from moral impairments (resulting from lovesickness or the emotional instability of their mothers). Pinel diagnosed the savage boy similarly, deducing that he was suffering from a defective physical *organisation* as well as *lésions manifestes* in his moral faculties. This pathological condition was probably caused by his mother's fright during pregnancy or birth, the boy's fright or convulsions in childhood due to parasites *(affections vermineuses)*, or particularly difficult and painful teething.[135] This list reveals the double discourse of physiology and morality within Pinel's positivist applied science. The doctor concluded that the savage's antisocial behavior and apparent stupidity were not (as most earlier scientists would have had it) the result of his isolation; rather, they were imputable to mental retardation, a congenital and incurable affliction that probably prompted the boy's initial departure from society. But Itard dared to hope that the boy could be brought out of his lethargia, and the institution entrusted him with the experiment.

In contrast to Pinel's somber prognosis, Itard's 1801 report was highly optimistic. Human science appeared to have come a long way since Arbuthnot tried to investigate the potential of Peter of Hanover. As Candland reminds us, Arbuthnot's work amounted to an observation, not an experiment. Whereas experiments are designed to distinguish between alternatives, observations simply state the evident and classify it in logical patterns.[136] Unlike those who had earlier tried to humanize wild children, Itard did not stop at observation but rather invented a systematic set of methods to test the boy's capabilities and to draw him out of his "vegetative" existence into a heightened sensitivity to things, people, and feelings. But in one important way, Itard's methods resembled Arbuthnot's: both emphasized language lessons and hoped to discern important truths about mankind from conversations with the boy, as if teaching him to speak would help decide whether human intelligence was innate or learned.

Itard's method was to take the boy—now named Victor—through a series of sensory experiments, harnessing the boy's limited resources and devising ways around the intellectual, emotional, and motivational obstacles that blocked his development. He tried to stimulate the boy's memory by devising matching-to-sample experiments, for instance, which taught Victor to match pictures and objects in various colors. He sought to awaken Victor's nervous sensitivity through experiments with objects of different sizes, shapes, and textures, and succeeded in developing the boy's discernment of touch, taste, and cleanliness. The boy grew adept at communicating by gestures, as when he put the handles of a wheelbarrow in a visitor's hands to give him a ride or when he offered visitors their coats after an overly-long stay and "pushe[d] them gently towards the door, which he close[d] impetuously upon them" (*Wild Boy*, 35). His apathy gave way to expressions of interest and pleasure in certain people, such as the housekeeper, Mme Guérin, and for certain rituals he enjoyed, such as a daily walk.

Such success with the child's sensitivity, though modest, Itard concluded, provided material proof of "most important truths" concerning man's natural state. Judging from the cases of Victor and of other children found in the wild, Itard ascertained that man is inferior to many animals in "the pure state of nature" (that is, total solitude); he lacks any kind of innate morality, intelligence, or feelings, and is dependent on external factors for all his ideas and needs. It is possible to improve mankind, but only through rigorous, personalized forms of education. Echoing the ideas of the Edgeworths, noted above, Itard argued that one must appreciate the broad spectrum of capabilities that exist in human beings, from the genius to the feeble-minded, declaring, "[M]odern medecine . . . of all the natural sciences, can help most powerfully towards the perfection of the human species by detecting the organic and intellectual peculiarities of each individual and determining therefrom what education ought to do for him and what society can expect from him."[137]

One must recall that this report was written to account for Itard's work before the authorities who funded the experiment—this call for a change in policy was not only a rhetorical flourish but a pragmatic appeal to the people who controlled the institutions of medicine. When Itard's report was first presented to the Société des Observateurs de l'Homme in October 1801, it met with widespread applause. Joseph-Marie Degérando (who would soon become minister of the interior) declared that "the philosophers' dreams are starting to come true. . . . In a very short time, citizen Itard has obtained a success that is well nigh prodigious; I have seen it myself."[138] Once published, this report brought instant fame to Itard; by 1802 it was translated into English and became an overnight sensation. The emperor of Russia, Alexander I, was so impressed with Itard's work that he presented him with a saphire mounted on a golden pin and an invitation to join him in Saint Petersburg. By June 1803 Itard was named surgeon (de deuxième classe) at Val-de-Grâce Hospital, and after he defended his thesis, the government offered him a further promotion to surgeon aide-major, which he turned down to continue his clinical work in Paris.

In 1806 Itard published his second report, which seems far removed from the idealistic hopes of the first. Instead of calling for medical reform, this work reveals a resignation born of Victor's lack of progress and a disillusionment with the limits of "moral medicine." The program had advanced in some ways. He taught the boy to generalize, for instance, by devising more complicated experiments that matched objects to words, and then matched the same words with similar objects. His work on Victor's sense of hearing improved as well, so that the boy was eventually able to distinguish between simple sounds, such as a bell and a drum, then increasingly complicated sounds such as a rod hitting a shovel, a rod hitting skin, or a wind instrument. But overall, Victor's successes—his rudimentary reading and writing, his growing emotivity and understanding of moral values—paled by comparison with his general unsociability. He remained essentially selfish, unable to show cognition except after slow and laborious efforts. Despite Itard's special attention to the child's speech, Victor remained largely mute (apart from his ability to pronounce the word *lait* and the sound *o*). Victor's sexuality proved particularly problematic; although tortured by genital sensations, the adolescent had no notion of sexual functions or social decorum. He continued to spend hours in frenetic masturbation. Itard tells of trying to redirect his energy through rigorous exercise or to soothe him with cool baths, to no avail. The doctor's inability to cure became emblematic of the failure of his science in general: "I was obliged to restrain myself and once more to see with resignation these hopes, like so many others, vanish before an unforeseen obstacle."[139]

After six years, Itard abandoned the case and devoted the rest of his career to a medical practice specializing in deaf-mutes. Victor was initially transferred back to the Institution des Sourds-Muets, but his loud and public masturbation prompted the administration to seek other arrangements. Victor's bad example also influenced the institution to refuse admission to another wild boy discovered soon thereafter. Citing the "contagious example of vicious habits" that this boy would doubtlessly bring with him, the institution's administration recommended that he be interned at the local hospice instead (Gineste, *Victor de l'Aveyron,* 45–46). A governmental pension was arranged for Mme Guérin to care for the boy, who then fell completely out of the public eye and spent the rest of his life with her in an annex of the institution until his death in 1828.

To say that Itard's experiment with Victor ended in failure is misleading, since the second report, like the first, was widely acclaimed. The authorities who evaluated it praised Itard's intelligence, wisdom, and courage and argued that his modest success must be attributed to the boy's imperfect physical constitution rather than to the teacher's lack of talent.[140] His experience with Victor taught Itard the skills to become an excellent doctor and brought him fame among the wealthiest Parisian elite. Moreover, his innovative techniques inspired many pioneers in early childhood education, including Maria Montessori, who translated the reports into Italian to revamp her own teaching methods. Today Itard's works are widely read by students in developmental psychology, behavior analysis, and the "deprivation triad" (sensory-social-cultural development).[141]

Paradoxically, as Gineste has pointed out, Itard was a positivist who refused to make value judgments or to use mechanical methods of intervention with his patient (except in the most extreme circumstances). Although he came of age while studying the mechanical philosophy of La Mettrie, Condillac, and Locke, Itard ultimately rejected the notion of man as a mass of molecules, an organism like a machine whose defective mechanisms might be repaired with psychological or biological techniques.[142] Part of Itard's appeal lay in his humanity and commitment to the patient's well-being. In his writings on Victor, as in other works, Itard argued for a broad conception of humanity embracing the perfectible as well as the terminally marginal: deaf-mutes, the mentally ill, and the retarded. Echoing Locke's warning about the arbitrary nature of all efforts to classify mankind, Itard declared: "The boundaries which separate reason from madness, good from evil in our moral existence are staked out in a very haphazard, arbitrary manner, here by doctors, there by moralists, and are subject to variation."[143] Those once designated as "monstrous" are not only human, they embody the very essence of humanity: "in madness there is all that is human."[144]

Itard is often cited as the father of systematic experimental methods in psychology, and he invented many methods that have passed the test of time.[145] But perhaps he could have done more. Later scientists criticized Itard for not intervening forcefully enough with his patient and for remaining focused on the mind to the detriment of the body.[146] We must recall the caution Itard took not to interfere with the most vulnerable facet of Victor's psyche (his sexuality), even though this unresolved problem doomed the boy's chances for social integration. Physical "cures" did exist. Itard could have tried more intrusive physical means such as binding, therapeutic blood-letting, or electric shock, instead of stopping at cold baths and exercise. But instead he refrained and, in the name of "moral medicine," lamented his inability to do anything to assuage the boy's pain.

Many of his colleagues harbored far more ambitious goals, however, and used physical means to achieve them. Mechanical devices, such as rotating machines, were recommended for mentally disturbed patients, as were other means of inducing a "therapeutic" form of terror. The idea was that if one could detach the mind from an idea and replace it by another feeling or by terror, the convulsions, depression, or other pathologies could be cured.[147]

Although the practice of using electric shock to cure mentally ill patients had only been introduced in the early 1800s, the therapeutic use of electricity had been well known since the 1770s at least. The claims for electricity's curative role were nothing short of miraculous: many believed it could reawaken a destroyed memory, reestablish a wandering reason, endow a failing eyesight with renewed vigor, and most significant, impart speech to a mute tongue.[148]

Itard's unwillingness to make value judgments also ran counter to contemporary trends. More typical was the 1812 judgment of Victor rendered by F. J. Gall and G. Spurzheim, two doctors who invented and promoted the study of phrenology, a pseudoscience that claimed to assess people's character flaws by analyzing their skull's shape and protuberances. In their influential *Anatomie et physiologie du système nerveux (Anatomy and Physiology of the Nervous System)*, they traced Victor's stunted intellect to his abnormal anatomy and concluded succinctly that he was an "imbecile à un haut degré" because of his "defective" cranial anatomy—his low, narrow forehead, small, deepset eyes, and poorly developed cerebellum.[149] The portrait of Victor that serves as frontispiece to Itard's first report typifies the fascination with skull structure that marks this era, the heyday of phrenology and physiognomy (fig. 11). The silhouette makes it glaringly obvious that the subject suffers from such "defects" as a weak chin, an overbite, deepset eyes, and a receding forehead. The prominent scars and blemishes on the boy's skin reveal the hardships he had to overcome in order to survive—not only smallpox and the rough conditions of the wilderness but also a human attacker. The original caption reads: "Showing on the front of his neck a transversal scar due to a criminal attempt on the boy's life." Interestingly, a very different vision of this "wild boy" greets the reader of the English translation of Itard's report (1802; fig. 12). As if this boy were more successfully cured, here Victor's scars and blemishes have been erased, his eyes have been enlarged to appear less reptilian, his chin has been made more prominent, his nose has been straightened, and his hair has been combed. The resulting effect is quite the contrary of the 1801 image; this boy appears pleasant, not pathological; he seems reassuringly normal.

This kind of material rationale became increasingly important later in the nineteenth century. By 1859 anthropology had been largely remodeled along comparative anatomy lines: it was primarily physical anthropology and above all craniology.[150] The definition of *monstrous* humanity changed accordingly. As Marie-Hélène Huet has argued, the new science of teratology rejected the time-honored theory of maternal imagination and redefined monsters as simple variants in the orderly interplay of biological norms.[151]

FIGURE 11

Frontispiece of J. M. G. Itard, *De l'éducation d'un homme sauvage ou des premiers développements physiques et moraux du jeune sauvage de l'Aveyron* (Paris: Gouyon, 1801). Reproduced by permission of the Bibliothèque Nationale de France, Paris.

FIGURE 12

Frontispiece of J. M. G. Itard, *An Historical Account of the Discovery and Education of a Savage Man, or of the First Developments, Physical and Moral, of the Young Savage, caught in the woods near Aveyron in the year 1798* (London: Richard Phillips, 1802). Reproduced by permission of the British Library, G14680.

Human differences were widely conceived in terms of pathology or race; it was no longer assumed that all men were perfectible or could ascend to the top. Thus L. J. Delasiauve declared Victor "a mutilated being" in his famous 1865 article, adding, "the savage of Aveyron was what he was supposed to be, according to his crippled nature. Some potentialities did not exist."[152] Delasiauve also offered scores of methods to help cure unfortunates like Victor, however, and suggested that with physical techniques Victor might have achieved more progress than he did. The jury remained suspended on the case of the "savage of l'Aveyron" long after all the actors had died.

> I can never care for seeing things, that force me to entertain low thoughts of my Nature. [. . .] I could never look long upon a Monkey,without very Mortifying Reflections.
>
> —William Congreve

Monsters and subhuman creatures effect a great pull on the human psyche, writes Dennis Todd, because they seem to answer suspicions we may have about our identities, to point to the hidden shape of the self we may intuit or fear lies hidden beneath the convenient fictions of our quotidian identities.[153] This same dynamic of attraction and avoidance operates within the stories of *Homines feri:* their evocation of mankind's humble origins and need for contact touches us, but it also disturbs by reminding us of the "despotism of the passions" that afflicts us all.[154] Whether couched in terms of his deviance from *le physique* or *le moral,* the wild child incarnates the double-edged promise of science: being recognizably human, the child should be amenable to teaching or rehabilitation, but his peculiar habits and strengths challenge the possibility—and ethical viability—of a cure.

Of all the children, Marie-Angélique's humanization was most successful since she eventually mastered language, religion, and social decorum. Yet hers was also the most problematic because of the specters of bestiality and moral relapse that haunted her reputation. Narratives of all the *Homines feri* highlight five categories of wildness: diet, locomotion, nakedness, passion, and speech.[155] But whereas Peter's oddities were couched in a benign primitivism and Victor's difference was diagnosed as a mental disorder, Marie-Angélique's peculiarities were widely held against her as proof of her sin or unfitness for society.[156] Her one-time assault on a forest companion grew into a legend of murderous, even cannibalistic passions. Her physical strength was initially discouraged as "indecent" by the priests in Châlons; later, when her health and new-found modesty no longer permitted tree climbing or running, her benefactors demanded these feats as entertainment for visitors and royal guests.[157] As adolescents, all three children evidenced anxiety concerning the opposite sex. But whereas Peter's awkward embrace of Lady Walpole was deemed an endearing flirtation, and Victor's passionate leap onto the bed of a young lady was cited as evidence of his "mad gaiety,"[158] Marie-Angélique's rejection of male attention recalled her unsociable past and potential for violence. (Note that it was heterosexuality at stake here: Victor's impetuous gestures toward a woman were judged entertaining, but his later penchant for autoeroticism would occasion the harshest of reprisals.)

Schiebinger has documented the sexual conventions that marked eighteenth-century naturalists' portrayals of ape anatomy and behavior: the female was invariably represented as chaste and modest, the male as foolish and lascivious. Such images, Schiebinger argues, had implications beyond the domain of natural history: they "served to reinforce the notion that females—both human and beast—are by nature modest and demure."[159] Accounts of Leblanc persistently underlined her deviations from normative female conduct years after her taming and language learning were complete. This strategy of projecting the natural onto a state of culture that the *Puella campanica* could never attain was a potent caution, warning of the dangers awaiting those who strayed from rules of proper, civilized femininity. Although Marie-Angélique's lack of interest in men was deemed abnormal, even ominous, the uncouth aggressiveness of Peter and Victor toward women drew only laughs. Surely this is not unrelated to eighteenth-century popular imagery, which propagated a female moral code of chaste decency all the while titillating the public with images of savage man's irresistible sexual appeal. As the ballad commemorating the London visit of three Cherokee chiefs intoned: "Wives, Widows and Matrons, and pert little Misses, / Are pressing and squeezing for Cherokee kisses."[160]

Perhaps it was the very success of the wild girl that doomed her to be judged with apprehension. Because of their indomitable alterity, Peter and Victor remained safely on the margins of social intercourse; accounts of their lives inscribed the boys within the comfortable parameters of scientific observation and popular entertainment. Marie-Angélique's life, however, traced a spectacular rise from subhuman to sociable that belied any doubt of her humanity. Yet her notorious past, like the guttural noises that peppered her fluent French, dogged her for years, prompting "low thoughts" of human nature and "Mortifying Reflections" that readers would rather not admit.

Turning from the sensational to the philosophical, one can see in the texts on wild children how eighteenth- and nineteenth-century writers grappled with still-current questions concerning mankind's dominion over animals, the process of language acquisition, and the importance of social contact for mental health. Taken together, the most striking impact of these texts is the growing sense of optimism about science's power to improve on the human condition. The people who worked with Peter and Marie-Angélique resorted to traditional methods: language lessons and religious training. Even when they met with success, as in the case of Leblanc, superstitious fears of the girl's pre-social past made them despair of ever truly taming the child. By the time Victor was found in 1799, the institutions that had greeted Peter and Marie-Angélique—the court and convent—were thoroughly altered, and the mechanisms of integrating such individuals were firmly rooted in "science," not theology. Thus Victor received a state-of-the-art education that was exemplary for its sustained, methodical, scientifically based methods. Itard did not only try to teach Victor to speak (although that remained a crucial component), he also sought to draw out the boy's other mental, moral, emotional, and physical capacities. Much of this evolution in treatment can be traced to the different modalities of human science as it was practiced at the different moments seen here. The human science of 1720–1760 was dominated by methods of natural history that sought to observe and classify mankind according to pre-existing habits of thought and by religious concerns over mankind's proximity to the divine or the hard work of redemption. By the 1800s, when Victor was discovered, a thoroughly secular form of professional medicine had replaced earlier attempts at taming, and the wild child—now considered a case of mental pathology—benefited from a more humane, individualistic form of education. In real-life cases like this, it seemed the scientists' optimism was well founded.

—CHAPTER TWO—

The Animated Statue and the Plasticity of Mankind

Although fascinating, the cases of Peter, Marie-Angélique, and Victor were ultimately deemed failed experiments in human science. After the excitement of their discovery passed, observers realized these children would never provide answers to the aporia of mankind's origins and progress. But such questions remained at the center of period debates and prompted a variety of investigatory methods drawn from "experimental philosophy" to see how the human mind responds to—and could potentially be improved by—its environment. Narratives of statues or Adamic figures suddenly coming to life date back to antiquity in such authors as Herodotus, Arnobius, Ovid, and Cicero, but they took on particularly powerful currency during the Enlightenment.[1] Coming alive *ex nihilo,* like Locke's "blank sheet," the statue represented the logical point of departure for a psychology based on sequential development. As a means of visualizing the invisible, the figure also conjured up the technologies used to demonstrate hidden bodily functions, like the *écorchés* of human musculature in the *Encyclopédie* article "Anatomy," the gynecological wax model (or *femme invisible*) of Marie-Catherine Biheron, and Vaucanson's automated digesting duck. But the processes of human thought proved more difficult to visualize than digestion or anatomy. In order to demonstrate the methodological and ethical difficulties implicit in this experimental discourse, I have designed this chapter in three parts. The first analyzes how some eighteenth-century philosophers conceived the mind as a plastic entity responding to the senses, particularly through imagery of a new-born man or animated statue, and shows how such rhetoric created the illusion of performing science.[2] The second explains how contemporaries reacted to such tales in view of larger debates about experimentalism. The third part notes the darker implications of this model of human development by suggesting its ramifications for women and the working poor, as well as its role in large-scale efforts at social engineering through education. The first and second sections thus provide the conceptual definitions and rhetoric of the "sensationist" or "associationist" schools of thought that inform, to a lesser or greater degree, all the literary works analyzed in chapters 3, 4, and 5.[3] But the third section is most germane to our discussion of perfectibility. It is here that we see how period thinkers deduced from this abstract picture of mankind the social and educational conclusions that are our ongoing concern in this book.

SENSIBILITY AND ANIMATED STATUES

The image of a human consciousness brought to awareness *tabula rasa* is found in all kinds of period writing: in conjectural histories and ethnographic accounts it signified the transition from savagery to primitive sociability; in legal texts it signaled the ineffability of natural laws; and in libertine literature it represented mankind's reflexive impulse toward sexual pleasure (often by contrast to the rigid and arbitrary restrictions of marriage).[4] This imagery of Adamic men and statues coming alive responded to two tendencies in early eighteenth-century science and philosophy: (1) the impulse to explain complex phenomena by reducing them to their simplest components or earliest origins (what one writer called the "hankering after the bare Mechanical causes of things")[5] and (2) an appreciation of the sentient body as the central influence on human perception and thought.

Locke is generally cited as the father of the sensationist approach to human psychology because of his theory that the brain receives information from physiological sensations instead of innate, God-given ideas. Building on Locke's principles, many writers and physicians incorporated the lexicon of "nerves," "fibers," and "vapours" into their explanations of human behavior.[6] These terms—and the theories of sensibility behind them—were hugely popular because they offered a means to identify empirical causes for emotional responses. As Barbara Benedict notes, "with its tremblings and tears, flushes and faints, the body speaks a sincerity before which devious language resigns."[7] But one must recall that Locke also recognized the danger of positing physiology as the basis of human understanding. The sensory organs could be vitiated by illness or madness, just as the sensations they pass along could be compromised by the effects of custom or irrational antipathies.[8] Moreover, as Barker-Benfield has wisely pointed out, Locke's physiological model of reasoning could "seriously modify an individual's sense of personal control and freedom" by suggesting that biology dictates destiny.[9] Indeed, this deterministic rationale was used by some people to justify the prerogatives of the privileged. If the senses dominated the mind, it seemed quite logical to assert that women's minds—which were necessarily troubled by their heightened sensitivity to nervous disorders—could never attain works of genius, and that the lower-born, whose nerves were coarsened by menial labor, could never rise to the level of abstract thinking.

The figure of the sentient body was more than a rhetorical strategy or metaphysical concept; it also had roots in laboratory science. The concept of physical sensibility can be traced to the work of the Swiss experimentalist Albrecht von Haller, who from the 1730s to the 1750s performed hundreds of experiments on living animals and drew up an influential theory of bodily response. Haller's work went beyond traditional understanding of reflexes or "animal spirits" to distinguish two kinds of reactivity manifest in the body: irritability, which drew on involuntary, ongoing unconscious reactions, and sensibility, which was tied to voluntary, physical activities willed by the soul, using nerve fibers as a medium of communication with the body.[10] Haller's concepts helped scientists move away from mechanical models to seek out physiological bases for mental states.[11] According to Antonie Luyendijk-Elshout, Haller's concepts of irritability and sensibility summoned up a new view of the human body: "It became an organism with a mind, which was believed to be responsive to outside influences apart from the pathways of mechanical connections. The mind/body relation became crucial in a different way," giving rise to more studies in what we would now call psychology and medical anthropology, as well as education and physiology.[12]

Haller's pioneering work on the nerves was part of a massive effort to ground knowledge in verifiable, empirical data—an effort that we find in medical and literary discourse as well. By demonstrating an experiment before an audience or detailing every step of the experiment in writing, people felt they could guarantee the authenticity of results. As the anatomist William Hunter wrote, describing his lectures: "if a teacher would be of real service, he must take care not merely to describe, but to show or demonstrate every part. What the student acquires in this way is solid knowledge arising from the information of his own senses; thence his ideas clear and make a lasting impression on his memory."[13]

This autobiographical empiricism underscored the importance of witnessing in creating truth claims. But the demand for witnessing posed a problem for human science. Some tests could be arranged for study of human anatomy or the nervous system, but what about the mind? Many people lamented that the great inroads being made into animal physiology and cognition could not be pursued—or were wilfully neglected[14]—on human subjects.[15] As evidence of this frustration, one finds scores of proposals for work on human intelligence and language acquisition in the annals of period science.[16] Proposals ranged from the banal to the sadistic; indigent children stranded in uninhabited locales formed a particularly troubling test population.[17] One writer suggested that in order to determine how vision affects abstract thinking, a "king or magistrate endowed with public authority" should procure of group of orphans, blindfold them, and relegate them to some quiet place where they would live until adulthood. The superior senses of hearing and touch that these children would necessarily develop would well reward them for the sacrifice, the author asserted; their sensory acuteness would enable them to become "useful citizens, perhaps even illustrious citizens."[18]

Philosophical narratives of sentient statues belong to this genre of projected or virtual experimentation. The rhetoric of such philosophers as Buffon, Condillac, and Bonnet resembles the techniques of period experimentalists in its attempts to *stage* human science for the public eye. Eliding the barriers between fiction and reality, the thought experiment takes on the symbolic weight of an empirical event, thanks to the narrator's "eyewitness" persona and his serious or even scolding asides to the reader. Although their apparatus are vaguely defined, through figurative language these authors purported to experiment with invisible facets of human experience or, as Charles Bonnet put it, "to go back as far as possible into the mechanics of our ideas."[19] Such texts enjoyed the status of science (or "experimental physics") in their day.[20] Granted, "experimental methods" covered a huge array of practices in this period: over the course of the century, metaphysical geometry gave way to empiricist psychology, but writers remained rooted in introspection.[21] By perusing the best-known fictions about animated statues from this period, we can see how ideas of the human mind evolved gradually from mechanical or metaphysical models into an entity defined by physiology,[22] with an intelligence and a political destiny of its own.

Buffon

The section of Buffon's *Histoire naturelle* titled "De l'homme" (1750) exemplifies the mid-eighteenth-century shift from mechanical models to a more zoological vision of human life. Instead of relying on fixed laws of motion or atomic analyses of individual cells, Buffon argues that there are a panoply of influences—geography, climate, diet, reproduction, habits—that have an impact on human life. In the chapter "Des Sens en général"

("Of the Senses in General"), Buffon begins by explaining the two building blocks of human and animal bodies: unfeeling matter (bones, fat, blood, lymph) and feeling matter (membranes, nerves). Nerves form the core of volition and intelligence: the "active substances, which give spring and vivacity to all the members."[23] Since the senses in all animals are made up of the same thing—nerves—it should be possible to explain their functioning in common. This method works for sight, sound, smell, and taste, which function similarly (to different degrees) in humans and animals. But when he arrives at the sense of touch, Buffon must discriminate. Only humans and apes have hands. And since hands are the most effective transmitters of touch, and touch connotes sensitive intelligence, these animals must be the most intelligent of all.[24]

But how to explain the difference between ape and human intelligence? At this point in his analysis, Buffon's method breaks down. In the other chapters of *Histoire naturelle,* he was able to follow the same procedure: he carefully described the animals' appearance and behavior and sketched causal ties to material phenomena (such as diet and climate) in the animals' environment. But the natural historical method could not pertain to mankind, because there seemed to be no material reason why the human's senses enlightened him above all others. This methodological impasse led the author to depart from the realm of science to embark on a self-avowed "philosophical tale" *(récit philosophique),* which he justified by invoking the importance of the inquiry.[25] Thus he abandons the technical terms, objective stance, and taxonomical focus that organized the other sections of his work in order to make his reader *feel* the facts more readily ("[A]fin de rendre les faits plus sensibles," *De l'homme,* 214). But what exactly are those facts?

In order to explain mankind's superior powers of mind, Buffon imagined a man like Adam, full-grown at the "moment of his creation," waking up for the first time.[26] As the man progressively explores his five senses, he discovers many forms of pleasure and some hints of pain. Just as period illustrations figured Buffon's Adam as a muscular Adonis reaching to the heavens, so does the text wax poetic on this creature's perfect powers of *sensibilité.*[27] On opening his eyes, he recalls being enthralled by the sight of "the light, the celestial vault, the verdure of the earth, the transparency of the waters," and the sound of birdsong, which "excite[s] the most sweet and enchanting emotions."[28] The taste of a ripe red grape, he exclaims, "fill[s] me with astonishment and transport. Till now I had only enjoyed pleasures; but taste [gives] me an idea of voluptuousness."[29] Just as the sense of touch established the superiority of mankind's intelligence, the sense of touch proves crucial here, too. Through his hands, the new-made man discovers love and heterosexual pleasure, which cap his development into personhood. Awakening, he sees a body by his side that appears different from his own and, while reaching out to verify its existence with his hands, he instantly achieves that sixth sense—sexual passion and love—which inaugurates his participation in humanity:

> I ventured to lay my hand upon this new being: with rapture and astonishment I perceived that it was not myself, but something much more glorious and desirable; and I imagined that my existence was about to dissolve, and to be wholly transfused into this second part of my being. I perceived her to be animated by the touch of my hand: I saw her catch the expression in my eyes; and the lustre and vivacity of her own made a new source of life thrill in my veins. I ardently wished to transfer my whole being to her; and this wish completed my existence; for now I discovered a sixth sense.[30]

This passage is interesting as regards Buffon's "naturalization" of the body's propensity for pleasure and the inevitability of sexual desire. By placing humankind more or less on the same plane as other living creatures, Buffon reduced human intelligence to a physiological, rather than a divine, capacity.[31] As the sun sets on this amorous couple, the narrator concludes: "I perceived with pain, that I lost the sense of seeing; [but] my enjoyment was too exquisite to allow me to dread annihilation."[32] Although the sexual act is but vaguely evoked here, by couching it in terms of an irresistible and beneficial force, Buffon endowed human sexuality with what Aram Vartanian has called "metaphysical respectability." He suggested that man does not fully exist until, on discovering woman, he becomes conscious of himself as a sexual being capable of loving and being loved in return.[33]

This image of an innocent youth feeling sexual arousal for the first time was routinely used by pornographers, who, as Margaret Jacob notes, claimed "to speak honestly and openly about things sexual, either to instruct or to arouse by just using the words."[34] But Buffon claimed that his tale was meant not to arouse but to edify. As proof he cited his "delicacy of style, that philosophical apathy, which annihilate[s] every loose desire, and bestow[s] on words nothing more than their simple and primitive signification."[35] This professed reliance on words' "simple and primitive signification" recalls the charter of the Royal Society, which asked that "the Matter of Fact shall be barely stated, without any Preface, Apologies, or Rhetorical Flourishes."[36] But the analogy only goes so far. Although Buffon's Adamic narrative in

L'Histoire naturelle hid the act of copulation under a veil of pudicity, its poetic imagery hardly exemplified the "naked way of writing" espoused by Boyle.

As if to certify its status as a scientific narrative, in the 1772 edition the author appended to this story results drawn from a laboratory—namely, experiments to test the human body's tolerance of heat by putting people in super-hot ovens and baths. Gone are the flights of wonder and imagination; these sentient bodies are allowed only one sense. In this account, the people subjected to intense heat seem strangely cut off from their intellects; we learn nothing of the sight, hearing, taste, smell or psychic disturbances suffered by the girls who sat in ovens set at 120, 130 and 140 degrees Fahrenheit; they are said only to "withstand, without incommodity," the heat.[37] The resulting narrative—which must be one of the oddest hybrids of physiological information, experimental evidence, and lyric sensuality ever written—reveals the great latitude given to "matters of Fact" in eighteenth-century science.[38]

Condillac

As a major proponent of the inductive method, Abbé Etienne Bonnot de Condillac insisted that the proper way to learn any science was through analysis, that is, by duplicating the process of discovery in the student's mind. Elsewhere he applied this insight to mathematics; in the *Traité des sensations* (1754) he applied it to what would later be known as cognitive psychology.[39] Because of the nature of human memory, it is impossible for man to remember his earliest ignorance or the gradual process by which he first came to awareness. Locke had been stymied by just this problem in his *Essay Concerning Human Understanding;* he traced the origin of man's knowledge of laws of nature to sensations and abstract ideas but left undecided the question of the nature of the latter.[40] In the *Traité des sensations,* Condillac proposed to answer Locke's unresolved question by showing that abstract ideas could themselves be connected to sensations. Condillac strove to ban the arbitrariness of Locke's system; as John O'Neal points out, Condillac's definition of experience left nothing to chance, illness, or confusion.[41] Given the impossibility of testing real human beings, the only way to do this, Condillac claimed, was to invent an experimental subject and analyze how it develops sensations into abstract ideas.

Although the sequential chain of senses in Condillac's text resembles Buffon's,[42] his rhetoric reveals an even bolder attempt to engage the reader by means of what Shapin and Schaffer term "virtual witnessing."[43] Like other experimental philosophers working in an empiricist and inductive mode, Condillac tries to generate matters of fact (or a probable hypothesis) through perceptual experience. But his reasoning relies on a startling sleight of hand. Declaring that the only way to explain how sensations generate abstract knowledge is through recourse to a visual phenomenon, he demands that the reader imagine a marble statue brought magically to life: "we imagined a statue constructed internally like ourselves, and animated by a mind which as yet had no ideas of any kind. We supposed the marble exterior of the statue to prevent the use of its senses and we reserved to ourselves the right to open them at will to the different impressions of which they are susceptible."[44] Once this premise is established (irrespective of its impossibility), Condillac proceeds as if he were an experimentalist defending his work against charges of illegitimate performance. First he lays out the rules for the reader-witness: "I wish the reader to notice particularly that it is most important for him to put himself in imagination exactly in the place of the statue we are going to observe. He must enter into its life, begin where it begins, have but one single sense when it has only one, acquire only the ideas which it acquires, contract only the habits which it contracts: in a word he must fancy himself to become just what the statue is."[45] Only by adopting this introspective method, Condillac declares, will the reader will be able to analyze how the human mind gradually acquires sensations and then ideas.

Just as Boyle's air pump experiments depended on public approbation, Condillac defined the goal of his experiment in social as well as epistemological terms: its legitimacy depended on its being witnessed in the correct manner by many people.[46] Why else would he have prefaced the treatise with "Advice of some importance to the Reader" ("Avis important au lecteur")? Yet the burden of proof in this case lay not with the experimenter but with the witness. If, as Condillac suggests, the reader follows his rules and absorbs the narrative in the correct manner, he will attain knowledge of a real mental state that is otherwise inaccessible to the adult brain: the original ignorance of the newborn and its gradual awakening to the world. If the reader does not follow the rules, however, his understanding will be vitiated by his own fault. As the philosopher writes: "I believe that the readers who put themselves exactly in its place, will have no difficulty in understanding this work; those who do not will meet with enormous difficulties."[47]

But this thought experiment fails on several counts. The call for observation proves impossible given the vague nature of the observable phenomena and the logical leaps required to follow the theory. Although the narration uses simple language, the apparatus itself remains extremely imprecise. We find few details of the appearance of the statue or the objects it uses to make sensory discoveries (apart from allusions to a rose, a stick, a globe, and a cube). The reader does not know if the statue is standing or sitting, dressed or naked, male or female. The subject seems to exist in a state of physiological limbo, as when the experimenter tests the function of taste: "In endowing the inside of the statue's mouth with sensibility I am not supposing it able to take food. I suppose that the air brings to it, at my pleasure, all sorts of tastes."[48] Many chapters evoke the sterile atmosphere of a laboratory and propose simple experiments to demonstrate the cognitive functions that derive from the association of touch with sight, for example (part 3, chapter 3), or touch with smell (part 3, chapter 1). Although later chapters take place in natural settings of much greater complexity—fields, forests, plains—these settings are highly artificial as well. They resemble the theatrical artifice of Boucher and Watteau: the countryside as conventional *locus amoenus*.[49] Moreover, social isolation is assumed in every setting. As Yves Citton cogently notes, "These scenes in nature have the peculiarity of being *purely natural,* insofar as all traces of human contact have been carefully erased."[50] The statue will hear the murmur of brooks, gather fruit, and encounter animals, but it will never see a trace of human existence. It is difficult to extrapolate from such extremely artificial, isolated settings to the actual functioning of living human beings.

The sequential presentation of sensory functioning also leads to some confusion regarding mankind's power to reason and think accurately. First, Condillac demands that his reader-witness share his ontological assumptions regarding perception. He writes that the statue does not smell or see objects; rather, it becomes the sensations these objects generate: it *is* the smell of roses, it *is* the color red. And the ideal reader-witness must experience these same processes by careful observation and identification with the subject: "In order to judge we must put ourselves in its place," the author reminds us throughout.[51] Whereas Citton argues that gestures that ask the reader to "imagine the unimaginable" lend the work its conceptual strength (286), I see them as more evidence of Condillac's lapsed logic. After a succession of flowers pass under the nose of the statue, it realizes that the existence of one moment is not the same as that of another moment, leading to a comparison of the two existences. But if memory is "nothing more than a mode of feeling," how did the statue obtain that ability to compare?[52] This theory culminates in an extremely reductionist vision of human cognition in which all mental processes—recollecting, comparing, judging, discerning, imagining, wondering, having abstract ideas and ideas of number and duration, and so on—and all passions "have their origin in feeling alone" because "sensation contains within it all the faculties of the soul."[53] As Figlio aptly remarks, the sensationist philosophers of the Enlightenment "shunned mediation of any sort. Nothing could stand between the mind and the world, between knowledge and the postulated reality on which it was founded."[54] Whether the ideas formed by the mind were faithful representations of the external world remained a problem.

Another blind spot in Condillac's theoretical assumptions lies in the portrayal of the experimenter and his relation to the statue-subject. A philosopher-experimenter is omnipresent and omnipotent throughout the text: he alone stages the sensory experiences, yet one never sees him or witnesses his interactions with the subject. His invisibility lends an air of voyeurism to the scenario that is especially pronounced if one accepts Citton's contention that the statue represents a woman.[55] Yet Condillac maintains a high level of abstraction in this text, glossing over the sites where the statue discovers bodily pleasure, for example, and deliberately mixing male- and female-gendered nouns.[56] This imprecision may be an attempt at neutrality; it suggests that the statue's growing intelligence and implicit perfectibility are characteristics equally available to all sentient humans, men and women, no matter their social rank, education, or national origin. Indeed, in its final incarnation the statue no longer represents a disembodied sensorial potential but rather the prototypical perfectible human: the savage in a "natural" state. Faced with dangers on all sides, the statue survives by using all five senses, devising clothing and weapons, and learning to kill and devour other animals.

This work presents an empirical solution to the mysteries of human development posed by children found in the wild because, as if to prove the truth-value of his hypothesis, the philosopher ultimately tests it against the well-known case of the wild boy of Lithuania.[57] Such a case shows, Condillac admits, that the evolution of the senses depicted in the *Traité* might not always obtain and that one sense might dominate the others. Like deaf-mutes or wild children, any individual who suffers from physical deprivation of some kind—say, constant hunger—would have certain senses—for example, taste and smell—developed above and beyond all others. This explains why such individuals seem so unhuman—their senses, and by extension all their faculties, have developed awry. If one could somehow restore such individuals to their original environment, one might gain insight into how the senses develop in deviant cases and learn to help them recover equilibrium. Condillac imagines this process in the next chapter: "The Memory of one who has been given the use of his senses in succession." Once endowed with a voice, this individual (the statue/wild child) articulates a monologue highly reminiscent of Buffon's, listing the various stages in its sensory awareness. But the culminating moment of this individual's development is not its discovery of passions; rather, it is the ability to *control* his passions: "Taught by experience, I examine, I deliberate before I act. I no longer blindly obey my passions, I resist them, I conduct myself according to my own light, I am free."[58]

But this declaration of freedom from sensibility and passion rings false. Because of Condillac's insistence on the physical origins of mental processes, the whole economy of the *Traité* is predicated on a passive subject whose actions are essentially reactions.[59] Until the final chapters, the statue engages in no self-directed activity but rather reacts to stimuli upon demand and remains mute, thereby allowing the experimenter-philosopher to interpret from his perspective only. Such assumptions about the physical characteristics of mental processes had political ramifications. Although Condillac was primarily a logician or a metaphysician rather than a political theorist, he did venture into political writing at times, and his ideas are somewhat disconcerting as regards the concept of personal freedom.[60] Consider his vision of the ideal relationship between legislator and citizens as articulated in the *Traité des systèmes* (1749): "A people is an artificial body; it is up to the legislator . . . to maintain the harmony and the strength of its members. He is the mechanic who must adjust the gauges, and put the machine back into working order as often as circumstances require. . . . To lead the people, one must establish a discipline which maintains a perfect balance among all orders, and which thus makes each citizen identify his interest as the interest of the society. The citizens must . . . conform necessarily to the views of the general system."[61] Here we see the citizen as bereft of all personal interest, akin to an automaton mutely following directives from above. Such ambivalence about human agency would remain a problematic legacy.[62]

Bonnet

Although the Swiss scientist Charles Bonnet is probably best known today for his endorsement of preformationist and "panspermist" theories of human reproduction, he was very influential in his time. A corresponding member of both the Royal Society and the Académie des Sciences, Bonnet maintained contact with leading scientists of the day, and his works were translated into Italian, English, and German. Friend of the avid vivisectionist Haller, Bonnet early wrote energetically in favor of experimentalism and held that the microscope could wield far more useful information than any amount of philosophical study.[63] While a young man, Bonnet undertook numerous microscopic studies of worms and aphids and earned critical acclaim for his masterful *Traité d'insectologie ou Observations sur les*

Pucerons (1743). But at age twenty-five, with his eyesight dimming and his health failing, he was forced to give up microscopy. Bonnet's later works drew on methods both experimental and philosophical, for as he argued, "The science of the soul, like that of the body, rests equally on observation and experimentation."[64]

In his *Essai analytique sur les facultés de l'âme* (1759), Bonnet articulated a psychology that functioned using methods borrowed from physics. Like physics, Bonnet wrote, psychology must separate the exposition of facts from their interpretation. Thus his method analyzed all parts of the sensory process—chemical, neurological, and physiological: "I have studied what happens in the organ [the brain], when it transmits the impression of objects to the soul. I have tried to show the connections that link these sensitive fibers and the results created by them."[65] The *Essai analytique* echoes Buffon and Condillac with the now-familiar opening—"Let us imagine a man"—but Bonnet pretends to go deeper than his predecessors and to show how cognition occurs as a physical event, that is, he claims to "anatomize" sensation.[66]

Bonnet constructed his experimental apparatus from a wide array of sources and theories—materialist, Christian, and vitalist, among others. In one curious juxtaposition of vitalist and mechanical metaphors, he likens the statue's mind to a harpsichord that retains traces of music played, the "music" of thought circulating like water through its nerves: "The moral and physical value of our automaton will thus rely on its construction and the method that we use to operate this machine. . . . Vital movements already surge through the statue; spirits circulate and take the necessary nutrients to all of its parts."[67] Competing with Condillac but with the methods of physical science—including Hallerian notions of nerve fibers and sensible body parts—Bonnet explains the statue's first olfactory sensation by describing the action of microscopic entities *(corpuscules infiniment petits)*: "the infinitely small corpuscles that emanate from the rose create an odiferous atmosphere around it. They enter the nose through the air. They act on the nerve fibers that line the nose. This action results from the connections between the corpuscles and the fibers."[68] Unlike Haller's careful descriptions of animal physiology, however, Bonnet slips back and forth across the mind-body divide at will, as when he defines freedom as "subordinate to the will, as the will is subordinate to the senses, as the senses are to the organs, and the organs to objects . . . freedom is in itself indeterminate. It is a simple force, a simple ability to act or to move. The will determines that force to apply itself to one organ or another, one fiber or another."[69] Bonnet endows such authority to biological notions of "sensibility" and "fibers" that he glosses over fundamental unknowns.[70] After sketching the physiochemical chain of reactions above, for example, Bonnet does not explain how the odiforous corpuscules act on the nerves but rather concludes that it is simply a law of nature.

After a lengthy incursion into the minutiae of smell (four hundred pages), Bonnet concludes without following the statue to its full sensory awareness, although he notes that it could easily be done by applying his model.[71] This fictional apparatus, then, was designed primarily as a visual aid to a particular theory. Nevertheless, it marked a crucial step in the evolution of psychology by suggesting that the transcendental soul might be understood as a series of cognitive functions and by promoting the notion that psychological events could be described in a manner as naturalistic and objective as those of the physiochemical sciences.[72]

Perfectibility was at stake in this scenario as well. Bonnet was intrigued by the phenomena of wild children—and other substandard creatures, such as apes and American Indians—for what they might reveal about man's physical potential. As we saw above, Condillac associated perfectibility with habitual use of sensory organs. Bonnet elaborated on Condillac's theory and claimed that perfectibility lay in the ability to use the brain "fibers" stimulated through sensory experience to best advantage, notably through speech. "Language thus valorizes all the fibers of the brain. The brain of the Hottentot is surely not more poorly organized than that of an Englishman; but what a difference in their use of fibers!"[73] Admittedly ignorant of the actual functioning of fibrous relays, Bonnet nevertheless raised key topics for future research. In an effort to locate the physical origins of human speech, he called on anatomists to do more dissections of orangutan brains and to compare their results with work on human brains.[74] In the spirit of quantitative instrumentalism that would characterize later forms of human science, Bonnet even called for a physical device to measure the mind's capacity for thought: a "Psychometer."[75]

EXPERIMENTAL METHODS IN FLUX

Many people were not sanguine about the value of these texts and their introspective experimentalism. Even those who agreed with the principles of sensationist philosophy decried its limited applicability.[76] More significant opposition arose from thinkers who defended a different form of experimental method; members of the Edinburgh School were particularly cautious about—if not contemptuous of—such thought experiments. Although David Hume used an Adamic figure in his *Abstract of a Treatise of*

Human Nature (1740), it was only to demonstrate that such a person would be entirely incapable of making the slightest inference about natural phenomena because of his lack of experience.[77] Condillac's abstract construct had no appeal for this writer, who claimed that to understand mankind, the philosopher must study real people, not hypotheses, and "draw no conclusions but where he is authorized by experience."[78] Hume's refusal to resort to such heuristic devices gained him the praise of Dugald Stewart, who later declared, "Hume has very great merit in separating entirely his speculations concerning the philosophy of the mind from all physiological hypotheses" and added pointedly, "His works are perfectly free from those gratuitous and wild conjectures, which a few years afterwards were given to the world with so much confidence by Hartley and Bonnet, and in this his example has been of infinite use to his successors in this northern part of the island. I know of no part of Europe where such systems as those of Hartley and Bonnet have been so uniformly treated *with the contempt they deserve* as in Scotland."[79]

Although the Scottish school was famous for its conjectural histories, which resided on an inductive method, its adherents perceived themselves to be operating from very different assumptions than the sensationist philosophy of Condillac et al. It may be convenient to trace the progress of man's faculties separately, wrote Adam Ferguson in the 1790s, but speculation must not be taken for fact or seen as a normative description of human cognition.[80] Repudiating another form of evidence widely cited by French philosophes,[81] the Scot declared insights revealed by formerly blind and deaf people to be useless for science, for their sensory isolation is a symptom of pathology, not a guarantee of original integrity:

> As the anatomy of an eye which had never received the impressions of light, or that of an ear which had never felt the impulse of sounds, would probably exhibit defects in the very structures of the organs themselves . . . so any particular case of this sort would only show . . . the defects or imbecilities of a heart in which the emotions that pertain to society had never been felt.[82]

But Ferguson did not oppose conjecture on principle. Rather, he focused on the social body of the nation rather than the psychic or physical body of the individual. To that end the Scot proposed that instead of analyzing the minutiae of individual psyches, researchers put entire societies under the microscope, because "every experiment relative to the subject should be made with entire societies, not with single men."[83]

But how different were Ferguson's experimental methods from

Condillac's? What did it mean to undertake empirical investigations at this time? Since the practice was loosely defined, let us recall the multiple meanings of experimental method. Although many historians of science consider eighteenth-century techniques to be pre-scientific at best, texts from this period and earlier evince a concerted effort to refine experimental procedures. Already in the 1660s, Robert Boyle's researches in pneumatics exemplified how one could work and talk as an experimental philosopher. As Shapin and Schaffer have shown, Boyle's experimental program was based on three kinds of technology: material (the construction and operation of the air pump), literary (the texts by which phenomena produced by the air pump were made known to those who were not direct witnesses), and social (the conventions designed for scientists' dealings with each other, used to judge knowledge claims).[84]

Key to Boyle's program was a didactic, even a democratic purpose: not only did he insist that experiments be performed in the public places of a laboratory or in Royal Society meeting rooms (instead of the philosopher's cabinet), his books contained systematic advice allowing the reader to replicate the experiments. Perhaps most important, Boyle's narration made use of the literary technology that Shapin and Schaffer designate "virtual witnessing."[85] Yet Boyle almost never performed the physical manipulations in the experiments himself. This was done by various sorts of assistants, laypersons for the most part. What this meant is that when the candle in the glass globe went out, the air pump experiment successfully achieved its material realization, even if the observers came away with completely different theoretical interpretations. For Boyle, the fire's extinction meant that the air had vanished, whereas Hobbes attributed it to the violent winds produced by the pumping. This variability cast a shadow over the supposed truth value of the hypotheses that people sought to prove, even with empirically verifiable experimentation.[86]

The *Encyclopédie* articles "Experiment" and "Experimental Philosophy" show that the philosophes shared this concern for the "truths" resulting from experimental inquiry. The *Encyclopédie* defines *experimental philosophy* as a dynamic activity revolving around experimentation and observation. Whereas observation is limited to visible facts, and aims to provide detailed descriptions of nature, experimentation tries to "penetrate [nature] more profoundly, to steal what it hides, to create in some way, by different combinations of bodies, new phenomena to be studied: finally, it does not stop at listening to nature, rather it interrogates and presses nature."[87] As Moser notes, this last expression ("l'interroge et la presse") refers to the commonplace "judicial metaphor" of a scientific trial, although it supposes a rigorous judicial system "that does not allow the witness to keep silent, but makes him/her speak by means of interrogation and torture."[88] Rigor emerges as well in remarks on what kinds of practices to avoid. The article continues: "Descartes, and Bacon himself, notwithstanding how much philosophy is obliged to them, would have been more useful to it if they had been more practical and less theoretical physicists; but the idle pleasure of meditation and even of conjecture, carries away great minds."[89] The pejorative "idle pleasure" forms just one of the many vices to be avoided by experimental philosophers; Moser points out that "in these different formulations ["vain fancies," "supposed facts," and so on], the text systematically identifies the same disorder and deformation of scientific discourse: dissociating words from facts; allowing them to be used without referential control; giving them theoretical, conjectural and imaginative autonomy. This whole attitude amounts to producing a 'novel of supposed facts' and ought to be rejected."[90] Moser claims that this cleavage between fiction and science presages similar remarks in scientists such as Lavoisier, who sought to expel fictional elements from science and in so doing to give science the exclusive right to produce truth claims.[91]

But the cleavage between science and fiction was less clear than Moser alleges. Again, a look at the Scottish school is instructive, because there we find philosophers using the same rhetoric of experimentation but with very different assumptions about how sources might be "interrogated and pressed" to reveal new truths.[92] Of primary interest is the claim they made to cast aside the excessive minutiae of earlier methods in order to perceive more important continuities. As a witness wrote in 1803: "Instead of gazing . . . with stupid amazement on the singular and diversified appearance of human manners and institutions, Mr. Millar taught his pupils . . . to consider them as necessary links in the great chain which connects civilized with barbarous society."[93] Anti-French reaction was at issue too in the Scots' disdain for the hypothetical speculations on "natural man" so prevalent in French texts.[94] By arduously collecting data and testing hypotheses against ethnographic records, these writers believed that they could historicize the process of social development from its origins in the contemporary experience of "rude" and "primitive" peoples such as North American Indians.[95] *Natural phenomena* here designated events that typically happen in the course of human life or cultural progress, such as the physical processes of birth, infancy, maturity, and decline, or the Vicoesque cycles of national rise and decline.[96]

But while they disdained the excessive reliance on metaphysics in French theory, the Scottish historians took similar liberties in their treatment of evidence. As Mary Poovey has pointed out, "Just as one could not literally see the nerves or the moral sense, so one could not see, or read accounts of anyone who had seen, the transition from hunter-gatherer to agricultural society."[97] Blithely redefining what *empirical truth* might mean, some declared their work akin to a natural science. John Millar wrote in 1771, "By real experiments, not by abstracted metaphysical theories, human nature is unfolded; the general laws of our constitution are laid open; and history is rendered subservient to moral philosophy and jurisprudence."[98] One must keep in mind that "real experiments" here connoted the amalgam of methods we saw in the philosophes analyzed above: they ventured into induction and reasoning from observed phenomena, as well as deduction and reasoning from postulated axioms. Yet this kind of illogic caused very little consternation among practitioners. As Poovey notes, "That the coexistence of these methods was considered as noncontroversial to most of the conjectural historians as to the experimental moralists can be seen from the formers' tendency to rely both on eyewitness accounts, generally of so-called rude societies, and on a priori principles, which were derived from a combination of introspection and assumptions about providential design and the laws of human nature" (223). Finding the reliable sources for their histories was a far more troubling matter than practicing a rigorously coherent method.

The huge influence of all three groups attests to the wide variations in public expectations for science and matters of "fact" during this period.[99] Central to all of these visions of experimental method was the notion of successfully *staging science*. Boyle's methods were widely disseminated and cultivated an air of authenticity through public demonstrations and how-to descriptions of experimental procedures. The writers of animated statue tales experimented, too, in the sense of a coherent inductive study. The Scottish historians' experiments were equally rigorous in that they employed a self-consciously imposed methodology, accumulated a vast mass of particular cases, and traced plausible narratives of historical progress. Although the Scots' social science was qualitatively different from an exact science, "in applying their methodology to the study of history," Andrew Skinner explains, "the School evidently fulfilled the requirements of *scientific performance*. More, they quite obviously regarded their work not merely as science but also as amounting to a science."[100]

SENSIBILITY AND PERFECTIBILITY: POLITICAL DIMENSIONS

By defining the functioning of the human mind as an understandable and verifiable chain of events, sensationism crossed the boundaries into "science," as seen above, and into politics. The political valence of this theory derived from its assumptions about men's and women's potential to learn, or to be conditioned into, reasonable behavior. Grounding the intellect in physical criteria had no ideological significance per se. Some used sensationist logic to defend the status quo; others used it to found ambitious plans for social reform.

Defenders of the status quo position argued that social distinctions were grounded not on arbitrary criteria such as wealth or social status but on the concrete, material criteria of nervous refinement. Hume justified class privileges with this kind of physical proof when he argued in 1739, "The skin, pores, muscles, and nerves of a day-labourer are different from those of a man of quality: So are his sentiments, actions and manners. The different stations of life influence the whole fabric, external and internal; and these different stations arise necessarily, because uniformly, from the necessary and uniform principles of human nature."[101] As Christopher Lawrence has shown, Hume inspired many other authors of the Scottish Enlightenment to share his belief that the political and social interests of the landed minority were "natural" privileges. Because of their heightened capacity for exquisite feeling, this minority felt they had the right to govern what was otherwise a backward land.[102] Such reasoning was sometimes grounded in a hierarchy of civilization or intellect rather than landed interests.[103] But whatever the rationale, it was widely held in both Britain and France that "refined people and other persons of fashion are born with more 'exquisite' anatomies, the tone and texture of their nervous systems more 'delicate' than those of the lower classes."[104] Consequently, the potential progress of the human species was severely compromised. Education could have only a limited role in perfecting peasants, savages, or others whose innate coarseness of temperament irresistibly inclined them to particular courses of action.[105]

Such physical rationales could also undermine the abilities of women, who were reportedly enslaved to bodies that were "naturally soft" and "sensible all over."[106] Although many precedents could be cited among English authors, the French physician Pierre Roussel is arguably best known for promulgating this gender-specific sensationism in his *Système physique et moral de la femme* (1775).[107] As Lieselotte Steinbrügge usefully notes,

Roussel saw woman's sensory acuteness as both a gift and a liability: "The superior softness and mobility of woman's bodily organs resulted in a greater sensitivity of the nerves and thus in quicker and more subtle sensory perceptions. This intensity and simultaneity of the most varied perceptions, however, made women incapable of abstraction."[108] Typical of this reasoning was Roussel's claim that "[t]he difficulty of shedding the tyranny of her sensations constantly binds [woman] to the immediate causes which call forth [the sensations], preventing her from rising to those heights which would afford her a view of the whole."[109] Although Roussel warned both men and women against the sedentary life of the scholar, women were particularly at risk since, as the doctor noted, "Their delicate organs will feel more keenly the unavoidable ill effects that serious study brings with it!"[110] However, such a rationale could also be used to defend women's potential talents as creative artists. The historian Antoine Thomas claimed that because of women's "mobile senses," they "delight in creating an imaginary [world], which they inhabit and embellish."[111] Of course, this premise had a downside for more rational activities: "the presumption of great female powers of imagination that—in contrast to the male imagination, which was ruled and controlled by reason—continually threatened to slip into irrationality and superstition."[112]

These theories of the physiological origins of women's sensibility and, by extension, women's intelligence have recently given rise to contentious debates among feminist historians and critics.[113] Michèle LeDoeuff condemns Roussel for drawing "global consequences from his partial knowledge" of women's physiology and, based on a psychoanalytic reading of Roussel's *Système,* she argues that the author's repressed sexuality led him invert the qualities that should be assigned to woman's physical and moral registers.[114] Madelyn Gutwirth seconds LeDoeuff, labeling Roussel's work "technocratic" and his vision of women "irremediably bound to the telos of biology, their reproductive finality." In feminist indignation, Gutwirth decries Roussel's image of women as "frail beings, uteri cloaked in an evanescent and fragile, inherently decaying medium of flesh."[115] Countering such criticism is Anne Vila, who claims that Roussel should not be considered misogynist because "his tendency to moralize about physio-anatomical details, while also biologizing particular moral characteristics, is . . . applied just as systematically to man as to woman."[116] Although I agree that some critics err on the side of anachronism, I find it hard to reconcile Vila's claim with the facts of Roussel's influence and reception. Vila admits that eighteenth-century medical theorists used the putative physio-anatomical characteristics of the female body to argue that the maternal state was not only preferable but also biologically necessary for woman, and she also recognizes the derogatory conclusions that ensued, for example, the notion that "although woman's hyper-receptive system is aroused by everything, nothing—not passion, not tears, and certainly not ideas—ever leaves a strong impression on it" (252). Vila attempts to save such theories from feminist condemnation by arguing that period writers intended their work to be read primarily in scientific milieus, where it was meant to "save the reigning medical model of sensibility from its own internal contradictions" (256). Be this as it may, such intent was easily lost on readers. As we shall see in our consideration of revolutionary discourse, pseudoscientific rationales were often used to justify women's exclusion from the male world of ideas.[117]

Indeed, this kind of determinism alarmed some period thinkers. Consider the work of the English doctor and metaphysician David Hartley, who borrowed freely from both Locke and Haller to develop an "associationist" theory of human thought in his *Observations on Man* (1749).[118] Because of the overwhelming force of sensations and the associations they elicit from physiological receptors in the body (the nerves, the brain, and the spinal chord), Hartley argued that the human mind was eminently malleable to external forces—and thus free from the bonds of heredity or race. He interpreted the association of ideas as God's way of ensuring the continual improvement of mankind.[119] Ergo, mankind could be made better, more virtuous: "we may learn how to cherish and improve good [Affections and Passions], check and root out such as are mischievous and immoral, and how to suit our Manner of Life, in some tolerable Measure, to our intellectual and religious Wants."[120] All this seemed fine and good. But, as Hartley wisely pointed out, this plasticity might also be a liability: "The Doctrine of Association, when traced up to the first Rudiments of Understanding and Affection, unfolds such a Scene as cannot fail both to instruct and alarm all such as have any Degree of interested Concern for themselves, or of a benevolent one for others." Why such concern? Because, Hartley warned, this doctrine posited the possibility of making all human beings think and behave in exactly the same manner.[121] In the hands of an unscrupulous government, legislator, or other agent of social control, the felicitous differences among men might be annihilated so that they "become perfectly similar, or even equal." Equality here was not the optimistic principle that it would become in the discourse of the French revolutionaries; rather, it signified a dismal kind of social leveling that would rob human beings of all that they hold most dear.

Appropriated by Enlightenment political theorists, sensationism laid the groundwork for some egalitarian schemes of education as well as some very controlling models of legislation. These warring tendencies are exemplified by the work of the philosophes Helvétius and Condorcet. In *De l'homme* (1772), Helvétius trumpeted the sensationist premise in a celebratory mode, declaring that "the superiority of the understanding is not the produce of temperament, nor of the greater or less perfection of the senses, nor of an occult quality, but that of the well known cause, education."[122] Implicitly refuting the elitist and gender-specific rationales cited above, Helvétius argued that one's intellect does not depend on the refinement of the senses; all persons—no matter their culture, nationality, or sex—have the same organs of intelligence and the same aptitude to acquire knowledge.[123]

Condorcet pursued this line in two pamphlets, *Lettres d'un bourgeois de New-Haven à un citoyen de Virginie* (1787) and *Sur l'admission des femmes au droit de Cité* (1790), where he argued that all humans enjoy a common sensorium and intelligence and thus ought to enjoy more or less the same rights. Men are impressionable beings, susceptible to moral ideas and to reasoning from those ideas, wrote Condorcet. And since women have the same qualities as men, "either no one truly has any rights or all have the same ones."[124] To those who cited women's physical weakness and periodic incapacitation due to menstruation and pregnancy, Condorcet replied that the same objection applied to men, who had the gout every winter and who caught cold easily.[125] Like Helvétius, Condorcet countered claims of woman's intellectual inferiority and overly sentimental nature by citing the poor education they received and the laws that oppressed them. Condorcet acknowledged that some kinds of thinking were gender-specific, but he located the causes of this dimorphism in society, not physiology.[126] Education must be extended beyond the convent or classroom, Condorcet contended, to combat the subtle yet powerful discouragement induced by unjust social conventions. Voicing a refrain that sounds very familiar to modern-day women, Condorcet argued that social conditioning outweighs the impact of physiological determinants: "The kind of constraint imposed on women by traditional views regarding manners and morals has influenced their mind and soul almost from infancy; and when talent begins to develop this constraint has the effect of destroying it."[127]

Such liberalism did not necessarily characterize the philosophes' larger schemes of reform, however. Gutwirth reminds us that Condorcet retreated from his stance of unequivocal democracy in his educational writings of 1791 and 1792; already in 1790, he had retracted his bold statement on gender equality and posited instead that "except for a small number of enlightened men, equality is complete between women and the rest of men."[128] Helvétius took a rather cynical attitude toward reform, arguing that the only hope of changing people lay in coercion. Reducing understanding and talents to chance circumstances and "the produce of [men's] desires and particular situation," he concluded that the science of education resides in "placing a man in that situation which will *force* him to attain the talents and virtues required of him."[129] His hope for public education thus boiled down to a plan "to inoculate . . . good sense on the rest of the people."[130] Because of his distrust of the monarchy, Helvétius stopped short of proposing an immediate plan of action, although he recast Hartley's warning about public powers as a vision of eventual progress: "when the obstacles opposed by a stupid religion or tyranny to the progress of morality are removed, mankind may flatter themselves with seeing the science of education carried to the highest degree of perfection of which it is susceptible."[131] For all these hopes, *De l'homme* concludes in a mood of hopelessness: Helvétius describes France as a nation caught in the stranglehold of clerical obscurantism and declares that "in an era as superstitious as this one, the [Catholic Church's] emissaries will always have enough power to effectively block any useful reform."[132] Such pessimistic rhetoric was not lost on the powers that be: *De l'homme* was banned by the Parlement de Paris and ordered burned.

The programs of Helvétius and Condorcet were not so revolutionary as they may initially appear. Although Helvétius condemned despotism in *De l'homme,* he dedicated this book to Catherine II and Frederick the Great, "enlightened despots" both, and he did not flinch at advising coercion or absolute authority, provided that it was "enlightened." Highlighting this peculiar juxtaposition of liberalism and authority, Passmore comments: "Helvétius did not pause to explain precisely how, in a world where all other men are governed by their private interests, a legislator could arise who would be wholly dedicated to the general interest, prepared to devote himself to ensuring that everybody else's private interests would coincide, as his own automatically did, with the general interest."[133] As for Condorcet, we shall see in chapter 5 how the schemes he devised to reform public education during the revolutionary era were designed to promote an elite class of scientists and intellectuals who were supposed to bring the rest of the people along gradually toward enlightenment. His elaborate scheme of institutes, colleges, and academies did not explicitly exclude women; it simply assumed that they would not be involved. I thus agree with Passmore that most philosophes lacked the political experience that might have "tempered their enthusiasms" into more practical plans for reform, but I protest his Tocquevillian claim that they "despised the public."[134] True, some writers portrayed the people as ignorant and foolish, but they also held out the possibility that one day the masses' situation might be improved, their minds enlarged, and the conditions for social change thereby set in motion. In the early 1790s, it would appear, the French nation had arrived at that bright future, and the discourse of philosophes such as Helvétius and Condorcet provided some of the most powerful impetus for the social experiments of the revolution.

The thought experiments of sensationist philosophers such as Buffon, Condillac, and Bonnet were undertaken as a means of exploring the origins and processes by which human beings translate physical impressions into thought. Although they seem anodyne in themselves, the theories they defended were easily appropriated by later theorists with a particular ideology in mind. Armed with a new understanding of the nervous system, some theorists postulated connections between the nerves and the brain that excluded women and the poor from such progress, or, alternatively, argued for far-reaching reforms in education. Human perfectibility here took on very different connotations: for some it was an individual's capacity to live the best life possible as a thinker and agent for his own happiness, for others it was the process—stimulated on demand—by which the individual could be taught to think in a particular way. For a theory that began as an attempt to free Lockean psychology from arbitrary forces, there is a great irony in the way sensationism would ultimately feed the Jacobins' infamous attempts to "create a new people" during the Terror.

—CHAPTER THREE—

Compromised Idylls

NATURAL MAN AND WOMAN ENCULTURED

If it is good to use men as they are, it is much better to transform them into what one needs them to be.

—Rousseau, *Discours sur l'économie politique*

For a host of cultural and political reasons, the subject of human development and instruction was a hot topic throughout the eighteenth century; it inspired thousands of competing theories, manuals, and schemes to improve on existing practices. This literature was widely considered progressive in that it broke with earlier traditions, which stressed the child's fundamentally wicked character, treated children as miniature adults, and relied on a system of rote learning, to conceive a wholly new vision of the child as a being with its own intellectual integrity, stages of development, and a more or less infinite potential for learning.[1] Diderot incarnated this new attitude in his claim that "nature did not make us evil: it is bad education, bad examples, and bad legislation which corrupt us."[2] But there was a darker side to this supposedly enlightened literature. This chapter looks at how some writers defined and addressed new techniques to raise children, and it also pulls into the light of day some of the internal paradoxes, contradictions, and infelicities embedded in these writings that went more or less unseen by the writers. My analyses reveal the existence of a literary corpus that embraces some of the period's most "progressive" antitraditional ideas about human nature and yet projects an increasingly inhumane attitude toward the means required to reach their goals. Although these authors explicitly rejected Christian attitudes toward mankind's fallen condition in the name of a more optimistic vision of human potential, they seem impervious to the ethical problems raised by their own efforts.

The concept of civic morality runs through all these texts, although it is not always clear who is to embody this important virtue—the independent individual or a controlling state. This literature typically transposes the sensationist scenario we saw in chapter 2 into a prescriptive chronology: the subject's sensorial awakening leads to a moral experiment as the newborn grows into a child, and then an adolescent, and finally an adult. Adolescence forms the crucial pivot, for that is when the demands of mind and body enter into conflict and when the nascent desires of sexuality battle with the worldly obligations of citizenship. For the three French authors studied here—Rousseau, Beaurieu, and Dulaurens—the adolescent's unruly sexuality threatens to cast mankind adrift in a sea of primitive impulses. To establish the ideal society envisioned by these authors, one must either wage a mighty struggle against deep-seated human appetites or, conversely, reject the whole notion of morality.

Although my corpus is primarily French in this chapter, I draw contrasts to analogous works by the English authors Locke, Defoe, and Kirkby to underline the literature's ambivalence toward targets such as religion and the monarchy, as well as the concept of individual rights. All of the writers covered belong to a shared intellectual milieu, but the English seem less concerned about culture's power to suppress or absorb individual differences. They present a relatively sanguine attitude about protecting people's natural freedoms from the inroads of social pressures, perhaps because of their faith in religion's capacity to comfort the oppressed. Instead of aiming to reform society, the English writers seem mainly concerned with a pragmatic desire for self-improvement, cultivated through a strong sense of restraint, moderation, and self-control. Rousseau, Beaurieu, and Dulaurens, on the contrary, profess a much more wary stance toward the powers that be and express doubts about the capacity of individuals to exert self-control. Although (or perhaps because) they had no reasonable expectation of influencing governmental policy, they see themselves in opposition to the Catholic Church and the monarchy, institutions that in their works symbolize the corruption of modern society.[3] These authors suggest that, through radical methods of childrearing, one might allow the next generation to recover at least some vestiges of mankind's original good nature. But retaining that goodness might require strong intervention from the state. Like the young protagonist in Benjamin Martin's *Young Gentleman's and Lady's Philosophy* (1755) who justified his cruel experiments on animals by citing his desire to find out "how far the Power of Nature could operate" and "what could, or could not be done," the French writers resort to some rather unorthodox, even sadistic methods in their efforts to test mankind's potential for wholesale regeneration.[4] They had to take great risks in the experiment, it seems, because so very much work was yet to be done.

NATURE'S RESISTANCE TO CULTURE: LOCKE AND ROUSSEAU

Based on the Aristotelian dictum that "the further we are from a state of nature, the more we lose our natural tastes," Rousseau's *Emile ou de l'éducation* (1762) imagines raising a child who would not only become a good citizen but would also recover mankind's lost nature.[5] Raising Emile, as Pierre Burgelin has noted, relies on a paradox: it demands that man conserve his "natural" habits even in social life.[6] But how can one graft this second nature onto the first? Reconciling mankind's natural essence within a new, improved social order is the fundamental challenge Rousseau sets for himself, and even though it is never fully achieved, he clearly felt it was an important issue—perhaps the most important of his time.[7] And yet the author seems oblivious to an even greater paradox in his vision of society: his notions of what are "natural" and "civil" virtues for man prove startlingly incompatible with the virtues prescribed for woman. The conflicts inherent in man's internal warfare between self-interest and civility are magnified tenfold in woman's unpredictable corporeality. Together these conflicts undermine the carefully constructed idyll of *Emile* and lead to its destruction in the sequel, *Emile et Sophie ou les solitaires.*

Emile begins on a promising note. Following in the footsteps of John Locke's *Some Thoughts Concerning Education* (1693), Rousseau argues that human agency (as distinct from divine grace) is capable of leading men to virtue, and he proposes a more or less systematic program to follow.[8] Although *Emile* borrows many methods from Locke, in Rousseau we find a significantly more utopian tone. Whereas Locke neatly integrated his pupil into an existing society, Rousseau raises his in isolation; when Emile at last enters the world, his role is less to conform than to reform things as they are. Man is formed by three forces, Rousseau writes: nature, things, and other men. One might preserve and even improve man's relation to these forces by devising a careful program of experimental education. The healthy child's natural strength can be maintained through a rigorous program of conditioning, and his manual skills can be enhanced through an apprenticeship in useful arts and crafts. The last force to contend with, other men, poses the biggest challenge, but Rousseau suggests that the child's integrity may be bolstered by a regime of moral testing and social deprivation. These three programs in a nutshell organize the experimental program of *Emile.* Or at least the first goal, that is, to form a natural man *(l'homme de la nature).*

The second goal, to integrate the natural man into society and thereby form a citizen *(l'homme de l'homme)* is far more problematic, as Rousseau admitted.[9] A precarious balance is the ideal: mankind must be free, yet citizens must be dutiful; the state must satisfy all, without catering to the personal interests of any. We see this dilemma in *Emile* whenthe boy clings to freedom and eschews the corruption of civil society yet dreams of establishing himself as a benevolent landowner and *pater familias.* Moreover, the natural laws that made him strong and independent appear to play an opposite role in the character of his wife-to-be. Sophie's education, as it is sketched in book 5, offers only a pale version of experimental childrearing, basically replicating the traditional model of female upbringing in the home instead of the convent. Her freedoms are severely curtailed from childhood on, as per Rousseau's vision of a female nature that is always already encultured. Although the two marry and inhabit a utopian universe at the novel's end, the tug of war between personal liberty and social duties ends sadly in the devastating sequel to *Emile,* wherein the unruly woman is sacrificed in the name of republican virtue.

At the beginning of *Emile,* however, all things seem possible through education. Building on Locke's metaphor of the infant "only as white Paper or wax to be moulded and fashioned as one pleases,"[10] Rousseau sees experimental education as a way of renewing the species. As he declares in the novel's first line: "Everything is good, coming from God; everything degenerates in the hands of man."[11] Writing about the newborn, the author exclaims: "Would you keep him as nature made him? Watch over him from his birth. Take possession of him as soon as he comes into the world and keep him till he is a man."[12] To ward off meddling by the mother or father, and to apply his method in the purest form, Rousseau places a babe with a tutor immediately after birth and keeps the pair in relative isolation for the next fourteen years. This myth of origins, as Yves Touchefeu has argued, is not just a rhetorical convention but the basis for Rousseau's philosophy of human goodness in *Emile.* In abstracting the child from all familial bonds and inherited traits, Rousseau lays the groundwork for an analysis of the individual in absolute terms, freed from all the corruptions and limitations of bloodlines, nationality, religion, and history.[13] In this premise lies the weakness and strength of Rousseau's system. Critics attacked *Emile* as a chimera since its subject was so remote from any being ever known; admirers claimed that its novelty offered a vision of what might become possible.[14]

Called by turns "an automaton," "abstract man," and "the child," Emile is initially anonymous and without personality, like the subject of a medical case study or an experimental inquiry.[15] The child's mind is described as rising to consciousness gradually as sensory perception gives way to cognition, in keeping with the theories of Locke and Condillac.[16] But Rousseau adheres to a more rigorous materialism than does Locke. Despite his "blank sheet" metaphor, Locke believed that some natural inclinations did exist. Instead of standing idly by while such inclinations take root, Locke argued, the tutor must be vigilant and intervene as needed to cultivate socially sanctioned habits. Thus he claimed that "he that knows not how to *resist* the importunity of *present Pleasure or Pain* . . . is in danger never to be good for any thing. This Temper therefore, so contrary to unguided Nature, is to be got betimes; and this Habit, as the true foundation of future Ability and Happiness, is to be wrought into the Mind, as early as may be" (*Some Thoughts,* 111; emphasis in original). Yet Locke also warned that too much change should not be attempted, lest it interfere with God's great plan: "God has stampt certain Characters upon Mens Minds, which, like their Shapes, may perhaps be a little mended; but can hardly be totally alter'd, and transform'd into the contrary. . . . For in many cases, all that we can do, or should aim at, is to make the best of what Nature has given; to prevent the Vices and Faults to which such a Constitution is most inclined, and give it all the Advantages it is capable of" (122). This advice challenges the environmentalist label commonly attributed to Locke and suggests that his vision of mankind's potential was somewhat less optimistic than philosophers such as Passmore have claimed.[17] As opposed to Locke, with his directive methods aimed at instilling good habits, Rousseau claimed to practice an "inactive" method modeled on scientific procedures of observation and experimentation. His fictional tutor observes, records, and diligently protects the subject but without prejudicing the spontaneous evolution of phenomena, and the narrator counsels his reader to do the same: "Fix your eyes on nature, follow the path traced by her."[18]

Depending on their understanding of the child's innate goodness, critics have emphasized the kindness or the control exerted by Rousseau's tutor.[19] But one must see the tutor-child relationship in context: Rousseau envisions the tutor protecting nature and enabling the boy's natural growth in different ways at sequential moments in *Emile,* following Locke's advice to instill "fear and awe" in the child while young but to shift into friendship as he grows up.[20] The tutor's neutrality similarly dissipates as the imaginary pupil advances through childhood. By the novel's end, the methods of empirical inquiry have been discarded entirely for more explicitly prescriptive tactics. But in many respects the tutor-child relationship seems ideal, and indeed it was received by contemporaries as a marvelous innovation on the stultifying methods then practiced in traditional boarding schools and

FIGURE 13

Title page of Jean-Jacques Rousseau, *Emile ou de l'éducation*, book 2, engraved by C. P. Marillier, eighteenth century. Reproduced by permission of the Bibliothèque Nationale de France, Paris.

convents.[21] As flawed as Rousseau may appear to modern readers, one need only compare the advice on training Sophie discussed below to the harsh methods employed in convent schools that I discussed in chapter 1 to get a sense of the experimental, even radical character of *Emile.*

We see the tenets of experimental method in books 1–3, where tutor and child discover basic laws of nature. In accordance with period notions of scientific methods, Emile and his tutor observe natural phenomena under controlled or repeated circumstances, they compare and manipulate components, and then they draw general laws about nature. By taking sunrise walks to the same spot in summer and winter, for instance, Emile realizes how the sun's location is affected by seasonal change (this episode is depicted on the left of the title page in fig. 13). The tone is deliberately amateurish. Like Locke, who insisted on the superiority of hand-made toys, Rousseau calls for hand-made scientific instruments.[22] Refusing to take the child into a scientific *cabinet,* the narrator writes: "We shall make all our apparatus ourselves. . . . I would rather our apparatus was somewhat clumsy and imperfect, but our ideas clear as to what the apparatus ought to be and the results to be obtained by means of it. . . . Too much apparatus, designed to guide us in our experiments and to supplement the exactness of our senses, makes us neglect to use those senses."[23] The instruments foregrounded at the bottom of the title page, engraved by Clément-Pierre Marillier, include all the tools mentioned in *Emile.* Note that they are ordinary household items: a chair, a map, a stick with two weights tied to it, a basin, a magnet, a thermometer, a wax duck, and an assortment of carpentry tools. These homely objects underscore the accessibility of Rousseau's methods for would-be educators.

These simple tools also underscore what Rousseau liked to think of as the spontaneity or transparency of his techniques, in that no complicated machinery obscures the child's understanding. In this regard, *Emile*'s methods are consonant with contemporary science manuals for children. Popular texts such as Benjamin Martin's *Young Gentleman's and Lady's Philosophy* and John Newbery's series on Tom Telescope taught children how to perform basic experiments and to deduce scientific laws from ordinary household activities. Tom whips a top, for instance, to demonstrate Newton's laws of matter in motion.[24] Similarly, Emile acquires the basics of astronomy, geography, and physics not through written instructions but from his own hands and eyes. Rousseau depicts a simple lesson in physics to demonstrate how the method of "rough experimentation" *(expériences grossières)* works. As the tutor explains:

> For my first lesson in statics, instead of fetching a balance, I lay a stick across the back of a chair, I measure the two parts when it is balanced; add equal or unequal weights to either end; by pulling or pushing as required, I find at last that equilibrium is the result of a reciprocal proportion between the amount of the weights and the length of the levers. Thus my little physicist is ready to rectify a balance before he ever sees one.[25]

An eighteenth-century engraving after a drawing by Choquet (fig. 14) illustrates the simple apparatus in this scene.

But *Emile* differs from Martin's and Newbery's works on one significant point. Rousseau's experiments are decidedly simple; theirs are not. Anyone could do Rousseau's experiments and perceive the natural laws behind visible phenomena. The English texts lead from similarly basic principles to much more sophisticated knowledge and rely on an array of costly and delicate apparatus that Rousseau does not even mention—instruments such as the orrery, air pump, and electrical machine, which fascinatethe young protagonists in both books. It is the elaborate collection of paraphernalia that initially attracts Tom Telescope to the Marquis de Setstar's home, where he stages all his little lessons.[26] The infatuation of Martin's characters is even more pronounced, possibly because of Martin's other vocation as a proprietor of an instrument-making business in London.[27] In *The Young Gentleman's and Lady's Philosophy,* Euphrosyne exclaims, "nothing will appear so astonishing to me, as to hear any Gentleman of Fortune, Spirit, or Genius, should be without an Air-pump in his Possession."[28] Rousseau's self-imposed austerity must be understood as a reaction against this vogue. Although he seeks to reveal the secrets of nature to Emile, he wants the boy's interest to derive not from his concern with worldly trends but from sincere curiosity.

Rousseau manifests much greater concern about scientific charlatanism than do either of the English writers. Consider the magnetism lesson in book 3. Rousseau first depicts child and tutor discovering principles of magnetism at home, then attending a fair where they see an experimentalist leading a wax duck around a basin of water through no visible force. After experimenting with a magnetized needle and a wax duck at home, Emile eagerly returns to the fair the next day and tries to upstage the performer. But the duck avoids him entirely, performing all kinds of stunning feats at the conjuror's command. Publicly humiliated and confused, Emile returns home only to receive a surprise visit from the performer that evening (this scene is depicted on the upper right side of the Marillier title page, fig. 13). His conversation recalls the work of itinerant lecturers like Benjamin Martin,

FIGURE 14

"J'ajoute de part et d'autre des poids tantôt égaux, tantôt inégaux." Illustration for Jean-Jacques Rousseau, *Emile ou de l'éducation*, engraved by Choquet, eighteenth century. Reproduced by permission of the Bibliothèque Nationale de France, Paris.

who plied his trade all over England, but Rousseau casts such work in a pejorative light. Thus the *bâteleur* is made to complain, "My word, gentlemen! had I any other trade by which I could earn a living I would not pride myself on this." He goes on to berate both child and tutor for their arrogance, but he also reveals the illegitimate ruse behind his display (a boy hidden under the table). Justifying his subterfuge as a convention of the art, he explains: "[O]ne must not be so foolish as to display all one knows at once. I always take care to keep my best tricks for emergencies, and I have plenty more to keep young people from meddling. . . . I earn my pay by doing tricks not by teaching."[29] An aphoristic declaration on the dangers of vanity caps this episode and also suggests the possibility of other, invisible lessons to be absorbed along with the principles of magnetism. As the performer admits, he charges not for the lessons, but for the tricks. The real lesson, then, is about the dangerous subterfuges of scientific performance.

This mention of the bâteleur's sneaky procedures is hardly an isolated incident in eighteenth-century letters. As Barbara Stafford points out, "The potential for fraud lurked in any demonstration in which the performer created the illusion of eyewitnessing without informing the beholder how the action was done."[30] By the 1780s the wild popularity of "scientific" performances by such infamous characters as Mesmer, Marat, and Cagliostro would create an enormous rift between academicians and amateur scientists and elicit a flurry of pamphlets challenging the power of academies to define science.[31] We find a veritable obsession with charlatanism in Henri Decremps's 1789 work, *Les Petites aventures de Jérôme Sharp, professeur de physique amusante,* which aims, like *Emile,* to warn young readers against mistaking legerdemain for science. As Jerome travels from Marseille to Paris, he encounters a series of shady types and reveals the secret impostures behind their fraudulent schemes. A chemist who appears to change the color of liquids on command actually relies on a compatriot hidden under the table, who orchestrates chemical changes through an elaborate system of hidden tubes. A so-called doctor who fools a group of peasants by seeming to make air inflammable, it turns out, is relying on a secret receptacle with ether in it.[32] Although directed against peasants more than children, the charlatans' similarly unethical kind of science casts the whole edifice of scientific learning into question.

Rousseau's scenes of experimental learning do more than instruct, then; they also engage in timely polemics regarding the status of scientific knowledge. The narrator frames the physics lesson above with assertions that undermine the authority of the increasingly prominent Académie des Sciences, declaring: "Let him not be taught science, let him discover it. If you ever substitute authority for reason he will cease to reason; he will be a mere plaything of other people's thoughts," and "The scientific atmosphere destroys science."[33] Stressing the ease with which one can replicate his experiments, Rousseau portrays scientific knowledge as accessible to even unlearned parents and derides the academies' monopoly on such knowledge. But he also warns against the misleading lessons that one can absorb in popular milieus and insists that apparatus and performances be kept to a minimum. As we shall see, this ambivalence about the methods of scientific learning will be mirrored in Rousseau's ambivalence about his own role as master pedagogue. The artifice associated with *performance,* even when coupled with such anodyne topics as simple science and basic morality, was forever a source of anxiety for this philosopher who prided himself on his closeness to nature, and forever a source of righteous rationalization in his work. As we saw in chapter 2, the question of how to access truths about nature—by deliberate performance, spontaneous witnessing, or abstract speculation—was a fraught issue for many eighteenth-century thinkers.

Rousseau insists that his pupil is not a performer but rather an ordinary boy who learns and develops "naturally," that is, spontaneously. In practice, however, the child is carefully cultivated to ensure this natural development. For Rousseau it is not enough merely to use the senses; one must train them to perform optimally. He exhorts the would-be tutor: "Make the best use of every one of [the senses], and check the results of one by the other. Measure, count, weigh, compare. Do not use force until you have estimated the resistance."[34] Force is acceptable, even necessary. Along with the regime of rough experimentation for his intellect, books 2 and 3 of *Emile* offer a variety of Spartan methods to help the child's body grow up strong and healthy. Like Locke, Rousseau presents a program of bodily conditioning that begins at birth. Locke's program, one may recall, was designed to teach the boy "to *deny himself* his own Desires, cross his own Inclinations, and purely follow what Reason directs as best" (*Some Thoughts,* 103). Instead of protecting children from inclement weather and dressing them in stylish, tightly laced "Cloths that pinch," Locke argued, children should be exposed to all extremes of climate and dressed in light, loose-fitting clothes. As the ancients prescribed, children should be bathed in cold water, learn to swim, play often in the open air, sleep abundantly (but on a hard bed), and consume a rustic diet that consists mainly of bread, milk, gruel, some fruits, and very little meat.[35] The importance of self-restraint could not be overstated; Locke even proposed that such rigor be applied to babies. "The first thing they should learn to know should be, that they were not to have any thing, because it pleased them, but because it was thought fit for them" (108). By following these measures, the civil education is achieved: the child learns to submit to authority and "understand in whose Power he is" (109).

Rousseau echoes the advice in Locke's *Some Thoughts* but instead of habit, he couches his scheme in the pseudoscientific terms of conditioned response.[36] Rousseau wants the child to feel his powerlessness in the context of natural laws rather than social laws. *Emile* thus prescribes cold baths and vigorous exercise as the means to bend the child's soft and flexible "fibers" before they "harden" in adulthood.[37] Whereas Locke suggested that tutors watch for bad habits, Rousseau provides vignettes showing how to manipulate the pupil to achieve desired outcomes. His tutor's methods are somewhat sadistic. Following Locke's advice that children should be inured to infantile fears, Rousseau gives concrete examples of how to achieve the child's heightened tolerance for psychic distress of various sorts, encouraging tutors to upset children deliberately by wearing scary masks, for instance, or counseling them to raise the child's tolerance for noise by shooting guns within earshot.[38] These incidents recall the somewhat cruel forms of experimentation undertaken by period scientists—procedures such as electrifying living children (as in fig. 1) and self-experimentation like Newton's tests on his own eyes.[39] As Stuart Strickland has noted, the practitioners of this popular science treated the human body as they did other objects in their laboratories—no better, and no worse.[40] Suffering was a necessary adjunct to the important work of "science."

Emile's plan also includes an economic angle: he must work—or at least know how to work—for a living. The implications for this manual training suggest a very different political vision than that of Locke. For one thing, Rousseau insists that manual work is existentially superior to other forms of labor because it is "nearest to a state of nature."[41] Whereas Locke encouraged his charge to pick up some manual skills for recreation and health,[42] Rousseau insists that Emile surpass the mere performance of tasks to become, in every sense, an artisan. Carpentry being the chosen trade, Emile must adopt the life of an apprentice carpenter, obeying his master's orders, working long hours, taking meals with him, and producing useful objects to sell. Such training is not only healthy, it also affords financial freedom and makes the boy useful to his community. This is proven in book 5 when Emile settles in a village near Sophie, dispenses useful favors liberally to peasants in distress, and hires himself out to a master joiner like a "real worker," prompting Sophie's father to exclaim in delight: "Go and see that young man in the workshop . . . you will soon see if he despises the condition of the poor."[43]

The contrast with Locke puts Rousseau's republican politics plainly into focus. Locke promoted trade skills for the health benefits they provide as a respite from study. Even more important than trades, however, was what Locke called "*Merchant's Accompts*": "a Science not likely to help a Gentleman to get an Estate, yet possibly there is not any thing of more use and efficacy, to make him preserve the Estate he has" (*Some Thoughts,* 261). The protection of private property formed a crucial principle to be mastered: by learning the basics of accounting, the boy could gain a distinct notion of property and "know what is [his] by a peculiar Right exclusive of others" (171). With its pragmatic advice for ensuring the gentleman's health and financial well-being, it is clear that Locke's project focused on the self-improvement of an elite instead of social reform writ large. For Rousseau, on the contrary, peasants and workers should not be merely objects of the pupil's compassion, they should be admired and emulated as models of a good work ethic. Echoing the period illusion of a happy, industrious peasantry, Rousseau claims that, unlike the idle rich, who "are slain by dullness," the "lower classes [*le peuple*] are seldom dull" and they know how to live since their "many days of labour teach them to enjoy their rare holidays."[44] Rousseau thus transforms Locke's elitist advice on dilettante tradesmanship into a republican political statement about the value of manual labor in the state's moral economy.

Physical and mental conditioning, along with "rough experiments" such as the physics lesson shown in figure 14, were an integral part of Rousseau's "inactive method," a method long touted for its emphasis on physical education and participant teaching methods.[45] Although largely borrowed from earlier thinkers, Rousseau's innovations had a huge impact on the public and ensured that the author would be known for years as a kindly "friend of mankind."[46] But as Harari and others have argued, in practice Emile's education often appears to be anything but nonintrusive.[47] Images of the child at play alternate with vignettes projecting a controlled form of education. Consider the episode in book 2 in which Emile's ill-fated bean plants teach him the principle of private property or his humiliating incident with the fairground performer and his magnetic duck in book 3. After depicting Emile's disgrace at the fair and his embarrassing confrontation with the performer that night at home, the narrator admits in a note that "this little scene was arranged beforehand, and that the juggler was taught his part in it."[48] These scenes, in which the tutor manipulates the child's social and material environment to teach a particular lesson, resemble spectacles of human science staged for a rural audience. Like the experiments of period scientists, they are couched in a rhetoric of public instruction based on observable causes and effects, replicable methods, and verifiable results. After the bean plant incident, the narrator intones: "Young teacher; pray consider this example, and remember that your lessons should always be in deeds rather than in words."[49] As a postscript to the magnetic duck episode, he declares: "There is more meaning than you suspect in this detailed illustration. How many lessons in one!"[50]

Even as *Emile* gives a plan, it shows ambivalence toward the methods it encourages. Consider Rousseau's treatment of science. On one hand, the author portrays science experiments as a useful means to test hypotheses on the natural world; on the other, he argues that manipulation of nature may be dangerous. Rousseau erects limits to the child's researches, as when his Savoyard vicar comments scornfully on chemists' attempts to create hybrid species: "The mere generation of living organic bodies is the despair of the human mind. . . . [Nature] is not content to have established order, she has taken adequate measures to prevent the disturbance of that order."[51] Deferential toward nature's mysteries, the vicar describes himself as "like a man who sees the works of a watch for the first time . . . I do not know what this is for, says he, but I see that each part of it is fitted to the rest, I admire the workman in the details of the work, and I am quite certain that all these wheels only work together in this fashion for some common end which I cannot perceive."[52]

Remarks such as these provide a useful reminder of Rousseau's opposition to many of the goals of the liberal-minded eighteenth-century *philosophie.* In the *Discours sur les sciences et les arts* (1750) he ridiculed the Encyclopedists' worshipful attitude toward science, criticized period researches in biology, astronomy, and geometry, and argued that at any rate freedom cannot be secured by the sheer influence of scientific rationality alone.[53] Scientific ambitions, Rousseau concluded, need to be controlled: "Nature's intention was to keep you away from science, as a mother who snatches some dangerous weapon from the hands of her child."[54] This caution—and Rousseau's distrust of book learning in general—has prompted some critics to caricature the author as an obscurantist who promoted ignorance for its own sake.[55] Although his early (some say juvenile) *Discours sur les sciences et les arts* praised a "modest" or "reasonable" ignorance, in *Emile* (which Rousseau considered his "most important work") we have seen that the author created an elaborate program of education that covered lessons in physics, astronomy, geography, morality, and religion.[56] It was not knowledge as such that Rousseau opposed, but the means used to attain it. Hence the emphasis on hands-on learning, exempt from the mediation of books, theories, or institutional structures.

Through the character of the wise Savoyard vicar, whom Emile meets in book 4, Rousseau preaches a similarly nuanced approach to religion. There is a Supreme Being who directs the motion of the universe, the vicar declares, but one need not follow the methods of organized religion to discover His intentions. Instead of following the overly intellectualized, partisan methods of priests and scholastics, the vicar calls for direct, individual contemplation of the Almighty's works. In one of the passages that provoked the great ire of his Catholic critics, Rousseau's vicar criticizes the age-old tradition of exegesis and exclaims: "What! Nothing but human testimony! Nothing but men who tell me what others told them! How many men between God and me! Let us see, however, let us examine, compare, and verify."[57] Unlike the other philosophes, Rousseau did not deny the value of religion. Rather, he contended that religion is the linchpin of a stable state and exhorted people to listen "to what God says to the heart of man."[58] His opposition to the Catholic Church derived from the church's elaborate rituals and dogmas, which, he charged, promoted priestly arrogance rather than authentic spirituality. Rousseau would have the child appreciate God's works first-hand and draw his own conclusions. It is significant that Rousseau did not erect limits to this amateur theology in *Emile*. Whereas he argues that science must be limited and that some facets of nature must remain unknown, he confidently invites readers to bring new rigor to their study of religion. Firm in his faith, he refused to believe that some individuals might through this process arrive at more radically skeptical, even atheistic, conclusions.[59]

Rousseau's tortured attitude toward truth claims, whether revealed or empirically proven, comes out in his advice to the reader as well. In the preface the author claims that his work forms a feasible program of childrearing, declaring: "It is enough for me that, wherever men are born into the world, my suggestions with regard to them may be carried out" and envisioning the reader as "a good mother who thinks for herself."[60] In the science lessons discussed above, Rousseau insists that his methods are replicable and envisions the reader as a "young teacher" using *Emile* as a training manual. Yet the author was visibly uncomfortable with his own role as a provider of truth claims, for he wanted to envision a kind of being who did not presently exist. In book 3, then, he maintains that this program is merely a thought experiment with no practical value, commenting: "The real Emile, a child so different from the rest, would not serve as an illustration for anything."[61] The author later corresponded with readers from all over Europe, as we shall see in chapter 4, and his responses were characteristically ambiguous, reflecting the uneasy relation between his confidence in the philosophical integrity of *Emile* and his concern about blind worship of his principles.

Part of Rousseau's uneasiness as a provider of truth may derive from the difficulties he encountered in imagining *l'homme de la nature* in later life. In books 1–3 Rousseau's system protected the child by relegating him to the relative isolation of the country with a tutor. But in book 4 Emile arrives at adolescence, the crucial moment when he must begin to leave his tutor's protection and live among his peers as a citizen *(l'homme de l'homme)*. The sensationist rhetoric used in books 1–3 cannot describe the new challenges he meets, since Emile's mind no longer exists in harmony with his body. Reconciling these two parts of the individual would prove difficult. Whereas the child's sensory awakening was represented as a quiet process of unfolding, the adolescent's maturity takes on the dramatic aspect of a natural disaster—a tidal wave or volcanic explosion. Thus we read at one point: "As the roaring of the waves precedes the tempest, so the murmur of rising passions announces this tumultuous change; a suppressed excitement warns us of approaching danger." And, in another passage: "Little by little the blood grows warmer, the faculties expand. . . . The blood ferments and bubbles; overflowing vitality seeks to extend its sphere. The eye grows brighter and surveys others."[62] Rousseau's melodramatic prose reflects the tenor of period medicine, which associated the heightened blood flow of adolescence with a state of mind that is overly *sensible* or receptive to the sly and deceptive stimuli of carnal temptations.

Reflecting Emile's new status as a man, Rousseau's program henceforth stresses the social repercussions of his conduct. Hereafter the individual will not live in isolation but will inhabit a larger world of family and polity, and sublimation, not spontaneity, must be his guide. As the tutor admonishes the adult Emile in book 5: "To feel or not to feel a passion is beyond our control, but we can control ourselves."[63] But what about the individual's natural rights? Unlike Locke's pupil, who was raised with a constant concern for his social role, Rousseau's pupil is raised in isolation and only introduced to the world at adulthood.[64] His epistemological assumptions about the natural universe are thus poised for a direct confrontation with worldly conventions. Manipulation, force, and control now become crucial tools for the educator. Such means are justified by the very important ends of creating a chaste new citizen.

The transition from childhood to adulthood is symbolized in the one book Emile is allowed to read, *Robinson Crusoe,* for this novel forcefully redirects the boy's energies from sex to work. The critics Allan Bloom and James Hamilton have misread this novel and underestimated *Crusoe*'s didacticism by describing the island as a world where "there are no conventions" and by portraying Crusoe as a "man without moral relations."[65] Defoe's hero does not engender a new world; he imitates culture by replicating known patterns. Although living in an impoverished state, he is very rich, endowed with all the tools of an advanced civilization, such as fire, iron, guns, gunpowder, agricultural knowledge, carpentry tools, and literacy, not to mention a goodly fortune in gold and silver. The story of how Crusoe learns to use those tools symbolically retraces mankind's rise from primitivism to modern culture.[66] The spiritual metaphor of original man is thus inscribed in a very worldly plot: along with grace, Crusoe's solitude breeds initiative and invention.[67] Indeed, the plot articulates a capitalist message that has prompted some to declare Crusoe *Homo economicus* incarnate.[68]

Most important, Defoe's novel celebrates sublimation by describing Crusoe's ceaseless industry in a womanless world. "I was very seldom idle" forms a familiar refrain in this book, as does the hero's praise of his new diligence.[69] Work and study afford salvation from worldly needs; as Crusoe remarks on the anniversary of his fourth year of isolation: "by a constant study and serious application of the word of God . . . I had neither *the lust of the flesh, the lust of the eye, or the pride of life*" (139, emphasis in original). His womanless condition has troubled readers from Ian Watt, who remarked that Crusoe's lifestyle is "marked by an extreme inhibition of what we now consider to be normal human feelings," to pornographers bent on filling in this gap in Crusoe's activities.[70] But in Defoe's original, the hero accepts deprivation unflinchingly. On his return to England at the novel's end, Crusoe does marry but the relation lasts only a few years (six at most) and his wife is described merely as "not either to my disadvantage or dissatisfaction," bearer of his three nameless children, and soon thereafter dead (298). Even this brief interlude of domesticity is hidden from Emile, for the tutor cuts his copy so that it only contains Crusoe's journal of his thirty-five years on the island and ends with an image of triumphal individualism.[71]

This truncated text is one of a manifold arsenal of techniques used to reinforce Emile's self-sufficiency and work ethic—two elements that strengthen his body's sublimation to the demands of civil society. Once the boy becomes a man, he can no longer gratify his every desire because he must now compete with other men (a situation Rousseau historicized in his *Discours sur l'inégalité*). Hereafter he will inhabit a state of constant tension between his instinctive desires for self-gratification and his learned respect for social obligations. The *staging* of lessons becomes key; as Harari argues: "In Rousseau's staging the tutor holds the position of director, standing behind the floodlights, which both blind and illuminate the child-actor."[72]

Until the pupil is married, teachers should not openly discourage interest in intercourse but rather should offer scenes *(tableaux)* "calculated to repress the passions."[73] Such scenes should insist on the pain and suffering—including the possibility of death—that accompany childbirth and thus cover sexual intercourse "with a veil of sadness which deadens the imagination and suppresses curiosity."[74] Just as the child realizes natural laws by observing phenomena such as sunsets, so the adolescent learns of social dangers by witnessing scenes of moral depravity. In a passage that recalls the shock tactics used by period "museums of morality" that showed the oozing wounds of sexual diseases, Rousseau tells of a wayward boy's visit to a hospital ward where syphilis victims lay dying.[75] That "hideous and revolting spectacle" was a good pedagogical tool, writes Rousseau; it so sickened the boy that it put him off "harlots" *(filles publiques)* forever (193; Fr. 4:518).

But what about woman? It is clear that Rousseau considers Emile's unorthodox upbringing suitable for natural *man* alone when one arrives at book 5, which describes in much less detail the method to form a female "pupil of nature." As critics have amply noted, the education proposed for Sophie goes against the principles of Emile's in many ways.[76] Of course, Rousseau never claimed they were equal. He attributes the different curricula to the "laws of nature" that designed woman differently from man. "But for her sex," the author declares, "a woman is a man";[77] this one difference in sexual function justifies Rousseau's entire program of unequal, gender-specific moral and social roles.

As an experimental method, the apparatus of book 5 appears impoverished in comparison with the variety of techniques and vignettes laid out in the narration of Emile's early years. There are no experiments in physics, magnetism, or astronomy here, only homely scenarios of a young girl following her mother around the daily routine. Whereas Emile's tutor gave the boy great freedoms (or at least the semblance thereof), Sophie's mother keeps her close by the hearth, imposing a daily regimen of domestic tasks and moral constraints to make her docile and subservient. Rousseau's prescriptive notion of female nature emerges throughout book 5: boys and girls may share many games, he writes, but girls should be encouraged to pursue sedentary pastimes, especially dress-up and dolls. Most notorious for later feminist critics is Rousseau's vignette of a little girl playing with her doll, which concludes, "in due time she will be her own doll."[78] Dolls are not just toys; they represent woman's life's work *(sa destination):* baby care and coquetry. The author similarly recommends needlework rather than scholarship because "Little girls always dislike learning to read and write, but they are always ready to learn to sew" and "Most of them make a bad use of this fatal knowledge [reading]." [79]

The theoretical assumptions of Sophie's education counter those of the male model. Books 1–4 were based on an "inactive" method that demanded "rough experimentation," independent thought, and original discoveries. Book 5, on the contrary, presents a program based on the principle of dependency—moral, social, and physical—on societal norms. Whereas the male's education tried to repress his carnal appetites as long as possible, the female learns early that her role is to elicit and rebuff male lust. Just as sublimation allows men to become encultured, shame is crucial to women's education. Contrasting the lubricious longings of women with the orderly arousal of female animals, Rousseau constructs a vision of desire that elicits self-loathing, thus aiming to convince women that their most valuable talent is to appear uninterested in sex.[80] Indeed, woman is defined primarily by her body: "The male is only a male now and again," the narrator asserts, "the female is always a female, or at least all of her youth; everything reminds her of her sex."[81] As proof of this claim, Rousseau cites woman's delicate state during pregnancy and childbirth and the many demands on her life while her children are young.

One must remember the limited scope of activities available to *le sexe* during Rousseau's time and the rigid methods used to raise girls. Many of Rousseau's readers found this novel immensely inspiring.[82] After all, Sophie is allowed some physical pleasures denied convent girls, such as running and playing outdoors. Even her sin of gourmandise is tolerated while she's young and serves as a pedagogical tool on occasion.[83] But once she passes the threshold of adulthood, a woman's body and taste become much more charged with societal constraints. The ideal woman exemplifies a "pure" nature and rural simplicity: her food preferences should be blandly vegetarian, like Eve's before the fall, and foster a state of emotional calm.[84] Sophie's diet is thus aligned with her "feminine" taste for dairy products, pastries, and sweets and her aversion to meat and alcohol (4:749). Whereas the young girl was encouraged to enjoy physical exercise, the woman is taught to cherish her weakness. "Far from being ashamed of her weakness, she is proud of it . . . she would be ashamed to be strong."[85] Redefining "natural rights" to suit his prescriptive morality, Rousseau declares that woman must learn early to submit to injustice, but that she has "the right to be weak if she chooses" (323) ("le droit d'être foibles au besoin," 4:696).

Sophie's life revolves around what one might call a natural science of artifice. Consider her clothing. Emile is raised with a profound disregard for bodily comfort: his scanty clothing is analogous to the savage's nudity—it embodies his natural strength and unashamed humanity. But Sophie cannot afford such negligence; as the critic Philippe Roger reminds us, "The desirable body, in the eighteenth century, is never the 'natural' body."[86] Woman's social function requires a careful balance of aesthetics and integrity. Thus Sophie is described as "fond of dress" although she "hates rich clothes" (356). Moreover, what appears plain and unadorned is actually carefully calculated to seduce: "Her dress is very modest in appearance and very coquettish in reality; she does not display her charms, she conceals them, but in such a way as to enhance them. . . . While you are with her, you cannot take your eyes or your thoughts off her, and one might say that this very simple adornment is only put on to be removed bit by bit by the imagination."[87] In this passage Rousseau makes clear that woman exists primarily for man—to stoke the fires of male fantasy, as here, or to guarantee the routine comforts of man's daily life.

Echoing many of his contemporaries, Rousseau posits that woman has most value when her personal desires are sublimated to a greater good—be it self-control, marital cohesion, or the creation of future citizens. This theme runs throughout *Emile*. Already in book 1 the author emphasized the crucial role that mothers could play in reforming the *polis* if they would cast aside urbane diversions for the simpler pleasures of home and hearth. When women assume responsibility for their own children, especially through breast-feeding their infants, a chain reaction of moral and civic regeneration will begin. Rousseau declares: "[N]atural feeling will revive in every heart; there will be no lack of citizens for the state; this first step by itself will restore mutual affection. . . . The noisy play of children, which we thought so trying, becomes a delight; mother and father rely more on each other and grow dearer to one another; the marriage tie is strengthened. . . . Thus the cure of this one evil would work a wide-spread reformation; nature would regain her rights."[88] As Gutwirth points out, motherhood becomes the cornerstone of moral regeneration: "only motherhood, it is promised (or threatened), will redeem women from 'their' fallen actuality, and men from the vices of culture."[89] Implicit in this rhetoric of a 'return' to maternal sacrifice and domestic pleasures lies a denunciation of period mores, which Rousseau perceived as degenerating at an alarming rate.

Of course, this political rhetoric of self-denial for the welfare of the whole was not exclusive to women. As Rousseau prescribed woman's compliance with man's will in the family, so he called for the subordination of the individual man to the public will in civil society. Indeed, this concept was one of the fundamental tenets appropriated by revolutionary leaders, who also inherited the difficulties inherent in the premise. For how does the natural man retain his primitive freedoms of movement and thought when he becomes a dutiful husband, father, and citizen? As Mona Ozouf has pointed out, a crucial challenge for the Jacobins was admitting that enlightened men could think differently and that individual opinion could maintain its right to refuse the yoke of the collectivity.[90]

The end of *Emile* represses such concerns by envisioning a singularly happy future for the young couple in the bosom of a grateful rural community. Thanks to his training as a carpenter and the fortune (conveniently) left to him by his parents, it appears that Emile will realize his dream of becoming an independent landowner, a farmer, and a benefactor to neighboring peasants. Although details are left vague, it seems likely the couple—who will soon be parents—are ultimately enjoying the idyllic lifestyle Rousseau also portrayed in *La Nouvelle Héloïse,* that is, the "patriarchal, rural life, the earliest life of man, the most peaceful, the most natural, and the most attractive to the uncorrupted heart."[91] Furthermore, they are laying the foundation for a new, improved generation of people for the future, as the tutor exclaims:

> I like to think what benefits Emile and Sophy, [*sic*] in their simple home, may spread about them, what a stimulus they may give to the country, how they may revive the zeal of the unlucky villagers. In fancy I see the population increasing, the land coming under cultivation, the earth clothed with fresh beauty. Many workers and plenteous crops transform the labours of the fields into holidays. . . . Men say the golden age is a fable; it will always be for those whose feelings and taste are depraved. . . . What is needed for its restoration? One thing only . . . we must love the golden age.[92]

This poetic vision of a future golden age was extremely powerful for Rousseau's contemporaries, because it overturned centuries of Christian doctrine to suggest that mankind could revive the God-given goodness and strength it once enjoyed here and now, on earth. It was politically stirring because it took seriously the small contributions of individual citizens, declaring that such initiatives could bring immense rewards for the whole human race.[93] The repeated metaphors of growth, cultivation, and regeneration made a huge impact on readers in the late eighteenth century. Indeed, Rousseau's image of the strong and virile *homme régénéré* in *Emile* would be one of his most lasting legacies and become a veritable fetish of republican ideology during the revolution.[94]

But the story is not quite over yet. Two years after Rousseau's death in

1778, his works were rereleased in a massive edition of his *Oeuvres complètes* and gained critical acclaim anew.[95] The sequel to *Emile, Emile et Sophie ou les solitaires,* was only now discovered in the *Oeuvres* and caused quite a stir, with rival translations quickly published for new markets in Britain. It is hard to judge why readers were devouring this unfinished fragment so eagerly, however, because in many ways it puts the entire system of *Emile* in doubt. *Emile et Sophie ou les solitaires* presents a devastating view of the young couple years after their marriage. After their rural utopia is shattered by the deaths of their baby daughter and Sophie's aged parents, the couple leaves their country home and goes to Paris with their young son in the hope of curing their melancholia in society. But Emile soon becomes preoccupied with his own affairs, leaving lonely Sophie to fall prey to a couple of unscrupulous *débauchés* who take advantage of her naivete. In one of the rare moments when Sophie speaks directly, she explains her fault with metaphors of corrupted ownership and defiled purity, telling Emile: "I am no longer anything for you. Another man has soiled your bed."[96] In keeping with Rousseau's one-sided vision of sexual politics, Sophie's adultery is ascribed not to her own desire but rather to her lack of resistance.[97] Her guilt—symbolized by the illegitimate child growing in her belly—forms a visible proof of her untrustworthiness, at least on one occasion.[98] But what about her irreproachable past?

Emile was supposed to be the "man of nature" who would follow his own principles regardless of social conformity, yet in this circumstance he defers to public opinion and abandons mother and child forever. Presenting himself as a kind of melancholy postlapsarian Adam, he laments, "the delicious charm of innocence has disappeared." And like an Old Testament patriarch, he rules with an iron will, declaring: "Yes, all our bonds are broken, broken by her. In breaking her vows she frees me of mine. She is no longer anything for me, didn't she tell me that herself? She is no longer my wife . . . I will never see her again. I am free."[99] Sophie thus destroys the idyll created in *Emile,* prompts the hero to depart on a pointless journey in exile, and condemns herself to the lot of the abandoned woman. Although the text ends without describing her future, aside from an allusion to her untimely death, one thing is sure: this experiment in creating a natural couple is a resounding failure.

But was it the fault of Sophie, female nature, or human nature more generally? Was the author undermining his own system, showing that *Emile*'s idyll is impossible to achieve? It is unclear why Rousseau penned this pessimistic coda, but it is revealing that his hero manifests the same intolerance for human frailty that we saw governing his early education in *Emile.*

Allan Bloom celebrates this aspect of *Emile* as an attempt to "attain the sublime condition of idealism."[100] I see it in a less positive light. For all the nonconformism and resistance to authority he exemplified in life, Rousseau's textual view of the adult world is loaded with guilt and shame, so much so that it is hard to reconcile with his oft-cited belief in mankind's original goodness. Whether they are meant to save man from his own demons or to protect society from internal warfare, the moral prohibitions laid down in *Emile* allow for totalitarian and sadistic practices—a feature that Beaurieu and Dulaurens would amplify with terrifying results in their works. As Graeme Garrard has argued, Rousseau leaves us with the message that "social life is, at best, always a precarious balance built upon the intractable tendency for private interest to dominate human action."[101] In a very "counter-Enlightenment" move, Rousseau shows that the Enlightenment project to liberate man from traditional moral and social constraints was more likely to aggravate latent problems rather than to achieve any lasting liberation.[102] Natural man, and especially natural woman, must be encultured for their own good.

ISOLATION AS A PHILOSOPHICAL CONCEIT: DEFOE, KIRKBY, BEAURIEU, AND DULAURENS

Before turning to Rousseau's imitators, we must make a short step back in time to an important genre that informed their visions of mankind developing in isolation, the "Robinsonad," or desert island fiction inspired by *Robinson Crusoe*. By looking a little more closely at *Crusoe* and at one popular Robinsonad published in its wake, we will gain a better sense of the special religious tone that this genre carried in England and the harsh materialism of its cousins from across the Channel.[103] Defoe's 1719 novel uses the hero's isolation to depict a symbolic trajectory of human industry through the ages whereby Crusoe's eventual mastery of agriculture, metallurgy, Christian devotion, and ultimately civil government depicts the progress of the human spirit from barbarity to civilization. This plot was reworked in many ways by later writers, notably by John Kirkby in *The Capacity and Extent of Human Understanding Exemplified in the Extraordinary Case of Automathes* (1745), whose subtitle describes the novel's basic premise: *A Young Nobleman, who was Accidentally left in his Infancy, upon a Desolate Island, and continued Nineteen Years in that solitary State, separate from all Human Society. A Narrative Abounding with many surprizing Occurrences, both Useful and Entertaining to the Reader.*[104] Most significant for our purposes is how Kirkby transforms Crusoe's utilitarian attitude about the natural world into a more explicitly reverent appeal to Christianity's power as a revealed religion.

The narrative of *Automathes* runs in a circle: we first hear of the hero through a manuscript found in a bottle by the editor, who transcribes it as a "Service to the Cause of Religion and Virtue."[105] Written by an English priest, the manuscript describes his experience being shipwrecked on a remote island that turns out to be an exemplary Christian nation. The wise laws and educational practices of this country are clearly based on Lockean principles of self-denial and discipline, but with a harsher attitude toward the "wretched Frailty" of man's "corrupt nature" (18, 39). A man named Automathes is the governor of this precious place; the narrative relates his life from infancy to adulthood. Like *Crusoe*, *Automathes* is heavily indebted to Christian doctrine and includes generic features of forms such as the spiritual autobiography and the providence book.[106]

In *Crusoe* the debt to such genres is seen in the hero's encounters with events both wondrous and quotidian. Wondrous events such as the "miraculous" corn that thrives on barren soil and the frightening earthquake start the hero on his journey toward conversion (94, 96). But it is not until he is visited by a terrible dream of a fiery man that he understands the presence of providential forces. The next day he suddenly realizes his "stupidity of soul," that is, his estrangement and alienation from God while a young man, and starts to suspect that the shipwreck was divine punishment for his sins.[107] Following this revelation, he learns to scrutinize his daily life as well as his soul and to see his isolation as a blessing, not a curse. Thus with renewed vigor he throws himself into the hard work of building up his "empire"on the island.

Crusoe's is a Puritan God who smiles on human industry. The hero's scientific enterprises thus go hand-in-hand with his spiritual growth: he undertakes a series of investigations—agricultural experiments and observations of the island's flora and fauna, tides, seasonal change—that supplement his Bible study.[108] Crusoe writes, "by a constant study and serious application of the word of God, and by the assistance of his grace, I gained a different knowledge than I had before. . . . In a word, the nature and experience of things dictated to me, upon just reflection, that all the good things of this world are no farther good to us than they are for our use" (139–40). Thanking God for his good fortune, Crusoe learns to grow corn, master some mechanical trades, and create a number of ingenious inventions: earthenware pots, a sieve, and a canoe, among others. Although the hero does not consistently retain a pious attitude, this narrative meets the generic requirement of a spiritual autobiography in its plot of gradual conversion and its imposition of "a purposeful pattern" on the hero's account of his possessions and chronology.[109] The focus of this tale is self-improvement and eventual redemption, culminating in Crusoe's conversion of the savage Friday into a good Christian. Although Crusoe does establish a small colony on the island, Defoe does not present it as a nascent utopia or vision of man's perfectibility but rather as evidence of the hero's successful improvement of his self and his natural world. The greatest legacy of *Crusoe* is the useful knowledge he discovered on the island, his self-sufficiency, and the reverence for God he gained on the way.

Automathes follows a similar trajectory, but with less attention to the details of material existence and a more systematically didactic aim. Automathes' parents were worldly people, the hero writes, shipwrecked on a desert island and making a belated conversion to Christianity in their new solitude. But the mother dies soon thereafter, and the father, while searching for life on a neighboring island, is swept away by rogue tidal currents. Automathes is thus abandoned to nature from the age of two. The narrative traces his rise to cognition in a few pages, with an evident debt to Lockean theory but with a much stronger commitment to Christianity. As soon as his mind is fully aware, Automathes embraces "the principal Truths of revealed Religion." Why? Because he (innately) realizes the "wants and Imperfections" of mankind's fallen condition, and he deduces from the island's natural beauties that an intelligent agent of creation must exist (*Automathes,* 79, 116). Borrowing a gesture common to providence tales, he claims that this seemingly spontaneous religiosity was actually the work of an "invisible Instructor"—the spirit of his dead mother—who spoke to him in dreams, "secret Hints and Intimations, which I then frequently perceived upon my Mind" (80).[110] Perhaps even more important for the theme of education, however, is his claim that the example of his parents' devotion, however short-lived, had so impressed his infant mind that it was ready to receive religion. This character lives in a universe pregnant with supernatural signs and omens that he readily interprets as signals from God.

Other ordinary and extraordinary events further confirm this hero in his devotion: the changing seasons and movement of the tides, for instance, reveal "an apparently wise Design, where the least Design of all was expected" (119). The death of his faithful dog, although it initially incites a fearful recognition of his own mortality, ends by confirming the hero in his belief that "this Dissolution of the Body, whenever it came, [was] a welcome Deliverance of the Soul from those Burdens and Miseries, to which I saw her continually exposed" (159). After igniting a forest fire by accident, he has an even more powerful epiphany: "I discovered, to my Sorrow, the natural

Depravity and Perverseness of my whole Temper" (155–56), and he vows to practice prayer and supplication to make up for his fallen state. God returns the favor, it seems, when a group of friendly beavers save Automathes from drowning, an occurrence that inspires "grateful Acknowledgements to Heaven" (207). When he is finally reunited with his father and rejoins society at age twenty-one, Automathes is quickly disgusted by the cruelty, arrogance, and stubbornness of mankind, but eventually he finds the means to realize his fondest dream: a colony (Soteria) where civil and religious governance work hand-in-hand and whose residents are all devout Christians who practice "a steady Adherence to the Apostolical Doctrine and Discipline in their original Purity" (5).[111] As if this were not sufficiently edifying, in the final pages of *Automathes* the hero warns those who have not yet accepted the truth of revelation to "open their Eyes before it is too late, that they may not *tremble* with [the Devils]!" (270). This heavy-handed preaching, superimposed on a tale of adventure, discovery, and intellectual growth, reveals one use to which the Robinsonad was put in an English context.

Twenty years later, Gaspard Guillard de Beaurieu penned *L'Elève de la nature* (1763) and demonstrated how the same plot could serve very different purposes when integrated into French habits of thought. This novel, which enjoyed considerable popularity in the last decades of the eighteenth century,[112] adopts the double education of *Emile*. But instead of presenting the natural and the social as equally important components of humanity, *L'Elève* announces an explicit preference for the latter. In the preface to the 1766 edition, the bookseller states Beaurieu's two goals: (1) to form "a decent man [*un honnête homme*] content with himself" and (2) to make that man happier still by making him a good citizen.[113] Thus the pupil's life culminates in a position as respected patriarch and founder of a colony that replicates certain tendencies of *Automathes*' utopia, but with an even stronger system of control.

Compared to the psychological complexities of Rousseau's fiction, with its troubling vision of tutor-pupil manipulation and self-contradictory messages to the reader, Beaurieu's novel most resembles an intellectual comic book (but not a very light or entertaining one).[114] The isolation of Crusoe, Automathes, and Emile is made even more literal in *L'Elève*'s experimental apparatus: the "pupil" spends his first fifteen years imprisoned in a wooden cage. The history of this apparatus is interesting in itself as a reflection of Beaurieu's intellectual milieu. The author did not call his project an *experiment* until he revised *L'Elève* for the 1771 edition.[115] In the first edition (1763) the premise was justified by politics: the pupil was locked up as a political reprisal against his English parents, who angered a prominent member of George II's court.[116] From the 1771 edition onward, the boy's isolation would be explained as a systematic "philosophical education" devised by French émigré parents and sanctioned by the English government. Before their marriage, the boy's father had convinced his wife that if they had more than six children, the babes should be given to "Nature," abandoned "to instinct alone." The father then seeks and obtains the help of "public power" because "[t]he government saw that an experiment of this kind must turn to the advantage of human nature."[117] Note that human experimentation was deemed a perquisite of monarchs, who could transcend ethical constraints in the name of a higher good. This image of cooperation between French philosophy and enlightened English governance was a sign of the pre-revolutionary times.

But none of this history is revealed to the reader—or to the pupil—until the middle of volume 2, when the pupil has already endured twenty years of solitude, met and married a woman, and begun his own family. In the early pages, we read only that he lived in a cage with "a small box of pasteboard, a fly, some straw, a stone; meat, bread, fruits, and water, with which I was supplied by means which I could not discern."[118] Other details follow: his straw was changed every six months by the invisible custodians because "it was determined that I should neither hear nor see a human being till the time I should be restored to society."[119] Even the construction of his toilet facilities *(des lieux 'à l'Angloise')* are made available in a footnote.[120] This is clearly a prison cell.

The theoretical assumptions of this work reiterate the sensationist theories of Locke and Condillac: the pupil slowly acquires knowledge through sensory perception and, "rather like a plant than like an animal," grows up. The so-called course in philosophy begins in earnest at age fifteen when his cage is removed to a desert island and opened for the first time. (See this liberating moment in fig. 15, a 1778 engraving by Marillier). Whereas Crusoe and Automathes were providentially blessed with environments free of dangerous animals, in *L'Elève* the island is mechanically sanitized and tamed before his arrival. Its dangerous animals are destroyed, decrepit trees are felled and young ones planted, fruit is hung from branches around his cage, a dog is tied to a nearby tree, meat is hung in baskets in the shade, and a few necessary tools are stowed for his later discovery and use. The nameless benefactors even leave a trail of water bowls leading up to a pond on the other side of a distant hill. In the absence of a tutor or a benevolent God, Beaurieu's setting plays a similarly pedagogical function.

Like Crusoe, Beaurieu's pupil explores and observes his island in detail.

FIGURE 15

"Je voyois le ciel!" Frontispiece, engraved by C. P. Marillier, of Gaspard Guillard de Beaurieu, *L'Elève de la nature*, vol. 1 (Lille: C. G. J. Lehoucq, 1778). Reproduced by permission of the Bibliothèque Nationale de France, Paris.

But whereas Crusoe studies nature for its use-value, discerning which tree has the best wood for canoe-making, for instance, or which reeds might make the best baskets, Beaurieu's pupil explores nature looking for invisible laws of cause and effect. When he spills his water bowl on his body, Beaurieu's pupil discovers the first law of physics.[121] His observations do not incite him to engage in any useful labor, but rather bring forth reflections couched in the language of Buffonian natural history on the wind and shadows (1:41–42, 1:103–4), the cause of dew (1:130–31), the natural cycle of birth, death, and putrefaction (1:127–28), and astronomical phenomena (stars, an eclipse, and lightning, 1:140–41, 1:186–87). That the author considered this novel a work of serious scholarship is clear in the frequent footnotes to scientific authorities such as Dr. Tissot (2:18), Dr. Levat, a surgeon at the Military Hospital of Rouen (2:202), the author's own *Cours d'histoire naturelle* (2:18), and Buffon's *Histoire naturelle* (3:16–18).

Echoing the contemporary preoccupation with the mechanisms of reproduction, the pupil gives a detailed description of a deer giving birth and a vivid account of the dissection of a pregnant rabbit (1:173–74).[122] His dissection report is a striking example of the popularization of science through fiction. The pupil describes the rabbit's heart, stomach, womb, membranes, internal organs, and fetuses in very accurate terms by period standards, which reminds the reader that Beaurieu's first vocation was as a naturalist.[123] But when he lifts the membrane of her womb, the pupil's description veers into a horrifying spectacle of infanticide:

> A veil that I trembled to rip open hid something that seemed to be a mass of uneven, shapeless flesh. I looked closer, and through the veil, which was of a delicate and transparent texture, very tightly stretched, I thought I saw heads and eyes. My stone dropped from my hand, I pick it up, and to overcome my repugnance I cut open the body quickly. . . . What a sight! *[Quel spectacle!]* Six little unborn rabbits, already living, squirm around, hideously opening their mouths, and reproach me with horror for having dared to penetrate the sacred haven where Nature had brought them from out of nothingness; they breathe, I throw the unhappy hare and her little ones into a bush. . . . Crying and screaming, I run toward my cave, and curse myself.[124]

This emotional reaction to the death of an animal marks another departure from the Crusoean model of practical survival. Defoe's character shows no compunction about shooting animals for food or butchering domesticated pets, and he delights at discovering that he had killed a pregnant turtle full of eggs (*Crusoe,* 101). Beaurieu's hero, on the contrary, clearly suffers from his sense of transgressing against nature. This instance may be read as a gesture to the growing concerns about vivisection in the scientific milieus Beaurieu inhabited as a natural historian.[125] Nevertheless, the character quickly recovers from his qualms and continues his inquiries. Soon after his traumatic experience with the rabbit, the pupil reproaches himself for not having taken more time to investigate the "warm and humid smoke" that came out of her stomach (1:194). When he finds a dead crow, he seizes his knife to see if its internal organs resemble those of quadrupeds, and when he soon thereafter finds a bird egg, he kills the baby by cracking open the shell (1:195; 1:201).

A useful contrast to Beaurieu's amateur anatomist can be found in Martin's *Young Gentleman's and Lady's Philosophy*. With a macabre attention to detail, Martin's young protagonists describe such gruesome exploits as electrical experiments on a titmouse (who dies as a result) and pneumatic experiments on a rabbit in an air pump. Although the description of the air pump experiment seems graphic and sadistic to modern readers, this sort of experimentation was very common as a parlor game of sorts. Describing the rabbit's reactions, Cleonicus explains to his sister Euphrosyne:

> As the Air is more rarified, the Animal is rendered more thoughtful of his unlucky Situation, and seeks in vain to extricate himself.—He leaps and jumps about.—A Vertigo seizes his Brain.—He falls, and is just about expiring.—But I turn the Vent-piece, and let in the Air by Degrees.—You see him begin to heave, and pant.—At length, he rouzes up, opens his Eyes, and wildly stares about him.—I take off the Receiver, and shall now deliver it as recovered from the Dead.

After recovering from her emotion, Euphrosyne exclaims: "The Usefulness of this Machine seems unlimited. What a prodigious Variety of Experiments are shewn thereby to explain the Nature of Things, and the important Properties of Air!"[126]

What are we to make of these troubling images of juvenile science? It is tempting to group Beaurieu's pupil with what Barbara Benedict calls the "blasphemously curious men" of nineteenth-century fiction, such as Victor Frankenstein or Beckford's Vathek, who pursue curiosity until, Faust-like and aiming too high, they plunge into hell.[127] But such moral tensions are strikingly subdued in eighteenth-century texts. Instead what we find in Martin, as in Beaurieu, is that experimentalism, regardless of its ethical implications, is promoted as a useful pastime.

Looking back to Rousseau's warring concerns with control, charlatanism, and transparency might help us understand this paradox. As we saw in

Emile, Rousseau promoted an active, engaged kind of study so that the child could gain first-hand knowledge of nature's laws, although he sometimes staged the lessons in a highly artificial manner to manipulate the child's emotions. Like others, he believed that since the Fall, man's senses had been dimmed. If experimental philosophy could restore knowledge to its prelapsarian state, through direct and verifiable means, then such work was necessarily worthy. The ethical improprieties it demanded of the (animal or human) subject were merely part of the means to achieve this noble end.

Beaurieu's pupil has neither the industrious, goal-oriented approach to life that characterized Emile and Robinson Crusoe nor the reverence of Automathes. Instead of sublimating his physical urges into work or worship, his growing awareness culminates in an intense desire for sensual gratification. Awakening one morning enraptured by the sunlight, birdsong, and smells of the earth, he rolls and frolics in dewy lilies, releasing a heady perfume that sends him into an erotic dream of sexual longing. "I squeeze the hands of my charming companion, I fall on her bosom, I awaken with a start, open my eyes, and see that I am alone."[128] Once awakened, his desire becomes insatiable and inflames his imagination, coloring everything he sees: the island appears inhabited by loving couples of doves, insects, fish—even the flowers and plants seem to enjoy each others' presence.[129] This eroticized landscape recalls the imagery of period natural history, such as the "bridal beds" of Linneaus's plant morphology and the vignettes of floral connubial bliss in Erasmus Darwin's *Loves of the Plants* (1789), not to mention Buffon's Adamic narrative.[130] It also implies an essentially materialistic vision of sexuality as the dominant impulse in mankind as in all other living creatures.

This carefree hedonism abruptly disappears from the second part of *L'Elève,* however, which traces the pupil's "second birth" as a social being. Wandering about the far side of the island, he stumbles into a trap and finds himself captured by an old man and his lovely young daughter, shipwreck victims who have been living there for several years. We learn that Julie has been tending the hut and maintaining domestic order in spite of their isolation. Here again, woman is always already in culture. And man's education, here as in *Emile,* must lead him out of nature into culture by way of sublimation. In a swift metamorphosis from his earlier existence as a contemplative, pleasure-seeking primitive, the pupil soon learns the French language and the principles of agriculture, acquires a name (Ariste, or "well-taught") and a set of clothes, starts a family, and assumes a clearly defined social function. The evocation of sensual pleasure, which played such an important role in volume 1, disappears from Beaurieu's text in volume 2.

Hereafter sexuality is solely identified with procreation: the serious work of populating the desert island. Individual desire is thus sublimated to the welfare of the group; the unruly natural man fades from view as the obedient civil subject takes his place. Instead of submitting to an omniscient God, Beaurieu's pupil submits to monogamy and places his faith in the patriarchal family order.

The rest of volume 2 forms a hybrid of the various topoi culled from Locke, *Crusoe, Automathes,* and Rousseau. Ariste is reunited with his father (whom he welcomes with open arms and no reproaches about his bizarre childrearing techniques), he makes a hasty visit to Europe (and proffers a rather stale version of "savage critic" commonplaces), he writes his new knowledge into a set of formal discourses on topics such as agriculture and architecture, and he makes a triumphant return to the island with a group of disciples in tow. The colony that takes shape in volume 3 exemplifies the Physiocrats' dream of integrating the country and the city (indeed, Beaurieu cites the Physiocrats' journal, *Les Ephémérides du citoyen,* to make this connection clear to the reader).[131] As in the alpine utopia of Rousseau's *Nouvelle Héloïse,* its houses are surrounded by fruit trees, grass, and tame animals, and its inhabitants' lives revolve around the demands of communal agriculture and a domestic sphere designed to maintain "the calm of the passions" (3:86). Julie acts as a model for the other women by tending to her daughters' education, gardening, feeding the chickens, cooking, and cleaning every inch of her house so that it harbors no "disagreeable odors" (3:86). As in *Crusoe,* industry is key to this domestic happiness. The only texts available for women are the community readings of La Fontaine or Virgil that they attend in the evening. Women are allowed no leisure reading, especially not *livres bleus* or popular fiction (3:88). Ariste's portrait stresses his robust health and skills in agriculture and canal-building; it makes no mention of his feelings other than his empathy for fallen trees and his ardent interest in his children's education (3:85–91).

Beaurieu's final solution thus bypasses the troubling tensions between individual drives and social duties in *Emile,* but the idyll of L'Isle de la Paix relies on a sinister notion of citizenship. The last pages of *L'Elève* include a detailed inventory of techniques for maintaining order in the social sphere. Here we find advice on communal dining, child care, sexual division of adolescents (at age fifteen) and segregation of adults (during daywork), labor assignments based on sex and age, a blueprint of the streets and buildings in the city-state of Aristie, even a building-by-building and room-by-room analysis of the uses to be assigned to architectural space. In keeping with his vague deism, Ariste requires communal worship of God and of "the strongest and most perfect being after God," by which he means not Jesus Christ but the sun (3 : 59). Instead of struggling to maintain their integrity, as do the characters of Defoe and Rousseau, Beaurieu's protagonists appear to have achieved permanent perfection. They inhabit a geometrically perfect, pastoral city-state, where each citizen receives a list of social duties to fulfill and moral regulations to respect in order to keep their nature well in check.

But as Gillian Beer and others have reminded us, the choice of an island casts a certain pessimism over the reformative potential of this project of social perfection.[132] Some of the governor's measures, here as in *Automathes*, suggest that the utopia is actually a despotic regime. Beaurieu's Ariste punishes a child who steals by confining him in a dark room with only bread and water for three days (3 : 104–5). He alone governs all the male children and determines which ones have artistic talents so that he may warn them never to use those talents except for the public good (3 : 123). He prides himself on purging all vices from the children because "he radically cured them in childhood" ("il les en a guéri radicalement dès leur enfance," 3 : 127). The spontaneous "pupil of nature" has undergone a radical evolution into this control-minded panopticon. By an odd paradox, this weighty fiction (more than six hundred pages) projects a utopia based on a preliterate stage of human society. In a gesture eerily prescient of the Terror, when deputies argued that libraries should be burned since the revolution wanted no memory save that of its own history and laws, Beaurieu bans all books from his colony and warns that would-be authors "will be regarded as sacrilegious and disrupters of the public peace."[133] Although three or four citizens keep the art of writing alive, they use it only to engrave in marble the principal events of the colony's history. Since *L'Elève* is supposedly motivated by public instruction, the author announces that once it is finished so is his writing career: "Myself, to set the example, I will burn my pen."[134] As this utopia concludes, one is left with a disturbing vision of the natural man-cum-lawgiver maintaining his privileged status over a populace forced into a life of preliterate labor. Although Beaurieu did not pursue his fiction to its logical end, this endless accumulation of rules and forced sharing of public life is already a dystopia. During the revolutionary era Beaurieu proposed to found a boys' school *(pépinière de jeunes hommes)* that would operate upon some of the principles in *L'Elève,* but to no avail.[135] After perusing this troubling fiction, one can only be glad that the project failed.

The plot of human perfectibility in Dulaurens's novel *Imirce ou la fille de la nature* (1765) ends with a situation of similarly high-minded virtue, but what a different trajectory leads there! Like most of Abbé Dulaurens's works,

Imirce was banned and confiscated in France for its irreligious and pornographic content. But this public notoriety must be seen in context: *Emile* and *L'Elève de la nature* were also banned because of irreligious and "philosophical" claims, and even *Crusoe* was criticized for its "dangerous" religious attitudes.[136] All three of the French works figure in Robert Darnton's corpus of illegal or "clandestine literature" circulating in France between 1769 and 1789.[137] Whereas the other authors were respected for their work, however, Dulaurens seems to have been dismissed as something of a crackpot.[138] Among other bizarre experiences, he was apparently confined for several months by his superiors at a Trinitarian monastery in a kind of wooden cage suspended above the ground. His experience resembles Imirce's deprivation. With no pen or pencil, he used a piece of metal to inscribe epigrams and quolibets all over the wooden bars.[139] In 1767 Dulaurens was condemned to prison in perpetuity for his impious and antireligious writings; he spent the last twenty-seven years of his life in the "convent-prison" of Marienbaum, where he slowly declined into madness.

But although the author has largely disappeared from literary history, his works were widely read in the eighteenth century.[140] Between 1765 and 1782, *Imirce* caused quite a stir—at least nine editions were published in French and one English translation.[141] This novel may be reemerging from oblivion today, thanks to Annie Rivara's 1993 reedition. Perhaps *Imirce* will contribute to what Peter Cryle sees as the "sexual liberation" occurring in modern-day French literature—as witnessed by the increasingly visible presence of early works of erotica on publishers' lists and bookstore shelves in the United States and in France.[142]

Illustrated editions have drawn attention to the most titillating episodes in this text and created an image of *Imirce* as erotica (as in fig. 16). This is arguably one of the attractions of this strange little book, but Dulaurens's text is also interesting for its restaging of the human experiment. The novel's apparatus makes literal the *degré zéro* of Rousseau's experiment in startlingly cruel ways. "A rich philosopher bought me a few days after my birth," writes Imirce, and for the next twenty-two years she sees neither sky nor earth. She is confined in a stone cellar *(la cave)* encircled and paved with iron, having only two small windows for light.[143] Once a day, a basket descends with bread. Originally blindfolded, the child is only allowed sight when the invisible "master of the cellar" wills it (81). Although Rivara sees these material details and eyewitness narration as realistic devices aiming to make Rousseau's abstraction more tangible, I see nothing realistic about such a setting.[144]

FIGURE 16

Woodcut by Sylvain Sauvage from Abbé Dulaurens, *Imirce ou la fille de la nature* (Paris: J. Fort, 1922).

Rather, this novel recalls the extremely stylized decor of late eighteenth-century erotica and Gothic fiction. The stark cruelty of the cellar, the diet of bread and water, the nudity and squalor of the characters—who witness their dead baby's putrefaction while the philosopher watches from above—presage the suffering found in the Gothic horrors of Matthew Lewis's *The Monk* (1796) and Sade's *120 Journées de Sodome* (1785). Just as the sight of mothers grieving their dead children thrills Sade's characters, the sight of his experimental subjects discovering primal instincts gives pleasure to Dulaurens's philosopher-voyeur.[145]

Dulaurens's "scientific" premises bear some resemblance to period practices. Consider the cruel pneumatic experiments in Martin's *Young Gentleman's and Lady's Philosophy,* for instance, or the scenes of experimental philosophy popularized by Wright of Derby's famous painting *Eperiment on a Bird in the Air Pump* (c. 1767–68; fig. 17). Here as in Dulaurens, the

FIGURE 17

Joseph Wright of Derby, *An Experiment on a Bird in the Air Pump*, c. 1767–68. Copyright Tate Gallery, London/Art Resource, New York.

subject's fate is entirely dependent upon an apparently sadistic experimenter's will and skill with the procedure. The art historians Judy Egerton, David Solkin, and David Fraser have documented the ambivalence inspired by Wright of Derby's work: if one presumes the bird in the air pump's glass receiver is dead, the scene can be read as a *vanitas* underlining the transience of earthly existence—an interpretation seconded by the decaying human skull glimpsed on the jar on the table. But the lecturer may turn the stop-clock just in time to revive the bird, and if so, one may read the painting as a comment on the awesome power of the researcher over his subject.[146]

The moral implications were not necessarily so obvious as one might think. At least one critic interpreted the bird in the air pump as a family pet, but not to criticize the painting for its insensitivity. Instead the critic applauded Wright of Derby's rendition of the child "whimpering for her pigeon" as a "tender and ingenious touch."[147] Although many criticized Hunterian medicine for its callous treatment of human subjects and condemned the use of live animals in air pump experiments, others defended similarly inhumane practices as effective methods of teaching moral lessons.[148] The children in Martin's *Young Gentleman's and Lady's Philosophy* and Newbery's *Newtonian System of Philosophy* express qualms about suffocating and electrocuting animals, but they perform the experiments anyway and thus learn elements of physics and what can or cannot be done to direct "the Power of Nature."[149]

The radically contrived, impoverished setting of *Imirce* demonstrates the materialist's vision of mankind's original abjection and mounts a blank screen onto which the characters' innate ideas and social apprenticeship are clearly projected. The apparatus includes a boy (whose name, Emilor, recalls Rousseau's hero) and a series of objects sent down to test the children's ability to translate sensation into thought. Echoing Locke and Condillac, Dulaurens's philosopher first tries a rose, then a parrot (as in fig. 16), a mirror, and a monkey. These objects replicate the sensationist scenario of mental awakening; they are designed to elicit a sequence of increasingly complex mental reactions.

The isolated social unit was itself another common leitmotiv in contemporary philosophy.[150] Since Herodotus, savants had dreamed of raising an entire society in isolation and thereby observing the "natural" development of human ideas, language, and social relations. Dulaurens builds on this premise but couches it in an approximation of primitivist rhetoric, as when Imirce describes the children's language: "We already understood one another; but our words were few, as well as our ideas. The sounds we uttered were guttural, and resembled a good deal the disagreeable cries of certain animals" (83).[151]

Along with this transparent language, uninhibited sexuality was supposed to be a given among primitive peoples.[152] *Imirce* thus shows the characters growing to maturity not by accumulating social learning but by acquiring sexual knowledge. As the heroine writes: "We were for ever touching and examining one another: our hearts, pure as the light of day; and our innocent hands found nothing indecent in these natural caresses" (84).[153] The conclusions this entails for social commentary are evident: relocating the primitive's authenticity from some exotic locale to the early years of childhood, Dulaurens makes it accessible to all. As the narrator declares: "This instinct among children is doubtless that of nature, and was ours" ("Cet instinct, chez les enfants, est sans doute celui de la nature" 72; 84). Instead of seeing shame as an integral part of human nature, as did the Christian writers Defoe, Kirkby, and Rousseau, the materialist Dulaurens dismisses the concept by declaring it unnatural.

The protagonists leap from birth to puberty in the space of four paragraphs: a strategy common in erotic texts that dismiss childhood as a useless time of waiting.[154] Sexual awareness emerges as a result of physical proximity and sensory stimuli, as when they discover the pleasures of her budding breasts: "He saw my bosom increase in prominence, and, delighted with this object, caressed it incessantly . . . to my great satisfaction, [he] learned by degrees to touch it with more gentleness" (84).[155] Although they first have sex "without knowing what [they] were about," the characters soon realize the great pleasure to be had by this act and practice it frequently: "The slight pain that attended it was amply re-paid by a transport of delight; and I felt that pleasure was preferable to bread, to the basket, and to the master of the cellar" (85).[156]

As pornographers would revise Defoe's novel by giving Crusoe a sex partner,[157] so *Imirce* revises the abstract narratives of Condillac and Rousseau to give "the girl of nature" sexual desires and the will to gratify them. The use of a female narrative voice makes this text all the more titillating and inscribes *Imirce* in the female tradition of pornographic materialism alongside *Fanny Hill* (1748) and *Thérèse philosophe* (1748). Like the narrators of those books, the "female voices move the texts along," writes Margaret Jacob, "just as their bodies are compelled by their desires."[158] But in this regard Dulaurens is less innovative than other pornographers. Although his heroine is free of Judeo-Christian guilt about sexuality, she still inhabits the social role conventionally assigned to woman. Imirce and Emilor are described as a typical heterosexual couple: he is intelligent, she is vain and inconstant.[159] The dynamic between experimenter and female subject is explicitly sexualized here as well. When the philosopher (satirically named Ariste, like Beaurieu's hero) finally allows Imirce out of the cellar in her twenty-second year, the liberation is described as a gesture of licentious self-interest.[160] After initiating sexual intercourse with Ariste and finding him pleasurable, Imirce placidly accepts her new condition and "from that moment, poor Emilor was forgotten" ("dès le moment, le pauvre Emilor fut oublié," 95; 76).

This formation is supposed to retain her uninhibited nature intact, but one might rightly wonder, to what end? Imirce's later self-identification with a prostitute reveals one of the blind spots in Dulaurens's libertine primitivism. Observing some camp-followers carousing with soldiers, she comments: "[They] suffered themselves to be handled with as little reserve as I did in my prison," concluding, "they are indeed chastised because they offend against decency; are confined because the vicars have not given them permission to sleep with these soldiers; and are despised, and called whores. At this rate then, am I a whore too?"[161] This remark reveals the ambivalence in Dulaurens's vision of female sexuality and highlights the persistence of tradition—which defined the female body as the recipient, not the agent of desire—even in this *libertine* text. That Imirce should care about what people think proves she has already been "denatured."

The shock value of *Imirce* lies less in its treatment of gender than in its materialist principles, which lead to a callous disregard for the sanctity of human life and justify the philosopher's manipulation of the human subjects. Imirce's pregnancy, childbirth, and care of her infant son are evoked in mere half-dozen lines, after which the baby dies. Gazing in horror on the rotting, worm-infested body, Imirce and Emilor conceive a primitive cosmology: they call death "the bad smell" *(la puanteur)*, day is "the master's eye" *(l'oeil du maître)*, and night is "the eye of death" *(l'oeil de la puanteur)*. Fearful of these invisible powers, they express a materialism that distorts Locke's famous dictum—"our business here is not to know all things, but those which concern our conduct"—into an amoral egoism.[162] Emilor's credo—"we cannot make a cellar as he has done; let us live in his; love one another, and eat his bread" (88)[163]—can be seen to presage the ethos of Sade, who would announce thirty years later: "it is less important to understand nature than to draw pleasure from it and to respect its laws."[164] In this and other passages, *Imirce* delineates how materialism can twist the relation between nature and culture into a justification for human abjection. The squalor of the cellar, with its slopheap and rotting cadaver, forms a shocking contrast to the sterile or benevolent settings we saw above.

Once Imirce is above ground, the narrative adopts a new register: the pseudo-exotic "spy novel," or satire of contemporary manners.[165] But the criticisms of French culture we see through her eyes offer nothing new. They simply reiterate commonplaces about the poverty of peasant life, the absurdity of aristocratic fashions, the injustice of penal institutions, and the gluttony of the rich. Ultimately, Dulaurens abandons his desire to challenge the nature-culture debate and places the characters firmly in the dominant social order. Imirce accepts a position in the aristocracy she once condemned as the legal wife of Emilor, who is finally allowed out of the cellar to ensure the posterity of the dying Ariste. In an abrupt reversal of their original nudity, Emilor and Imirce take on complex new social roles, new names—the comte and comtesse d'Albin—and end their story as the resident landowners of a country estate. By marrying off Imirce and rechanneling her search for pleasure into domesticity and good works *(bienfaisance)*, Dulaurens negates the principles of his initial experiment and produces a textual monster instead of a cohesive work of erotica, libertinage, psychology, or pedagogical theory. This novel is often considered libertine in its hedonistic disregard for socio-moral norms, but it lacks the crucial feature of libertinism, that is, didactic unity.[166] Although Imirce's radical beginning suggests a substantive effort to rethink human beings' metaphysical status in the natural world, by the end this novel merely reasserts the status quo. As in *Emile* and *L'Elève,* whatever good emerges from Imirce's final incarnation will be the work of her individual aristocratic *bienfaisance* rather than any effort to change existing attitudes or institutions. The conclusion of all three novels merely reverses the initial situation and invents a new site of benevolent isolation: the country estate.

It is tempting to sweep away all the inconsistencies of these books by citing their speculative nature, which absolves the authors of the need for sustained, responsible plans. As Norman Hampson reminds us, the French *hommes de lettres* of the mid-century "moved in an atmosphere that encouraged speculation for its own sake, and the audience for which they wrote was more interested in bold and original concepts, especially those which *sentaient le fagot* [flirted with heresy], than in the systematic study of how things came to be as they were and in detailed plans for improving them."[167] To say that they are simply speculative, however, underestimates the polemical nature of these texts. Although couched in the genre of the novel, all three works contain proposals for social reform. All three writers express palpable suspicion of existing governments and a desire to empower individuals to undertake reforms that might improve on current practices. The increasingly aggressive interventions they envision under the rubric of experimental education shift the goal from Locke's values of virtue and self-mastery to a "nature" that is supposed to free mankind from its bondage to corrupt social institutions.

Yet their solutions give the reader pause. We have seen how the manipulative practices of Rousseau's tutor coerce the child into learning the right lessons and how the rude stoicism inculcated in Emile fosters a moral inflexibility that ultimately undoes the utopia in *Emile et Sophie.* The materialism of Beaurieu and Dulaurens deals a heavy blow to the potential for human freedom, as well. As Owen Bradley has shown, this kind of reasoning argued that organic life obeys natural laws (in Cartesian terms, the laws of matter in motion). But to this it added more dubious claims: first that such laws were mechanical, and second, that not only animals' organic functions but their sensibility or intelligence could be reduced to purely mechanical processes. Whereas the first could be considered a felicitous contribution to the history of physiology (the understanding of man as a natural being free of theological determinants), the second leads to perplexing conclusions. By excluding nonmechanical motivation from the conduct of human beings, such writers "contributed to the emerging ideology of man as the engineering master of nature."[168] But in attempting to engineer nature, Beaurieu and Dulaurens's characters were also engineered by it, as part of a vast, unthinking machine.

Oddly, this materialist strain was not untainted by sociocultural concerns. All the while trying to desacralize human conduct, Beaurieu and Dulaurens relied on moral codes inherited from the past. In *L'Elève* and *Imirce,* as well as in *Emile,* the conflict between sensory impulses and sociocultural rules is ultimately resolved by allusion to man's need for monogamy and woman's naturally submissive supporting role in monogamy. Echoing age-old Christian dogma, all of these texts—including the most radically materialist—represent sexual instincts, especially female desires, as a primitive urge or vestige of the savage living within. Even in Dulaurens's erotica, the "girl of nature" is ultimately dealt the fate of all unruly elements in the enlightened social order: she is channeled, for better or worse, into domestic concerns serving the public good. The new orders they envision at the end prove just as stultifying as the original societies they were intended to repair. For all their utopian rhetoric, these visions of perfecting mankind raise troubling questions about the value of individual freedom—questions that later fictions would exploit to devastating effect.

—CHAPTER FOUR—

Raising the Rational Child

REAL-LIFE EXPERIMENTS AND ALTERNATIVES TO ROUSSEAU

—How difficult a thing it is to bring up a child.
—Assuredly it is, because the father and mother are not made by nature to bring it up, nor the child to be brought up.

—Exchange between Louise d'Epinay and Jean-Jacques Rousseau

Attempts to apply Rousseauian principles to "perfect" actual children were not as rare as one might suppose. Although *Emile* was banned almost on publication in France for its irreligious ideas and was confiscated by police for the next two decades, with its author forced into a long and painful exile, many readers cherished the book and considered its author an expert on raising children the "rational" way.[1] Gilbert Py has signaled the considerable impact of *Emile* among progressive parents in Germany and Switzerland; also noteworthy is the novel's popularity among the leading upper-class families of Ireland, France, and England. Thus we find mothers applying Rousseauian practices in sites as far-flung as the Tighe estate in rural County Kilkenny, the fashionable Fitzgerald mansions in Dublin and London, and the Mirabeau *hôtel particulier* in Paris.[2] When *Emile* was first published in English, it was attacked by intellectuals but touted in the popular press as a manual for middle-class family life. The 1762 *London Chronicle* excerpted passages urging mothers to nurse their children, and the *London Magazine* (August 1762) cited book 5 as an illustration of the different kinds of compatibility necessary for a successful marriage.[3] No fewer than two hundred treatises on pedagogy were published in English from 1762 to 1800, the majority of which show the influence of Rousseau.[4]

Not only did the popularity of *Emile* transcend national borders, so did the public's trust in Rousseau during this time. Scores of readers of various nationalities wrote to the author with requests for advice. The author's responses, however, were characteristically ambiguous. Although in *Emile* he insisted on the abstract nature of his treatise, when the prince and princess of Wurtemburg expressed their intention to raise their daughters along

Rousseauian lines, the author responded with many enthusiastic letters of support and advice for coping with problems such as the babies' teething pains and crying—their correspondance amounted to more than fifty letters.[5] But when a bourgeois from Strasbourg claimed to be educating his son à la Emile, the author scolded: "So much the worse, sir, for you and your son, so much the worse."[6] When one reader rebuked him by calling his system "utopian," Rousseau agreed: "You are quite right to say it is impossible to create an Emile; but do you really think that was my intention and that the book that bears this title is truly a treatise on education? It is quite a philosophical work based on the principle, advanced by the author in other writings, *that man is naturally good*."[7] Implicitly encouraging another would-be experimentalist, the author challenged: "If it is true that you have adopted the plan I tried to sketch in the Emile, I admire your courage; for you are too intelligent not to see that, in such a system, it is all or nothing."[8]

Such ambivalence is unsurprising, coming from the author of *Emile.* What is surprising is the fervent following he enjoyed as an authority on childrearing. True, Rousseau's pedagogical ideas were considered impractical for the more urgent development of much-needed public schools, and his notion of "inactive" education was blamed for encouraging neglect.[9] But *Emile* remained potent for decades after its publication. Most parents integrated Rousseau's ideas within a more conventional framework and adopted his recommendations on breast-feeding, physical education, clothing, diet, and hygiene, while disregarding or criticizing the author's views on religious education, discipline, and book learning in general. But for better or worse, *Emile* was a major feature on the European intellectual landscape.

In this chapter I propose to explore the writings of three notorious parent-pedagogues—Richard Lovell Edgeworth, Thomas Day, and Manon Roland—who followed the precepts laid out in *Emile* to devastating ends. I present these cases not because they typify period practices but rather because their experience provides a fascinating glimpse of what went wrong when real children were held accountable to Rousseauian theories and how experience forced the would-be pedagogues to rethink their concept of perfectibility. This foray into real-life experimentation is followed by a discussion of two of the most famous writings on education from the period: Mme de Genlis's novelistic *Adèle et Théodore* (1782) and Maria and Richard Lovell Edgeworth's encyclopedic *Practical Education* (1798), both of which purport to rework Rousseau's scheme into a more feasible, responsible, even "scientific" kind of childrearing. These cases and texts will provide us with a good control model for understanding just how far-fetched the plots of fiction were vis-à-vis the practices and reflections of real parents, and conversely, how deeply pedagogical theory had penetrated contemporary habits of thought.

THREE FAMOUS CASES

What is most striking about the cases of Edgeworth, Day, and Roland is the experimenters' overinvestment in predetermined notions of human nature as something pure that, if kept intact until adulthood, might produce superior beings. Judging from their letters and memoirs, and from contemporary accounts of their activities, these teachers were less committed to raising real children than to acting out an ideal of physical and moral perfection. When their pet theories were proved false by the vagaries of child development or the child's psychology turned out to be too difficult to manage, the whole edifice of experimental learning fell down. In all three cases, the performance of Rousseauian education ultimately ended in a challenge to the master's notion of human perfectibility. Like the wild children discussed in chapter 1, the subjects of real-life experiments made a poor showing, revealing human frailty and limitations instead of confirming notions of unlimited progress.

Richard Lovell Edgeworth and Richard Jr.

Perhaps the earliest documented long-term experiment in Rousseauian pedagogy is the case of Richard Edgeworth (born 1764), educated at the hands of his father, Richard Lovell Edgeworth. Richard Sr. is most famous today for his mechanical inventions, notably his conveyor belt, and for his membership in the progressive Lunar Society of Birmingham.[10] Although Richard Jr. was not well known during his lifetime, his story has emerged since, thanks to the published memoirs and correspondence of his father and sister, the biography of Maria Edgeworth by Marilyn Butler, and the biographies of Thomas Day, an Edgeworth family friend, by Peter Rowland and George Gignilliat Jr.[11] True to his experimentalist spirit, the young and idealistic Edgeworth weighed the "many plausible ideas" of *Emile* against the "obvious deficiencies and absurdities" of contemporary social customs and, with his wife's consent, he "determined to make a fair trial of Rousseau's system" on their firstborn son.[12] This project was by no means easy, as Edgeworth later admitted: "I steadily pursued it for several years, notwithstanding the opposition with which I was embarrassed by my friends and relations, and the ridicule by which I became immediately assailed on all quarters" (*Memoirs,* 1 : 173). Although Edgeworth does not spell out the details of his method, clothing and outdoor play were key to this regime, as they were for Emile. From age three to age eight, "little Dick" was dressed in an "extraordinary" fashion, with no stockings and a jacket that left the arms bare. He was allowed to run about wherever he pleased and follow his will in everything. According to Edgeworth, the project created a "bold, free, fearless, generous" youngster with a "ready and keen use of all his senses" (1 : 174). Moreover the boy proved to be "capable of bearing privation of every sort" and had a good mind for mechanics—doubtless a result of witnessing his father's constant invention (1 : 173).

But the child's stunted social skills ultimately proved problematic. Traveling through Paris en route to Lyon in 1771, Edgeworth took seven-year-old Dick to meet Rousseau. After chatting with the child for a couple of hours, the philosopher appreciated the boy's abilities but warned that his resolute stubbornness and chauvinism boded ill for his character—a prophetic perception, Edgeworth later commented (*Memoirs,* 1 : 253–54). The situation came to a head while Dick was living with father in Lyon, where the latter had been drawn by plans to divert the Rhône—a fascinating opportunity to see and implement new technology. Remembering the child at age nine, the father admitted: "Whatever regarded the health, strength, and agility of my son, had amply justified the system of my master; but I found myself entangled in difficulties with regard to my child's mind and temper. . . . It was difficult to urge him to any thing that did not suit his fancy, and more difficult to restrain him from what he wished to follow" (1 : 268, 269). Richard Sr. became engrossed in the more pleasant technical problems of engineering and turned away from his obstreperous son.[13] After an English tutor found the child incorrigible, Edgeworth placed him in a nearby seminary in 1772.[14] It was rumored at the time that the boy had been disrupting the household for years and that even the Catholic regimen could not cure his relentless disobedience. Later the elder Edgeworth would regret this project, although he divided the blame between Rousseau ("the error of a theory") and himself, realizing that he had abandoned Dick's education when the child needed him most (1 : 269–71). He took a much firmer hand with his other children, insisting that they be well disciplined and begin performing household chores by the age of three.[15]

When Richard Jr. later returned to Edgeworthstown, his parents sent him off to school again until in 1779 they gave him their blessing to go off to sea at age fifteen. "I found it better to comply with his wishes, than to strive against the stream," wrote his father (*Memoirs,* 1 : 348). The boy was alienated from his family; he did not even ask to come home until 1783, after deserting ship—and he was refused.[16] In 1784 he was allowed to return to England, and Edgeworth wrote to Day asking if the young man might stay at his home for a while. Day's reply reveals his anxious memories of the boy's character: "I should be glad to see the young gentleman for a limited time, but that I could not possibly engage for more, till I know the state of his manners and behaviour." Warding off any possible reproaches for this inhospitable reply, Day added: "Until the stains of his past conduct get washed, Mr E. cannot be surprized at this [as one] who does not choose to have him in his own house."[17] In July 1784, Edgeworth defended himself and expressed his own coolness toward the boy: "I hope he [will beco]me an amiable man; & and also am sure you will be the first to sy[mpathise] with me & to throw a veil over his past failings; but till then I believe myself capable of acting towards him with steadiness and justice."[18]

Although Dick visited the family a few times in later years and received financial support from them, when he married and settled in South Carolina, he apparently led a rather dissipated life. Reflecting on his son's death in 1796, the father would icily appraise this misspent existence: "his way of life had become such as promised no happiness to himself or his family—it is therefore better for both that he has retired from the scene."[19] Years later, this story would still be circulating in the popular imagination as the tale of an ungovernable "child of nature."[20] Even more mortifying for the Edgeworths' pride was the unflattering resemblance between the elder Edgeworth son and the elder Musgrove son depicted in Jane Austen's novel *Persuasion* (written 1816). Austen's description of Dick Musgrove recalls many of the painful facts of Richard Edgeworth Jr.'s life. He was "a very troublesome, hopeless son," she writes, who was sent off to sea before age twenty

> because he was stupid and unmanageable on shore . . . [and] had been very little cared for at any time by his family, though quite as much as he deserved; seldom heard of, and scarcely at all regretted . . . though his sisters were now doing all they could for him, by calling him 'poor Richard', [he had] been nothing better than thick-headed, unfeeling, unprofitable Dick Musgrove, who had never done any thing to entitle himself to more than the abbreviation of his name, living or dead.[21]

This is a sorry eulogy for one who had once incarnated the hopes of "natural" pedagogy.

Thomas Day and Sabrina

Edgeworth's zeal for pedagogy was not limited to his family alone; he also supported the notorious experiment of his friend Thomas Day. Day is a somewhat enigmatic figure. Eyewitnesses offer wildly contrasting accounts:

Richard Lovell Edgeworth's *Memoirs* presents the sympathetic view of a lifelong friend, whereas Anna Seward's *Memoirs of the Life of Dr. Darwin* (1804) denigrates Day's life and works in a most acerbic manner.[22] Thanks to the thoughtful attention of Day's biographers, we have access to a more accurate account of his accomplishments and eccentricities.[23] Like Edgeworth, the youthful Day admired Rousseau unreservedly; he declared to his friend in 1769: "Were all the books in the world to be destroyed . . . the second book I should wish to save, after the Bible, would be Rousseau's *Emilius*. . . . Every page is big with important truth."[24] Inspired by Rousseau, Day vowed to marry a woman who would share his spartan lifestyle and cater to his rigorous views on wifely duties. But after driving away more than one lady-love with his eccentric ideas, uncouth table manners, gruff disposition, and unkempt appearance, Day became determined to create the ideal woman, like a philosophical Monsieur de la Souche.[25]

At age twenty-one, then, Day adopted two girls (aged eleven and twelve) from foundling hospitals in the London area, drew up a legal agreement for financial support, named them Sabrina Sidney and Lucretia, and placed them in a widow's home.[26] Seeking to avoid the inquiries of London acquaintances and to achieve greater isolation, Day soon moved with his two charges to Avignon, where he taught them to read and write and endeavored to make them adopt a Rousseauian contempt for dress, luxury, and titles. His teaching followed the course laid down for Emile at age twelve. He demonstrated basic principles of geometry and prodded the girls to observe natural phenomena such as sunrises and seasonal changes. That fall, he sent back a glowing report of their progress to Edgeworth: "I have made them, in respect to temper, two such girls, as, I may perhaps say without vanity, you have never seen at the same age. They have never given me a moment's trouble throughout the voyage, are always contented" (Edgeworth, *Memoirs,* 1:220–22). By the spring of 1770, however, Day had had enough of this experiment; the girls frequently quarreled and, when they both fell ill with smallpox, he was forced into playing nursemaid to two querulous patients. Lucretia proved to be "invincibly stupid" and France intolerable. On returning to London, Day placed Lucretia with a milliner and gave her a dowry of three hundred pounds, which paved the way to her marriage a few years later with a respectable linen-draper.[27]

Sabrina was Day's favorite; in the summer of 1770 he leased a house for the two of them in Lichfield, near his friend Edgeworth and members of the Lunar Society. The town's intelligentsia observed this household with interest, if not astonishment.[28] It appears that Day applied rather cruel methods to develop his charge's physical and mental strength. Witnesses claim that he fired pistols at Sabrina and dropped melted sealing wax on her arms to inure her to fear and pain.[29] Although these methods were bizarre, they are taken directly from books 1 and 2 of *Emile*.[30] Sabrina reportedly endured these tests out of love for her teacher, but after a year of disappointments and in view of the superior charms of another young lady, Day abandoned the experiment and sent Sabrina to a nearby boarding school on the condition that she not be trained in either music or dancing.

In 1774, with more amorous defeats and continental travels behind him, Day returned to find Sabrina a "feminine, elegant and amiable" young woman of sixteen. His letters to Edgeworth speak warmly of her beauty and good temper; Day appears to have been intending to marry her, and Sabrina seems to have been in love with him. But something happened—perhaps she wore the wrong sleeves, carried the wrong handkerchief, or told a secret—and Day abruptly abandoned the project. He cited her supposedly weak mind and inadequate attachment as irremovable barriers to improvement, and he left her forever (Edgeworth, *Memoirs*, 1:334). Day eventually married in 1778, when he finally found a woman (Esther Milnes) who shared his predilection for thrifty living and philosophical debate; the two lived happily until his death in 1789. True to his original agreement, Day ensured a pension of fifty pounds a year for Sabrina, which allowed her to move out of the school and into a boarding house. But he never saw her alone again.

Day appears oblivious to his injustice; later he dismissed the four years spent educating Sabrina as "the extravagancies of a warm heart, and of a strong imagination."[31] He would imagine a more successful female education in the person of Miss Simmons, a character in his best-selling didactic novel *Sandford and Merton* (1783–89). Miss Simmons's education can be seen as an idealized version of Sabrina's. In order to prevent excessive delicacy and form a strong character, Miss Simmons's uncle makes the girl "accustomed, from her earliest years, to plunge into a cold bath at every season of the year, to rise by candle-light in winter, to ride a dozen miles upon a trotting horse." She reads the best English authors, learns the laws of nature and some geometry, becomes adept at all domestic tasks, and learns how to read but not speak French.[32]

But Sabrina's trials were not yet at an end. After several years as a lady's companion, in 1784 Sabrina married Day's friend John Bicknell (who had been present when Day originally chose the orphans). When she was widowed with two infant sons only three years later, Bicknell's old friends—especially Edgeworth Sr.—were a lasting source of friendship and financial support for her. But her peculiar upbringing again became the topic of popular discussion when Anna Seward's scathing *Memoirs of Dr. Darwin* was published in 1804 and revealed Day's project in the most unflattering light for tutor and pupil.[33] Other contemporaries presented contrasting views as well. Frances Burney claimed that Sabrina was not abandoned by Day but that she left him in the lurch to marry Bicknell, and long lived to regret it.[34] When Maria Edgeworth visited Mrs. Bicknell in 1818 before publishing the memoirs of her father, she heard a different story: she cites the anguish suffered from Sabrina's son in 1804 on learning of his mother's peculiar origins and quotes Sabrina as saying that Day "made her miserable—*a slave*!"[35]

Manon Roland and Eudora

Thanks to the published correspondence and memoirs left by Manon Roland after her untimely death and the research of scholars such as Gita May, Madeleine Clemenceau-Jacquemaire, and Mary Trouille, we can piece together Roland's peculiar story of Rousseauian childrearing.[36] Several years after Day gave up on Sabrina, this young wife of an up-and-coming government official would embark on an experiment with her baby daughter in Amiens, France. Like Rousseau, Marie-Jeanne (Manon) Roland (née Phlipon) was daughter of an artisan—a Parisian engraver. At about age seventeen she discusses Rousseau in her correspondence with a friend, yet she claims to have become infatuated with Rousseau only after reading *La Nouvelle Héloïse* upon her mother's death.[37] She reportedly read and reread *La Nouvelle Héloïse* and *Emile* several times over the years and cited these books as strong supports for the trials she endured as a mother and a wife.[38] Soon after her baby Eudora was born in October 1781, the mother fell ill and could no longer breastfeed. But instead of sending off the infant to a wet-nurse, she defied the advice of her doctor, her mother-in-law, and other local authorities, concocted a special diet (in consultation with medical books and the *Encyclopédie*), managed to restore her milk supply, and surprised everyone by successfully bringing both baby and mother back to health.[39]

But their first months together were clearly difficult. Her letters are full of anxious accounts of her milk supply, the baby's diet and weight, and complaints about the infant's incessant demands. Six weeks after giving birth, this fervent disciple of Rousseau began to question the principle of mankind's natural goodness. As she wrote to her husband:

> I have concluded that the fable of Eve is not so stupid and that gluttony is truly an original sin. You philosophers, who do not believe this, who

> tell me that all the vices originate in society through the development of the passions and the clash of interests, tell me why this six-week old child, whose imagination is not yet awakened, whose peaceful senses should have no other master than need, is already overstepping its limits?[40]

Moreover, although she had kept up with the latest trends in science since her precocious youth and attended lectures on natural history after her marriage, Roland refused to have her child inoculated.[41]

Roland's childrearing gives evidence of many contradictions. Although she was a strong-minded woman who would play a crucial role in her husband's career and ultimately go to the guillotine for her unwavering support of the Girondins, she also held vigorously "antifeminist" views. Gita May and Mary Trouille have stressed this incongruity: in spite of her prominent public role in revolutionary politics, Roland insisted that a woman's life should revolve around her duties to home, hearth, and family.[42] In her daughter's early years, Roland followed an idiosyncratic combination of Rousseauian teachings, combining Emile's intellectual development and physical activity with Sophie's domestic skills, religion, and morality. Every day mother and daughter were up at six to read catechism and do needlework; the daily routine alternated between maternal lessons, physical recreation, music, and readings.[43] By the time her daughter was five, Roland wrote that "Eudora reads well, is beginning to know no other plaything but the needle, enjoys making geometric figures . . . and is afraid of nothing."[44]

Like Edgeworth, however, Roland found Rousseau's system most deficient when it came to discipline. She frequently cites her battles with Eudora and her efforts to remain calm despite the child's tantrums, writing, "Eudora is strong and inflexible proportionately; I always win, but my heart bleeds over the victory," and, a year later, "Our major work is obedience; there have been tantrums; I pronounced a punishment, and she screamed at the top of her lungs."[45] By the time Eudora was six, her mother's belief in Rousseauian pedagogy had been seriously compromised by what she saw as the flightiness and incorrigibility of her child. In her letters, her attitude swings from optimism to despair. To her husband in 1787, she suggested a compromise: "Since nature didn't make her for great knowledge, let's not insist on instruction, let's form her character to be open to everything, and let the rest arrive of its own accord, through inspiration, not constraint."[46] But a year later, she wrote to a friend in frustration: "Teach me to conquer, to control this rebellious, careless character, upon which gentle caresses have no more effect than severity or punishments. This is my daily torment.

Childrearing, that most cherished of tasks for a loving mother, seems to be the hardest trial I have ever had to face."[47] Stressing the difficulties of having a child underfoot when she and her husband were both trying to read and write, Roland argued that Rousseau's system was insufficiently tailored for their lifestyle. Although she tried to come up with a feasible solution (*Lettres,* 1:716–19), when Eudora reached age nine Roland sent her to a nearby convent and thus freed herself to concentrate on the more interesting demands of her husband's increasingly prominent political career.

In retrospect, Roland blamed her failure on the impracticability of hands-on pedagogy for busy parents: "One would have to devote oneself entirely to the child, without reserve, and you have to admit that there are few stations in this world that would allow you to concentrate and devote yourself solely to the education of one child."[48] But the fault lay not only in an impractical system; it was also due to the subject's inferiority. Assessing her daughter's achievements in 1791, Roland glumly concluded that all her efforts at enlightened mothering had come to nought because of her child's "cold and indolent" nature. As she wrote ruefully to her husband: "There is no use disguising it, your daughter . . . hasn't an idea, not a grain of memory; she might just have come from a wet-nurse, and she gives no promise of wit. She has embroidered me a very pretty work bag and she does a little needlework; beyond this she has a taste for nothing."[49] Two years later, in prison while awaiting her appearance before the revolutionary tribunal, Roland again cited her child's mediocrity to explain this failed experiment: "I nursed and raised [my daughter] with all the enthusiasm and solicitude a mother could have . . . but never will her stagnant mind or lackluster spirit give my heart the sweet pleasures I hoped for."[50] In bitter irony, the public prosecutor later seized on Roland's engrossment in childrearing as proof of her threat to the nation. When her maid Fleury was brought in as a witness, the girl was compelled to admit that "Roland and his friends wished to rule over France" and moreover that she had been enjoined to consider Roland's daughter "as if she were the daughter of a king."[51]

Why did this experiment end in such defeat? Historians have faulted Roland's coldness toward Eudora, her impatience, or nostalgia for her own childhood brilliance.[52] Although Maria Edgeworth was well aware of the risks involved in experimental education (witness her brother Richard), she took Roland to task for what she saw as her inconsistencies and lack of attention toward Eudora.[53] Others have defended Roland's view that Eudora was congenitally dull and incapable of intellectual engagement.[54] Roland clearly found the frustrations and boredom of raising a rambunctious child to be far less rewarding than the tender duties of caring for an infant. The physical bond between mother and infant was the most powerful, and palatable, aspect of parenting for her. Her letters frequently emphasize breastfeeding as a sign of good parenting. When Eudora failed to recognize her mother at the convent, Roland wrote that she felt unfairly slighted, treated "like one of those women who didn't nurse their children"; musing on her daughter's loss of dependency, she sighed, "I wish the child still needed milk, and that I had some to give her."[55]

Roland's experiment would soon be forgotten in the shocking devastation of political upheaval, however. During the revolution Manon Roland was castigated in the popular press as a dangerous, conniving plotter, the secret muse of the Girondins. Accused of aiding a rival political faction, she was imprisoned by the Montagnards for five months before being executed on 8 November 1793. Eudora was left orphaned by the subsequent suicide of M. Roland, but family friends took her in, and she eventually married the son of her mother's editor, Champagneux. With the publication of Roland's *Mémoires* in 1795, Manon Roland's story reentered the public sphere cast in a more positive light. Thanks to the heartrending depiction of her own mother's death and the poignant instructions to her daughter included in the *Mémoires,* Roland is known today not only as a revolutionary martyr and outspoken woman but also as an exemplary figure of mother love.[56]

Let us consider the gendered implications of these human experiments. Richard Edgeworth Jr. was raised in the spirit of books 1–3 of *Emile,* that is, he was basically left to his own devices and his "natural character" was thereby kept intact. It wasn't until later that the boy was found to be boorish and uncooperative: the "progress of nature" made him unfit for society. The programs of Day and Roland, in contrast, combined the "inactive method" of Emile's education with the moral training of Sophie. Day claimed to have inculcated in Sabrina and Lucretia "manly" virtues of physical hardiness and moral stoicism, but he also expected the girls to display "feminine" virtues of docility and subservience. Bragging about his early success, Day wrote that the girls "think nothing so agreeable as waiting upon me (no moderate convenience for a lazy man)" (Edgeworth, *Memoirs,* 2:220). But Sabrina's youth ultimately did her in; Day wanted a mature mind as well as a comely servant.

We have already seen how the political circumstances surrounding Manon Roland's life led her to incarnate in the public eye the very opposite of the domestic ideals she espoused in private. This paradox marked her relation with her daughter as well. One would think Eudora's modest intelligence amply adequate for the domestic duties her mother expected her to perform and for the acquiescence toward male authority she was expected to practice. But in this as in Day's scheme, the subject's display of inferior traits led the experimenter to abort the project. In both cases we see how abstract notions of human nature and perfectibility conflicted with culturally specific values of femininity. Once they judged their subjects incapable of achieving the predetermined ideal, Day and Roland both lost interest. Although passionate about social reform, these authors gave precedence to abstract philosophical principles over tangible improvements in women's education. All three of these experiments proved Rousseau wrong in various respects and demonstrated the difficulties of applying theory to practice. But still the hope remained that somehow childrearing might be made into a more controllable activity.

ALTERNATIVE SCHEMES FOR RAISING THE RATIONAL CHILD

Reasserting Parental Authority: *Adèle et Théodore*

Madame de Genlis's novel-treatise *Adèle et Théodore, ou Lettres sur l'éducation* (1782) is an exemplary work of what one might call High Enlightenment pedagogy in its strenuous promotion of human perfectibility and its intolerance toward human weakness.[57] The author herself was an illustrious devotee of the cause of social improvement and committed all of her considerable energies to raising the level of achievement in France's youth—among the nobility and the lesser ranks.[58] Governess of the Chartres-d'Orléans children in the 1770s and 1780s, and mistress of their father the duc de Chartres, (later duc d'Orléans, notorious during the revolution as the regicide republican Philippe Egalité), Genlis oversaw and conducted most of the lessons for an entire brood of youngsters. Her charges included the five young princesses and princes (including the future king Louis-Philippe), her two daughters, and a number of adopted children and visitors. According to the many accounts of her former pupils, Genlis was a demanding yet remarkably effective pedagogue.[59] Her duties involved spending twelve- to fourteen-hour days in teaching, correcting, cajoling, and observing the children as they performed their many tasks, only to toil away her nights writing an enormous corpus of educational treatises and novels for adults along with scores of edifying plays, stories, and lessons for children, many of which received critical acclaim.[60] Although *Adèle et Théodore* was written at the beginning of her career as governess, the author was already well known for her "théâtre d'éducation,"which had brought her considerable attention and respect in 1780.[61]

Adèle et Théodore reveals a vision of education as total engagement—on the part of parents and children—that Genlis would exemplify during her long and busy life. Although it is very impressive in its achievements, the educational program of Adèle—to whom most of the novel is dedicated—nevertheless gives the reader pause, not only because of its somewhat unrealistic expectations but also because it rests on a claustrophobically intimate relationship between mother and child that leaves nothing to nature, chance, or the child herself. Dominated by the mother's directive energy, the child absorbs a great many useful skills and important facts, but such accomplishments pale in comparison to the modeling on which they rely. Little by little, the child comes to incarnate her mother's will.

As a collection of letters by the baron and the baronne d'Almane and their relatives and friends, the novel presents the d'Almanes' pedagogical model alongside among a number of other, largely disastrous examples of children who turn out badly and adults who suffer from poor upbringings.[62] Although it is presented as a work of fiction, the author's interventions—which grew more numerous in succeeding editions—blur the boundaries between real life and fantasy in this novel so that it becomes obvious that Mme d'Almane *is* Mme de Genlis, the adopted Italian waif Hermine *is* Genlis's adopted daughter, and the fictional methods of raising Adèle and Théodore form a tried and true plan of childrearing that the reader would do well to emulate.[63] The novel's considerable popularity may be due to its reputation as a *roman à clef* as much as to its pedagogical methods, however, for the latter seem strikingly infeasible for the vast majority of the populace.[64] In this lies the sinister potential of *Adèle et Théodore,* for its conception of human nature is anything but inclusive. Although Genlis has justly been celebrated for her sensitivity and devotion to female education,[65] it remains that her vision of perfectibility is extremely narrow. Only a few superior beings are capable of realizing such grandiose ambitions.[66]

The curriculum changes over the course of the twelve-year period reported in this book, but the basic routine and philosophy remain the same: every minute is used in practical lessons that allow the children to display their growing virtue and mastery. The author's omnipresent concern with time management is doubled by a desire for environmental control. Every aspect of the d'Almanes' universe serves an educational function. The walls of their chateau are decorated with maps, instructive tapestries, and historical portraits, which the children explicate with ease when visitors come to call (*Adèle et Théodore,* 1:47–58). Whether speaking English, Italian, German, or French (depending on the time of day), they respond to their masters' bidding in a prompt and obedient manner, gradually absorbing topics and skills such as mathematics, geography, history, Christianity, mythology, harp playing, dancing, carpentry, drawing, charitable works, and literature. The only topics that appear to surpass the baronne's abilities are technology and the sciences. For the former, she pores over the illustrations of manufacturing techniques in the *Encyclopédie* and leads the children on visits to workshops and factories to learn how things are made. For the latter, which are not studied until the children are in their teens, the baronne secures access to a series of lectures on chemistry and natural history taught by experts in the capital. The children enjoy a Rousseauian exposure to the elements, sleep on hard beds, and use the natural environment to learn gardening and gain an eye for distances, as well as to master such physical skills as swimming and running. Even their toys serve a purpose: Adèle practices her lessons by repeating them to her doll and learns to sew by making doll clothes (1:78–83).

Behind this wonderful array of learning there lies the mother's voracious will to control. She herself creates or commissions all the tableaux that decorate the house, including the panorama depicted in her own bedroom (which represents Genesis). From seven in the morning until nine at night, she devotes herself entirely to her children and never leaves Adèle's side, either chatting with her, teaching her, supervising lessons taught by others, or doing her own work in Adèle's presence (the baron maintains a similarly symbiotic relationship with Théodore).[67] After putting the children to bed, she spends the evening discussing them with her husband, falls asleep thinking of them, and dreams of her children all night long (1:33). She writes the books they will read and the plays they perform (and later edits other authors' works for her purposes), she performs their custom-made magic lantern shows, and she devises moral "experiments" to test their budding virtues.[68]

In a pattern that runs throughout this novel, for each of the courses in "experimental virtue" *(vertu expérimentale)* that the child inevitably fails, the baronne inserts a correct precept that the child then vows to obey. After befriending a "dangerous" young woman in the convent and suffering the uncomfortable consequences, Adèle learns that her mother had been watching all along and declares: "Oh, what imprudence I have been guilty of! I will never do so again."[69] The baronne maintains the same sort of relationship with other correspondents, too, so that their letters often begin with an admission of penitent gratitude, as in Mme d'Ostalis's declaration, "I have followed your advice, and I have found all my happiness again" or the vicomtesse de Limours' humble comment, "Our disputes always end in the same manner. I find you in the right, and I am obliged to confess my faults. . . . Yes, my dear friend, you are still right."[70] As if the baronne's influence were not sufficiently clear, she announces to Adèle toward the end that "you cannot pride yourself on the qualifications and talents you possess, without recollecting it is to me you owe them."[71] This image of infallible female authority justifies the mother's final advice to Adèle before her marriage. Now that Adèle has become a product of the baronne, she too should exercise a formative function on those around her, beginning with her husband. "What an interest have you in correcting all his defects, and in forming his temper and mind as much as possible!" exclaims the proud mother.[72]

Genlis's notion of experimental virtue resembles Rousseau's scheme to stage-manage the child's character development in *Emile.* But her program relies on a more pessimistic, traditional Christian vision of human nature than Rousseau's; indeed, her philosophy more closely resembles that of the pious Kirkby or Louis Racine than the free-thinking philosophe. Because of the d'Almanes' religious devotion, the baron categorically refutes Rousseau's notion of human goodness on one occasion, declaring: "*Rousseau* has said with great eloquence, 'that a man born naturally good, if he is left to himself, will always remain so'[;] I am not of this opinion," and elaborating later, "Man is born good . . . but his reflections cool, change, and make him selfish. He is inconsistent, because he is naturally an imperfect and confined being. It is religion alone that can give him a constant taste for virtue."[73] This wary attitude toward the child's character informs all the d'Almanes' practices. Given mankind's basic propensity toward vice, even the obedient child must be closely watched, the baronne writes, because

> when you have forced a mind, naturally imperious, to submission, you must never leave her to herself a single moment; for if you ever lose sight of her, you may be sure that she will make herself amends the very first opportunity, for the constraint you impose on her . . . therefore never put her into hands on which you cannot depend, as well as yourself. Keep your eyes on her, till time, reason, and habit, shall have absolutely changed her disposition.[74]

Note the insistence on *changing* the child's natural disposition. This goes directly counter to Rousseau's concern for protecting the child's individuality. Unlike Rousseau's progressive unfolding, Genlis's model is quite clearly designed to perfect the child from the outside in, with regular training and conditioning that will break natural tendencies and replace them with improved, socially admired traits.

Genlis's relation to Rousseau is complex. Her program borrows standard procedures from *Emile* concerning physical education, hygiene, dress, and childhood fears, while explicitly rejecting other issues regarding punishment, empathy, and the basic concept of natural goodness.[75] Yet the tone is generally sympathetic to the great philosophe. Over the years, however, her attitude toward Rousseau and other philosophes became increasingly hostile. In the 1800s Genlis would undertake an ambitious rebuttal of key philosophical writings (what she called "*mon cours antiphilosophiste*") that culminated in her 1820 publication of a copiously annotated and truncated "purified edition" *(édition épurée)* of *Emile* that discards passages on sexuality and religious education.[76] As Laborde points out, after the revolution Genlis blamed the philosophes for their abortive effort to rescue human nature from a supposedly corrupt society. By loosening the bonds of traditional morality, the philosophes thought they could improve mankind's condition; yet they only made things worse, according to Genlis.[77] This issue of the citizen's responsibility to the polis proved vexing to Rousseau, as we have seen in our discussion of *Emile.* Although trying to retain the best of l'homme de la nature, Rousseau's final image of Emile is that of the benevolent patriarch and landowner—leading the regeneration of his village's social and agricultural well-being. For all her criticisms of Rousseau in *Adèle et Théodore,* I contend that Genlis's vision of the child's final "perfection" exemplifies this same kind of civic ideology.

In fact, Genlis's position is more consistent than Rousseau's because she sees no conflict between individual autonomy and the civil order. Individuals are destined to obey the enlightened few and to accept social rules, even if they include such issues as censorship and policing thought.[78] Superior individuals should share their good fortune in individual good works, as a gesture of intellectual *noblesse oblige.* Although Genlis's novel contains bucolic scenes of grateful peasants and healthy children enjoying the outdoors, I absolutely disagree with Gilbert Py's claim that the educational setting of *Adèle et Théodore* is nature, or that its goal is to "prepare the regeneration of the species, in conformity with the myth of innocence popularized by the 'eloquence' of Rousseau."[79] Rather, I see *Adèle et Théodore* as a highly stylized, manipulative program that resembles nothing so much as the ultimate dream of a despotism run by initiates of "enlightened" social control.

As proof of their successful training in *bienfaisance,* the children's final performance is the establishment of a charity school for ten young girls, who will depend for all their learning on Adèle. She in turn will replicate the model of maternal control learned at the hands of the baronne, thereby creating so many smaller copies of herself. In the last letter of the novel, the baronne recounts her conversation with Adèle on her wedding day. Even though the girl is now married, the mother-child compact is still the dominant force in Adèle's life. In a bizarre appeal for dependency, Adèle begs her mother to continue teaching her with the same discipline and rigor as before, exclaiming, "I vow you the same submissive obedience I have ever paid you. The first and dearest wish of my heart is; to take you for my model, to copy you, if it be possible; to observe all your advice, to devote my love to you. I am sensible, that all your happiness depends on my conduct. Ah! I will justify your expectations!"[80]

Genlis's vision of society in microcosm—the family—revolves around a panoptic maternal authority who exercises complete control over the individual ad infinitum.[81] In the words of a wife vowing eternal love, obedience, and submission to her mother at marriage we can see a perfect example of Rousseau's dictum that "Good social institutions are those best fitted to make a man unnatural, to exchange his independence for dependence . . . so that he no longer regards himself as one, but as part of the whole."[82] Although rewritten as mother instead of the king, priest, or husband, this authority rightly overrules all others, for it alone has the superior wisdom and virtue needed to continually watch, correct, and improve the child—and the nation.[83]

A New Kind of Experimentalism: *Practical Education*

Published nearly twenty years after *Adèle et Théodore,* after the massive turbulence of the French Revolution and the reprisals that followed it, *Practical Education* appeared on the scene in the midst of another violent political upheaval. It was published almost simultaneously with the Great Rebellion that took the lives of twenty-five thousand Irishmen, ruined Irish hopes for parliamentary reform, and devastated the landscape for miles around the authors' holdings in County Longford. And yet the Edgeworths' writing seems untouched by the disillusionment and anxiety that were rampant in the country.[84] Reading this confident, optimistic scheme for raising the rational family, one is struck by how little has changed since Mme de Genlis's 1782 work. This impression is not an accident; rather, it is a deliberate gesture on the part of two writers who were schooled in eighteenth-century theories and who refused to let political setbacks dampen their hopes for human improvement through secular, progressive methods. The world in *Practical Education* scarce extends beyond the walls of the family manor: its message is geared primarily to parents, to help them manage the quotidian demands of raising young children.

A prominent inventor, landholder, and one-time member of the Irish Parliament, Richard Lovell Edgeworth early embraced Rousseau and raised his first son accordingly, as we saw above. Yet he showed less interest in his daughter Maria's education and sent her to boarding school at the age of seven. During Maria's childhood Edgeworth married again, fathered several more children, and busied himself with mechanical experiments until in 1782, when, after assessing the sorry state of his Irish holdings, he moved the family to Edgeworthstown in rural County Longford.[85] There he tried to set up the cheerful, progressive model idealized in *Practical Education* and boasted of its success to Erasmus Darwin: "I do not think one tear per month is shed in this house, nor the voice of reproof heard, nor the hand of restraint felt."[86] Edgeworth's children, however, had very different views of their father's methods. After hearing one of the Edgeworths complain about their strict upbringing, Coleridge noted the irony of this situation: "J. Wedgwood informed me that the Edgeworth's [*sic*] were most miserable when children; and yet the father in his books is ever vapourizing about their happiness."[87]

Although his daughter Maria's life was less eventful, it too poses many a paradox. Maria Edgeworth wrote scores of books touting domestic virtues yet refused to marry herself. Instead she devoted her life to the management and education of her father's growing family, a major task indeed considering that Richard Lovell fathered twenty-two children in all (borne of four wives), and that thirteen of them received their primary and secondary educations at home during this time. This odd conjunction of household management, childrearing, and spinsterhood has given rise to many myths about Maria. For some she is an "obsequious puppet," for others she is a tragic case of stunted potential: the promisingly "wild," spontaneous author of the ribald *Castle Rackrent* who was later tamed into a "pattern of prudence" by her controlling father.[88] The works of both Richard Lovell and Maria Edgeworth propose many a prescription for rational living that their lives seem to disavow.

Modern readers are more likely to be familiar with Richard's mechanical inventions or Maria's literary output—her Irish novels or didactic tales for children—rather than the encyclopedic *Practical Education*. Buoyed by recent interest in Irish romanticism and retrospectives on the Great Rebellion of 1798, Maria's four Irish novels (*Castle Rackrent,* 1800; *Ennui,* 1809; *The Absentee,* 1812; and *Ormond,* 1817) have lately enjoyed a resurgence of popularity. Forerunners of a long tradition of national literature, the novels present clearly articulated responses to crucial moments in Irish history: the state of the landed gentry before 1792, the rebellion of 1798, and the Act of Union in 1800.[89] The continuing popularity of these novels surprised the author, however. A product of eighteenth-century progressive thinking, she felt that the Edgeworthian contribution to education was far more important than her fiction. Her own efforts at pedagogical writing began at age sixteen, when she translated Genlis's *Adèle et Théodore* (only to learn that another author beat her to the prize).[90] In the *Memoirs* she expressed the wish that her father be remembered for his pioneering efforts in pedagogy more than for any of his other endeavors, because he was the first to make education a truly "experimental science."[91] Indeed, historians of pedagogy have long touted *Practical Education* as the "most significant contemporary work on pedagogy" and the "most important work on general pedagogy" to appear between Locke and the mid-Victorian era.[92]

Practical Education is an attempt to disseminate the tenets of progressive education to a wider audience, and in a more hands-on manner, than any novel or treatise might do. Unlike the contrived settings of *Emile,* with its focus on the individual in isolation, or the rarefied demands of the elitist *Adèle et Théodore, Practical Education* argues that the best site for education is the bustling haven of a large, middle- to upper-class family. Its founding apparatus is the country estate: a household complete with dogs and horses. Although it is apparently an ordinary house, the setting includes some special features to make childrearing easier for busy parents: a special room for the children to run and play and an abundance of materials such as "rational toys."[93] But the authors also include recommendations for public education and take care throughout to mention the feasibility of their methods for parents in various social milieus, including "persons of narrow fortune."[94]

The rhetoric of *Practical Education* returns repeatedly to the concepts of rationality and experimentalism, but always keeping sight of the limited abilities of children. In transforming education into what they call an "experimental method," the Edgeworths signal their support for individual initiatives and hands-on experiments of all kinds. Consider the notion of "rational toys." Appealing to the common sense of the adult reader while arguing from a child's point of view, the Edgeworths maintain that many of the fashionable toys that are given to children are not only frail and useless, they also wreak injustice on the child's curiosity. A vignette of a young boy playing with a tiny gilt coach, much to the "terrors" of his parents, concludes: "As long as a child has sense and courage to destroy the toys, there is no great harm done; but, in general, he is taught to set a value upon them totally independent of all ideas of utility, or of any regard to his own real feelings" (1:2). Instead of wasting money and fruitless anxiety on such items, the Edgeworths encourage people to invest in sturdy, lasting toys that children can really play with, for example, models of furniture, engines to take apart, wood for carpentry projects, chemicals and scientific instruments, and a large library of age-appropriate books, prints, and maps.

But this call for practical, experimental education also constituted a warning against speculative theories and grandiose schemes; indeed, the Edgeworths' attitude toward reform in general is a cautious, localized pragmatism. In a passage on public education that echoes the authors' political conservatism, they write:

> Mankind, at least the prudent and rational part of mankind, have an aversion to pull down, till they have a moral certainty that they can build up a better edifice than that which has been destroyed. . . . We do not set up for projectors, or reformers; we wish to keep steadily in view the actual state of things, as well as our own hopes of progressive improvement; to seize and combine all that can be immediately serviceable; all that can assist, without precipitating improvements. (2:501)

This desire for modest change is felt in their advice to the reader, too. The book presents hundreds of ideas on how to teach children all manner of topics and skills, yet it also counsels people to maintain reasonable expectations. Unlike Genlis's sanguine assurance, the Edgeworths often seem cowed by the immensity of the parents' task. As we read in "Toys," "Let us do what we will, every person who has ever had any experience upon the subject, must know that it is scarcely possible to provide sufficient and suitable occupations for young children: this is one of the first difficulties in education. Those who have never tried the experiment, are astonished to find it such a difficult and laborious business" (1:14). One feels a keen sense of the authors' will to engage in solidarity with their readers. Unlike Rousseau, the Edgeworths actively recruit disciples, writing: "we sincerely wish that some intelligent, benevolent parents may verify our experiments upon their own children."[95]

Although the authors include personal examples throughout, they claim that such asides are meant only to suggest the effects one might produce through the techniques of *Practical Education*. Indeed, they stressed the contingency of their advice in the "Advertisement" to the second edition (1801), which they retitled *Essays on Practical Education* so as to avoid its appearing like a "system."[96] Contrasting their work with that of such French theoreticians as Condillac, the authors assert: "without examples from real life, we should have wandered, as many of far superior abilities have already wandered, in the shadowy land of theory" (2:722). Empirical to the last, they append to the text transcripts of actual conversations by which the reader "will distinctly perceive the difference between practical and theoretical education" (2:734).

The Edgeworths criticized *Emile* for its artificially staged lessons, but their methods reveal a similar desire to purify the child's environment. They argue that books, for instance, must be carefully altered because "few books can safely be given to children without the previous use of the pen, the pencil, and the scissars [*sic*]" (1:322). The social universe must be limited: children should steer clear of servants lest they pick up their "awkward and vulgar tricks," and visitors must be supervised so as not to confuse children with nonsense talk (1:122, 140). This clinical atmosphere may recall the dubious authoritarianism of the pedagogues we studied in chapter 3, with its recurring images of the paternal or tutorial gaze watching over the scene, but it also allows the authors to foreground the complex mental life of children.[97] Similar to the stated goals of their predecessors, though with a more felicitous eye for endearing details, are the Edgeworths' respectful portrayals of the infant learning about its environment or the child engrossed in play, which encourage readers to see even the youngest children as full-fledged humans, naturally gifted with reason, the capacity for invention, and the desire for autonomy.[98]

Most significant for our purposes is the Edgeworths' confident attitude toward amateur science. Unlike Genlis, who subcontracted this portion of her curriculum to experts, the Edgeworths endorse a full-fledged course in topics such as physics, mechanics, chemistry, mineralogy, and botany—all of which are presented as eminently feasible and useful for nonspecialists. This assurance contrasts with the general trend in the 1790s to consider the pursuits of chemists and physicists as difficult and even dangerous enterprises inaccessible to the nonspecialist.[99] Adopting a child's perspective on the subject, the Edgeworths debunk science of its intimidating aura. To find instructions for simple chemical experiments, for instance, they direct readers to borrow freely from scholarly sources such as the works of Benjamin Franklin, Joseph Priestley, or the *Memoirs* of the Académie des Sciences, which contain "a variety of simple experiments . . . which will at once amuse and instruct." Readers should not let such weighty titles frighten them, write the Edgeworths, because "the names of Dr. Percival, or Dr. Wall, will have no weight with children; they will compare only the reasons and experiments" (1:28). Accessibility is key. Although somewhat more complex than the expériences grossières recommended in *Emile,* the chemistry experiments in *Practical Education* are described as requiring "no great apparatus," only common household substances such as vinegar, sugar, and salt, and the experiments in optics require only a "cheap microscope" (1:26, 30).

This attitude of populist *bonhomie,* however, slips a bit in the chapter titled "On Mechanics," written by Edgeworth Sr. As a highly skilled engineer and inventor, Edgeworth expresses frustration that the tools of his science are so unknown to the majority of the population and exhorts itinerant lecturers (presumably the primary authority for many middle-class readers) to do a better job teaching the technical language of physics (2:453–54). The common household could serve as an excellent source for simple lessons in engineering, Edgeworth claims; visits by workmen to repair locks and pumps, for instance, could be put to good pedagogical use (2:460). But to gain deeper understanding of "mechanic powers," Edgeworth recommends the construction of an apparatus of his own invention called a "Panorganon" and offers instructions on how to build it and experiment with it for about twenty pages. Despite his assertions to the contrary, this machine requires a good deal of ingenuity and mechanical expertise—indeed, it seems rather intimidating—and one wonders just how many readers of *Practical Education* were able to enjoy the "entertainment" it promised "for many a vacant hour" (2:487). Clearly, Edgeworth was able to promote amateur science with such confidence because he himself—and his son-in-law, the famous experimentalist Thomas Beddoes, and many of their friends from the Lunar Society—kept up with latest developments and lived in a milieu where science and technology were topics of everyday conversation.[100]

Perhaps this explains why *Practical Education* expresses such concern for the pseudoscience of fairground performers and how-to books for children. As does *Emile,* this text denounces those who purport to teach science through "magic and deception," arguing that one should not aim to produce "amazement" but rather seek to give children "a permanent taste for science." The authors recommend revising a well-known source book and replacing titles of experiments such as "Changing winter into spring" or "To produce the appearance of a phantom" with more "rational" titles. The truth-value of performance is crucial. Just as experimentalists must test phenomena instead of accepting theories at face value, children are encouraged to search for causes behind effects instead of wallowing in "blind admiration of the juggler's tricks" (1:26–28). Here as elsewhere in Enlightenment writing, we see the supernatural treated as an obstacle to progress and first-person eyewitnessing treated as the surest form of evidence. Echoing the tenets of Condillac and other philosophers of the sensationist school, the individual serves as the ultimate judge of physical phenomena, through his senses, which are the most reliable source of information.

Practical Education had a profound effect on its progressive Continental readers. One witness reported to Maria Edgeworth, "In Paris they read your book on education—in Geneva they gobble it up.—In Paris they admire your principles—in Geneva they practice them."[101] But this rational, secular approach to understanding the natural world coincides with what appears to be a very old-fashioned attitude toward morality, especially as regards women.

Like Rousseau, Maria Edgeworth corresponded with female readers who reported their results or asked for advice.[102] This relay from woman writer to woman reader evokes a female community of sorts, but one must exercise caution about what Mitzi Myers has called "Edgeworthian feminism."[103] In her *Letters to Literary Ladies* (1795) Edgeworth's spokesman declares: "Do not, my dear sir, call me a champion for the rights of woman . . . I am more anxious for their happiness than intent upon a metaphysical discussion of their rights."[104] Her vision of domestic happiness includes intellectual stimulation, but Edgeworth cannot be considered feminist: indeed, the "new woman" forms the target of some of her most vitriolic writing (as in the character of Harriet Freke in *Belinda*). Seamus Deane best captures her spirit when he writes: "She is *au fond,* a provincial writer in the English 'Protestant' tradition of Hannah More."[105]

The vision of gender roles in *Practical Education* is best aligned with the Edgeworths' political ideal of paternalism. Although the authors strike a liberal tone in their call for independent thought, their gender-neutral language, and their "affirmation of the child's freedom to feel and judge for herself," their vision of female potential is essentially paternalist.[106] In her Irish novels Maria resolved the social problems of the poor by depicting a new breed of absentee landlords. Unlike their much-hated predecessors, these heroes leave behind the lures of the capital, return to their estates, and assume the duties of a modernized, benevolent feudalism. In *Practical Education* the authors contend that such happiness might be achieved in miniature if women would take responsibility to maintain traditional social forms. Boys are encouraged to aim high with precepts such as: "no great man ever formed a great design which he was not also capable of executing" (2:599); girls are discouraged from such dangerous ambitions. The one truth to "engrave upon the memory of our female pupils" is: "Begin nothing of which you have not well considered the end" (2:700). Such passages echo Genlis's similarly mitigated vision of Adèle's pursuits, which she is careful to describe as "resources against idlenesss" instead of learning for its own sake.[107]

Although Rousseau is taken to task throughout the book for his most egregious errors, particularly his promotion of dolls and his depiction of female cunning, one finds many echoes of Sophie in the chapters written by Maria for female readers.[108] The major authority cited in "On Female Accomplishments" is Rousseau's ardent disciple Manon Roland, who, like Edgeworth, insisted that women not publicize their talents: above all, girls must not aspire to *perform* (2 : 527). A woman's crowning accomplishment is to "be a good oeconomist, a good mistress, as well as a good mother of a family" (2 : 549, 527). As in *Emile,* woman is always under the prying eye of the public.[109] Thus in "On Prudence and Economy," Edgeworth advises that girls be taught more caution and self-discipline than boys, since "they cannot always have recourse to what *ought to be,*" nor can they "rectify the material mistakes in their conduct" (2 : 699). Although the author earlier rejected "that debasing cunning which Rousseau recommends," here she warns against women "hazarding opinions in general conversation" and encourages conversation only with friends or family members (1 : 167, 2 : 700). Girls should develop their minds in wide readings and reflections on topical issues; however, the audience for their thoughts remains the home.

A tension runs through this advice. On one hand, Edgeworth advocates women's intellectual growth on political grounds, arguing that "it will tend to the happiness of society in general, that women should have their understandings cultivated and enlarged as much as possible." On the other, she undermines her support for women's learning by depicting the myriad difficulties it entails for the individuals involved. To ward off dissatisfaction with her lot in life, Edgeworth writes, woman's "imagination must not be raised above the taste for necessary occupations, or the numerous small, but not trifling pleasures of domestic life: her mind must be enlarged, yet the delicacy of her manners must be preserved." The choice of reading material poses particular problems and demands "early caution, unremitting, scrupulous caution." Edgeworth admonishes soft-hearted mothers to remember the girl's ultimate function in life: "a mother ought to be answerable to her daughter's husband for the books her daughter had read, as well as the company she had kept" (2 : 550). Female ambition is finally rechanneled into an emotional peak involving the whole family—"domestic happiness"—instead of the more individualistic, mercenary commonplaces of "success in the world" or "fortunate establishments" (2 : 725).

This conflict between public and private is particularly poignant in the appendix. It is useful to contrast the Edgeworths' authorial strategy with

Genlis's in *Adèle et Théodore* here; again we see that the later work eschews Genlis's coy roman à clef mannerisms to represent itself as a document of scientific value. Whereas Genlis simply announced, rather disingenuously, that "Monsieur and Madame *d'Almane* never speak of what passes in the family to those to whom it does not concern" (regardless of all Genlis's personal footnotes to the contrary), these authors take a more "scientific" approach to the potentially embarrassing mixture of private and public.[110] In the appendix the authors present transcripts of actual conversations in their family in which the Edgeworth children demonstrate, through amusingly naive comments, their curiosity about everything in the world. But the authors preface these exchanges with two gestures of scientific rigor. First, they cite the philosopher Thomas Reid's call for a "distinct and full history of all that hath passed in the mind of a child from the beginning of life and sensation till it grows up to the use of reason"; second, they align their work with the principles of Bacon. In the spirit of Baconian inquiry, they claim, such conversations constitute data to be shared with the community of scholars who seek further knowledge on the "history of the infant mind" (2:734, 735). After citing forty pages' worth of cute remarks by children ages two to thirteen, however, they conclude with a caveat: "We hope, that candid and intelligent parents will pardon, if they have discovered any desire in us to *exhibit* our pupils . . . we have hoped, that only such conversations or anecdotes have been produced as may be of some use in Practical Education" (2:775).

Exhibition of family members—opening the home to the public eye—is admissible only in circumstances where its use-value dominates its entertainment-value. Otherwise it would be a violation of the domestic ideology, which posits the home as a universe closed to the outsider. This anxiety about public exposure haunts Edgeworth's writings on Ireland as well, possibly because of her protective attitude toward the Irish poor. Describing the Colambre school set up by the landlord's agent and his wife in *The Absentee,* the narrator declares that "it was just what it ought to be—neither too much nor too little had been attempted. . . . Nothing for exhibition, care to teach well."[111]

But the prioritization of the home as school raised problems having to do with the *spectacular* or *demonstrative* nature of this pedagogy. Perhaps because she conceived of the home in her novel as a formal educational institution rather than as an intimate space of family life, Genlis appears untroubled by such concerns. Indeed, she seems to have courted publicity in *Adèle et Théodore* (and was attacked for her *éducation de parade*).[112] *Practical Education* presents a more bourgeois concern about personal privacy and asks an ethical question with broad ramifications: How can one intervene in the private life of family members without violating the sanctity of the home? Although the authors justify their vignettes of the Edgeworth children in the name of "experimental science," their concern for the sanctity of family space pervades the program—as seen in the strictures on contact with visitors and servants, for instance.

This was the ultimate quandary confronting "scientific" efforts to improve on man. Any scientist worth his salt accepted that publicity was vital for responsible experimentation. Yet it was an extremely delicate matter for those working on human subjects. What to do? In *Adèle et Théodore* we saw one solution: the illusion of full disclosure couched in the artifice of fiction. By the end of Genlis's novel both children are proved to be well-bred; they both marry successfully and the author declares her system a success. It was not as easy to evaluate the people subjected to the methods of *Practical Education*. Many of the children were still young when the book was published, and there remained the embarrassing specter of Edgeworth's earlier failure with Richard Jr. It is important to recall the high stakes involved in such experiments. Just as the Edgeworths' text depicts self-experimentation as key to advanced research on pedagogy, the experimentalists performing in European fairs and salons performed their most compelling demonstrations on themselves. And, as the painful examples of the electrified boy and Richard Edgeworth Jr. suggest, when one experiments on oneself, one risks getting burned.

In the final analysis, the case histories and treatise-novels we've studied here set a dangerous precedent for childrearing because of their reliance on the problematic metaphors of perfectibility. Although Rousseau and Diderot originally defined perfectibility as a potential for decline as well as progress, this literature presupposes only the possibility of improvement. The issue of freedom is at risk. As in the educational reforms of the revolution, to which we will turn shortly, the works of the parent-pedagogues want to ensure that improvements would take place at the same time as they ensured the child's freedom. But one cannot have it both ways. Just as the revolutionary government justified the destruction of churches and persecution of the clergy on the grounds of liberating the people from its "superstitious" notions and "Gothic" prejudices, the progressive parents seen here wield a heavy hand over the child's imagination and propensity to daydream, be silly, bicker, and all the other "irrational" diversions that children constantly devise to keep themselves amused. But the writers' sense of goodwill and confidence is obvious; it is as if they were blind to their own shortcomings. In conclusion, let us consider the paradox of *Practical Education*'s "laissez-faire" philosophy. The first chapter concludes: "The danger of doing too much in education is greater even than the danger of doing too little. As the merchants in France answered Colbert, when he desired to know 'how he could best assist them' children might perhaps reply to those who are most officious to amuse them, 'Leave us to ourselves'" (1:35). And yet the hefty tomes that follow contain hundreds of ways to fill the child's time and keep him occupied. Then as now, it was easier to tell people how to be the ideal parent than to do it oneself.

—CHAPTER FIVE—

Perfectibility in the Revolutionary Era

UTOPIAN POLITICS AND DYSTOPIAN FICTIONS

A revolution posits the notion not only that individuals are malleable, but also that the whole body politic may be changed. What happened to the notion of mankind's malleability and perfectibility in the years of the French Revolution? Did the metaphors of testing and improving mankind that we have been following through the eighteenth century take on a special resonance in this period of social and political turmoil? In reply I would have to answer, no and yes. No, because much of the revolutionary political discourse articulated concepts and borrowed terms from philosophes like those we have already studied. Many of the deputies to the Assembly were learned men, lawyers and professionals who built their plans for reform on a foundation of progressive principles that sound very familiar to the readers of Genlis, Locke, and Rousseau. The idea of progress was one of the most common metaphors in eighteenth-century thought, as was the assumption that it (that is, mankind's progressive improvement in morality, philosophy, technological expertise, or scientific knowledge) would unfold naturally under the proper circumstances.[1]

But yes, the discourse of perfectibility did take on a new resonance in the revolutionary years, notably in the imagery of *l'homme régénéré* (regenerated man). Revolutionary writers recast the age-old biblical figure of l'homme régénéré to underline the nascent republic's rupture with the past. As Daniel Gordon has aptly noted, "revolutionary authority was inherently creative, rather than preservative, because the revolutionaries believed that they were regenerating a world in a state of total corruption."[2] Alongside celebratory images of the republic as a strong and virile young man creating his own future were darker views coined by royalists and other critics that presented the revolutionary state as a squalling, ignorant infant or murderous son attacking the venerable *patrie*. Regeneration was also allegorized as a female. In this discourse too heroic characterizations overlapped with demonic ones, although there was a shift over time toward more threatening imagery. As Gutwirth has suggested, in the early years of the revolution, one often finds the new nation conflated with images of an active, strong, and nurturing mother.[3] Although this imagery remained popular, in the later years of the revolution there also emerged a corpus of imagery representing the nation as the victim or the monstrous progeny of a perverted or dangerously radical *sans-culotte* mother.

This chapter aims to analyze these dialectical images in the revolutionary period to show how the schemes for human improvement that we saw in authors such as Genlis and Rousseau seemed to be coming true, if only in illusion, and if only for a brief moment, before the reality of violence, injustice, and political infighting led people to realize how difficult it was to effect self-reform on a national level. Lynn Hunt has shown how the concept of liberty evolved unsteadily from imagery of a brawny Hercules to the figure of a buxom but chaste Marianne in the 1780s and 1790s "because the political class found it difficult to agree on where the Revolution ended."[4] I have discovered a similar pattern of cultural change related to the concept and imagery of regeneration during this period, taking 1797–98 as my endpoint. Regeneration assumed multiple meanings in the highly charged politics of these years in France and England; for some it was a metaphor of welcome change and much-needed reforms; for others it was an emblem of reckless disregard for a cherished heritage. Images of the French republic as a "new man" coming spontaneously to life or a capable mother watching over her brood later gave way to more sinister visions, such as that of a monster encroaching on French soil, an ugly sans-culotte and her ghastly infant, or a vast machine running amok. This shift in political imagery and agency presaged the increasingly strong-arm tactics that would be adopted by the governments of the Convention, the Directory, and the empire. After surveying the imagery of regeneration in a variety of political writings, in the second part of this chapter I focus specifically on literary texts that depict misguided, sometimes terrifying efforts to meddle with humankind through aggressive interventions both pedagogical and physiological. Whereas the first section of this chapter adopts cultural history's "linguistic approach" to suggest the diverse connotations of regeneration in period writings, later sections explore the ramifications for fiction of an interpretation of the revolution as conspiracy.

As François Furet and Lynn Hunt have noted, the notion of the revolution as plot or conspiracy lent itself to a variety of political positions in the 1780s and 1790s.[5] Republican propagandists disseminated images of the young nation struggling against "aristocratic plots" in order to cement the connection between the people and its new leaders, whereas counterrevolutionary writers cast the revolution itself as an evil plot in order to challenge the morality of its leaders and to scrutinize their assumption of power.[6] In the powerful counterrevolutionary rhetoric of émigré journalists and of authors such as Edmund Burke, Abbé de Barruel, and Joseph de Maistre, the notion of a plot "no longer served to nurture the charismatic appeal of power by the people, but to fuel the pretended or real opposition to the usurpation of that power by those who used the Revolution for their own ends."[7] My literary readings depart from this important point to show how fiction from the late 1700s magnified political fears of secret plots against *la patrie* into stories of cruel ministrations on vulnerable female subjects. These novels' pessimism built on existing foundations, combining political antagonisms of the 1790s with older strains in Enlightenment thought regarding the ethics of meddling with human nature, be it through pedagogy (*Belinda*, *Secresy*) or scientific research (*Pauliska*, *Justine*, *Juliette*, and *Les 120 Journées de Sodome*). My analysis of these often overlooked novels thus complements the better-known history of political rhetoric during the revolutionary era and shows how literature at the turn of the century cast a glaring light on the fault lines we have detected all along in the edifice of "enlightened" progressivism.

THE REVOLUTIONARY HOMME RÉGÉNÉRÉ

The image of regenerated man was one of the most prevalent metaphors of the revolutionary period. One might say it was a logical corrective to late eighteenth-century worries about the decadence and decline of the ancien régime. From the 1770s on, scores of brochures and pamphlets lamented the weakness and effeminacy of the French monarchy and the degeneracy of the nobility. King Louis XVI's impotence was a common leitmotiv in the anti-aristocratic pamphlets that proliferated in the 1780s, such as *Les Amours de Charlot et Toinette*, which used the king's penis (described as "no bigger than a straw, / Always limp and always curved") as a metaphor for the administration's flabby, ill-conceived plans to save the state from ruin.[8] Novels such as Laclos' *Les Liaisons dangereuses* (1782) and Sade's encyclopedic *120 Journées de Sodome* (1785) evoke a world of bored aristocrats who can find nothing better to do than to pervert what little remains of the goodness and beauty in their world. Mercier's topical vignettes in *Le Tableau de Paris*

(1781–88) present a similar scenario of brutal injustice, juxtaposing images of industrious workers scraping out a miserable subsistence alongside images of arrogant aristocrats gambling and gorging themselves, while their once noble race dies out unseen.

Running counter to this tendency toward decay and decline was a cult of virtue promulgated by Jean-Jacques Rousseau. With his genius for iconoclasm, Rousseau had long presented himself as a model of auto-regeneration. In his *Confessions* (1778) he described how he spontaneously metamorphosed from a simple artisan into the dazzling writer and reformer that he became. Perusing a newspaper one day, he experienced an epiphany and instantly "became" another man.[9] The transformation was complete when he earned his first public recognition as a philosopher: "I no longer saw anything great and beautiful except to be free and virtuous, above contingency and public opinion, and to suffice unto myself!"[10] Although he had many critics, Rousseau was popularly viewed as Europe's most extraordinary individual, what Carol Blum calls "the living wellspring of goodness in a wicked world."[11] The same virtues Rousseau exemplified—freedom, energy, transcendence above time and circumstance—would reappear in various guises in the revolutionary homme régénéré. These values, however, would create problems for the revolutionary leaders, for they learned too late that civic virtue cannot be legislated into existence, and energy cannot necessarily be harnessed toward a given goal.[12]

Rousseau clearly perceived himself as unique, but he argued that other men could attain a measure of superiority as well, through education. Rousseau exhorted readers to think for themselves and enjoy their natural freedoms; as he wrote in *Emile* (1762): "Liberty is not to be found in any form of government, she is in the heart of the free man, he bears her with him everywhere."[13] Yet he also warned readers that some liberties must be sacrificed to achieve social harmony. As he wrote in the *Considérations sur le gouvernement de Pologne* (1772): "It is education which must give national strength to the [people's] souls, and direct their opinions and their tastes, so that they become patriots by inclination, by passion, by necessity."[14] We saw in chapter 3 that this concept of enlightened self-denial for the good of the whole was widely shared by his contemporaries, even though it belies a basic instability.[15] For how can a man retain all his "natural" rights and freedoms while living in civil society? Rousseau's model in both *Emile* and *Le Contrat social* (1762) presupposed that when the individual enters into a relation with the state, he voluntarily curbs his acquisitive appetite so that he might live in peace with others and "his self-perfection miraculously becomes an end in itself."[16] Although Rousseau admitted the temerity of this scheme, he did not acknowledge its impracticability.[17] When he demanded that the citizen submit to the commonweal, he assumed that such *alinéation* of rights was merely a temporary arrangement, because the state was expected to restitute all rights eventually and to cement the contract as a public mandate. Countering those who criticized Rousseau for providing the ideas that were later used to justify the Terror, Paul Janet reminds us that it was not in the interest of a despotic state that Rousseau required this exchange of natural for civil rights, but in the interest of freedom.[18]

But Rousseau's theory gave no notion of how long it might take to achieve a state of balance. As the revolutionary leaders realized to their dismay, it took much longer than they predicted—a crucial issue for the anxious and impatient populace of the 1790s.[19] The citizens' actions fell short of the virtuous profile imagined by Rousseau, as did the state in respecting the people's sovereignty. A crucial challenge for the Jacobins was admitting that their countrymen had the right to refuse the yoke of the collectivity and that the church might play a valuable, stabilizing influence in the new polis.[20] These unresolved issues, when combined with the government's dubious attitude toward the sister states that were conquered by revolutionary armies, the leaders' increasing obsession with internal enemies, and the widespread financial turmoil that continued to wreak havoc on a hungry populace, contributed to the schemes for social control devised by the Robespierristes and led to the mass purges of the Terror. All of this elicited the ire of conservative critics, who blamed the revolution for assuming that one could—and should—change human nature in such radical ways.

The struggle between liberty and loyalty emerges forcefully in early images of l'homme régénéré, for after the revolutionaries celebrated their renewal, the more difficult task of governing began. Thanks to the ground-breaking work by Antoine de Baecque and Mona Ozouf, among others, we can sketch out relations between this imagery and the changing political climate during the revolutionary period.[21] Starting in the 1760s, the concept of regeneration had been linked to the idealized, Rousseauian image of a warm, nurturing mother. Since the nation's fate lay in the hands—and wombs—of Frenchwomen, women were held to a high standard of physical and moral health. Women's diet, clothing, and especially their conduct as mothers were of great interest to a nation that saw women's conduct as a barometer of national mores.[22] Some reformers seized on this connection to argue that, by improving women's status, one might strengthen future generations. Thus one polemicist declared in 1779, "Let us apply ourselves to making [women] strong, robust, courageous, educated and even learned as much as is possible and we will see, in the first generation to succeed us, humanity enter into all its vigor, all its splendor."[23] Commenting on the atmosphere in the 1770s, Mme de Miremont noted, "It has been good form to be a nursing mother. Mothers have become more interesting."[24] Running contrary to this imagery was the slanderous propaganda attacking Queen Marie-Antoinette, who was widely cast as a negligent mother, adulterous wife, and ambitious plotter.[25] Unlike Marie-Antoinette, who undermined the state through secret ministrations with enemies abroad, the ideal mother would stay quietly at home and attend only to her husband and children, leaving public matters to men.

Thanks to the euphoria surrounding the convocation of the Estates General, the king enjoyed a major resurgence of popularity in 1788, and the discourse of regeneration—which had long circulated only in maternal rhetoric or agricultural reform—was extended to the monarchy.[26] Thus we find the press praising Louis XVI as "le régénérateur de France."[27] Although in December 1789 the king would be praised for supporting "la régénération de la France," after the fall of the Bastille the term also took on the meaning of spontaneous national rejuvenation.[28] Taking agency away from the king, one well-known pamphlet transformed popular unrest into a cure for the aging body politic; as the 1789 *Catéchisme d'un peuple libre* declared: "What is a revolution?" "It is a crisis through which the people, who had grown old by suffering, regain the vigor of youth, and escape the grip of death."[29] This metaphor of corporeal renewal was so widespread that one (apocryphal) account cites a victim of the guillotine begging the National Assembly to have his blood, which would no longer be of any use to him, transfused into the veins of an older man to help rejuvenate the nation.[30]

We find a similar image of renewed physical strength in another pamphlet from July 1789 that describes the nation harkening back to a pre-Bourbon historical precedent that was above all virile: "Frenchmen, you have regained your freedom, that freedom which your ancestors the first Franks held in such esteem; you are going to rejoin them, strong and healthy, like them you will let your beard grow and wear your hair long. . . . Farewell to hairdressers and tailors, a rough homespun cloth will suffice for you."[31] This new discourse of virility salvaged Frenchmen—who had long been caricatured as effeminate fops—as agents of regeneration.[32] Such images fostered the republican ideal of virtue as a profoundly homosocial bond of fraternity between men.[33] The shift in gendered agency is important: although women could provide the vehicles and props to sustain the process of regeneration, it is only the men—the state itself—who could build a new future.

The release of energy from the collapsed monarchy formed another topos of regeneration. Building on the connotation of bodily renewal from a medical perspective, Philippe Pinel declared in the November 1789 *Gazette de Santé* that "the nervous maladies which were during preceding years so common in Paris, seem to have disappeared since the beginning of the Revolution, doubtless because the indolent and apathetic sloth of the rich gave way to reborn caring and to agitations capable of engaging the activity of the soul." Diagnosing the new body politic as physically fit, Pinel concluded, "Politics has thus come to the rescue of medicine."[34] A year later Pinel reiterated his positive diagnosis, claiming to hear many a Frenchman say, "I feel better since the revolution."[35] This sense of politics restoring life to the nation through spontaneous, collective action is also seen in descriptions of political clubs as "associations régénératrices" and symbolic rituals such as the planting of liberty trees.[36] These trees had their origins in the maypoles planted by peasants as an act of rebellion against local lords, but they quickly became appropriated in the organic metaphor of earthly regeneration, linking the nation's fate to that of a healthy young plant.[37] As de Baecque has cogently noted, regeneration thus formed a utopian program for the French people's political, moral, and physical health—and one that was not necessarily dependent on the king.[38]

Although virile men needed republican wives, opportunities for women to contribute to political processes directly as independent agents were limited, and when women's clubs began to vie with male groups for a say in the course of revolutionary politics, their activities were gradually cloaked in a fear-inspiring imagery that wrecked any hopes of political legitimacy. After the assassination of Marat on 13 July 1793, the radical Club des Citoyennes Républicaines Révolutionnaires appropriated the symbolism of maternity in a powerful series of events. They kept watch over Marat's body and collected the blood that continued to flow from his wound. In the night of 16–17 July, they paraded Marat's bloody chair and bathtub through the streets of Paris, mixing the blood of the slain hero with their own, as symbols of women's fertility and strength. Replying to an orator's appeal that "the blood of Marat shall give rise to intrepid republicans," the women swore to give birth to a whole brood of little Marats.[39] This collective female energy made a memorable impact on the public; as one witness recalled: "Marat's body is decomposing and rotting, to be reborn, thanks to the women, in a sublime form."[40] But as Godineau and Gutwith have noted, these intense symbolic gestures may have damaged the women's hopes for political participation and alienated the male leadership of the Cordeliers and the Jacobins. "The delirium of intensity they demonstrated . . . may well have unsettled a political regime striving to embed itself in patriotic abstractions."[41]

This incident was not an isolated episode; such imagery of female political agency through sexual or bodily functions appears rather widespread. This is unsurprising when we recall that the women expressly justified their contributions through reference to their maternal responsibility; as Gutwirth notes, "The Nation, their family, was summoning up their protective maternal ardor."[42] Nevertheless, the menacing aspect of such work was blown out of proportion by the media. Note the frightening image of the nursing mother-cum-*tricoteuse* that we find in the infamous periodical *Le Père Duchesne:* "These women so scary / Feed one and feed all / From miraculous teats / At a vast public feast / And the liquid goes flowing / The dread crowd a-growing / It's not milk at all, but blood."[43] Because women were valued above all for their childbearing potential, intelligent, politically informed women were viewed as unnatural, and their activities were questioned. Conflated with news of horrible mob actions and bloodthirsty sans-culottes, the women's groups were slandered in hostile media, which reported their acts as efforts to annihilate the infant *patrie* in a bloodbath of murderous rage against the clergy, the aristocracy, and other ill-defined enemies of the people.[44] Most frightening was the specter of radical women taking over through the work of their capacious fertility. An anonymous print from this era, "Citoyens né libre [*sic*]" (fig. 18), captures that awesome possibility. This image shows a bulky sans-culotte woman frowning in pain, minutes after giving birth to an oversized infant. Instead of using the supine position favored by the aristocracy, she has apparently given birth standing up. As she lifts up her rough dress to reveal the fruits of her labors, her newborn son, a brawny, scowling "freeborn citizen," struts out to enter the fray. This image associates the infancy of the new republic with an alarming, almost superhuman energy.[45]

Allegorical goddesses peopled many of the revolutionary festivals, notably in the Festival of Unity choreographed by Jacques-Louis David (10 August 1793). This festival, which represented what Michelet called a "history of the Revolution in five acts," began at the Bastille, which had been transformed into a great site of baptism.[46] There one found the Fountain of Regeneration, an enormous statue of Hathor (an Egyptian mother-goddess) whose "fertile teats" *(fécondes mamelles),* discreetly covered by her crossed arms, flowed with water. Delegates lined up to drink this water from a communal cup and found themselves refreshed. Afterwards, they paraded around the city in a quasi-masonic ritual; as Ewa Lajer-Burcharth points out, such festivals led the participants' bodies through a kind of urban site of memory that redefined them as republican subjects.[47] Under the "waters of regeneration" individuals were initiated as deputies of the new

FIGURE 18

"Citoyens né libre [*sic*]." Anonymous engraving.

republic—the state-sponsored purification replacing the participants' earlier baptism at the font of the Catholic Church.

The importance of a particularly maternal femininity is obvious in the tableaux staged for the second station on this procession, a triumphal arch recalling the women's march to Versailles. There Hérault de Séchelles harangued the crowd in language that stressed the maternal role expected of female citizens: "O women! Liberty attacked by tyrants needs a people of heroes to defend it. It is for you to give them birth. Let every martial and generous virtue flow with your mother's milk into the hearts of the infants of France!"[48] Gutwirth questions the efficacy of such rhetoric, wryly noting, "In its drive to make a figure of nurturance into a symbol of the Nation Indivisible, Frenchmen had ignored the fact that nurture, like freedom itself, cannot be wrested or imposed upon a people,"[49] but she underestimates the impact of this event. Although staged during a time of mass unrest and panic in the new republic, the Festival of Unity apparently struck a profound chord in participants. Ozouf documents witnesses writing of the festival as visualizing "the great beauty" *(le grand beau)* of the revolution that had been promised but unrealized for so long.[50] Regardless of their workaday concerns with low salaries and the high price of bread, and their fears for personal safety—because of foreign intruders or unannounced *visites domiciliaires* (house searches)—Parisians responded enthusiastically to this massive spectacle of willed rebirth. One could always hope that the myth would become reality.

There was no one dominant metaphor for regeneration; writers and artists drew on diverse conventions to capture the extraordinary sense of newness. Metaphors of organic growth, maternal care, paternal love, and virile self-sufficiency co-exist alongside more traditional images of Christological rebirth. Like the American revolutionaries before them, the French initially celebrated their nation's turbulence as manifesting millenarian myths.[51] Taking God as their witness, the citizens emerged triumphant from the events of 1789 as from their own judgment day. One pamphlet declared: "Then will be the day of anger, justice, and vengeance! . . . The call of the convocation . . . like a vengeful lightning bolt, will summon all—the guilty and the innocent alike—to emerge from their distant Provinces and to gather around the king's throne. . . . Then will the book of Truth open wide: everything is written there."[52] The famous chemist and Dissenting minister Joseph Priestley is perhaps the best-known proponent of this millenarian view in Britain. In his *Letters to the Right Honourable Edmund Burke occasioned by his Reflections on the Revolution in France* (1791), Priestly argued that, since the world began in 4004 B.C., creation was nearing its end. Although he noted that the revolution might bring "calamities to many, perhaps to many innocent persons," he insisted that the result would be "eventually most glorious and happy." [53] Some legislators tried to maintain this vision of a nation regenerated by the Gospels, but the coupling of revolution and Christianity was a tenuous one indeed.[54] Unlike the American model, the French revolution's adhesion to a myth of religious redemption was sorely tested by its increasingly aggressive and hostile measures against the clergy.

Indeed, many supporters of the revolution were forced to withdraw their allegiance in mid-stream. The British poets Wordsworth, Southey, and Coleridge are famous examples of this trend; all embraced the revolution at its inception, only to recoil in disgust as time wore on.[55] Wordsworth's autobiographical poem *The Prelude* (written between 1799 and 1805) exemplifies the shift from approval to horror. Looking back to his youthful sojourn in revolutionary Paris, he incarnates the euphoria of 1789 by exclaiming: "Bliss was it in that dawn to be alive, / But to be young was very Heaven!" [56] The leitmotiv of regenerated man emerges here from an exchange with a patriotic French friend; after a passionate discussion of politics, the two young men beheld "a people from the depth / Of shameful imbecility uprisen, / Fresh as the morning star. Elate we looked / Upon their virtues; saw, in rudest men / Self-sacrifice the firmest, generous love, / And continence of mind, and sense of right, / Uppermost in the midst of fiercest strife" (*Prelude*, IX:383–89 [560]). Since this passage is followed by an apostrophe celebrating the pleasures of political discussion "in academic groves, or such retirement, Friend! As we have known," one suspects that it represents an ideal rather than an actual vision. Nevertheless, it captures much of the hope and civic virtue associated with regeneration. Although in retrospect Wordsworth expresses bitterness for the sad fate of his friend and the revolution overall, it is unclear what he blames most for its failure—its violent mob actions or its cold-blooded leaders. Both pale in comparison to the new enemy, Napoleon. Justifying his retreat into a stance of "wise passivity," Wordsworth concludes his recollections with disgust. He recoils in indignation and, citing the book of Proverbs, laments the French people, who "once looked up in faith, as if to Heaven / for manna" only to end up at Napoleon's coronation "[taking] a lesson from the dog / Returning to his vomit" (XI:362–64 [573]).[57]

For a graphic example of these shifting attitudes toward revolutionary "regeneration," consider the following two images. The first, drawn by the English poet and artist William Blake to celebrate the American Revolution is named "Albion Rose" (fig. 19) and dated 1780 (although scholars argue

FIGURE 19

William Blake, *Albion Rose (or Glad Day)*, c. 1790. Reproduced by permission of the British Library.

that it was probably executed in the early 1790s).[58] This engraving shows a naked youth who symbolizes the new or infant nation celebrated by Tom Paine in his tracts. He exemplifies the millenarian topoi of light, youth, and innocence, unfettered by the shackles of ancient injustices. The second, drawn by the French artist Jacques Louis Perée, is titled "L'homme régénéré" and dates from 1795 (fig. 20). Here we find another muscular male nude, but, armed with an enormous pick-axe, this man carries a threat of violence. Instead of looking out toward the spectator, as Blake's figure does, he stares up at an unseen God in the dark sky and waits for a response. The art historian Klaus Herding contends that this image "expressly condones" the destruction of the old regime, but I believe its message is more ambiguous.[59] True, the "regenerated man" tramples underfoot the insignia of royalty, nobility, and the Catholic Church, which are engulfed in flames from a strategic lightning bolt, and true, he holds out a majestic manuscript of the declaration of the rights of man. But he stands alone in an empty landscape and appears at risk of future lightning strikes.[60] Unlike Blake's naked innocent, he has covered his loins with a drape, symbol of postlapsarian guilt. Although he may be triumphant, this regenerated man inhabits a barren and desolate environment and seems uncertain of his fate.[61]

By 1795, of course, the revolution had undergone a massive shift from the heady days of 1789 to the dour atmosphere of apathy and counter-Terror experienced during the Directory. But already in August 1789, the metaphor of regeneration had shifted meanings as deputies struggled to define which rights should mark the citizens' new status. Whereas earlier writers had cited the American example to bolster their cause, France's difference from America now became painfully visible. As Mirabeau declared, "We are not savages, arriving naked from the banks of the Oronooco to form a society. We are an old nation" whose institutions date back more than thirteen centuries.[62] The British Americans were not savages, either. What Mirabeau meant to evoke here was the Americans' resemblance to the fortunate society depicted in Rousseau's second *Discours:* a society that, because it had only a small population and a simple social structure, existed in perfect balance between barbarity and hierarchy.[63] Unlike those happy people, the French had to clear away accumulated injustices to make room for freedom. But, although Mirabeau underlined the weight of France's history and government, this did not dissuade him or others from believing in the possibility of sudden change, for they believed that the dynamism of the revolution would ignite man's latent perfectibility and make all things possible. Education thus became most important. But what kind of education?

FIGURE 20

Jacques Louis Perée, *L'homme régénéré*, 1795, engraving. Reproduced by permission of the Bibliothèque Nationale de France, Paris.

Legislators spent countless hours designing and debating schemes of national education, but they were notoriously unsuccessful in effecting practical change. Gregory Dart reminds us that it was not until after the fall of Robespierre in 1794 that the government managed to pass a bill providing public instruction.[64] Nevertheless, the proposals are interesting insofar as their use of the metaphor of regeneration reflects the rapidly deteriorating political situation by enlisting the increasingly aggressive involvement of the state. Whereas Condorcet's schemes presumed that the nation would perfect itself spontaneously under propitious conditions, Lepeletier's invoked a more interventionist model of reform.

Condorcet had established himself as a proponent of reform long before making his reports to the revolutionary government in 1791 and 1792 and his famous *Esquisse d'un tableau historique des progrès de l'esprit humain* (published posthumously in 1795). In his work as secretary of the Académie des Sciences, Condorcet had often preached a model of self-governance by the enlightened few. Justifying such elitism, he claimed that it would serve the public good by taking decision-making out of the hands of traditional guilds and families and putting it into the hands of scientists, whose actions—he blithely maintained—were determined solely by the objective rationale of experimental inquiry. His proposals for public instruction belie a similar confidence in the perspicacity and integrity of academicians. If the masses would cast aside their unfounded faith in the clergy and follow the lead of scientists and intellectuals instead, he claimed, they could all achieve greatness. Through a system of early vocational training, grade schools, colleges, and institutes free and open to all, Condorcet envisioned the state both serving its own purposes and helping citizens attain their potential: "to cultivate . . . in each generation, their physical, intellectual, and moral faculties, and in so doing, to contribute to the general and gradual perfection of the human race . . . such must be the object of education."[65]

Without such guidance, Condorcet argued in his *Mémoires sur l'instruction publique* (1791), even the best-made laws would give rise to a monster more dangerous than the powers they had abolished, because as the revolutionary legislation allowed more independence to the masses, the masses became an increasingly dangerous force in the hands of unscrupulous demagogues.[66] Despite the evidence of just such a threat in the events of 1791 and 1792, however, Condorcet opposed schemes that would curb individual rights and put the state in control of public education, arguing instead that a properly credentialed intelligentsia should be entrusted to form the citizenry.[67] The diverse kinds of learning offered to the populace would make them immune to the false consolations of religion and philosophical in the face of adversity.[68] The physical sciences held an especially privileged place in this meritocracy. Condorcet biographer Keith Baker defends the philosophe's scheme, arguing that its stress on the sciences was not meant to accustom people to "accept the dictates of the 'scientist' without considering the basis of his authority," but rather to teach the masses an ideal model of rational thought, "because the physical sciences—accepting no authority but that of fact—developed the critical faculties to the highest degree."[69] Condorcet's fellow deputies politely applauded this costly and ambitious proposal and put it aside, because, as one critic noted later, "Condorcet obviously had no practical sense."[70] Although some facets of Condorcet's program would later become institutionalized under the Directory and the First Empire, the philosophe incurred the wrath of conservatives for his apparent arrogance concerning mankind's perfectibility.[71] For Joseph de Maistre, writing in 1796, Condorcet was the worst kind of blind optimist, one who "used his life to prepare the unhappiness of the present generation, graciously willing perfection to posterity," all the while averting his gaze from the "terrible purification" caused by his doctrines.[72] Ridiculing the philosophe for his credulity, Sainte-Beuve more pointedly caricatured Condorcet's proposal as operating on the absurd assumption that by changing the nation's institutions, one might somehow transform each citizen, as if by magic, into a reasonable, rational philosopher.[73]

Other deputies advanced more coercive means to mold the citizenry into the kind of "new men" idealized by the revolutionaries. By the time the martyred Lepeletier's proposal was brought before the legislature in 1793, political events had revealed a darker side of *le peuple,* that is, their suspicion of democratic processes, their impatience with governmental solutions, and their tendency to resort to violence when food supplies ran low.[74] Lepeletier agreed with Condorcet that mankind was malleable, but he saw this quality less as a virtue than as a potential danger. Strong state intervention was necessary, since, he declared, "considering the extent to which mankind was degraded by the vices of our old social system, I am convinced of the necessity of carrying out a complete regeneration, and if I may express myself thus, of creating a new people."[75] Inspired by his spiritual master Rousseau and the dictum that education begins at birth, Lepeletier devised a program that takes hold of the populace at a younger age and in a more forceful manner than Condorcet's. It mandates a neo-spartan model of compulsory education in which children would be raised together from age five to twelve in state-owned "maisons d'égalité" under the vigilant eye of state-sanctioned teachers. Following the "sacred law of equality," all children would thus receive the same frugal clothing, food, and instruction and would be governed by the same constant surveillance. Parents who refused to comply would lose their rights as citizens and pay higher taxes.[76] From here it was only a small step to Saint-Just's cold-blooded assumption that "[c]hildren belong to their mother until the age of five, if she has [breast-fed] them, and to the Republic afterwards . . . until death."[77] Like an effort to create thousands of Emiles, Lepeletier's program controls the budding citizenry through a regimented lifestyle of physical exercise, vocational training, and a rudimentary knowledge of morality, economics, and political science.

This proposal, which was warmly endorsed by Robespierre and ultimately adopted (though never realized) by the Convention, reflects the increasingly strained relations between Jacobin leaders and the citizenry as a whole in 1793. It demonstrates the Jacobins' fear that nothing less than a total cultural training could control the populace.[78] Whereas the earliest visions of l'homme régénéré celebrated a spontaneous rediscovery of natural freedoms, here we see an effort to enforce national loyalty through totalitarian, mechanistic structures. Ironically, these structures negate the values of individual autonomy and freedom of thought upon which the revolution was supposedly based. A year later, in the midst of the Terror's worst crimes against humanity, Lepeletier's fellow deputy Abbé Grégoire would voice an even more urgent appeal for regeneration. Here too we see that the process was no longer assumed to be spontaneous or natural; rather, it is a willed, imperative change in habits. As Grégoire urged the Convention: "The French people have gone beyond other peoples; however, the detestable regime whose remnants we are shaking off keeps us still a great distance from nature; there is still an enormous gap between what we are and what we could be. Let us hurry to fill this gap; let us reconstitute human nature by giving it a new stamp."[79]

Each new regime would appropriate such rhetoric in its own interest, although one senses a growing distance between political discourse and popular sentiment. After Thermidor, the Directory claimed its mission to be, among other things, "to regenerate the mores," revive patriotism, and bring back the peace.[80] Just four years after its conception, there were appeals to the people to help "regenerate the first Republic of the world."[81] But such rhetoric was often mixed with nostalgia. As one commentator wrote in 1796, "We have used, or rather abused, violent means too much in the past; let us employ a softer means of seduction; let us create new friends of freedom . . . and the past will no longer bring regrets to mind. We will return to those beloved days of memory, and the present, however hard it may be, will at least be sweetened by hopes of a good future."[82] Putting the lie to notions of spontaneous renewal, a similar rhetoric announced the coup d'état that ushered in the Consulate; as we read in November 1799, "From this moment a new order of things begins. The government was oppressive because it was weak; its successor has undertaken the duty to be strong in order to be just."[83]

This shift from images of autonomous regeneration to notions of imposing strength from without goes hand-in-hand with the innovations introduced by the governments of the 1790s. In spite of claims that there would be no major changes, the Directory, and then the Consulate, gradually did away with certain rights brandished by the rebels of 1789, such as the right of "resisting oppression" (1789) and of "insurrection" (1793), and restored the supremacy of the law. Other rights also fell by the wayside, including the right to work, social aid, and education. Instead we find by 1795 a new list of "duties" installed that prescribed obedience to the law, productive labor, and service to the patrie. As Furet reminds us, such measures were "all aimed at avoiding the tension between the unlimited nature of rights and the necessity for social order based on the law: since 1798, the internal revolutionary dynamic had found its source in that gap."[84] Significantly, Napoleon would ultimately ridicule the entire concept of a balanced republican state as a "wild dream, with which the French are infatuated, but it will pass like so many before it."[85] When he took charge a new order of things was under way: a revolutionary dictatorship, based no longer on virtue but on interests.

The strong-arm tactics increasingly adopted by governments after Thermidor challenged the notion that the revolution had been a liberal, democratic attempt to collectively *empower* the French masses as a sovereign whole. Rather, by the late 1790s many people began to suspect that such rhetoric veiled an effort to force the populace into a new kind of subjection to a bureaucracy. Emphasizing what he saw as the menacing philosophical materialism that lay beneath revolutionary discourse, Maistre, for instance, vilified the new republic as a vast and heartless machine. Juxtaposing the positive values of traditional, cyclical organic life to the negative values of a cold, mechanical governmental apparatus, Maistre declared: "Open your eyes and you will see that it does not *live*. What an enormous machine! What a multiplicity of springs and clockwork! What a fracas of pieces clanging away! What an immense number of men employed to repair the damage! . . . Everything is artificial and violent, and it all announces that such an order of things cannot last."[86] It was not only reactionaries who condemned the revolution; many former republicans shared Maistre's skepticism about the promises of national regeneration. Given the mounting evidence of government-sanctioned violence during the Terror and the volatile factionalism of the power elite after Thermidor, many people began to wonder if the revolution would have any positive effects at all. Paradoxically, the drive for greater individual liberties had in the long run underscored the need for order in society, thus making Napoleon's firm assumption of power all the more welcome to a weary populace. As Vaughan and Archer point out, "The incapacity of successive governments to achieve [order], or to exercise or even retain power, made an authoritarian regime appear as a refuge against outbursts of uncontrolled violence."[87]

Skeptics had doubted the feasibility of national regeneration all along, of course. From the beginning there existed a countercurrent of ironic and pessimistic images of *l'homme nouveau.* Hence one pamphlet dated January 1790 damned the "new French creature" to a rapid fall, declaring: "A plague on this creature who is so pleased with herself . . . she will soon be the unhappy victim of her own pride."[88] In Britain, Edmund Burke's *Reflections on the Revolution in France* (1790) took on the counterrevolutionary cause with great gusto, recasting the proud new man of the revolutionaries as a weak and vulnerable figure. In a deft inversion of the values of youth and newness, Burke depicted the revolutionaries' will to overthrow old institutions as a mad passion to discard wisdom for a brutish state of ignorance, where, as he wrote, "all the decent drapery of life is to be rudely torn off" and "the defects of our naked shivering nature" are exposed for all to see.[89] (Maistre concurred with Burke's dismissal of youth, sneering: "America is often cited. I know nothing so provoking as the praises bestowed on this babe-in-arms. Let it grow.")[90] According to conservatives, revolutionary innovations could only end badly, because they were based on the conceit that the child knows more than the father. In his mania to overthrow traditional ways, the regenerated man was considered a potential assassin and exemplar of oedipal rage. In one of many memorable images, Burke compared the revolutionaries to another murderous plotter, Medea, and warned readers to "look with horror on those children of their country who are prompt rashly to hack that aged parent to pieces, and put him in the kettle of magicians, in hopes that . . . they may regenerate the paternal constitution, and renovate their father's life" (3:146).[91]

Burke's counterrevolutionary rhetoric found a mighty adversary in Tom Paine, who had already established a formidable reputation as a polemicist on behalf of the American Revolution. Paine was well known and liked in progressive circles in France, and during the Convention he was even elected deputy (though he was later imprisoned by the Convention, too, when his popularity waned). His experiences in France and America, along with his powerful prose, made Paine a force to contend with.[92] In *The Rights of Man* (1791, 1792) Paine overturned Burke's major theses in a peremptory manner. He refutes Burke's contemptuous vision of l'homme régénéré, for instance, with two strategies of reversal. First, Paine inverts the temporal value that Burke attached to traditions such as the monarchy. Instead of assuming that age-old structures must be better than new, Paine claims that the monarchy is a mode of government that by its very age had always already "counteract[ed] nature." It "turns the progress of the human faculties upside down," he writes. "It subjects age to be governed by children, and wisdom by folly."[93] Second, instead of Burke's "cold and trembling nature," Paine rewrites the "regenerated" nation as a figure of virile charisma, arguing that in its nudity lies its strength. Challenging Burke with his greatest fear, that is, boundless revolutionary energy, he represents the new nation as a strong and vigorous form of life that gathers momentum with each new person it touches. The populace has no need for Burkean "draperies," Paine writes, because "it possesses a perpetual stamina, as well of body as of mind, and presents itself on the open theatre of the world in a fair and manly manner. . . . It exists not by fraud and mystery; it deals not in cant and sophistry; but inspires a language, that, passing from heart to heart, is felt and understood" (110). Borrowing metaphors from Rousseau and the pamphlet literature we surveyed above, Paine envisioned the revolution as a process working on transparence, universal understanding, and collective energy—ideas that went directly against Burke's image of the revolution as a clandestine conspiracy of intellectuals.

But the specter of secret plots ultimately won out over such idealism. Although Jacobin sympathies lived on in certain progressive circles in Britain, Seamus Deane has shown that the English responded to the revolution in the mid-1790s with violence and fear and that they embraced any number of conspiracy theories to explain the contamination they saw spreading through France and to warn against its influence on Britain.[94] Suggesting that the unrest might have physical causes, one polemicist claimed that the English dissenters had found a way to compress French ideas into what he called a "spiritual regenerating pill" that helped pregnant mothers produce children capable of imbibing the "cursed doctrine" at the contaminated breast.[95] (Inflaming popular fears about the revolution's power to corrupt the innocent, a 1795 newspaper announced the "remarkable" story of a woman—whose husband was member of a revolutionary commission—who gave birth to a "monster" posed like a *guillotiné* [a headless victim of the guillotine].)[96] Extending such metaphors of physical corruption to their logical conclusion, a French newspaper in 1797 advertised an antidote for revolutionary ideas—medical baths designed to cure the "crazy ideas" *(les égarements d'esprit)* fomented by the revolution.[97]

The most well-known proponent of the fear-inspiring rhetoric of conspiracy was the émigré priest Abbé de Barruel, who penned the surprisingly popular, two-thousand-page *Mémoires pour servir à l'histoire du jacobinisme* (1797–98).[98] Following Burke's lead, Barruel not only castigated the philosophes as idle theorists who meddled in affairs beyond their ken, he charted a vast plot linking well-known men of letters with freemasons, atheists, illuminati, and rabble-rousers from all over Europe—a secret society just waiting for the moment to usurp a weak government and establish anarchy in its place. L'homme régénéré is seen here as a member of a shadowy clan who mysteriously appears on the scene to wreak havok with all that we hold sacred: "Who are these men who suddenly arose, so to speak, from the bowels of the earth, with their doctrines and their venom, all their projects, their ways, and all the ferocity of their resolution? What is this devouring sect? Where did this swarm of adepts come from, with those systems, and that delirious rage against all the altars and all the thrones, against all the religious and civil institutions of our ancestors?"[99] Although Barruel saved his most vitriolic diatribes for Voltaire, he traced the upheaval of the revolution to a tight-knit network of sophists, atheists, and antigovernmental plotters working in clandestine haste to hatch their diabolical schemes. Such claims were certainly fictional, yet they held the populace in thrall. Why? According to the scholarship on secret societies, conspiracy theories offered a welcome answer to "the bewildering variety of changes which suddenly showered upon Europe." As J. M. Roberts points out, "Educated and conservative men raised in the tradition of Christianity, with its stress on individual responsibility and the independence of the will, found conspiracy theories plausible as an explanation of such changes: it must have come about, they thought, because somebody planned it so."[100] The assumption of individual agency was key. Unlike more modern explanations, which rely on social and economic factors, late eighteenth-century writers commonly targeted a single man, or a small group of schemers, as responsible for the devastation.

Ronald Paulson has astutely noted how some literary figures from the 1790s live out analogous plots in Gothic fiction. Working as a solitary mastermind, the evil monk Ambrosio sets up a diabolical scheme to destroy a whole society of saintly women in Lewis's *The Monk* (1796). Radcliffe's equally dastardly priest Schedoni (in *The Italian,* 1797) is the second kind of schemer—he works in concert with other sinister miscreants, only to be swept into a maelstrom of his own making at the end. Literature mirrors history; both Ambrosio and Schedoni suffer the ghastly fate that is their due, "like the Jacobin Club or Robespierre, who eventually loses his head, and ultimately a Napoleon."[101] Turning now to our own corpus of post-revolutionary fiction, we shall see how the persona of the experimenter—in pedagogy or in science—takes on the similarly despicable aura of the solitary plotter in the novels of Fenwick, Edgeworth, Réveroni Saint-Cyr, and Sade.

PEDAGOGICAL DYSTOPIAS: EDGEWORTH AND FENWICK

The plot of "perfecting" mankind—or rather, womankind—is linked to anti-French reaction in the dystopian fictions of the British writers Maria Edgeworth and Eliza Fenwick. As we have seen above, in war-torn Britain in the 1790s, many perceived the fascination with French politics as a particularly troublesome matter. Warning readers to be on their guard, T. J. Mathias declared in 1797 that "[l]iterature, indeed, at this hour, can hardly be divided from the principles of political safety. . . . We must be preserved from the tyranny and power of France; from all her principles, and from all her arms, open or concealed, mental, moral, or political . . . we must die, or defend ourselves from THE MONSTROUS REPUBLIC."[102] The critic David Simpson, among others, has explained how the British rhetoric of hostility to French theory defended national interests against political bugbears from across the Channel.[103] Loosely defined, French "theory" could connote metaphysics, rationalist inquiry, or Jacobin politics—all of which were easy targets for English traditions of empiricism, plain speaking, and common sense. I propose to show how aspects of Edgeworth's "moral tale," *Belinda* (1801), and Fenwick's Gothic fiction, *Secresy* (1795), focus on skirmishes over a related issue: efforts to improve on human nature as applied to the domestic sphere of woman.

Although far from the scathing critiques of the Roman Catholic Church incarnated in the villains of *The Monk* and *The Italian, Belinda* delivers a mordant satire of Rousseaian pedagogy in the foolish antics of Edgeworth's antihero, Clarence Hervey. Although hardly feminist, the pedagogical vignettes in *Belinda* serve as a corrective to Rousseau's limited vision of female nature. On one hand we see the happy Percival children, whose well-organized household and involved parents ensure that they will turn out well. On the other we must piece together the story of Virginia St Pierre, the idle romance-reader raised under the tutelage of Clarence Hervey's ineffectual French theories. Almost as condemnable as Hervey's project is the aristocratic approach of Lady Delacour, that is, parental noninvolvement and paid surrogacy. The tension between these different models reveals the author's effort to work through what were crucial unresolved issues in her time regarding the role of mothers in early education, and more significantly, the desirability of changing current practices in favor of attractive yet untried theories of childrearing. Much of the novel is constructed in the form of scenes in which the reader watches the three systems as they function, disintegrate or self-destruct, thereby teaching the characters important moral lessons.

We saw Edgeworth's concern for protecting the sanctity of the family home in *Practical Education;* in *Belinda* the author avoids those problems by means of an explicitly artificial genre. Artfully arranged performances make up the action in *Belinda:* they illustrate the didactic message and sustain the interest of readers with a penchant for sensibility. Let us recall that the late eighteenth century was a high moment for sentimental, theatrical styles in literature and art—witness the enormous success of the *drame bourgeois* and the melodramatic paintings of Greuze, David, and their English imitators.[104] This kind of art relies on the construction of highly legible tableaux depicting emotional moments of human drama. Read or gazed upon, the sentimental text or tableau becomes a public site—much like the site of scientific experimentation figured in Wright's *Experiment on a Bird in the Air Pump* (fig. 17)—where a "community of like minds [is] drawn together by their common reaction to a common scene."[105] Just as Greuze, David, and Wright foreground the individuals' reactions to create a spectacular effect, Edgeworth ends her tale with a spectacle of her own. Taken collectively, the scenes in *Belinda* show how the "experimental science" of *Practical Education* might play out in three social and psychological milieus.

As the heroine of a novel that is both *Bildungsroman* and a debate on educational methods, Belinda's background is strangely absent from the text, apart from vague mention of her living in the country. But Belinda's upbringing is less interesting than the ongoing variations on the theme of education we see in the plots of Virginia St Pierre, the Percival family, and Lady Delacour. Education takes on three very different meanings here: in the first case it ironizes a man's seduction of an innocent girl with "romantic" *(romanesque)* and potentially dangerous French ideas; in the second it connotes the ideal techniques—apparently spontaneous, yet carefully orchestrated—employed by exemplary parent-pedagogues; in the third it connotes a psychological awakening—the return of the repressed maternal instinct—in a negligent mother and aging *débauchée.*

In view of our interest in Rousseau, it would seem logical to focus on

Virginia St Pierre, a thinly veiled pastiche of Sophie and of Thomas Day's Sabrina. But like the romance heroine that she is, Virginia remains offstage for most of the novel, generating suspense and mystery but playing a passive role until her identity is finally revealed in volume 3. Hints of her extraordinary story wind through this novel of English manners like an exotic refrain in an otherwise familiar orchestra of plots, yet Lady Delacour is the real heroine of *Belinda.*[106] Her character has the wittiest voice and most endearing foibles, and she must reveal the most painful secrets and make the most difficult changes before closure is achieved. As she introduces Belinda into a breathtaking whirl of balls, visits, and masquerades, the *ingénue*'s sober reserve contrasts forcefully with this woman's artificial gaiety and affected, French-inflected speech.[107] (Here as elsewhere in Edgeworth's novels, familiarity with French connotes a kind of worldliness that bodes ill for domestic happiness.)[108] When Lady Delacour eventually admits her real feelings to Belinda, we see that inside this *mondaine* lies a frightened and insecure wife and mother. Thanks to Belinda's wise counsel, she finds the strength to reinvent her life in keeping with her newly discovered nature. By the novel's end she reconciles with her newly sober husband, accepts responsibility for her estranged daughter, moves to the country, discovers true happiness as wife and mother, and incarnates *la femme comme il y en a peu* (the woman with few peers) of Marmontel's popular *Contes moraux,* thereby realizing Lady Percival's prophecy: "[T]he period of her enchantment will soon be at an end, and she will return to her natural character.— I would not be at all surprised, if Lady Delacour were to appear at once, 'la femme comme il y en a peu'. . . . when she is tired of the insipid taste of other pleasures, she will have a higher relish for those of domestic life."[109] Note how retreat to the domestic sphere translates as a return to woman's "natural character."

But Lady Delacour's home is not the only site of reform in this fiction; other homes also fall under Belinda's scrutinizing gaze. The Percival home (an idealized vision of the Edgeworth estate) exemplifies how education and domesticity can work hand-in-hand. The name *Percival* itself signified progressive science to many readers. Thomas Percival was a well-known chemist, philanthropist, and peer of luminaries such as Joseph Priestley, Benjamin Franklin, and René Antoine de Réaumur (cited in *Practical Education,* 1:28).[110] The Percival home replicates the central dicta of *Practical Education:* its founding apparatus is a country estate complete with pets and well-managed servants. Close at hand are all the tools necessary for the children to learn about chemistry, gardening, painting, and music. The children apparently have a room of their own somewhere in the house since they occasionally run into the drawing room to report on their discoveries. Proponents of progressive childrearing, the parents do not speak down to their children or exclude them from serious conversations. Even the youngest exhibit a well-honed scientific curiosity; after looking at some goldfish in a bowl, they interrogate a family friend about fish anatomy and prompt him to proffer an anecdote worthy of *Practical Education:* "Dr X— observed, that this was a very learned dispute, and that the question had been discussed by no less a person than the Abbé Nollet; and he related some of the ingenious experiments tried by that gentleman to decide, whether fishes can or cannot hear" (90). The eager curiosity and attractive physiognomy of these children (with their "healthy, rosy, intelligent faces") give ample proof of the system's success (88).

Chief among Mr. Percival's many virtues is his ability to make everything serve a pedagogic purpose: "From the merest trifles he could lead to some scientific fact, some happy literary allusion or philosophic investigation" (204). Like Sophie, Lady Anne Percival makes her greatest contribution by facilitating the enjoyment of others: "Every body was at ease in her company, and none thought themselves called upon to admire her" (89). Their marriage is companionate in the best of senses, thanks to Lady Anne's careful use of learning: "[she] had, without any pedantry or ostentation, much accurate knowledge, and a taste for literature, which made her the chosen companion of her husband's understanding, as well as of his heart." After spending a few days in their company, Belinda draws the conclusion that will orient the rest of her plot: "domestic life was that which could alone make her really and permanently happy" (204).

The Percival family serves as the control model against which Lady Delacour and Clarence Hervey are compared and condemned. Not only do Hervey's techniques epitomize the worst kind of manipulative, domineering attitude toward his pupil, his entire enterprise—the apparatus, experimental style, and theoretical assumptions—are described in language borrowed from the highly suspect French traditions of speculative philosophy and romance. Hervey himself resembles a caricature of Rousseau: he is presented as a self-avowed "man of genius" who imagines himself "entitled to be imprudent, wild, and eccentric" (10). When his scheme turns sour, he laments his fate as the martyrdom of a great man: "I shall pay too dear yet for some of my experiments. 'Sois grand homme et sois malheureux,' is, I am afraid, the law of nature, or rather the decree of the world" (260–61).

When the mystery that has been hinted at since the beginning is finally revealed in volume 3, the twin influences of French philosophy and romance dominate. Hervey's scheme, we learn, was originally inspired by

Rousseau's *Emile.* After visiting revolutionary Paris, Hervey developed a rabid disgust with the "perverted" tastes of modern Frenchwomen and a great enthusiasm for the more conservative Rousseau: "He was charmed with the picture of Sophia . . . and he formed the romantic project of educating a wife for himself" (*Belinda,* 343). He later realizes this dream with all the accoutrements of romance—a chance encounter in a woods, a beautiful girl, and a man-hating grandmother who conveniently dies and leaves the girl orphaned. Disobeying the grandmother's dying wish, Hervey takes the girl away, renames her Virginia St Pierre (after the heroine of Bernardin de St-Pierre's 1787 idyll *Paul et Virginie*), installs her in an isolated cottage, and begins "educating a wife for himself" (343). As an experimental apparatus this house is barely described at all apart from mention of its high garden walls. Hervey's methods are few: he abandons all pretense of education after one short-lived attempt to teach her writing, and claims that she is better off unschooled after extolling the "purity" of her mind (355, 351). Virginia's trivial pastimes contrast forcefully with the female industry extolled in Rousseau and in Edgeworth's other works. She spends her time playing with a pet bird, reading romances, dreaming about mysterious lovers, and awaiting the infrequent visits of Hervey. Her companion is not her mother but a paid servant (the worst company, according to every pedagogue since Locke), an old woman who supports the girl's unthinking obedience to Hervey and encourages her overly developed sensibility. She retains a total ignorance of society, science, or politics. In short, this "inactive method" produces a lazy, irrational creature. Moreover, after meeting commonsensical Belinda, Hervey abandons the project entirely.

By now an obvious amalgam of Rousseau and Thomas Day, Hervey is thus proved to be fickle and self-serving.[111] If the novel ended here this experiment would appear an extremely callous exercise in personal manipulation. But thanks to Edgeworth's nationalist agenda and romance plot, Hervey retains our sympathy. Once he gives up his French theories and regains his English good sense, he realizes that happiness was within reach all along.

The novel rapidly ties up all loose ends in the final pages. Virginia becomes an heiress after being reunited with her long-lost father and finds a suitor at the same time; Belinda's erstwhile love interest proves himself unworthy, Hervey admits his love for Belinda, and she accepts his proposal of marriage. As if to underline the artificiality of this denouement, Edgeworth lends her narrative voice to the notoriously theatrical Lady Delacour, who lists the surprising coincidences that led to this point and then stages a final tableau vivant of domestic contentment. "Let me place you all in proper attitudes for stage effect," she exclaims as she directs the characters around an imaginary stage, placing the newly betrothed in tender proximity and urging newly reunited family members to embrace: "What signifies being happy, unless we appear so?" (450). The resulting pose brings to mind the didactic sentimentalism of artists such as Greuze, or in the scientific genre, Wright of Derby. Conforming to the conventions detailed by Bryson, "the characters freeze in their gestures—the moment of arrest coinciding with the expression of heightened emotion—and the spectator can take in 'as a whole and all at once' the full significance of the stage-spectacle."[112] At the end Lady Delacour steps forward with a final injunction to the reader-observer: "Our *tale* contains a *moral;* and, no doubt, / You all have wit enough to find it out" (451). What began as a more or less realistic depiction of a young woman's entrance into the world thus ends in a highly artificial *coup de théâtre.*

Critics have long been puzzled by this odd conjunction of realism, romance, and theatricality.[113] Although the eccentric schemes of female education concocted by Rousseau and Day are obviously implicated in the story of Virginia St Pierre, looking back to *Practical Education* offers a more compelling insight into *Belinda*'s ending. As subjects in a manual of experimental science, the Edgeworth children had to be reproduced in *Practical Education,* for only their felicitous example could prove that the authors' ideas constituted a sound program of childrearing. Nevertheless, this exhibit was fraught with concern for the authors' home and family. *Belinda* embroiders on *Practical Education* in the more expansive realm of fiction. In the plot of Virginia St Pierre, Edgeworth criticizes theories purporting to improve on female nature and blames the tutor's excessive reliance on French ideas for the disastrous result. In the plot of Lady Delacour, the author suggests that it is possible to redeem a world-weary débauchée and make her into la femme comme il y en a peu. The significant absence in the final tableau vivant is the Percival family. But this makes sense as well, for the Percivals need no final representation. Like the control against which an experimental subject is measured, they have undergone no dramatic changes nor altered their views. They simply live on, happily spreading the word that education succeeds best when progressive principles are guided by traditional domestic virtues, rather than by radical, untried theories.

Secresy; or, The Ruin on the Rock (1795) pushes the critique of experimental pedagogy farther by representing a heroine who never achieves domestic happiness but rather is doomed to a life of wild and tragic idiosyncracies because of her uncle's secret plot for her life. In *Secresy*'s heroine, Sibella Valmont, we find an incongruous hybrid: the voice of progressive Enlightenment ideology speaking for a victim of Gothic romance. When Sibella rebels against her uncle's cruel confinement, she borrows the fiery rhetoric of Wollstonecraft, yet she never tries to leave. Her moonlight wanderings around the castle and woods do not invite escape; her impassioned diatribes and daring pronouncements affect no one but herself.

Although *Secresy* is enjoying something of a revival today, thanks to three recent reprints, for many years Eliza Fenwick was forgotten or cited only for her children's literature.[114] First issued anonymously as "By a Woman," *Secresy* elicited a minor controversy in the London periodical press in 1795 and was reissued twice that year in London and Boston.[115] Whereas the reactionary *British Critic* criticized the novel's "French" extravagance, charging that *Secresy* was "one of the wildest romances we have met with . . . worthy enough of modern France, but far removed (we trust) from the approbation of Englishmen," the reviewer for the *Monthly Magazine* applauded the serious message of the novel, which bespeaks "a more philosophic attention to the phenomena of the human mind than is generally either sought for, or discovered, in this lighter species of literary composition."[116] These conflicting reviews may reflect the reviewers' tolerance for the progressive politics of Wollstonecraftian feminism, as the novel bears unmistakable homages to the eminent feminist in rhetoric, philosophy, and plot.[117]

Secresy's most striking feature is its didactic division into two registers: Gothic romance and philosophical diatribe. These two voices are strung along in an epistolary exchange between two female alter egos: the rational Caroline Ashburn, who reports on events in fashionable society and expounds her feminist ideas, and the tempestuous Sibella Valmont, who knows only the remote estate of her uncle George Valmont. When the novel opens Sibella and her foster brother Clement are nearly adults. For the past two years Clement has been traveling and enjoying worldly pleasures while she has remained a prisoner at home. We read the letters of other characters, too, and in so doing piece together the tragic fate of Sibella and the Valmonts.

Like a good number of other novels from this period, *Secresy* condemns the Rousseauian ideal of female confinement to the home. "The melodramatic entombing of the heroine by a powerful, often paternal figure is a conventional, even obsessional topos in eighteenth-century women's writing," notes Terry Castle; "it is frequently amalgamated with a sort of Bluebeard motif."[118] The story of a beleaguered daughter or wife who fights off the tyranny or incestuous passion of a father or husband figure is particularly common in the "female Gothic."[119] Although it borrows much from these conventions, *Secresy* also belongs to the corpus of fictional experiments. On a philosophical level, it perpetuates the feminist rebuttal of Rousseau begun by Macaulay and Wollstonecraft and illustrates many key points in *A Vindication of the Rights of Woman.* On a narrative level, under its Gothic trappings one finds the same story as in *Belinda* and *Imirce:* that of a Rousseauian tutor and his scheme to create an ideal, "natural" woman. The heroines differ widely in these novels, however, because of the different visions of female nature. Dulaurens celebrated the "girl of nature" as a shameless hedonist whose appetites sustained a cheerful sensuality, whereas Edgeworth painted a less flattering image of an eternal child. Fenwick breaks with both traditions to depict a heroine who is at once a romantic dryad and a woman endowed with "manly" intelligence.[120]

The Rousseauian experiment here becomes the springboard for a Gothic mystery. Incarnating the demand for public scrutiny, Sibella's would-be rescuer Caroline launches the inquiry that will direct much of the plot, writing to Valmont on the first page:

> As your seclusion of Miss Valmont from the world is not a plan of yesterday, I imagine you are persuaded of its value and propriety, and I therefore see nothing which should deter me from indulging the strong propensity I feel *to enquire into the nature of your system;* a system so opposite to the general practice of mankind, and which I am inclined to think is not as perfect as you are willing to suppose. (39, emphasis added)

But Valmont does not respect her wishes and keeps his project secret for pages to come. In this respect and others, Fenwick's villain echoes the French villain of Choderlos de Laclos' *Liaisons dangereuses* (1782), but in a paternal mode. The tension between Valmont and Caroline—one seeking information, the other guarding it—is one of the main mobilizing forces in the plot in *Secresy,* just as a similar tension between Valmont and his female partner in crime Merteuil motivated the plot of *Les Liaisons dangereuses.*[121] As in the latter, however, neither Valmont nor Caroline has wholly altruistic motives; both have a "system" to prove.

As the novel unfolds, all the requisite Gothic topoi crowd the pages, magnified as emblems of Valmont's mysterious scheme. The apparatus of this novel is the Gothic castle-cum-prison with its subterranean vaults, dilapidated tower, and omnipresent master. As in many Gothic novels, the reader is led into the site as an outsider who encounters "frowning battlements," "turrets all cheerless, all hostile, and discouraging" before wandering "through carved saloons and arched galleries, into which the bright sun of spring can only cast an oblique ray" (52). Valmont's experimental style might have been lifted straight out of Burke's attacks on Rousseau in *Reflections on the Revolution in France;* as Caroline writes, "it is singularity and not perfection that [Valmont] is in search of . . . he now bravely resolves to enforce the wonder of his compeers, if he cannot claim their reverence" (60).[122] The actual project recalls the sensationist premise of a humanity *degré zéro* combined with Day's dream of patriarchal control. According to Caroline, "His darling wish [is] educating two children, and one of them a female, to whom . . . nothing should be granted beyond the instinct of appetite" (65). Valmont himself declares: "I have purposefully educated [Sibella] to be the tractable and obedient companion of a husband, who from early disappointment and a just detestation of the miserable state of society is willing to abandon the world entirely" (182).

But Valmont's theoretical assumptions put a counterrevolutionary twist on the age-old dream of creating the ideal wife. He is not a progressive but a reactionary, an arrogant aristocrat "loaded with the punctilio of the last age" who tries to "instruct a new race" to compensate for the privileges he lost with the end of feudalism (63–64). Sibella's imprisonment, like that of many other Gothic heroines, critiques the old regime model of the patriarchal father/king and submissive family/populace. Her untimely death is a harbinger of the family's imminent extinction and puts a definitive end to her uncle's archaic plot. But one cannot give the heroine too much credit for destroying the edifice of patriarchal control. Valmont's chateau is no maze or monstrous labyrinth. Its exit is clearly marked and its sinister allures are mere stage effects. When offered a chance to escape, Sibella declines with rhetoric that could have come right out of Sophie, saying: "I am not convinced that the time is arrived when my submission ought to cease" (104). As for the villain, he may issue stern words and "terrifying" frowns, but Valmont proves far less abusive than most of the philosopher–father figures we have seen. He even initiates a reconciliation at the end.[123]

Secresy holds greatest interest for its description of the pathological mental state fostered by an unhealthy education. No bars need keep Sibella in her room; she is controlled by what Jacques Blondel calls the Gothic's "metaphysical prison"—that is, the fears and anxieties conjured by the thought of leaving the confinement of Valmont's system.[124] Although she eventually disobeys her uncle, even then she rationalizes her behavior as an act of philosophical integrity: "I am about to do nothing rash, I obey no impulse of passion, I have not separated duty and pleasure. I have examined the value of the object I would obtain with calmness; and . . . still duty points to the part I have chosen" (128). The heroine's only true release is in her correspondence with Caroline, in which she declares a spirited defense of women's rights. This feminist conversation is sometimes clumsy, but at moments it rings forcefully in a manner akin to Wollstonecraft's best passages.[125] Yet, although Sibella borrows the feminist language that Caroline uses, it ultimately proves powerless against the moral code she has interiorized—a code so stultifying that it endows her very existence with generic guilt.[126] At the end, when she realizes her lover's betrayal, even her wit evaporates and she seems to freeze up physically and intellectually. Her calm composure after the death of her child embodies a monstrous kind of self-control; Caroline writes: "the oppression she endured for want of this salutary relief [of tears] was dreadful to behold" (353).

This novel can be read as a cautionary tale about secrecy and clandestine experimentation, with a special warning against the victimization of female subjects. As in *Belinda,* the rhetoric of "bad" education veils a private, antisocial scheme that stunts one person's growth to test another's theories. And yet one cannot help but wonder just how new are the traps we've uncovered in *Belinda* and *Secresy.* Under a Rousseauian veneer, both fictions stage tales of gendered struggle that harken back to older tensions regarding English women's status in the law and their lack of proprietary rights. It is no accident that Virginia and Sibella are orphans and that the pedagogues to whom they are entrusted act as legal guardians.[127] Seen in this light, the heroines' dilemmas appear akin to the sufferings of a well-known sisterhood of English heroines, from Evelina, Monimia, and Fanny Price right up to Jane Eyre.[128] The antiheroes are dealt some measure of punishment for their mistreatment of the heroines, but that punishment pales against the travails they endure. The political subtext thus builds on the age-old subtext of so much women's writing: the character of the domineering father-pedagogue is not just a bogey of the postrevolutionary age, he incarnates the far more sinister because invisible reality of domestic terrorism.

Belinda and *Secresy* foreground the twin themes Colley has charted in the revolutionary era: the safety of the British women and the danger they face from France.[129] However passively the heroines succumb, their submission to ill-founded theories of female nature belies a glaring injustice that must be undone by a sensible English friend. The characters of Belinda, Lady Percival, and especially Caroline (in *Secresy*) incarnate the authors' hopes for self-help within an idyll of female society. Where the French menace is symbolized by a wild-eyed theorist or a tyrannical father figure, the heroine's rescue is made possible by the intervention of a sensible female. Politically divergent, the works of Edgeworth and Fenwick—like those of their compatriots Hannah More and Mary Wollstonecraft—should be seen as cautionary tales, tales that also serve as what Colley terms "survivors' handbooks."[130] Although we may not agree with their politics today, at the time the advice of *Belinda* on adapting to the status quo and of *Secresy* on urging action to change things were both regarded as a benefit for women.[131] Although they were largely confined to the private sphere in this very conservative age in Britain, such texts argued that no more females should suffer the silent plague of domestic terrorism.

SCIENTIFIC DYSTOPIAS: RÉVÉRONI SAINT-CYR AND SADE

Throughout this book I have traced a subtle shift in literature concerning science's responsibility for the living body. By this I mean the general move away from a stance of confidence in science's powers to a more ambivalent realization of the scientist's potentially dangerous impact on the natural order. As Emma Spary reminds us, "By the time of the French Revolution, concerns about de- and regeneration were associated with a view of the living body as extremely malleable in its functions: as subject to change in response to external conditions and internal will."[132] I posit that this shift followed the rising professionalism of scientific practice that became manifest in the 1790s. Part of the tension over experimental procedures derived from the diverse status of practitioners: although some experimentalists were prominent scientists or members of erudite assemblies, others were merely showmen or itinerant lecturers. Medicine was in a particular state of disarray. Thanks to the revolution's dissolution of all the old teaching institutions, including the Société Royale de Médecine, and the government's imposition of standard titles on all practitioners (as *officiers de santé*), the 1790s were a catastrophic period for medicine. As the historians Gelbart and Ramsey note, "Instruction was totally disrupted and marginal healers, empirics, and charlatans flourished"; "At no other time in modern French (or European) history have the legal distinctions between professionals and irregulars been so blurred."[133] Controversies erupted over this uncontrolled marketing of science. Just as the specter of charlatans killing patients with their ignorance made people wary of medicos in general, experimental science came to be perceived as a tool of deception, or worse yet, as a practice that might accidentally unleash powerful forces of destruction.[134]

Yet the 1790s are typically described as a propitious moment for the development of modern tools and methods. The diverse activities of experimentalists in the laboratory, the salon, and the coffeehouse defy classification, but a certain advance can be seen the techniques and apparatus that characterize the fin de siècle. As J. L. Heilbron has noted, after 1780 both the quality and quantity of physical apparatus commercially available increased sharply. These instruments included (1) increasingly elaborate apparatus sought by wealthy amateurs and teachers of natural philosophy; (2) more precise measuring devices such as barometers, standardized thermometers, and the newly invented electrometer; and (3) the air pump, the electrical machine, and their many accoutrements. Found in every respectable cabinet, these instruments were used for research as well as demonstration. Thanks to this new technology, scientists of the period felt more pressure to establish quantitative explanations for the physical phenomena they studied, and did so by devising procedures built on more refined theory, instrumentalism, and quantification.[135]

Historians often portray the late eighteenth century as a time of great prestige for science, citing the creation of the Institut de France and the Ecole Polytechnique as improvements on the sectarian academies of the ancien régime and noting the many technological innovations that were generated by the wartime economy. As Martyn Lyons declares, "the revolutionaries were intent on banishing the charlatanism of hypnotisers and mesmerists, and on making science directly useful to the nation. Science was no longer to be a pastime for aristocratic amateurs, nor was research to be directed in future by parasitical and monopolistic royal academies. . . . Science was now to become a citizens' science . . . less abstract and more directly useful."[136] Citing the influence of the Idéologues on French science, Lyons praises the period's new orientation toward observation and "cold analysis."[137] But did the Idéologues' claims to "democratize science" reflect widespread practices? Or were they a symptom of wishful thinking, as were the other schemes to improve public mores devised by the Directory government? Like the quixotic decision to distribute thousands of copies of Condorcet's *Esquisse d'un tableau historique des progrès de l'esprit humain* to the public free of charge, such celebratory claims on science's new utility must be seen in the wider social context of a period that is commonly portrayed as unsettled, apathetic, and nostalgic for lost certainties.[138]

Indeed, some have argued that the increasing reliance on sophisticated apparatus and theories was making scientific practice more opaque to the uninitiated. The ramifications of such change did not go unheeded by practitioners. Already in the late 1770s, Priestley's protégé Adam Walker insinuated that the scientist's manipulation of natural phenomena through complicated apparatus was tantamount to a secret corruption: "In all our experiments, we find that NATURE will not suffer herself to be violated with impunity; her struggles to restore the lost equilibrium of air, of fire &c. are not more conspicuous to the philosophic eye than those she makes against the fury and madness of those curses of mankind called conquerors!"[139] Thanks to the liberal if not radical politics of Priestley, Condorcet, Lavoisier, Beddoes, and other prominent scientists of the day, in the eyes of many people science took on the connotations of a potentially dangerous pastime.[140] As A. Patterson notes, by the early 1800s, "experiments with electricity had become confounded in the public mind with the construction of infernal machines."[141]

Such images were especially prevalent in Britain. Fearing that a revolutionary disease might undermine the health of the English state, English conservatives conflated experimentalism with ill-fated political practices and condemned both as arrogant attempts against a God-given natural order. In his long list of abominations foisted on the English people by French influences, Mathias included anatomical experiments performed at the Royal Society on virgin rabbits. In a passage that clashes forcefully with the blithe justifications of science's utility that we found in Martin's *Young Gentleman's and Lady's Philosophy,* Mathias condemned vivisection in his 1797 tract as an immoral and godless act: "Surely to sit calmly and watch with an impure, inhuman, and unhallowed curiosity the progress of the desires, and the extinction of the natural passions in devoted animals after such mutilations and experiments, is a practice useless, wicked, foolish, degrading, and barbarous."[142] Such concern extended beyond the natural sciences to physics and pneumatics as well. Electrical experimentalists, who were once celebrated as titans who "wrestled thunder from the gods," now found their work vilified as a diabolical effort to seize forbidden knowledge.[143] Seizing on the period's anxious concern for the nuclear family, Burke caricatured the Jacobins as irresponsible monsters who displayed "nothing of the tender parental solicitude which fears to cut up the infant for the sake of an experiment."[144] Burke's rhetoric is well known; what is less well known is how the French writers Sade and Réveroni Saint-Cyr contributed to a similar strain of foreboding in French thought.

The heroine of *Pauliska ou la perversité moderne: Mémoires récents d'une Polonaise* (1798) is another victim of inhumane experiments, although her story puts a different twist on the material we have seen thus far. In its bizarre scenes of experimentation, Réveroni Saint-Cyr borrows from contemporary work in pneumatics, chemistry, and electricity and mixes in the titillating effects of pornography.[145] He conjures up the émigré mentality of postrevolutionary political angst by inventing fearful characters moving through a landscape that is physically varied but consistently nightmarish. The heroine is a young mother of noble Polish blood who must flee the Russian soldiers who have killed her husband and captured her home. As she makes her way through a war-torn landscape, she encounters melancholy foreigners, impoverished peasants, and other miserables who lament their misfortune and whisper of evils wrought by secret societies and political plots. Although *Pauliska* was not well known during its time (only two editions were printed in 1798), recently this strange little book has received considerable attention.[146] Its conflation of émigré conventions, postrevolutionary politics, pornography, and bizarre scientific machinery exemplifies the sociopolitical forces converging in the 1790s.[147]

Unlike the novels discussed above, *Pauliska* does not harken back to Rousseau or follow the pattern of an experimental education. Rather, it is a first-person reminiscence of escape that bears a striking resemblance to the marquis de Sade's work. Like Sade, Révéroni exaggerates the sinister potential in the notions of "system" and experimenting on nature seen in *Emile, Belinda,* and *Secresy* and brings a French perspective to the political antagonisms of the 1790s. The evil connotations of system emerge forcefully in the publisher's preface to *Pauliska,* where it is hoped that this novel will help "stop those torrents of perverse maxims and absurd systems that... are presently destroying the foundations of morality and society in almost all nations of the world!"[148] Although this sweeping effort at reform may appear over-ambitious, Pauliska's plot does allow for a critique of many evils of the postrevolutionary age—or at least a symbolic critique, for the characters' sufferings are so exaggerated that they only allow a metaphorical reading.

It is true that Russia conquered Poland in 1793–95 and forced many to flee their homes, but Pauliska's travails take on the metaphorical dimension of a Sadeian horror show when one sees her passing from one assault to another, bravely defending herself and her young son from a series of villains who harbor increasingly dangerous ambitions. Pauliska begins by describing how, after surviving the hostilities of foreign armies and escaping the amorous attempts of a hideous guard, she and her son finally arrive at the home of a noble Hungarian host in Ust. She does not realize her peril until the maid whispers that her room is actually a laboratory rigged with listening tubes and ventilators that fill it with sinister gases. Her host the baron d'Olnitz, she learns, is not a kindly humanitarian but "a frightful maniac, atheist and profound chemist" ("un maniaque effroyable, athée, chimiste profond," 56). As if that were not bad enough, it turns out that d'Olnitz is also a member of some secret society whose "celestial pleasures" and "profound sciences" he wants her to learn. His "barbarious doctrine," detailed on pages 64–65, resembles the theories of *air vital* and animal magnetism propounded by Mesmer and his followers. The author appends a note linking it to "a sect recently established in Torino," warning, "women are invited to skip this whole paragraph" ("les dames sont invitées à passer tout ce paragraphe," 64), as if the mere act of reading it could corrupt delicate minds.

What is so potent about this science? The way it leeches into the body in secret: it is entirely physical and allows for no resistance. Firmly grounded in materialist principles, d'Olnitz's experiment begins by extracting bits of Pauliska's flesh and hair, which he distills and ingests in order to make her desire him (fig. 21). He justifies the vampire-like procedures with scientific rhetoric, claiming: "Love's fever may be tempered [*inoculé*] by a bite" ("L'amour est une rage, il peut s'inoculer . . . par la morsure," 58). This metaphor of love-sickness satirizes contemporary medical efforts to promote vaccinations against smallpox and rewrites the touching scene in Rousseau's *La Nouvelle Héloïse* (1761) in which Saint-Preux shares Julie's germs.[149] While she struggles in vain against his embrace, Pauliska is even more powerless to fight off other aspects of this experiment. The environment she inhabits is imbued with the baron's will: the food is intoxicating, the air filled with his breath. Despite her repugnance and terror, the heroine submits to the atmosphere and shamefully admits feeling a languor that was "almost delicious," a "giddy state which still makes me blush . . . I stammered words of desire and fell into a swoon."[150] Although this titillating passage stops there, the image of a sexually aroused yet virtuous woman reveals Révéroni's debt to the pornographic tradition.

Indeed, readers of Sade find much that is familiar in Révéroni's descriptions of the hapless Pauliska. *Pauliska*'s horrendous experiences bear a striking resemblance to the evil ministrations of villains in Sade's *Justine ou les malheurs de la vertu* (1791), *L'Histoire de Juliette* (1797), and, to a certain extent, *Les 120 Journées de Sodome* (written 1785). Misplaced scientific ambitions generate much suffering in novels by both Sade and Révéroni. Like the characters in Sade's novels, Révéroni's villains manifest the belief that their superior learning and social position give them special rights to break the laws of man and God. As Pierre Klossowski notes, "It is an *experimental right,* which could not be extended to the common run of mortals without danger . . . this *right to conduct forbidden experiments.*"[151] I suggest that this perquisite was not simply an apanage of the libertine sensibility; rather, it responded to the anxieties about science that marked the revolutionary age. *Pauliska*'s Baron d'Olnitz and *Justine*'s incestuous Dr. Rodin both work in private, submitting the female body to strange and cruel scientific experiments. Like a distorted echo of Condorcet's meliorist rhetoric, villains in both books justify their schemes through a utilitarian rhetoric of scientific "progress" that will benefit all mankind—at the slight cost of a few victims. Echoing the draconian measures endorsed by the Committee of Public Safety during the Terror, Sade's Rodin claims, "Anatomy will never reach its ultimate state of perfection" until one can determine how

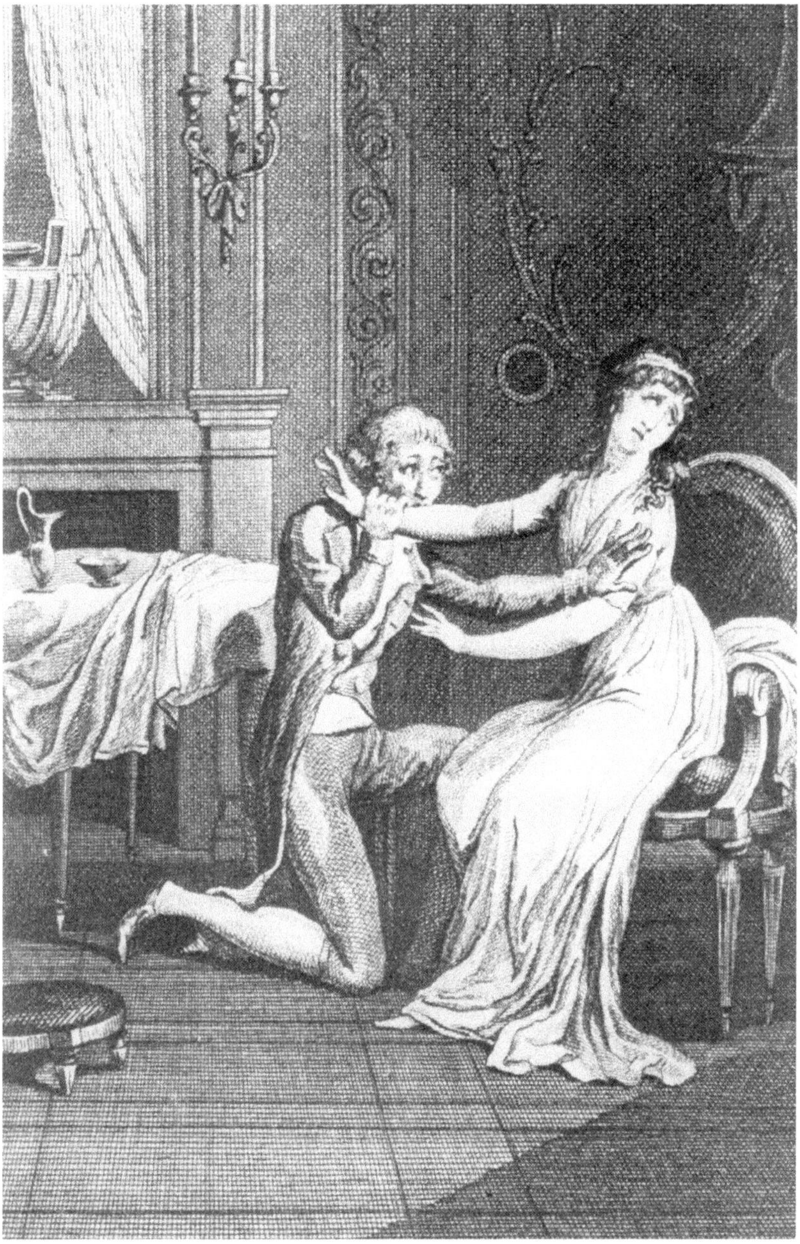

FIGURE 21

"L'Amour est une rage; il peut s'inoculer par la morsure." Frontispiece of Jacques Antoine Réveroni Saint-Cyr, *Pauliska ou la perversité moderne: Mémoires récents d'une Polonaise* (Paris: Chez Lemierre, an VI [1798]). Reproduced by permission of the Bibliothèque Nationale de France, Paris.

much the vagina of a young virgin contracts with violent death, and he expresses indignation against the "futile considerations" that thwart his efforts.[152] Révéroni's Italian *illuminati* express similar ambitions and frustration over the "apostles of humanity" who oppose efforts to test the human body's response to "condensed breath" and other secret substances (*Pauliska*, 170).

A philosophical materialism grounds the science of both authors. The villains of *Pauliska* and Sade's works stage gruesome experiments that rely literally on the materialist metaphor that "everything is physical." Thus Révéroni's decrepit d'Olnitz tries to regain his youth by ingesting the heroine's blood and breath, just as Sade's grotesquely obese, impotent comte de Gernande (in *Justine*) can only get his own juices flowing by watching rivers of blood spurt out of his beautiful young wife.[153] Sade extends materialist theory into an entire system of behavior and justifies the relentless abuse foisted on his victims through recourse to a host of explanations that recall the sensationist rhetoric discussed in chapter 2. Since all ideas—including pleasure—arise from physical causes, Sade claims that his characters' recourse to physical violence arises from their need for fresh new sensations. As the judge-torturer Saint Fond in *Juliette* declares:

> He who also would know the whole wild power and all the magic of lubricity's pleasures must thoroughly well grasp that only by undergoing the greatest possible upheaval in the nervous system may he procure himself the drunken transport he must have if he is properly to enjoy himself. For what is pleasure? Simply this: that which occurs when voluptuous atoms, or atoms emanated from voluptuous objects, clash hard with and fire the electrical particles circulating in the hollows of our nerve fibers. Therefore, that the pleasure be complete, the clash must be as violent as possible.[154]

Confident in her new learning, Juliette later concludes: "Cruelty is itself but an extension of sensitivity."[155]

Révéroni's and Sade's novels conjure up a universe rent asunder by cataclysmic forces beyond the heroines' control, but the origins of that upheaval, and the heroine's role in it, suggest very different visions of what *order* might mean. In keeping with the structure of an émigré novel, *Pauliska* drags its plucky young heroine through any number of trials to expose the political, moral, and social dangers of postrevolutionary Europe, then rewards her in the end by restoring the nuclear family, endowing her with a new husband and a new home in Switzerland "in the bosom of ease and peace" (211). Sade's *Justine* follows a similar voyage-type plot, but instead of rewarding her long-suffering virtue at the end, he kills her off with a symbol of divine wrath—a lighting bolt through her chest. In Sade's other works, order, or stasis, takes on an even more radically aberrant face; indeed, much of his fiction exists in a universe separate from the "dreary mediocre portion of mankind" *(les gens froids)*—that is, in the rarefied torture chambers of aristocratic libertines (*Juliette,* 340; 3:481).

In order to illustrate this contrast, let us look at *Pauliska* first. An amalgam of 1790s political anxieties and Gothic conventions, Révéroni's text leads the widowed Pauliska into hair-raising incidents with hostile soldiers, rugged hikes over alpine crags, and encounters with refugees who pass on news of political turmoil. Echoing contemporary suspicions about electricity and political radicalism, one of these unfortunates teaches her the melancholy truth that freedom, like electricity, "engenders brilliant phenomena" only to wreak destruction and storms in its wake.[156] The Europe she traverses shows traces of destruction everywhere: soldiers roll through villages inhabited by dispossessed noblemen and shell-shocked émigrés. This landscape of nomadic wanderers would have been very familiar to readers in 1796–99, for it seems there was a widespread sense of *déracinement,* or uprooting, felt by people during this time. Witness these lines from a period newspaper: "No one is what he used to be in 1789, or what he, in retrospect, expected to be in 1796. . . . We are all 'former' [*des ci-devant*], some former rich people, others former paupers: some former noblemen, others former commoners. . . . The reason is that at present we are all out of place."[157]

After arriving poor and homeless in Buda, Pauliska seeks work as a bookkeeper only to fall into the grip of Gothic conventions; that is, she slips through a trapdoor into a subterranean vault. There she is surrounded by a group of printers who are preparing counterrevolutionary propaganda and counterfeit *assignats* to spread new troubles in France. Forced to prostitute herself to this group, Pauliska manages to survive intact though her body takes on a monstrous new function when she is strapped onto a printing press and told to "make it moan" ("faire gémir la presse," 97). Pulling with all her weight, she hears a sigh only to realize that her force on the lever has strangled a kindly Frenchman and imprinted on his chest the words "Death, damnation for traitors!" ("mort, damnation pour les traîtres!" 98). In Révéroni's litany of modern evils, this scene perverts the printing press—which was vaunted for its liberating political potential during the heady days of the 1780s—into an instrument of torture wielded by foreign agents of counterrevolution. Although Sade staged a similar scene in *Justine,* where his heroine is enslaved by counterfeiters who make her turn an immense stone wheel,[158] Révéroni's revision injects the drama with a more pointedly political perspective. When Pauliska is surrounded by filthy rapists on all sides, it is the Frenchman—a discreet and kindly gentleman—who saves her honor. The Englishman who leads the counterfeiters is not only a dangerous brute, he is also a criminal and a political threat, seeking to disrupt the delicate balance of French national security.

In this and many other subplots of *Pauliska,* the villain science is coupled with various other demons, such as the sinister machinations of the Catholic Church, secret societies, and mercenary counterrevolutionaries. The entire narrative conveys the uneasy feeling of vulnerability and unpredictable dangers that penetrated the public consciousness in this postrevolutionary age. Presaging modern science fiction, some of Révéroni's most terrifying scenes revolve around apparatus that existed at the time but are grossly distorted for sinister new purposes. In the grueling finale, the heroine is trapped in apparatus that are monstrous in both size and intention. First we see her in an odd glass room that on closer inspection turns out to be a man-sized glass globe, recipient of an enormous air pump. Clearly informed about period pneumatics, d'Olnitz explains that this pump will not generate a vacuum and kill the subject (like the unfortunate cockatiel in Wright of Derby's painting, *Experiment on a Bird in the Air Pump,* fig. 17). Rather, it serves merely to gather breath. Sucking her breath into the head of the still, the pump condenses it through contact with cold water and liquefies it into a serum (186). Once again, however, science is perverted to amorous ends: her liquefied breath will not serve study or analysis; rather, it will rejuvenate d'Olnitz's feeble old body. Echoing the attempts to rejuvenate the national body in revolutionary discourse, the author intervenes here as elsewhere to verify the probity of his tale, noting, "This experiment, which is the height of madness, is nonetheless presently in vogue, and has been transported from Berlin to Paris."[159] Fanning the reader's anxiety, the author thus mixes fact with fiction so as to confuse the parameters of the possible. Such monstrous inventions are not only real, they are encroaching on the reader's space and moving ever closer to home!

Worse yet are the experiments concocted by the baron's conspirator, the Italian magnetizer Salviati. Dissatisfied with the slow process of harvesting breath with an air pump, Salviati proposes to build an immense machine that would generate "natural electricity" from the friction of a glass wheel rubbing against human bodies (189). These monstrous machines form another link to Sade, whose novels include a number of machines that give pleasure and then destroy their female victims.[160] Machines were a common motif in the marriage of Gothic and erotic genres that marked the 1790s; thus one finds a "magnetico-electric bed" in one novel of 1803 and a variety of armchairs—designed either to seduce or rape women—in other texts of the day.[161] But Révéroni's machines perform a wry reinterpretation of the metaphors of regeneration we saw above. Reinventing the known procedures for making light from rubbed glass,[162] Salviati perverts science by incorporating human subjects in the machinery and using the resultant energy to regenerate himself. First he tries the machine with two children and exalts over the effect imparted to him through the conductor: "soon his eyes shine . . . his face tightens, his hair stands on end and pushes up his wig," and he claims to have gained fifty years of life.[163] The next step is to attach Pauliska and another woman to the apparatus, but the experiment is stopped in the nick of time by the arrival of soldiers. At the trial that ensues, Pauliska finally has the chance to denounce her tormentors, but d'Olnitz, now deflated from his illusory youth, dies on the stand and Salviati, after being sentenced to life for atheism and immorality, blows up the court and prison and dies in the process. While the English counterfeiter escapes unscathed, at least some of Révéroni's villains are punished in the end.

In Sade's universe, it is the heroine, not the villains, who is punished. As noted above, when Justine survives, miraculously, all the assaults on her mind and body to rejoin her profligate sister Juliette at the end, Justine's prattling talk of virtue seems to invite the lightning bolt that strikes her dead. Despite her sister's reaction to the tragedy (her decision to join a Carmelite convent, where she becomes a model of piety), it is obvious that such rhetoric is but empty verbiage in Sade's universe.[164] In Sade I see one vein of Enlightenment scientism meeting its logical end. Like the masochistic self-experimenters and the callous juvenile scientists I noted in chapter 3, Sade does not shrink from even the most inhumane experiments in his effort to uncover all the laws—physical and moral—that control human nature.

Les 120 Journées de Sodome gives ample evidence of Sade's rigor in this respect. The author's list of "passions" enjoyed by his characters not only includes 150 "simple" ways to experience pleasure (sodomy, masturbation, whipping, voyeurism, coprophilia) but also embraces 150 "complex passions" (child rape, rape of priests and nuns and other sacreligious acts, assault and torture of pregnant women), 150 "criminal passions" (bestiality, torture, mutilation, abortion, cannibalism), and 150 "murderous passions" (a variety of methods for murdering people, with an array of machines constructed for that purpose). The characters' motivations and methods project a similarly exhaustive distortion of concepts considered edifying or scientific. Perverting the much-lauded practice of charitable *bienfaisance,* for instance, Sade's magistrate Curval admits that "the downtrodden classes were those upon which he most enjoyed hurling the effects of his raging perfidy" and that he oftentimes would lure paupers home in order to poison, rape, or murder them.[165] Building on contemporary curiosity about hybrids and other "monsters" of nature, Sade's libertine impregnates goats and cows and watches with interest as they give birth to creatures half-way between man and beast. However, such experiments appear less motivated by scientific reasons (for example, to see what traits the hybrid would perpetuate) than by the desire to invent new creatures for sexual abuse. After the birth of the man-goat Sade's libertine notes: "Monster though it is, he embuggers it."[166] In a nightmarish parody of quack medicine, another libertine operates on a young man's gallstone, anus, and eyes and "knows just enough about surgery to botch all four operations; then he abandons the patient, giving him no further help and watching him expire."[167] These kinds of scenarios project a universe where ordinary people easily fall victim to the atrocious experiments of fiendish aristocrats, and there is no escape.

But Sade's ambitions transcend those of any other novelist we have seen. Although one might see his *120 Journées de Sodome* as manifesting the natural historian's concern for classification and taxonomy, and his prerevolutionary novel *Justine* as inscribing a distorted yet more or less accurate portrait of period fears (about anatomical study, for example, or rule by a scientific elite),[168] in the postrevolutionary *Juliette* Sade suggests an even more radical vision of scientific practice. In one of Sade's long philosophical digressions, Pope Braschi explains to Juliette why he finds such solace in murder. Nature is indifferent to mankind, Braschi states, and seeks only to create. Nature is a "great murderess herself"; thus she delights in the wars, famines, and pestilences that annihilate mankind because they give new energy to her re-creative powers (*Juliette,* 768). The scientist, like the murderer, is equally impotent to wreak a permanent alteration on nature's creatures, Sade writes, for she always puts them back together again after death (772).

How, then, can puny mankind try to serve nature? Through meddling, tampering, or otherwise destroying her creations. In a passage that directly counters the Enlightenment's image of civilization's powers to improve on things, Braschi expresses a cynical pessimism about mankind's capacity to effect change or even understand the world at all.[169] Unlike the confident images of rebirth or rejuvenation that we saw above, which expressed hopes of building a new nation on the foundations of the old, Sade's text argues that even total annihilation of existing structures would not change a thing. "So rend away, hack and hew, torment, break, massacre, burn, grind to dust, melt, in a word: reshape into however many forms all the productions of the three kingdoms [animal, mineral, vegetable], and you simply shall have done them so many services." Challenging writers such as Rousseau, who warned that man's technological ambitions might trespass against nature, Sade's "Holy man" scoffs: "How dare we think that Nature could instill in us impulses which cross her purposes? Eh, indeed, we may rather believe this: that she took all good care to place well outside our reach the power to do anything that might really discomfort or harm her." In conclusion, he exhorts his young charge to give free rein to all her impulses, no matter how cruel, for they too are created by nature. "As for what [nature] has put in our power to do, we have thereby her authorization to do it; all that is inside our grasp is ours to have; let us tamper with it, destroy it, change it without fear of harming her."[170]

This powerful passage creates a stunning endpoint to our discussion of perfectibility in the Enlightenment. Whereas the other writers we have studied have couched the discourse of perfectibility in terms of studying nature, observing her works, or attempting to help her achieve her highest perfection through mankind, Sade disavows any such anthropocentric hubris. In a gesture of unprecedented humility, he sees mankind as having no more impact than any other living creature such as a maggot, a blade of grass, or a mite (*Juliette,* 773; 3:878). Perfectibility was thus a ridiculous concept for Sade—unless one construes it to mean perfection of technique, skill, or vision, for in his profile of the libertine, Sade did eye a kind of perfection.

The works of both Réveroni Saint-Cyr and Sade symbolize the dangers of science and politics in the postrevolutionary age. Réveroni added an edge of *actualité* to Sadeian scenarios in two ways: by taking them out of the libertine's isolated torture chambers and placing them right in major European cities, and by using them to indict the freemasons, Rosicrucians, and other secret societies who supposedly misused science to serve their twisted schemes.[171] Conflating experimentalism with masonic secrets and counterrevolutionary plots, *Pauliska* provided a screen onto which readers could project their own fears about the unpredictable forces of nature and politics in the revolutionary age. But Sade's works pushed this sense of anxiety much farther, by evoking a world dictated by natural laws that deny everything people hold most dear—their individual significance, their knowledge, and their sense of belonging on earth. These works thus form nightmarish successors to the ambivalent *Emile* and prescient predecessors to Mary Shelley's *Frankenstein.* Whereas the villains in *Belinda* and *Secresy* realize their mistakes and make some effort to undo the damage, the mad scientists of *Justine, Pauliska,* and *Frankenstein* prove less tractable. The comic-book contrasts of good and evil in Sade and Réveroni leave no room for redemption; similarly, despite the blood shed in his name, Shelley's antihero never abandons the dream of scientific progress. These dystopias paint a world in which the human subject is prey to dangerous forces on all sides and private systems take precedence over humanitarian concerns. Although the regulatory public eye hovers in the background, its salutary power is rarely felt or sustained in any meaningful way. Their theories and apparatus may be antiquated, but in this uneasy tension between public exposure and private design these fictions foreshadow the ethical problems that human science has acquired in our own age.

EPILOGUE

Monstrous Imperfection

The flipside of perfecting or regenerating mankind is the potential for degenerating or destroying the human race. Fault lines ran through even the most optimistic Enlightenment writing on perfectibility, but in the 1790s they opened into an ideological schism. The idealism of republican discourse, which borrowed so much from progressive *philosophie,* degenerated in the works of counterrevolutionary writers into images of blood-thirsty sans-culottes committing murder and parricide and annihilating all that was good and humane. Regeneration could serve as a trope for nation-building, but it could also signify a monstrous attempt to challenge divine prerogatives to make or take away life. Sade's visions of perverted libertines creating monstrous hybrids or feeding a vicious force of nature played into this discourse, as did the hideous scientist in *Pauliska.* Equipped with his ill-begotten serum, Réveroni's villain achieves the ultimate feat and overturns nature by regaining his youth. His character and morality mirror the hubris of this experiment: the wrinkled, stooped old body rapt in lecherous desire suddenly becomes plump and rosy, only to disintegrate when called to a higher power at the end. In many respects, Mary Shelley's *Frankenstein* (1818) capped this vein in counter-Enlightenment thinking, for in this novel the perfected man *is,* literally, a monster, and the specter of his gigantic, virile wrath embodies all that could go wrong when the dream of perfectibility goes awry. The monster's threat draws on a vein of scientific writing that coupled biology with aesthetics to establish the increasingly normative human science that would dominate nineteenth-century thought. Because we have inherited this legacy, it is worthwhile to investigate its premises and to see how it complicated the issues of perfectibility.

As Roland Barthes has noted, "the *monstrous* is . . . never based on more than a shift in perception."[1] Although the Enlightenment imagination strove to imagine the ideal citizen of the ideal state, it was haunted by the possibility of failure. Failure took many forms. Some of the most frightening images of failure are found in the literature of miscegenation and degeneration, that is, the natural history writing about individuals who manifest symptoms resulting from racial mixing, hereditary inbreeding, or other aberrations on European notions of "normal" generation and aesthetics. The sight of individuals who defied classification troubled observers because it challenged beliefs in civilization's boundaries.[2] As a parting thought, I would like to return to the issues of defining mankind and defining monstrosity raised in chapter 1 and see how portrayals of three individuals—an albino named Geneviève, Edward Lambert ("Porcupine Man"), and the nameless giant in Shelley's *Frankenstein*—demonstrate the role of perception in the creation of that normative, infinitely perfectible creature known as mankind.

A tension between monstrosity and ordinariness figures prominently in eighteenth-century images of monsters. In broadsides, the names and costumes of performers at fairs conjured up an ambiance of showmanship, yet their physical descriptions insisted on ordinariness. Advertisements framed the anomaly with reassurances of normality, picturing the "Bearded Lady" playing a harpsichord, emphasizing the maternal instincts of the "French Female Hercules," or offering a maternal chaperone for private showings of the "Windsor Fairy."[3] This rhetoric served to normalize the monstrous[4] and to prove its authenticity.[5] Then as now, freak shows demonstrate how easy it is to trouble the ontological boundaries between man and beast, or the aesthetic distinctions between beautiful and ugly, with the appearance of a furry skin, a mute countenance, or a startling birth defect.

A different mode of perception characterized eighteenth-century "scientific" accounts of monsters. Instead of gawking at wonders, the scientific eye purported to penetrate the mysteries of humanity by weaving together observations and theories on aberrant genetics, improper obstetrics, or deviations in physiology. Yet much scientific writing proves highly subjective, particularly as regards aesthetics. The case of albinos illustrates this point. Many scientists were fascinated by the question of inheritance and found ample material for their theories in the albinos ("spotted" or "white Negroes") exhibited in Paris and London during the 1700s. They could readily be seen in sideshows such as Curtius's Palais Royal wax museum or in scientific circles such as the Académie des Sciences or the Royal Society.[6]

The theories of albinism that one finds in period science reveal the normative aesthetics that marked eighteenth-century debates about race. In the *Encyclopédie* entry "Nègres blancs," one finds four oft-cited causes for the albino's whiteness: racial mixing, maternal imaginations; leprous skin disease, and intercourse between an ape and a Negro woman.[7] But this article neglects the explanation favored by most scientists of the day, that is, the original whiteness of *Homo sapiens.* In Buffon's hugely popular *Histoire naturelle,* by contrast, mankind's original whiteness serves a powerful ideological function. Contrasting the frequency of albino birth among Negroes with the paucity of Negroes born to whites, Buffon declares: "Nature, in her most perfect exertions, made men white; and the same Nature, after suffering every possible change, still renders them white: but the natural or specific whiteness is very different from the individual or accidental."[8] The albino's whiteness represented an accidental vestige of an ideal prototype, occurring in a strain otherwise doomed to the fate of other sickly and degenerate types.

Just as eighteenth-century showmen tried to garner public interest by citing the physical beauty of their freaks, writers on race often invoked the category of aesthetic ugliness to support theories of degeneration. The Berlin *académicien* Maupertuis, for instance, emphasized the albino's homely appearance to argue that such traits were inferior inheritances. Calling the albino a "monster" whose pallor "only emphasizes his ugliness," Maupertuis posited that such individuals do not constitute a separate race but rather an "accident" of nature.[9] The revulsion felt by parents of albino children ought to keep such anomalies at a minimum, Maupertuis contended: "[W]e see only too often . . . races of cross-eyed, lame, gouty, and consumptive types: and unfortunately it does not take too many generations to establish them. But wise Nature, by the disgust that she inspires for these defects, did not want them to be perpetuated; all fathers and mothers do their best to smother them."[10] Although he sanctioned the forcible tactics used to repress such flaws, Maupertuis does not seem confident that even infanticide can limit mankind's degeneration. Despite their weak and unattractive appearance, the albino and other undesirable types threatened to beget generations of substandard beings in perpetuity.

Buffon, by contrast, sings the praises of two particularly attractive cases of albinism in the 1777 addition to his *Histoire naturelle.* Buffon's appreciative assessment of albinism may derive from his theory that it is an entirely innocuous, untransmittable trait. At issue are Marie Sabina, a "Spotted negro" *(enfant nègre pie),* and Geneviève, the woman seen in figure 22, a steel engraving from the 1836 edition. Both of these persons were key to Buffon's argument on skin pigmentation, although his comments draw more

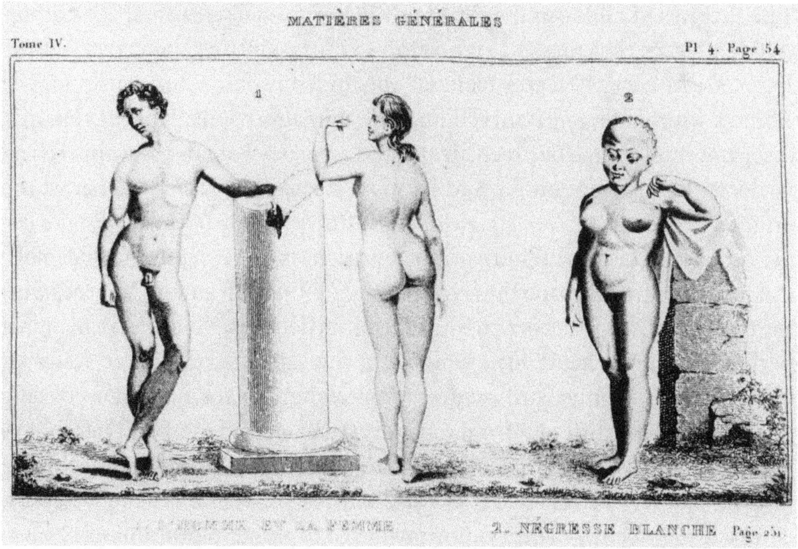

FIGURE 22

1. "L'Homme et la femme." 2. "Négresse blanche." Engravings for Georges Louis Leclerc, comte de Buffon, *Oeuvres complètes de Buffon avec les Supplémens* (Paris: P. Duménil, 1836), 4:54. Reproduced by permission of the Department of Special Collections, University Libraries, University of Notre Dame.

on aesthetics than on genetics. Describing his examination of Geneviève, Buffon reveals a voyeuristic eye probing every inch of her firm, sweet-smelling young body. Although he notes that her head is disproportionately large and her neck is too short, most of the author's comments compliment her aesthetic appeal. Her hands may be prematurely wrinkled, but her bottom is firm, as are her breasts which, we read, are "fat, round, very firm, and well placed."[11] Moreover, she conforms to Occidental norms of hygiene: her teeth are straight and beautifully white, her breath pleasant, and her armpits hairless. Enhancing this voyeuristic effect, Buffon comments on the emotions elicited by his probing. Sometimes her cheeks would blush, he writes, when she came near the fire or when she felt ashamed of disrobing in front of a man ("lorsqu'elle s'aprochoit du feu, ou qu'elle étoit remuée par la honte qu'elle avoit de se faire nue," 4:252). But Geneviève's superficial beauty could not change her morphological deficiency. Although she appeared nubile, if coupled with one of her own kind, Buffon asserts, she could never have a child because white Negro males cannot reproduce (4:253).

For all her comeliness, then, the albino was ultimately the last of her kind, a vestige of original integrity.

The engraving of Geneviève develops this theme of racial degeneration with significant details. Note the contrasting accessories provided for the Negro and the Caucasian models: the "White Negress" leans against a ruined wall, the remains of which are crumbling with age and the organic forces of nature, as seen in the plants growing on and around it. The normative "Man and Woman," on the contrary, pose alongside a powerful-looking Doric column whose base is cleanly delineated from the environment. Although the top is possibly broken, the column's smooth vertical lines evoke strength and solidity. These visual clues provide a powerful hint that the albino was perceived as a degenerate strain of the human race.

Like the albino, Edward Lambert—the so-called Porcupine Man—was considered to be the product of aberrant genetics. Lambert elicited much scientific discussion in England and in France when he appeared before the Royal Society in 1731 and 1755, the second time accompanied by one of his six children, who were born with the same condition. Buffon does not probe the mechanics of this inheritance, he merely notes Lambert in his *Histoire naturelle* as a dermatological enigma or kind of human snake (4:255). Others saw a more sinister potential in this man and his clan, claiming that their unusual inheritance could portend the beginnings of a monstrous new race. Quoting in 1758 from a report in the *Philosophical Transactions* (1755), the English scientist and artist George Edwards suggested the genetic havoc that could be wreaked by the virile Porcupine Man: "a race of people may be propagated by this man, having such rugged coats or coverings as himself: which, if it should ever happen, and the accidental origin be forgotten, it is not improbable that they may be deemed a different species of mankind." The visible difference of Porcupine Man thus supported a theory of monogenism, as Edwards concluded: "if all mankind were produced from one and the same stock, the black skin of the Ethiopians, &c. might be owing originally to some accidental cause."[12]

Most intriguing is the iconography that accompanies this text, in which we see a human being treated as a zoological anomaly. In the illustration to Edwards's *Gleanings of Natural History* (fig. 23), the human hand is juxtaposed to a botanical specimen, the branch of an apple service-tree. Edwards depicts the tree in the conventional botanical mode, thus visualizing the process of fructification by detailing buds, seeds, and a cross-section of a fruit.[13] But this tree branch is held aloft by an arm that has a dark brown bumpy growth on its skin. The reader's eye is drawn away from the careful

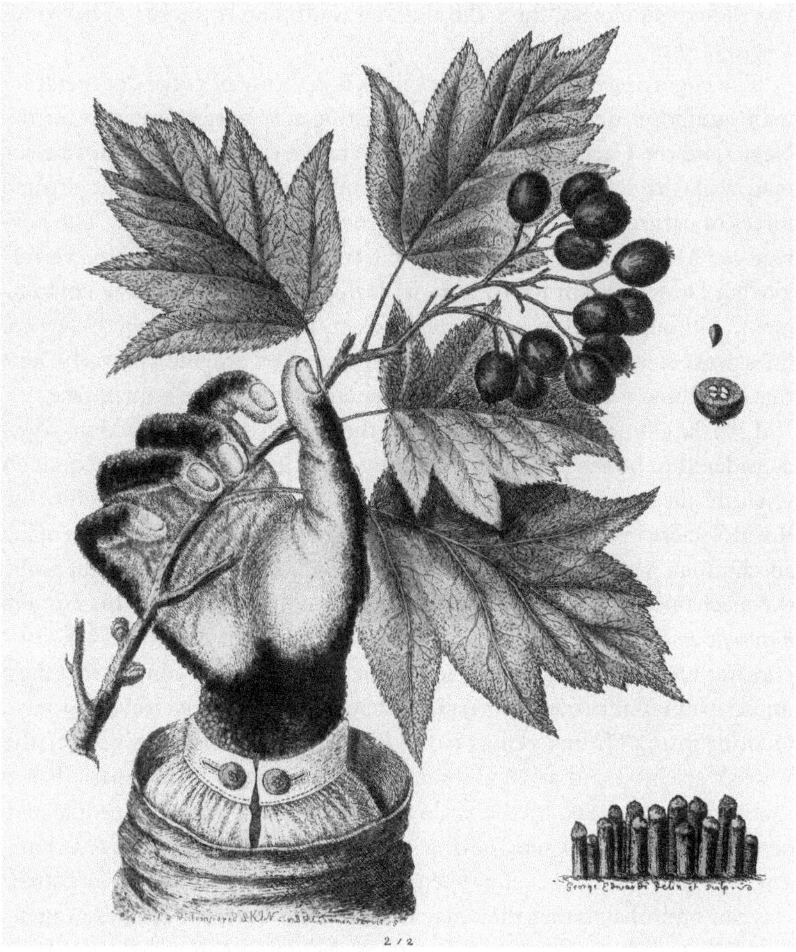

FIGURE 23

"The Hand of a Boy with a Distempered Skin, and a Branch of the Common Service-Tree." Copper-plate engraving by George Edwards in George Edwards, *Gleanings of Natural History* (London: Royal College of Physicians, 1758), plate 212. Reproduced by permission of the Department of Rare Books and Special Collections, Princeton University Library.

depiction of tree morphology to puzzle over the peculiar skin condition. This sense of estrangement is compounded by the magnified cross-section of the hand's wartish growth in the bottom right. This cross-section, which represents a topographical profile of protuberances ranging in size from 1/2″ to 3/4″ tall, was a monstrous exaggeration, to be sure. Here text and image reinforce the potent powers of generation and reiterate the morphological similarity between plant and human reproduction that was much discussed in eighteenth-century natural histories.[14] If planted in fertile soil, this tree will perpetuate itself indefinitely, just like the ugly Porcupine Man and his hearty clan.[15] Lambert's reproductive potential clearly troubled more than one observer, as did his celebrity. The wise Chinese philosopher in Goldsmith's *Citizen of the World* (1762) notes, à propos: "A man, though in his person faultless as an aerial genius, might starve; but if stuck over with hideous warts like a porcupine, his fortune is made for ever, and he may propagate the breed with impunity and applause."[16] Why did these unfortunates receive such anxious attention—and why do we continue to share the concern and fascination with degeneration?

In *Imagining Monsters,* Dennis Todd has advanced a theory of monstrosity relying on aesthetic response. As Todd explains, the visual appeal of people like the bearded lady, the albinos, and the Lambert clan relies on the observer's blindness toward his own faults, a titillating sense of danger, and a disregard for the ethics of isolating some people as less human than others. If the monster looked back, what might he see? In *Frankenstein,* Shelley adopted the monster's perspective to demonstrate how tenuous are distinctions between repugnance and aesthetic beauty and to warn readers about the devastating effects suffered by those whom society deems monstrous.

Whereas the environment was the key variable of the experiments discussed thus far, *Frankenstein* relies on a radically different theory of human mutability. Its scientist creates a new man not by manipulating external factors, or by inspiring a spiritual regeneration, but by rearranging human physiology. Unlike the omnipotent philosopher-artists of Condillac and Bonnet or the tutor-fathers of Rousseau and his followers, Shelley's scientist experiments in biology, not psychology or sociology. He creates a hybrid of dissimilar flesh, bones, and organs, thereby effecting a profound alteration in human-primate morphology: dead flesh reanimated, human and animal cells joined. The result is a man who bears visible traces of his difference. Although he is as uncultured as a newborn child, the creature's gigantic body is scarred by science and embodies a sinister kind of artificiality that challenges his human status.

The creature displays many key attributes of mankind as it was defined by the discourse of Enlightenment human science that I have discussed in this book. When the monster begins his tale, he describes his early existence as akin to that of feral children.[17] Like Victor de l'Aveyron, he survives an attack on his life and roves through the wilderness living on a vegetarian diet of roots and berries, forever on guard against the approach of beasts and men. He possesses the material self-sufficiency of *Homo ferus*—prodigious strength, agility, and the ability to withstand extremes of heat and cold—but he is emotionally weak and needy. As he later recalls: "I was a poor, helpless, miserable wretch; I knew, and could distinguish, nothing; but, feeling pain invade me on all sides, I sat down and wept" (68). When he finally enters society, people turn from him because of differences that are primarily aesthetic: his skin is a strange color, his body too big, his voice inarticulate. Speech is crucial here as it was in the earlier texts, but even after he learns to speak eloquently and express intelligent thoughts, society shuns him.[18]

The creature's early life also resonates with the sensationist texts discussed in chapter 2. Shelley's narrative of the creature's coming-to-awareness includes "animated statue" topoi: after an initial fear of the dark and feeling of chaos, he gradually learns that the natural environment is a source of pleasure, indeed a lyrical, anthropocentric *locus amoenus:* "I gradually saw plainly the clear stream that supplied me with drink, and the trees that shaded me with their foliage. I was delighted when I first discovered that a pleasant sound, which often saluted my ears, proceeded from the throats of the little winged animals who had often intercepted the light from my eyes" (69).[19] Like *Emile* and its sequels, *Frankenstein* is all about social reproduction.[20] But what or who was the scientist trying to create? And how did his theory lead to such devastating results?

As an experimental model, Frankenstein's project initially appears worthy because it respects the injunction to share results.[21] But its sinister potential quickly emerges when the scientist lets his dreams of personal glory outweigh his altruistic impulses, as when he marvels that "among so many men of genius . . . I alone should be reserved to discover so astonishing a secret" (30). Like the Gothic villain Valmont, Frankenstein refuses to share his secret system; and here as in *Secresy* the experiment eventually turns against its creator. Yet the novel's message about science and ambition is ultimately ambiguous. In his dying speech to Walton, Frankenstein justifies his actions and exhorts Walton's crew to try and find the Northeast Passage in order that they may "be hailed as the benefactors of your species; your name[s] adored . . . Oh! be men, or be more than men. Be steady to your purposes, and firm as a rock" (149–50). In the 1831 edition, Shelley would render Frankenstein a more culpable and penitent character, but in the original much ambivalence still cloaks his promethean dreams.[22] Beneath all the horrendous actions committed in this novel, there remains a belief in the nobility of great ambitions.

Frankenstein's practices reveal direct connections to the amateur experimentalism I have discussed. He practices vivisection, studies lightning, and experiments with the biological process of decay. Other real-life referents lie beneath his methods, too, such as robbing of graves and dissecting of corpses, which were widespread though unapproved practices among eighteenth- and nineteenth-century surgeons.[23] Like Beaurieu's remorseful "pupil," Frankenstein alludes to the guilty nature of his research by admitting: "I collected bones from charnel houses; and disturbed, with profane fingers, the tremendous secrets of the human frame" (32). As Révéroni does in the footnotes in *Pauliska,* Shelley makes references to contemporary scientific discoveries to stress the plausibility of Frankenstein's project. It does not seem so outrageous to animate dead tissue when we consider the work of Erasmus Darwin, who supposedly elicited spontaneous generation from a piece of vermicelli,[24] or the great feats of electrical experimentalists. The author declares: "galvanism has given token of such things: perhaps the component parts of a creature might be manufactured, brought together, and endued with vital warmth" (1831 ed., 172). Yet the 1818 preface undermines this sense of plausibility with an ambivalent disclaimer: "I shall not be supposed as according the remotest degree of serious faith to such an imagination; yet, in assuming it as the basis of a work of fancy, I have not considered myself as merely weaving a series of supernatural terrors" (5).

Ambivalence does not affect young Frankenstein's enthusiasm for science, however. Before discovering the electrical "principle of life," the eager student is urged on by his teacher Waldman, who describes modern-day scientists as men who "penetrate into the recesses of nature, and shew how she works in her hiding places. . . . They have acquired new and almost unlimited powers; they can command the thunders of heaven, mimic the earthquake, and even mock the invisible world with its own shadows" (28). As the historian Jan Golinski has shown, this rhetoric of unlimited potential echoes the writings of the famed chemist Humphry Davy, who was a family friend of the Godwins and widely considered a genius in the 1800s for his ability to manipulate chemical reactions into showy, reliable demonstrations.[25] In his writings Davy exulted the new instruments and powers of investigation available to scientists of his day, claiming that they enabled man "to interrogate nature with power, not simply as a scholar, passive and seeking only to understand her operations; but rather as a master, active with his own instruments."[26] Such excessive ambitions were not Davy's alone: researchers in chemistry celebrated their new techniques, such as the isolation of oxygen, with similarly messianic fervor. Thus John Robison remarked in 1803: "We are now admitted into the laboratory of nature herself."[27]

But Waldman goes beyond Davy, who admitted being concerned about uncontrolled experimentation, by endorsing the equivocal morality that will guide his student in *Frankenstein:* "The labours of men of genius, however erroneously directed, scarcely ever fail in ultimately turning to the solid advancement of mankind" (28). Frankenstein transcends all in his ambitions; he envisions ushering in a new and superior form of life on earth: "Life and death appeared to me ideal bounds, which I should first break through, and pour a torrent of light into our dark world. A new species would bless me as its creator and source; many happy and excellent natures would owe their being to me" (32). As the preface warned, this experiment may stray from the plausible into the Gothic realm of "supernatural terror."

The budding scientist's excessive ambitions betray his inexperience, but they also strike a timely note, speaking to the popular distrust of experimentalism that we saw so clearly in chapter 5. Contrary to earlier scientists such as the physiologist Haller, who proudly listed the hundreds of vivisections he performed as evidence for his nerve theories,[28] Frankenstein expresses shame and horror over his lab work: "Who shall conceive the horrors of my secret toil, as I dabbled among the unhallowed damps of the grave, or tortured the living animal to animate the lifeless clay?" (32). When he glimpses the creature's first sign of life, he is stricken with horror, as is the creature himself on seeing his own body. (These emotions are powerfully evoked in the frontispiece engraved by Chevalier, fig. 24). Responding in part to the hostility that greeted her first edition, Shelley amplified Victor's guilt in the 1831 edition by stressing the scientist's unhappy destiny. Whereas chapter 2 originally described Victor's visit to Waldman's laboratory as a "memorable" day that gave his life a new sense of purpose, the 1831 edition interrupted such hopes with a doleful warning: "destiny was too potent, and her immutable laws had decreed my utter and terrible destruction."[29] It is no coincidence that Frankenstein commits his work in secret or calls his laboratory a "workshop of filthy creation" (32). The awful figures created in the confines of his Ingolstadt garret and his Scottish hut form a stunning reminder of the public-private dichotomy we earlier saw in Boyle's writings on the experimental method. *Frankenstein* shows by default the crucial function played by the public eye in regulating scientific inquiry.

This moral ambivalence is particularly marked in the account of Frankenstein's second experiment: the attempt to create a female. By the time he agrees to make a second creature, the scientist is no longer driven by ambition and he is well aware of his awful power. To hide this scheme from the public eye, he travels to a remote isle off the coast of Scotland. The hut he inhabits is miserably primitive, but at least it allows him to work "ungazed at and unmolested" (113). The apparatus is but vaguely described, apart from mention of "chemical instruments" and a collection of necessary

FIGURE 24

"By the glimmer of the half-extinguished light, I saw the dull, yellow eye of the creature open: it breathed hard, and a convulsive motion agitated its limbs. . . . I rushed out of the room." Frontispiece by W. Chevalier for Mary Shelley, *Frankenstein; or, the Modern Prometheus* (London: H. Colburn and R. Bentley, 1831). Reproduced by permission of the British Library.

"materials," but en route to Scotland Frankenstein makes a significant stop in London to meet with philosophers whose knowledge and discoveries are of "indispensable use" for his plan (104–5).

This stopover is interesting for what it reveals about *Frankenstein*'s borrowings from contemporary science. Marilyn Butler has convincingly argued that Shelley is referring here to the celebrated "vitalist debate" of 1814–19: a series of public lectures by two professors at the Royal College of Surgeons, the vitalist John Abernethy and the materialist William Lawrence.[30] Desacralizing human reproduction and calling it an issue worthy of national concern, Lawrence proposed bold experiments in human breeding to improve what he saw as a degenerate species. Placing mankind on the same level as domestic animals as regards inherited traits, Lawrence declared:

> A superior breed of human beings could only be produced by selections and exclusions similar to those so successfully employed in rearing our most valuable animals. Yet, in the human species, when the object is of such consequence, the principle is almost entirely overlooked. Hence all the native deformities of mind and body, which spring up so plentifully in our artificial mode of life, are handed down to posterity, and tend by their multiplication and extension to degrade the race.[31]

These poor habits were worse among the civilized than the savage, Lawrence claimed, and worst of all among the ruling class, where the fatal effects of inbreeding had created generations of idiots. Given his desire to embrace the cause of mankind, it is somewhat ironic to learn that Lawrence was immediately denounced by his colleagues at the College of Surgeons for "propagating opinions detrimental to society" and "endeavoring to enforce them for the purpose of loosening those restraints, in which the welfare of mankind depends."[32] The memory of the recent "experiments" in France were perhaps too raw to allow for this kind of speculation, even in the name of the public good.

It is significant that Lawrence's proposal was to be enacted through organic, not artificial means—by marriages between strong and handsome people. In the debate on vital energy, Lawrence ridiculed the vitalist notion that the life principle was some kind of extraneous element, analogous to electricity, that could be added or extracted from bodies. Rather, he argued, animation was an integral component of organic life, to be studied only by close observation of living creatures' actions over time. According to Butler, Shelley undermines her scientist's authority in *Frankenstein* by showing him operating on "superseded" vitalist ideas, such as using chemical instruments to infuse the "spark of being" into dead matter ("Radical Science," 307). But the fact remains that his methods are successful. The failure of the second experiment is due not to the scientist's lack of expertise but rather to his own decision—prompted by moral qualms—to abort.

Alone in his squalid hut, Frankenstein becomes haunted by visions of female potency run amok. His suspicions about female sexuality mushroom into a full-fledged panic about uncontrollable reproduction. This anxiety emerges powerfully in a hallucinatory list of the female monster's potential crimes:

> she might become ten thousand times more malignant than her mate, and delight, for its own sake, in murder and wretchedness. He had sworn to quit the neighbourhood of man, and hide himself in deserts; but she had not; and she, who in all probability was to become a thinking and reasoning animal, might refuse to comply with a compact made before her creation. They might even hate each other. . . . She also might turn with disgust from him to the superior beauty of man; she might quit him, and he be again alone, exasperated by the fresh provocation of being deserted by one of his own species. Even if they were to leave Europe, and inhabit the deserts of the new world . . . a race of devils would be propagated upon the earth, who might make the very existence of the species of man a condition precarious and full of terror. (114)

This list recalls contemporary medical theories of the female body, such as the abnormal passions and cannibalistic desires invoked by La Mettrie and other doctors in chapter 1, as well as the melodramatic discourse of women's dangerous "regeneration" in French revolutionary writings we saw in chapter 5. Woman's potency—for good or evil—was believed to lie in her procreative potential, which was also a political force as in the image of the mother as nursemaid to the citizenry. Once Frankenstein realizes his inability to control this creature's fertility, he has no other choice but to tear the body limb from limb (114). As Judith Halberstam aptly remarks: "[Frankenstein] can build a man from the corpses of animals and humans but fashioning a woman demands that he construct and enervate a subject that is, in its future function at least, all body."[33] Ironically, it is the scientist's decision to abort this experiment for moral reasons that generates the greatest immorality of the novel: the creature's killing spree, which destroys the entire Frankenstein family.

But why does Frankenstein endow his first being with such dangerous strength and enormous bulk? Why create a giant? He claims that the decision was based on practicality. "The minuteness of the parts formed a great hindrance to my speed," he writes, so he made a being of "gigantic stature" about "eight feet in height, and proportionately large" (31–32). I contend that the choice of a giant was also motivated by the author's eye for aesthetics. Giants were traditionally associated with the grotesque, but they also carried an air of menace.[34] Walter Stephens reminds us that "[t]hrough most of his history in Western thought, the Giant was not only defined as Other, that is, from a differing and threatening culture, but he was often also conceptualized as inhuman, thus becoming a symbol of . . . cosmic terror."[35] Shelley transposes this connotation into a Gothic-Romantic mode. Her giant mirrors the landscape behind him—as when his dark form is silhouetted against the wild chiaroscuro of trees lashing about in a lightning storm or the stark blue whiteness of alpine glaciers. He is not only an inhabitant of this wild landscape, he incarnates its attributes. To stop him would be like trying to "overtake the winds, or confine a mountain-stream with a straw" (50). Both share the "greatness of dimension" praised by Burke for its sublime effects. Like the peaks and crevasses of awesome Mont Blanc, the creature excites ideas of superhuman pain and danger.

For personal and professional reasons, Frankenstein soon regrets the decision to build an oversize man. When provoked, the giant proves a mighty adversary. The specter of his angry presence lurking in the shadows after William's murder or jeering fiendishly through the window after Elizabeth's death is daunting indeed (48, 136). One might interpret the creature's menacing aspect as a political metaphor of the French Revolution: he looms over the Frankenstein household like the "many-headed monster" of the masses who threatened the French nation with their ferocious energy *(le peuple, mangeur de rois)*.[36] More pointedly, the creature threatens Frankenstein by revealing the shortcomings of his skills as surgeon and scientist. Once he comes to life it becomes obvious that his skin and lips are horribly discolored, his eyes are watery, and his skin is uneven—it barely covers the body at some spots, it is excessively wrinkled at others (34). Clearly, this scientist's handiwork has failed. By moving off the laboratory table and into real life, the creature loses any cachet of humanity that he once had for the scientist, who admits in horror: "I had gazed on him while unfinished; he was ugly then; but when those muscles and joints were rendered capable of motion, it became a thing such as even Dante could not have conceived" (35). But Frankenstein had endeavored to make his creature a thing of beauty. In spite of excessive height, the monster was supposed to be handsome: "His limbs were in proportion, and I had selected his features as beautiful . . . his hair was of a lustrous black, and flowing; his teeth of a pearly whiteness" (34). The 1831 frontispiece (fig. 24) captures this often forgotten aspect of the story by showing the creature as a physically attractive figure.

As Todd has noted in descriptions of sideshow freaks, the device of superimposing pleasing aesthetics onto deformed bodies normalizes the monster and stresses his ordinariness (*Imagining Monsters,* 157). This same strategy structures key passages in *Frankenstein.* By stressing the creature's ordinary virtues, the narrator is able to parry the observer's repugnance and suggest that "human" and "monstrous" are not mutually exclusive categories. The breakdown of this dichotomy manifests itself in two ways: in juxtapositions of the grotesque and the sublime, and in the psychological oscillation between repugnance and fascination. It is most clearly seen in scenes in which other characters respond to the creature. When they listen to him with eyes closed, the creature's appealing sensitivity and intelligence make them sympathize with him and pity his dilemma.[37] It is only when sight is allowed to influence hearing that the creature becomes a supernatural terror whose "unearthly ugliness rendered it almost too horrible for human eyes" (65). Examples of this kind of oscillating perception run throughout the novel, as seen in the creature's encounter with old blind man De Lacey (vol. 2, chap. 7), or the creature's final exchange with Walton on the Polar Sea (vol. 3, chap. 7). Most significant is the scene where he tells Frankenstein the long narrative of his life and requests a mate in the flickering shadows of firelight. After listening in silent fascination to the creature's voice, Frankenstein recalls: "His words had a strange effect upon me. I compassioned him, and sometimes felt a wish to console him; but when I looked upon him, when I saw the filthy mass that moved and talked, my heart sickened, and my feelings were altered to those of horror and hatred" (99).

Is aesthetics alone to blame for this repulsion? Perhaps not. Mellor has argued that it is the creature's morphological make-up, that is, his mix of dead and living matter, animal and human flesh, that repulsed observers and relegated him to bottom of the evolutionary ladder (*Mary Shelley,* 101). But such reactions may also be due to his virile giantism, which had particular significance for Shelley's readers. Although sideshow giants were almost invariably strongmen, in the texts of teratology—a new science that emerged in the early nineteenth century—giants were portrayed as weak and dull-witted.[38] Their origins were believed to be accidental and their progeny impossible. Like the dwarf, the giant was thought to be sterile. In the "Moral and Physical Profile of Giants," presented in Isidore Geoffroy Saint-Hilaire's groundbreaking 1832 work of teratology, for instance, the giant is characterized by his lymphatic temperament, delicate complexion, physical deformity, and impotence. To explain the apparent incongruity between the giant's huge size and puny strength, Geoffroy Saint Hilaire used an organic metaphor of excess energy expended in development: "The principle of life seems to wear out faster in them because of the extremely increased volume of their organs, and most [giants] perish as if exhausted, after achieving their enormous and rapid growth."[39] *Frankenstein*'s giant, however, suffers none of these flaws; his virility underlines his terrifying powers.

Mellor posits that the monster's genesis—the mechanical rather than evolutionary means by which he was created—made Frankenstein's project all the more objectionable.[40] She neglects to mention, however, the earlier case of a philosopher who was attacked for attempting just such a feat, that is, trying to grow a giant. According to a variety of sources, Frankenstein had a real-life predecessor in the 1750s who created a giant through physiological means. This tale concerns Bishop George Berkeley, a controversial figure in eighteenth-century metaphysics, who supposedly created a kind of hothouse in his home, confined an indigent youth named Cornelius MacGrath (or Magrath) therein, and created the famous seven-foot-tall "Irish Giant" who would go on to earn a living as a sideshow attraction and specimen of abnormal development. After he died in 1760, his cadaver was seized by students of Trinity College, Dublin, where his skeleton was preserved and exhibited for many years.[41]

The story of Berkeley and MacGrath is only partially true—MacGrath did stay with Berkeley for a while[42]—but it is most intriguing as evidence of how experimentation could be articulated in Frankensteinian terms well before the publication of Shelley's novel. It is equally significant, in view of our history of experimentalism, that explanations of Berkeley's experiment became invested with increasingly alarmist undertones in the postrevolutionary period. For eighteenth-century chroniclers, the case was merely the whim of an already notorious eccentric. Thomas Campbell, in his *Philosophical Survey of the South of Ireland* (1778), ridiculed Berkeley as that "subtle doctor, who denied the existence of matter" and described the experiment thus: "The bishop had a strange fancy to know whether it was not in the power of art to increase the human stature. . . . He made his essay according to his preconceived theory, whatever it might be, and the consequence was, that he became seven feet high in his sixteenth year."[43] Although the boy "contracted an universal imbecility of body and mind, and died of old age at twenty," this scheme is plausible and even forgivable, declares Campbell, because Berkeley was known to try the most extravagant experiments and almost killed himself in one foray into self-experimentation (*Philosophical Survey*, 187–88).

By the 1830s, however, observers evinced more serious misgivings about this scheme. Despite his objective stance, the teratologist Isidore Geoffroy Saint-Hilaire expressed righteous indignation at Berkeley's experiment in the *Histoire des anomalies* (1832), declaring: "The experiment succeeded completely, I mean for the philosopher; for poor Macgrath, who had suffered from symptoms of old age even in his youth, died at age twenty, victim of an experiment that we cannot entirely excuse, even knowing the laudable intentions behind it."[44] Twenty years later this story was inflated into a kind of Faustian nightmare in Michel Masson's collection of famous children (*Les Enfants célèbres,* 6th ed., 1859). Here we find MacGrath in a chapter on "martyred children" *(les enfants martyrs)* alongside Kaspar Hauser, in a narrative that demonizes Berkeley in terms reminiscent of the moralistic 1831 *Frankenstein:* "Alas! yes, science can be impious! thus that sublime knowledge, given to man for the betterment of humanity, is more guilty than the rudest ignorance, when it inspires the learned to bring about the misfortune of one individual, even if it were for the good of all others."[45] Its origins may be obscure and its methods may be organic instead of mechanical, but the legend of Berkeley and MacGrath tapped into many of the same anxieties as the story of Victor Frankenstein and his monster. There is one crucial difference, however, and that is the potential to reproduce. Whereas MacGrath's premature senescence rendered him a figure of pathos, the strength and virility of Frankenstein's giant made him terrifying.

Frankenstein synthesizes ambient fears about human science in its scientist and his awful creature. In his persona of ambition gone berserk, Frankenstein incarnates the dangers of amoral science and unchecked technology that haunt our nightmares still today. But the image of the gigantic yet morally immature creature forms an even more compelling site of postrevolutionary anxieties. Like the much-maligned albino and the ugly Porcupine Man, the creature's aesthetically loathsome body symbolizes the flaws within and its potential to contaminate the species. His body also symbolizes the unsuccessful science of his maker, proof of Frankenstein's imperfect knowledge and poor workmanship. For his part, Frankenstein tries to respond to the creature's dilemma, but there too he fails miserably. As if following the recommendations of scientists such as Maupertuis, who urged the annihilation of such degenerate strains, Shelley's scientist blocks his creature's capacity to reproduce. But even he cannot stop the creature's desire for companionship and learning. Failing these key ingredients of social acceptance, the creature spirals into a murderous hatred of all mankind.

In the dialectic between the creature and the creator, we see a metaphor for the exalted dreams of Enlightenment perfectibility in a fatal confrontation with the sobering realities of the postrevolutionary age. *Frankenstein* resonated with readers who looked back on their recent past as a "horrible time" and considered the revolution not a happy new beginning but rather "a monstrous phenomenon" that "nothing regular could explain or produce."[46] Like the early reformers of the revolution, Shelley's scientist appeared to have the expertise to perfect mankind, but his experiment was ultimately a failure. It sank for technical reasons—the limitations of his science—and moral reasons—the scientist's stunted sense of empathy for the "child" of his labors. He may have manifested more humanity than Maupertuis's cold-blooded infanticides, but Frankenstein withheld the crucial care needed to humanize this monster.

Our own age's fascination with genetically altered livestock, vegetables, and "Frankenfoods" has launched us into a real-life confrontation with a later version of this same experimental mentality that seems to be running amok. In the name of progress, scientists have penetrated nature's secrets and forced her into strange new combinations. But is mankind ready to bear the consequences? Only time will tell.

NOTES

INTRODUCTION

1. Eighteenth-century texts typically describe general traits belonging to all humankind under the umbrella term *l'homme* (man). *L'homme* only takes on the gender-specific value of "male" in passages that specifically contrast *man* and *woman* (*la femme* or *le sexe*). In order to capture the universalistic flavor of period language, throughout this book I use the terms *mankind, humanity,* and *humankind* interchangeably. When issues of gender are at stake, I use *man* and *woman.*

2. Adam Kuper, *The Chosen Primate: Human Nature and Cultural Diversity* (Cambridge: Harvard University Press, 1994), 102.

3. Although Stafford is right about the abundance of pseudoscientific paraphernalia in fiction of the 1790s and 1800s, she underestimates the ideological charge carried by such objects, claiming: "The old-regime fascination with magic, illusion, and science thus flowed unimpeded into an outlandish romanticism, equally smitten by electrical charges, moving gadgets, freaks, and funambulism. . . . Paintings and novels during the first two decades of the nineteenth century likewise served up a curious mixture of scenes culled from the laboratory, hospital, studio, and sanctuary." Barbara Maria Stafford, *Artful Science: Enlightenment, Entertainment, and the Eclipse of Visual Education* (Cambridge: MIT Press, 1994), 186.

4. Juvenel de Carlencas, *Essai sur l'histoire des Belles Lettres, des Sciences et des Arts,* 3d ed. (Lyon, 1740–44,): 2:86. On the epistemological implications of this terminological indeterminacy, see Georges Gusdorf, *Dieu, la nature, l'homme au siècle des Lumières,* vol. 5 of *Les Sciences humaines et la pensée occidentale* (Paris: Payot, 1972), 5:243–69.

5. Mary Terrall, "The Gendering of Science" in *The Sciences in Enlightened Europe,* ed. William Clark, Jan Golinski, and Simon Schaffer (Chicago: University of Chicago Press, 1999), 260.

6. Kenneth MacLean, *John Locke and English Literature of the Eighteenth Century* (New Haven: Yale University Press, 1936), 140.

7. *Journal de Bruxelles,* 10 January 1784, 81, cited in Robert Darnton, *Mesmerism and the End of the Enlightenment in France* (Cambridge: Harvard University Press, 1968), 27.

8. "La pratique de faire des *expériences* est fort en usage en Europe depuis quelques années, ce qui a multiplié les connoissances philosophiques et les a rendues plus communes." Denis Diderot, Jean le Rond D'Alembert et al., "Expérience," *Encyclopédie, ou dictionnaire raisonné des sciences, des arts, et des métiers* (Neuchâtel: Samuel Faulche, 1765), 6:297. All translations in this book are mine unless otherwise noted.

9. Cited in George Warren Gignilliat Jr., *The Author of Sandford and Merton: A Life of Thomas Day, Esq.* (New York: Columbia University Press, 1932), 80.

10. Popularizations include such best-sellers as Francesco Algarotti, *Il Newtonianismo per le dame* (1737); Abbé Pluche, *Le Spectacle de la nature* (1732–50); John Newbery, *Tom Telescope's Philosophy of Tops and Balls* (1761); Abbé Jean Antoine Nollet, *Lettres sur l'éléctricité (III) dans lesquelles on trouvera les principaux phénomènes qui ont été découverts depuis 1760* (1767). For more on scientific societies, see Roger Hahn, *The Anatomy of a Scientific Institution: The Paris Academy of Sciences, 1666–1803* (Berkeley: University of California Press, 1971); R. E. Schofield, *The Lunar Society of Birmingham* (Oxford: Oxford University Press, 1963); and J. E. McClellan, *Science Reorganized: Scientific Societies in the Eighteenth Century* (New York: Columbia University Press, 1985). The influence of these societies was so pervasive that by the 1780s the proceedings of scientific societies were widely used as textbooks. See Henri Roddier, *Jean-Jacques Rousseau en Angleterre au XVIIIe siècle: L'oeuvre et l'homme* (Paris: Boivin, 1950), 172.

11. Vandermonde's vision of prenatal care is indebted to traditional concerns, such as the importance of arranging suitable matches, avoiding infelicitous times of conception, and cautions about maternal imagination. For more on this discourse in the early modern age, see Marie-Hélène Huet, *Monstrous Imagination* (Cambridge: Harvard University Press, 1993). After birth, the child's existence is conceived in a mechanical model of cause and effect, i.e., his potential may be enhanced by a careful combination of diet, clothing, pedagogy, physical training, and so forth.

12. "Puisque l'on est parvenu à perfectionner la race des chevaux, des chiens, des chats, des poules, des pigeons, des sereins [sic], pourquoi ne ferait-on aucune tentative sur l'espèce humaine?" Vandermonde, *Essai sur la manière de perfectionner l'espèce humaine* (Paris, 1756), x. For more on this proto-eugenic vein in eighteenth-century thinking, see Anne Carol, *Histoire de l'eugénisme en France: Les médecins et la procréation XIXe–XXe siècle* (Paris: Editions du Seuil, 1995).

13. Robert Boyle, "Of the Usefulness of Natural Philosophy," in *The Works of the Honourable Robert Boyle* (London: A. Millar, 1744), 1:465.

14. Cited in J. L. Heilbron, *Electricity in the 17th and 18th Centuries: A Study of Early Modern Physics* (Berkeley: University of California Press, 1979), 318.

15. For some particularly graphic cases showing the ill effects that human subjects could suffer from experiments using electricity, see Stuart Strickland, "The Ideology of Self-Knowledge and the Practice of Self-Experimentation," *Eighteenth-Century Studies* 31, no. 4 (summer 1998): 453–71.

16. Schaffer's work has been particularly illuminating; see Simon Schaffer, "Self-Evidence," *Critical Inquiry* 18 (1992): 327–62; and Schaffer, "Natural Philosophy and Public Spectacle in the Eighteenth Century," *History of Science* 21 (1983): 1–43. See also Jan Golinski, *Science as Public Culture: Chemistry and Enlightenment in Britain, 1760–1820* (Cambridge: Cambridge University Press, 1992), and Geoffrey Sutton, *Science for*

a Polite Society: Gender, Culture, and the Demonstration of Enlightenment (Boulder: Westview, 1995). Stafford's *Artful Science* has been useful for understanding the visual conventions governing scientific entertainment.

17. G. S. Rousseau, "Science Books and Their Readers in the Eighteenth Century," in *Books and Their Readers in Eighteenth-Century England,* ed. Isabel Rivers (Leicester, U.K.: Leicester University Press, 1982), 197–255.

18. Serge Soupel, "Science and Medicine and the Mid-Eighteenth-Century Novel: Literature and the Language of Science," in *Literature and Science and Medicine,* ed. Serge Soupel and Roger Hambridge (Los Angeles: William Andrews Clark Memorial Library, UCLA, 1982), 3–43, esp. 31.

19. Anne C. Vila, *Enlightenment and Pathology: Sensibility in the Literature and Medicine of Eighteenth-Century France* (Baltimore: Johns Hopkins University Press, 1998), chap. 5.

20. John Bender, "Enlightenment Fiction and the Scientific Hypothesis," *Representations* 61 (winter 1998): 6–28, esp. 20.

CHAPTER ONE

1. Lucien Malson, *Les Enfants sauvages* (Paris: UGE 10/18, 1964), translated as *Wolf Children and the Problem of Human Nature,* trans. Edmund Fawcett, Peter Ayrton, and Joan White (New York: New Left, 1972). For the list of cases, see 39–43.

2. The most prominent scholarship on wild children includes Harlan Lane, *The Wild Boy of Aveyron* (Cambridge: Harvard University Press, 1976); J. A. L. Singh and R. M. Zingg, *Wolf-Children and Feral Man* (New York, Harper and Brothers, 1939); Douglas Keith Candland, *Feral Children and Clever Animals: Reflections on Human Nature* (New York: Oxford University Press, 1993); Roger Shattuck, *The Forbidden Experiment: The Story of the Wild Boy of Aveyron* (New York: Farrar, Straus and Giroux, 1980); Franck Tinland, *L'Homme sauvage: 'Homo ferus' et 'Homo sylvestris,' de l'animal à l'homme* (Paris: Payot, 1968); Thierry Gineste, *Victor de l'Aveyron: Dernier enfant sauvage, premier enfant fou* (Paris: Hachette, 1993); and Arnold Gesell, *Wolf Child and Human Child: Being a Narrative Interpretation of the Life History of Kamala, the Wolf Girl* (New York: Harper and Brothers, 1940). See also Michael Newton, *The Child of Nature: The Feral Child and the State of Nature* (Ph.D. diss., University College, London, 1996).

3. Victor has largely been appropriated by educational psychologists and behavioralists who have used his case to prove that any child can be socialized by proper stimulus-response techniques, whereas Kaspar's ongoing attraction has derived mainly from his mysterious origins and untimely death. For a brief summary of popular literature on Kaspar and Victor, see Leslie Fieldler, *Freaks: Myths and Images of the Secret Self* (New York: Simon and Schuster, 1978), 154–62.

4. Tinland, *L'Homme sauvage,* and Madame H——t [Hecquet], *Histoire d'une jeune fille sauvage trouvée dans les bois à l'âge de dix ans,* ed. Franck Tinland (Bordeaux: Editions Ducros, 1971).

5. The "bizarre episode" summation is from an anonymous reader's report on my application for a fellowship for college teachers, National Endowment for the Humanities, 1994. Malson includes Marie-Angélique in his list of hoaxes, writing that her story is "filled with details more reminiscent of fairy tale than fact," *Wolf Children and the Problem of Human Nature,* 62. Robert Zingg perpetuated this assessment in his 1939 work by echoing earlier writers who lamented that "the sources on the *Puella campanica* are

inadequate, or at least incommensurate with the importance of this case" and concluding that "through the defect in the records as to her exposure to isolation no scientific conclusions seem justified" (Singh and Zingg, 258).

6. Among the many great thinkers and *philosophes* of this age who practiced medicine or had received medical training are Linnaeus, Locke, Tyson, La Mettrie, Barthez, Maupertuis, Mandeville, Jaucourt, Hans Sloane, Vicq d'Azyr, Pinel, and Cabanis. As Ménuret de Chambaud—a principal contributor to the *Encyclopédie*—remarked: "Perhaps it is true that in order to be a good moralist, one must be an excellent doctor." Cited in Roselyne Rey, "Hygiène et souci de soi dans la pensée des Lumières," *Communications* 56 (1993): 25.

7. Ann Thomson, *Materialism and Society in the Mid Eighteenth Century: La Mettrie's 'Discours préliminaire'* (Geneva: Droz, 1981), 41.

8. Locke, *An Essay Concerning Human Understanding,* ed. Alexander Campbell Fraser (1690; reprint, New York: Dover, 1959), 2:73. Further references appear in the text.

9. Tinland, *L'Homme sauvage,* offers an illuminating analysis of these debates.

10. See, e.g., Diderot's rebuttal of the *méthodiste* Linnaeus in *Pensées sur l'interprétation de la nature* in *Oeuvres complètes,* ed. Jean Varloot (Paris: Hermann, 1981), 9:75–77. In his *Elements de physiologie,* Diderot takes a more conciliatory stance, admitting the difficulties of identifying the traits that distinguish one species from another and the necessarily slow process by which natural historians contributed to refine the chain of being. See Diderot, *Elements de physiologie* in *Oeuvres complètes,* ed. J. Assézat (Paris: Garnier, 1875) 9:253.

11. For more on European legends associated with apes, consult H. W. Janson, *Apes and Ape Lore in the Middle Ages and the Renaissance* (London: Warburg Institute, 1952; reprint, Nendeln, Liechtenstein: Kraus Reprint, 1976). Claude Blanckaert charts the fluid boundaries between man and ape in European thought of the early modern period in "Premier des singes, dernier des hommes?" *Alliage* 7–8 (spring–summer 1991):113–29.

12. Michel Foucault, *Discipline and Punish: The Birth of the Prison,* trans. Alan Sheridan (New York: Vintage, 1979), 149. On Linnaeus's concept of science as a process of logical classification, see James L. Larson, *Reason and Experience: The Representation of the Natural Order in the Work of Carl von Linné* (Berkeley: University of California Press, 1971).

13. Carl Linnaeus, *Systema naturae* (1735; facsimile of the first edition), trans. M. S. J. Engel-Ledeboer and H. Engel (Nieuwkoop, The Netherlands: B. de Graaf, 1964), 30.

14. Knut Hagberg, *Carl Linnaeus,* trans. Alan Blair (New York: E. P. Dutton, 1953), 93.

15. Linnaeus, *Systema naturae,* 18. Linnaeus's later experiments in hybridization, however, raised doubts over this doctrine of fixity; in later editions of the *Systema naturae,* Linnaeus no longer insisted on fixed species. See Roland Mousnier, *Progrès scientifique et technique au XVIIIe siècle* (Paris: Plon, 1958), 88–94, for more on this issue.

16. Jean Duvignaud claims that it was impossible for eighteenth-century thinkers to conceive of links between apes and man in *Le Langage perdu: Essai sur la différence anthropologique* (Paris: Presses Universitaires de France, 1973), 39.

17. Janson, *Apes and Ape Lore,* 335.

18. For more on Buffon's dispute with Linnaean method, consult Phillip R. Sloan, "The Buffon-Linnaeus Controversy," *Isis* 67, no. 238 (spring 1976): 356–75.

19. Georges Louis Leclerc, comte de Buffon, *Natural History, General and Particu-*

lar, by the Count Buffon, trans. William Smellie (London: T. Cadell and W. Davies, 1812), 10:25. "L'âme, la pensée, la parole ne dépendent donc pas de la forme ou de l'organisation du corps; rien ne prouve mieux que c'est un don particulier et fait à l'homme seul, puisque l'orang-outang, qui ne parle ni ne pense, a néanmoins le corps, les membres, les sens, le cerveau, et la langue entièrement semblables à l'homme, puisqu'il peut faire ou contrefaire tous les mouvemens, toutes les actions humaines, et que cependant il ne fait aucun acte de l'homme." Buffon, *Oeuvres complètes de Buffon avec les Supplémens* (Paris: P. Duménil, 1836), 6:259. In this and all other notes in which a citation from a published translation is followed by the original French, publication information is given first for the translation, then for the French text. Buffon's *Histoire naturelle générale et particulière* was a massive enterprise, lavishly illustrated and published in thirty-six volumes from 1749 to 1783 with the help of his collaborators (notably the naturalist Daubenton) and his successors.

20. "On voit que les pies et les perroquets peuvent proférer des paroles ainsi que nous, et toutefois ne peuvent parler ainsi que nous, c'est-à-dire en témoingnant qu'ils pensent ce qu'ils disent." René Descartes, *Discours de la méthode* (Paris: Garnier-Flammarion, 1966), 80.

21. The eighteenth century gave rise to a vast body of literature on the origins, nature, and function of language among human societies, as well as on animals' languages. Representative titles include Bishop Wilkins, *Essay towards a Real Character and a Philosophical Language* (1668); David-Renaud Boullier, *Essai philosophique sur l'âme des bêtes* (1728); David Hume, *Treatise of Human Nature* (1739; bk. 1, sec. 16); Condillac, *Traité des animaux* (1755); Rousseau, *Essai sur l'origine des langues* (1761); Condorcet, *Esquisse d'un tableau historique des progrès de l'esprit humain* (1795).

22. On the potential for speech in orangutans, see Edward Tyson, *Orang-outang, sive Homo Sylvestris* (1699).

23. Discussion of language acquisition and man's "natural" tongue has preoccupied thinkers since Pliny at least; most significant for the eighteenth century was Descartes' argument on the *langage des bêtes,* which was reworked in Samuel Butler's satirical *Hudibras* (1663–78); G. H. Bougeant, *Amusement philosophique sur le langage des bêtes* (1739); and the anonymous satire of Linnaeus, *A Letter from the Rope-Dancing Monkey in the Hay-Market, to the Acting Monkey of Drury-Lane* (London: J. Pridden, 1767), among many other works.

24. For more on this anecdote, attributed to Diderot, and contemporary interest in language, see Robert Wokler, "Perfectible Apes in Decadent Cultures: Rousseau's Anthropology Revisited" *Daedalus* 107, no. 3 (1978): 107–34.

25. John Hildrop, *Free Thoughts upon the Brute Creation: or, an Examination of Father Bougeant's 'Philosophical Amusement', &c. In Two Letters to a Lady.* (London: Printed for R. Minors, 1743), 63. Further references appear in the text.

26. For an overview of these debates and their theological implications, see Marie-Hélène Huet, *Monstrous Imagination* (Cambridge: Harvard University Press, 1993), 61–63; and Jacques Roger, *Les Sciences de la vie dans la pensée française du XVIIIe siècle: La Génération des animaux de Descartes à l'Encyclopédie* (Paris: Armand Colin, 1963), 397–418.

27. Jean-Louis Alléon-Dulac, *Mélanges d'histoire naturelle* (Lyon: Chez Benoît Duplain, 1765), 5:29.

28. Edward Tyson, in *Philosophical Transactions of the Royal Society* 21 (1699):

431–35; Delisle de Sales [J. B. C. Izouard], *De la Philosophie de la nature,* 7th ed. (Paris: Gide, 1804), 1:398–99. This list merely touches the surface of contemporary interest: accounts of hybrid humans can be found in the works of Locke, Voltaire, Buffon, Diderot, and Restif de la Bretonne, among others. For more on this phenomenon, see Léon Poliakov's excellent article, "Le Fantasme des êtres hybrides et la hiérarchie des races aux XVIIIe et XIXe siècles," in *Hommes et Bêtes: Entretiens sur le racisme,* ed. Léon Poliakov (Paris: Mouton, 1975): 167–81.

29. Oleg Neverov, "'His Majesty's Cabinet' and Peter I's *Kunstkammer,*" trans. Gertrud Seidmann, in *The Origins of Museums: The Cabinet of Curiosities in Sixteenth- and Seventeenth-Century Europe,* ed. Oliver Impey and Arthur MacGregor (Oxford: Clarendon, 1985), 54–61, esp. 60. On other human displays, see Amy Boesky, "'Outlandish-Fruits': Commissioning Nature for the Museum of Man," *ELH: English Literary History* 58 (1991): 305–30; and Barbara Kirshenblatt-Gimblett, "Objects of Ethnography," in *Exhibiting Cultures: The Poetics and Politics of Museum Display,* ed. Ivan Karp and Steven D. Lavine (Washington, D.C.: Smithsonian Institution Press, 1991), 386–443.

30. For more on the political implications of natural history, see Emma Spary, "Political, Natural, and Bodily Economies," in *Cultures of Natural History,* ed. N. Jardine, J. A. Secord, and E. C. Spary (Cambridge: Cambridge University Press, 1996), 178–96, esp. 184.

31. "[N]ous aimâmes mieux croire que des ours engendraient des hommes, que de penser qu'un homme pouvait produire un quadrupède." de Sales, *Philosophie de la nature,* 5:408–9.

32. Jean-Jacques Rousseau, *Discourse on the Origin of Inequality* in *The Basic Political Writings,* trans. Donald A. Cress (Indianapolis: Hackett, 1978), 45. "Pourquoi l'homme seul est-il sujet à devenir imbécile? N'est-ce point qu'il retourne ainsi dans son état primitif, et que . . . l'homme reperdant par la vieillesse ou d'autres accidents tout ce que sa *perfectibilité* lui avait fait acquérir, retombe ainsi plus bas que la bête même?" Rousseau, *Discours sur l'origine et les fondements de l'inégalité,* ed. Jacques Roger (Paris: Garnier-Flammarion, 1971), 171–72.

33. Rousseau argued that man's decline could, however, be obviated by adoption of the guidelines offered in works such as his *Contrat social* or *Emile.* See Wokler, "Perfectible Apes," 127–28. On the shifting meaning of this concept in eighteenth-century writings, see Michel Baridon, "Les Concepts de nature humaine et de perfectibilité dans l'historiographie des Lumières de Fontenelle à Condorcet," in *L'Histoire au dix-huitième siècle* (Colloque d'Aix-en-Provence, 1–3 May 1975) (Aix: Edisud, 1980): 353–74.

34. "La perfectibilité de l'homme naît de la faiblesse de ses sens dont aucun ne prédomine sur l'organe de la raison. S'il avait le nez du chien, il flairerait toujours; l'oeil de l'aigle, il ne cesserait de regarder; l'oreille de la taupe, ce serait un être écoutant. . . . L'espèce humaine n'est donc qu'un amas d'individus plus ou moins contrefaits, plus ou moins malades." Diderot, *Elements de physiologie,* 9:271, 272.

35. I have drawn these references from the best general sources on Peter of Hanover: Maximilian E. Novak, "The Wild Man Comes to Tea," in *The Wild Man Within,* ed. Edward Dudley and Maximilian E. Novak (Pittsburgh: University of Pittsburgh Press, 1972), 183–221; and Candland, *Feral Children,* 9–17.

36. Maria Edgeworth and Richard Lovell Edgeworth, *Practical Education* (London: J. Johnson, 1798), 1:64. Further references appear in the text. Biographers of Peter have

neglected this fascinating connection with the Edgeworths and thus have misrepresented Peter as losing all spectacle value when he leaves the capital.

37. For more on the epistemological underpinnings of early natural history and its vision of man's place in the universe, consult Georges Gusdorf, *Dieu, la nature, l'homme au siècle des Lumières,* vol. 5 of *Les Sciences et la pensée occidentale* (Paris: Payot, 1972), 244–353; Rousseau, *Discours sur l'origine,* 171–72.

38. James Paris, *A Short History of Human Prodigies and Monstrous Births, of Dwarfs, Sleepers, Giants, Strong Men, Hermaphrodites, Numerous Births, and Extream Old Age, etc.* (n.p., n.d.) [British Library, Sloane MS. 5246], 30.

39. These descriptions are from a work attributed to John Arbuthnot or Jonathan Swift, *It Cannot Rain but It Pours, or London Strowed with Rarities,* in George A. Aitken, *The Life and Works of John Arbuthnot* (Oxford: Clarendon, 1892), 471; and a work attributed to Daniel Defoe, *Mere Nature Delineated: or a Body without a Soul* (London: T. Warner, 1726), 8. Further references appear in the text.

40. Letter from Countess Shaumburg-Lippe to Count Zinzendorf, who had requested custody of Peter. Cited in Singh and Zingg, *Wolf-Children,* 185.

41. "His being so young was the occasion of the great disappointment of the ladies, who came to the drawing-room in full expectation of some attempt upon their chastity: so far is true, that he endeavoured to kiss the young Lady Walpole, who for that reason is become the envy of the circle." *It Cannot Rain,* 472.

42. "The Savage," in *Miscellaneous Poems by Several Hands,* ed. David Lewis (London: J. Watts, 1726), 305.

43. *The Manifesto of Lord Peter* (London: Printed for J. Roberts, 1726), 3.

44. *It Cannot Rain,* 473. Victor of Aveyron was also praised for his vegetarianism; Joseph Ritson lists Victor among the many people whose good health and vegetarian diet disprove the necessity for animal food in *Essay on Abstinence from Animal Food as a Moral Duty* (London: Richard Phillips, 1802), 192.

45. Lord Monboddo (James Burnett), *Antient Metaphysics* (1779–99; reprint, New York: Garland, 1977), 4:32.

46. Rousseau cites Peter as one of many quadruped wild children found in Europe since 1344: "Le petit sauvage d'Hanovre qu'on mena il y a plusieurs années à la cour d'Angleterre, avait toutes les peines du monde à s'assujettir à marcher sur deux pieds," *Discours sur l'origine,* 160–61.

47. "[I]l sera semblable à ce sauvage d'Hanovre et à cette petite fille ramassée dans les bois de Champagne: sans langage, sans signes et vraisemblablement sans idées." Marie-Jeanne (Manon) Roland, Letter LXII to Sophie (1 August 1774), in *Lettres de Madame Roland. Nouvelle série, 1767–1780,* ed. Claude Perroud (Paris: Imprimerie Nationale, 1913), 1:215.

48. Buffon, *Natural History,* 10:507–8; *Oeuvres complètes,* 4:204.

49. Buffon, *Natural History,* 5:141; "Ainsi l'état de pure nature est un état connu." Buffon, *Oeuvres complètes,* 5:157.

50. Buffon, *Natural History,* 5:141. "L'état de pure nature est un état connu: c'est le sauvage vivant dans le désert, mais vivant en famille, connoissant ses enfans, connu d'eux, usant de la parole et se faisant entendre. La fille sauvage ramassée dans les bois de Champagne, l'homme trouvé dans les forêts d'Hanovre, ne prouvent pas le contraire: ils avoient vécu dans une solitude absolue; ils ne pouvoient donc avoir aucune idée de

société, aucun usage des signes ou de la parole: mais s'ils se fussent seulement rencontrés, la pente de la nature les auroit entraînés, le plaisir les auroit réunis; attachés l'un à l'autre, ils se seroient bientôt entendus; ils auroient d'abord parlé la langue de l'amour entre eux, et ensuite celle de la tendresse entre eux et leurs enfans." Buffon, *Oeuvres complètes,* 5:157.

51. Peter's attributes are from *It Cannot Rain,* 471; *Mere Nature Delineated,* 24; Adam Ferguson, *An Essay on the History of Civil Society,* ed. Duncan Forbes (1767; reprint, Edinburgh: Edinburgh University Press, 1966), xv, 4; Johann Friedrich Blumenbach, *Beyträge zur Naturgeschichte* (1806), in *The Anthropological Treatises of Johann Friedrich Blumenbach,* trans. Thomas Bendyshe (London: Longman, Green, Longman, Roberts and Green, 1865), 333.

52. "Men, who have accidentally been brought up among beasts, not only lose the use of speech, but in some measure the power of acquiring it: an evident proof, that their throats are deformed, and that human speech is consistent only with an erect gait." Johann Gottfried Herder, *Outline of a Philosophy of the History of Man* (*Ideen zur Philosophie der Geschichte der Menschheit,* 1784), trans. T. Churchill (New York: Bergman, 1800), 89.

53. William Lawrence, *Lectures on Comparative Anatomy, Physiology, Zoology, and the Natural History of Man,* 9th ed. (London: Henry G. Bohn, 1848), 97.

54. This summary is based on the evidence of the major texts on Marie-Angélique's life: [M. A. M. N.], "Lettre écrite de Châlons, en Champagne, le 9 décembre 1731, par M. A. M. N. . . . au sujet de la Fille sauvage trouvée aux environs de cette ville," *Mercure de France* (December 1731): 2983–89; "Extrait d'une autre lettre sur le même sujet," *Mercure de France* (December 1731): 2989–91; Mme Hecquet [attr. to Charles Marie de La Condamine], *Histoire d'une jeune fille sauvage trouvée dans les bois à l'âge de dix ans,* ed. Franck Tinland (Bordeaux: Editions Ducros, 1971); Louis Racine, "Eclaircissement sur la fille sauvage dont il est parlé dans l'Epître sur l'homme," *Oeuvres de Louis Racine* (Paris: Le Normant, 1808), 6:575–82. N.B.: "d'Epinay" is often written "d'Epinoy."

55. Franck Rolin has traced Leblanc's life back to a Sioux or Fox tribe. Based on archival research, Rolin has determined that she was bought in 1712 by the widow of the commandant of Labrador, who brought her to France. They arrived on a fishing boat in Marseilles in 1720, only to be quarantined for a year and a half because of the plague epidemic that was then ravaging the city. She escaped in May 1722 and made her way more than 1,000 kilometers north to Châlons, where she was captured. Thus this "young girl" was actually twenty years old when found in 1731. I am grateful to Dr. Rolin for this information.

56. One must recall that at his capture in 1724, Peter of Hanover elicited a flurry of interest and literary productions: a number of pamplets, a sermon, a book-length satire by Daniel Defoe, and an anonymous poem, "The Savage." For more on this subgenre of "wild child" literature, see Novak, "Wild Man Comes to Tea," 183–221.

57. These details are from Charles, duc de Luynes, *La Cour de Louis XV, racontée jour par jour 1753–1754* (Paris: Henri Vivien, [1864–65]), 13:72. Further references appear in the text.

58. Monboddo cites her address as rue St. Antoine in 1765. She died in an apartment on rue Notre Dame de Nazareth (near Le Temple) in 1775.

59. *Inventaire après décès,* 5 January 1776. Archives nationales, Série MC; lxvi, 627.

I am extremely grateful to Franck Rolin for communicating this and many other precious archival sources on Leblanc to me.

60. *Papiers saisis à la Révolution,* Série T, doc. 930 (1). Documents concerning Leblanc and the prominent Lally Tollendal.

61. There is some ambiguity about the provenance of her name. In the archives of the Hôpital St-Maur (October 1731), we find mention of "une fille soy disant sauvage" named "Marie Angélique," suggesting that she called herself Marie-Angélique before her baptism. As Rolin has noted, she was listed twice in these records—on the list of children and on the list of women—so as to benefit from two allowances from the city of Châlons.

62. "Chaque situation de la vie scolaire suggère un modelage, qu'il s'agisse des heures passées par les écolières assises sur leur banc ou de leurs rares occasions de mouvement. En toutes circonstances les filles doivent respirer la modestie et la décence, leurs attributs les plus glorieux." Martine Sonnet, *L'Education des filles au temps des lumières* (Paris: Editions du Cerf, 1987), 157.

63. "[L]e règlement de l'internat organise l'espace et le temps éducatifs, comme il modèle le corps, pour que rien ne puisse se produire." Ibid., 161.

64. "Quand elles prendront leurs chemises elles feront en sorte que personne ne les voie nues, elles ne se regarderont point non plus elles-mêmes." Ibid., 155.

65. From the code of "les Dames de la Croix": "[L]es élèves prendront garde qu'il est très indécent de s'appuyer contre la muraille ou contre le dos de sa chaise; . . . de s'étendre les bras et les jambes, de montrer ses pieds, de ronger ses ongles avec ses dents et autres choses semblables." Cited in ibid., 158.

66. The extent of La Condamine's involvement with Leblanc is hard to determine. Most sources report that he interviewed her at length in 1747, sixteen years after her capture and subsequent taming in the convent. According to one source, however, La Condamine conducted a kind of experiment on her in 1731, right after she left the d'Epinay estate. As Buirette de Verrières wrote: "M. de la Condamine s'occupa à étudier les premières moeurs de cette sauvage, et par l'effet des objets qu'il soumettait à sa vue, chercha à démêler en elle l'âge de la nature, son origine et son premier état." However, Verrières concluded, "Mais cette étude ne lui laissa que des conjectures et rien de positif." Claude-Rémy Buirette de Verrières, *Annales historiques de la ville et comté-pairie de Châlons-sur-Marne,* pt. 1 (Châlons: Chez Seneuze, 1788), lxxviii.

67. Londa Schiebinger, *Nature's Body: Gender in the Making of Modern Science* (Boston: Beacon, 1993), 112–13.

68. "[E]lle n'est point de Norvège, (comme on l'a dit), on croit plutôt qu'elle est née dans les Isles Antilles de l'Amérique, qui appartiennent aux François, comme la Gadaloupe, la Martinique, S. Christophe, S. Domingue, &c. parce qu'un Particulier de Châlons, qui a été à la Gadaloupe, lui ayant montré de la *Cassave,* ou *Manioque,* qui est un Pain dont se nourrissent les Sauvages des Antilles, elle s'écria de joye sur ce Pain, et en ayant pris un morceau elle le mangea avec grant [*sic*] appétit." [M. A. M. N.], "Lettre écrite de Châlons," 2983–84.

69. For more on contemporary debates about language, see Hans Aarsleff, *From Locke to Saussure: Essays on the Study of Language and Intellectual History* (Minneapolis: University of Minnesota Press, 1982); Jacques Chouillet, "Descartes et le problème de l'origine des langues," *Dix-huitième siècle* 4 (1972): 39–60; and chapter 10 of Hans

Blumenberg, *The Legitimacy of the Modern Age,* trans. Robert M. Wallace (Cambridge: MIT Press, 1983).

70. "[E]lle appelle un Filet 'Debily,' dans le patois de son Pays; pour dire bon jour, Fille, on dit, selon elle; 'Yas yas, fioul,' ajoutant que quand on l'appelloit, on disoit 'Riam riam, fioul'; c'est ce qui fait connoître qu'elle commence à entendre la signification des termes françois, les interprétant par ceux de son Pays." [M. A. M. N.], "Lettre écrite de Châlons," 2987.

71. "On remarquoit que tout ce qu'elle mangeoit, elle le mangeoit cru. . . . Pour l'eau, sa boisson ordinaire, elle la boit dans un seau, la tirant comme une Vache, et étant à genoux." Ibid., 2985–86, 2987.

72. "Nous vîmes ce jour-là, avec une espèce d'horreur, cette fille manger plus d'une livre et demie de boeuf cru, sans y donner un coup de dent, puis se jeter avec une espèce de fureur sur un lapreau qu'on mit devant elle, qu'elle déshabilla en un clin d'oeil avec une facilité qui suppose un grand usage, puis le dévorer en un instant sans le vider." "Extrait d'une autre lettre," 2990.

73. As Jean-Louis Flandrin has argued, although the seventeenth and eighteenth centuries constituted one of the filthiest periods in history, contemporary manuals of civility reveal an obsession with cleanliness. Many new prescriptions for table manners, for example, date from this era: use of the fingers tended more and more to be forbidden, as did transferring food directly from serving plates to the mouth, and individual sets of silverware were *de rigueur.* See Flandrin, "Distinction Through Taste," in *A History of Private Life,* vol. 3, *Passions of the Renaissance,* ed. Roger Chartier, trans. Arthur Goldhammer (Cambridge: Harvard University Press, 1989), 265–67; and Georges Vigarello, *Le Propre et le sale: L'hygiène du corps depuis le Moyen Age* (Paris: Seuil, 1985).

74. George Cheyne, *The English Malady* (London: 1733), 174.

75. Claude Lévi-Strauss, *The Origin of Table Manners: Introduction to a Science of Mythology,* trans. John and Doreen Weightman (New York: Harper and Row, 1978), 505–7.

76. See Flandrin, "Distinction Through Taste," 267, for more on the ambiguous connotations of cleanliness and *propreté* in seventeenth- and eighteenth-century usage.

77. For more on the changing ambitions and administrative plans behind the many prisons, foundling homes, and insane asylums constructed in the eighteenth century, see Foucault, *Discipline and Punish; Deviants and the Abandoned in French Society: Selections from the Annales: Economies, Sociétés, Civilisations,* vol. 4, ed. Robert Forster and Orest Ranum, trans. Elborg Forster and Patricia M. Ranum (Baltimore: Johns Hopkins University Press, 1978); Jean-Pierre Gutton, *La Société et les pauvres en Europe (XVIe–XVIIIe siècles)* (Paris: Presses Universitaires de France, 1974); Owen Hufton, *The Poor of Eighteenth-Century France, 1750–1789* (Oxford: Oxford University Press, 1974); and Camille Bloch, *L'Assistance et l'Etat en France à la veille de la Révolution* (Paris: A. Picard et fils, 1908).

78. "M. l'Evêque a pris soin depuis de la placer dans l'Hôpital Général de cette Ville, où l'on reçoit les Enfans des pauvres Habitans, de l'un et de l'autre sexe, pour les y nourrir jusqu'à l'âge de quinze à seize ans, qu'on leur fait apprendre des Métiers. C'est là qu'on tâche de l'humaniser tout-à-fait, et de l'instruire. . . . La Supérieure de l'Hôpital dit qu'elle sçait bien broder. . . . On l'instruit cependant dans la Religion Chrétienne, elle dit qu'elle veut être baptisée dans le 'Paradis Terrestre,' terme dont elle se sert pour signifier nos Eglises." [M. A. M. N.], "Lettre écrite de Châlons," 2986, 2988.

79. "Cette étonnante fille, triste exemple de ce que nous serions sans l'éducation et la société." Louis Racine, "Epître II sur l'homme," in *Oeuvres de Louis Racine* (Paris: Le Normant, 1808), 2:124.

80. "Et ce qu'étoient alors nos sauvages aïeux, / Une fille en nos jours la fait voir à nos yeux. / Ce n'étoient point des mots qu'articuloit sa bouche: / Il n'en sortoit qu'un son, cri perçant et farouche. / Des vivans animaux que déchiroit sa main, / Les morceaux palpitans assouvissoient sa faim. / Dès l'enfance elle erra de montagne en montagne, / Et souilla ses déserts du sang de sa compagne. / Pourquoi l'immola-t-elle à ses propres fureurs? / Quel intérêt si grand vint séparer deux coeurs / Qu'unissoient leurs forêts, leur âge et leurs misères? / Reconnoissons les moeurs de nos antiques pères." Ibid.

81. "Les chaînes, les prisons, les gibets, les tourmens, / De la société furent les fondemens." Ibid., 2:125.

82. "De ces monstres affreux que veux-je ici conclure? / Le penchant où conduit la coupable nature. / Qui veut lâcher la bride à son emportement, / S'il peut tout ce qu'il veut, *devient monstre aisément.*" Ibid., 2:127, my emphasis.

83. "Le sang des animaux, si défendu aux hommes après le déluge, étoit son nectar." Louis Racine, "Eclaircissement sur la fille sauvage dont il est parlé dans l'Epître sur l'homme," *Oeuvres de Louis Racine* (Paris: Le Normant, 1808),6:578–79. On the significance of alimentary taboos in the Old Testament, see Jean Soler, "Sémiotique de la nourriture dans la Bible," *Annales: Economies, Sociétés, Civilisations* 28, no. 4 (July–August 1973): 943–55.

84. "[L]a plus violente de ses tentations, c'est celle de boire le sang de quelqu'animal vivant. Elle-même m'a avoué que quand elle voyoit un enfant, elle se sentoit tourmentée de cette envie. Lorsqu'elle me parloit ainsi, ma fille, jeune encore, étoit avec moi; elle remarqua sur son visage quelqu'émotion à l'aveu d'une pareille tentation, et elle lui dit aussitôt en riant: 'Ne craignez rien, Mademoiselle, Dieu m'a bien changée.'" Racine, "Eclaircissement," 6:581–82.

85. "Après toutes les peines que l'on a prises pour adoucir sa férocité, elle en conserve quelques restes dans les regards et les manières: elle n'aime ni notre nourriture, ni la société, où elle ne reste que par obéissance à Dieu. La religion dont elle est instruite, l'empêche, dit-elle, de retourner dans les bois." Racine, "Epître," 2:124.

86. These anecdotes are drawn from "Extrait d'une autre lettre," 2989; *La Belle Sauvage: The True and Surprising History of a Savage Girl*... (London: J. Bailey, [1820?]), 12; and Verrières, *Annales historiques,* lxxxv.

87. "[L]a plus violente de ses tentations, c'est celle de boire le sang de quelqu'animal vivant. Elle-même m'a avoué que quand elle voyoit un enfant, elle se sentoit tourmentée de cette envie." Racine, "Eclaircissement," 6:581–82.

88. "Notre sauvage la considère, la fixe avec des yeux avides, son visage change: Mlle de Net . . . croit qu'elle convoite son poulet. *Non,* dit-elle en se serrant les poings et en se faisant la plus grande violence, *ce n'est point ce poulet qui est l'objet de mon appétit, mais c'est toi-même . . . Comme je te!* . . . On n'eût que le temps de la retirer." Verrières, *Annales historiques,* lxxxiv.

89. Nicolas Venette, *La Génération de l'homme ou Tableau de l'amour conjugal considéré en l'état de mariage* (1685), cited in Herman Roodenburg, "'Venus Minsieke Gastuis': Sexual Beliefs in Eighteenth-Century Holland," in *From Sappho to De Sade: Moments in the History of Sexuality,* ed. Jan Bremmer (New York: Routledge, 1989), 89. See

also Théodore Tarczylo, *Sexe et liberté au siècle des lumières* (Paris: Presses de la Renaissance, 1983), 29–95; and Ludmilla Jordanova, *Sexual Visions: Images of Gender in Science and Medicine between the Eighteenth and Twentieth Centuries* (Madison: University of Wisconsin Press, 1989), 19–65.

90. Freud later invented the psychoanalytic category of "orality" in his theory of the libido to explain the interactions between sexuality and food. See the Paris VII Séminaire, "Discours sur le sexe et le sexe du discours," in *Aimer en France 1760–1860,* ed. Paul Viallaneix and Jean Ehrard (Clermont-Ferrand: Assoc. des Publications de la Faculté des Lettres et Sciences Humaines de Clermont-Ferrand, 1980), 302.

91. Michèle LeDoeuff, *The Philosophical Imaginary,* trans. Colin Gordon (Stanford: Stanford University Press, 1989), 155.

92. "On parloit beaucoup à Paris, quand j'y publiai la première édition de cet ouvrage, d'une fille sauvage *qui avoit mangé sa soeur,* et qui étoit alors au Couvent à Châlons en Champagne." Julien Offray de La Mettrie, *Traité de l'âme,* in *Oeuvres philosophiques* (Paris: Fayard, 1987), 1:240 (emphasis added).

93. Julien Offray de La Mettrie, *L'Homme machine,* in *Oeuvres philosophiques* (Paris: Fayard, 1987), 1:91. La Mettrie found most of these cases in the academic oration by Hieronymus Gaudius that he attended in 1747, which was published as *De regimine mentis quod medicorum est.* For the history of this borrowing and pertinent excerpts of La Mettrie's sources, consult Aram Vartanian, *La Mettrie's 'L'Homme machine': A Study in the Origins of an Idea* (Princeton: Princeton University Press, 1960), 90–92, 222–26. La Mettrie and Gaudius are not isolated examples of such ideas on the physical origins of cannibalism. The *Encyclopédie* entry "Anthropophagie" quotes (contemptuously, to be sure) from contemporary medical theories that purport to locate physical causes of cannibalism in a "bitter humor" found in membranes of a cardiac ventricle. Denis Diderot, Jean le Rond d'Alembert, et al., *Encyclopédie ou dictionnaire raisonné des sciences, des arts et des métiers* (Neuchâtel: Samuel Faulche, 1765), 1:498. These theories would later by satirized in the humorous *Album comique de pathologie pittoresque* (1823), with its outrageous illustration "The Desires of Pregnant Women."

94. "Si la raison est esclave d'un sens dépravé, ou en fureur, comment peut-elle le gouverner?" La Mettrie, *L'Homme machine,* 91.

95. The *Histoire d'une fille sauvage* was published in 1755, reprinted in 1761, and translated into English in 1760 and 1768 as *The History* [*Account*] *of a Savage Girl, Caught Wild in the Woods of Champagne.*

96. La Condamine noted that he had "facilité l'impression de l'ouvrage au profit de Demoiselle LeBlanc, dans la vue de lui procurer une situation plus heureuse, en intéressant à son sort ceux qui liraient son aventure." Charles-Marie de La Condamine, "Lettre à M. de Boissy, de l'Académie française," *Mercure de France* (April 1755): 75. Monboddo reiterated the claim of profits returning to the wild girl in his preface to the 1768 English translation, where he remarked that this text was rather hard to find, because most of the copies were "in the hands of Mademoiselle LeBlanc, the extraordinary personage whose history it contains, who makes a small profit by the sale of them." He added in a note, "For the satisfaction of any of the readers of this pamphlet who may happen to be at Paris, and have the curiosity of paying a visit to Mademoiselle LeBlanc, I here give her address in the year 1765; but whether she has since changed her lodgings, I do not know. It was thus: Rue St. Antoine presque vis à vis la vieille rue du Temple au troi-

sième étage, sur le Devant." Monboddo, preface to Hecquet, *Account of a Savage Girl Caught Wild in the Woods of Champagne,* trans. William Robertson (Edinburgh: A. Kincaid and J. Bell, 1768), xvi.

97. La Condamine, "Lettre à M. de Boissy," 75. This letter was strategically inserted in the *Mercure de France* soon after the appearance of the book (April 1755).

98. Indeed, Graffigny appropriated ethnographic data into her fiction with such artistry that her text was long considered a reference work or source book on Peru. For more on Graffigny's "Peruvian" exoticism, see chapter 2 of Julia Douthwaite, *Exotic Women: Literary Heroines and Cultural Strategies in Ancien Régime France* (Philadelphia: University of Pennsylvania Press, 1992).

99. One could not choose a race more repugnant to the French, except perhaps the squalid Hottentots; both peoples were felt to inhabit the extreme boundaries of humanity. On the etymology of *Eskimo* as "eater of raw meat," see Antoine, abbé Prévost, *Histoire générale des voyages* (Paris: Chez Didot, 1757), 15:13. Buffon asserts that Eskimos (like their cousins the Laplanders) are "all equally gross, superstitious and stupid" (*Natural History,* 3:305). Diderot argued that the Eskimos had so far degenerated that they no longer even belonged to the human species (cited by Tinland, *L'Homme sauvage,* 266).

100. Mme Hecquet [La Condamine], *The History of a Savage Girl, Caught Wild in the Woods of Champagne. Newly Translated from the French of Madam H...t* (London: R. Dursley, T. Davidson, et al., [1760]), 6–7. Subsequent parenthetical quotations of Hecquet's work will refer to this edition, unless otherwise noted.

101. Richard Bernheimer, *Wild Men in the Middle Ages* (Cambridge: Harvard University Press, 1952), 1.

102. Rousseau also mentions wild children in the *Discours sur l'origine,* but since he uses them only as examples of quadrupedal and bipedal locomotion, he enters into very little detail. See Rousseau, *Discours sur l'origine de l'inégalité,* 160–61n. 1.

103. Lord Monboddo (James Burnett), *Of the Origin and Progress of Language* (Edinburgh: J. Balfour, 1774), 1:191, 195. Further references appear in the text.

104. "Quelle conquête, quelle vraie gloire, si nous réussissions à rendre aussi habiles, et meilleurs que nous, des animaux qui n'ont été jusqu'ici que brutes et méchants!" Gaspard Guillard de Beaurieu, *Cours d'histoire naturelle, ou tableau de la nature* (Paris: Chez Lacombs, 1770), 1:332.

105. "N'a-t-elle jamais regretté les bois d'où on l'a tirée. . . . Quand en sortant des mains de la Nature, on voit nos moeurs, nos injustices, etc. si on ne retourne pas dans les forêts, au moins doit-on n'occuper dans la société, que la place du bon et honnête paysan." Ibid., 1:346.

106. Abbé M. Morelly, *Code de la nature ou le véritable esprit de ses lois* (Paris, 1755); René Louis de Voyer, marquis d'Argenson, *Considérations sur le gouvernement de la France* (Paris, 1764); Gabriel Bonnot de Mably, *Traité de la législation ou principe des lois* (Paris, 1776). Albert Soboul presents a comprehensive overview of these currents in eighteenth-century French literature and political thought in his "Lumières, critique sociale et utopie pendant le XVIIIe siècle français," in *Histoire générale du socialisme,* ed. Jacques Droz (Paris: Presses Universitaires de France, 1972), 1:103–94.

107. "Qu'on ne me cite pas le jeune sauvage de Hamel, la fille de la forêt de Songi et d'autres individus ainsi abandonnés. Ils vivaient isolés, et leur exemple, comme l'observe

très bien Mr. Schreber, ne nous apprend absolument rien touchant l'état naturel de l'homme, puisqu'ils n'y étaient point. C'est vouloir étudier la Physiologie, par l'observation d'un homme attaqué de la plus violente des maladies." Eberhard August Wilhelm von Zimmermann, *Zoologie géographique* (Cassel: De l'imprimerie française de Cassel, 1784), 203.

108. See book 1 of *Emile,* where Rousseau lays out the physical and mental qualities required of his pupil: "Je ne me chargerois pas d'un enfant maladif et cacochime, dût-il vivre quatre vingt ans. Je ne veux point d'un élêve toujours inutile à lui-même et aux autres, qui s'occupe uniquement à se conserver, et dont le corps nuise à l'éducation de l'ame." Jean-Jacques Rousseau, *Emile ou l'éducation,* in *Oeuvres complètes,* ed. Bernard Gagnebin and Marcel Raymond (Paris: Gallimard, 1969), 4:268.

109. Margaret Anne Doody, seminar on Rousseau and Frances Burney presented at the University of Notre Dame on 5 February 1999.

110. I thank Franck Rolin for this insight into Châlonnaise regional history.

111. Richard D. Altick, *The English Common Reader: A Social History of the Mass Reading Public, 1800–1900* (Chicago: University of Chicago Press, 1957), 69–77.

112. London: Printed and Sold by J. Bailey, n.d. A possible date of 1820 is given in the British Library catalogue.

113. As defined by Eric Hobsbawm, *invented tradition* connotes the rites and symbols of nationalism—such as the national anthem, flag, or animal emblem (the American eagle, the Russian bear, or French cock)—that were promoted in the nineteenth and twentieth centuries. Eric Hobsbawm, introduction to *The Invention of Tradition,* ed. Eric Hobsbawm and Terence Ranger (Cambridge: Cambridge University Press, 1983), 1–14.

114. "The Northern Ditty: or the Scotch-man Out-witted by the Country Damsel," in *The Euing Collection of English Broadside Ballads in the Library of the University of Glasgow,* ed. John Holloway (Glasgow: University of Glasgow Publications, 1971), 422. The front side includes the phrase "This may be printed" followed by the initials R. P. One Richard Pococke served as Licenser of the Press from 1685 to 1688, so we can presume that this text was printed then.

115. M. Foulquier-Lavergne, *Le Sauvage de l'Aveyron* (Rodez: Broca, 1875), cited in Louis Gayral, Pierre Chabbert, and Hélène Baillaud-Citeau, "Les Premières observations de l'enfant sauvage de Lacaune (dit 'Victor' ou 'Le Sauvage de l'Aveyron'), Nouveaux documents," *Annales médico-psychologiques* 2, no. 4 (November 1972): 466.

116. Paule F. Girard, "L'Histoire véridique de Victor, l'enfant sauvage de l'Aveyron, ou les origines lointaines de la psychiatrie infantile," *Lyon médical* 251, no. 8 (1984): 361.

117. Letter from M. Randon, commissaire central de l'Aveyron, to the municipal commissioner of Saint-Sernin (3 pluviôse an VIII), cited in Gayral, Chabbert, and Baillaud-Citeau, "Les Premières observations," 472.

118. Letter from Commissioner Guiraud (canton St. Affrique) to the Administration centrale, cited in ibid., 469.

119. "Sans bien connaître tous ces droits, / Jamais on ne fut vraiment libre, / Et notre ignorant, dans les bois, / Ne savait pas qu'il était libre, / Or, comme il est bien arrêté, / Que tout homme doit être libre, / Exprès nous l'avons arrêté, / Pour l'informer qu'il était libre." Dupaty, Maurice, and Chazet, *Le Sauvage du département de l'Aveyron ou Il ne faut jurer de rien.* Reviewed in *Le Journal de Paris* (30 March 1800). Cited in Gineste, *Victor de l'Aveyron,* 133.

120. "Je veux enrichir aujourd'hui / La médecine et la physique; / Souffrez que je fasse sur lui / Quelque recherche anatomique." Cited in Gineste, *Victor de l'Aveyron,* 134.

121. "On n'aurait pas cru possible / Chez les grecs, chez les romains / De voir la femme invisible / Et des acteurs à tout crins / Mais à Paris la science / Marche vite et prouve bien / Qu'en fait de génie en France / Il ne faut jurer de rien." *Le Sauvage du département de l'Aveyron,* 121. I thank Thierry Gineste for sharing this manuscript with me. For more on "la femme invisible"—the anatomical wax model of Mlle Biheron that could be opened and dismantled for inspection—see Mme de Genlis, *Mémoires de Mme la Comtesse de Genlis sur le 18e siècle et la Révolution française,* 2d ed. (Paris, 1825), 1:338–39.

122. Girard, "L'Histoire véridique," 363. Itard tells of naming Victor in *De l'éducation d'un homme sauvage ou des premiers développements physiques et moraux du jeune sauvage de l'Aveyron* (1801), cited in Gineste, *Victor de l'Aveyron,* 303.

123. These include a novel, J. A. Neyer, *Rodolphe ou le Sauvage de l'Aveyron* (1800); a vaudeville piece, Dupaty, Maurice, and Chazet, *Le Sauvage du département de l'Aveyron ou Il ne faut jurer de rien* (1800); and a song, *La Romance de l'enfant de la forêt, au moment où il quitte Clémence* (1800). For more on the popular representation of Victor's life, see Gineste, *Victor de l'Aveyron,* 29–32, 132–34.

124. For the exchange of letters on the boy's supposed charlatanism, see Gineste, *Victor de l'Aveyron,* 146–180.

125. Candland, *Feral Children,* 18.

126. "Ainsi son âme ignorante et sauvage est simple; elle est connue du premier abord; elle est exempte d'hypocrisie . . . elle est bornée, et rude; elle est grossière, égoïste, mais enfin elle est une, pure et franche." Julien-Joseph Virey, *Dissertation sur un jeune enfant trouvé dans les forêts du département de l'Aveyron, avec des remarques sur l'état primitif de l'homme* (1800), cited in Gineste, *Victor de l'Aveyron,* 234.

127. "Un roi devant lui ne serait pas différent à ses yeux du dernier des mortels; comme un nouveau Diogène, il dirait à un moderne Alexandre de s'ôter de devant son soleil." Ibid., 241.

128. "Va, jeune infortuné, sur cette terre malheureuse, va perdre dans les liens civils ta primitive et simple rudesse. . . . Comment perdras-tu ton absolue indépendance dans les entraves politiques, dans nos institutions civiles! Que de larmes tu dois verser! Ah, puisses-tu vivre heureux au milieu de tes compatriotes! Puisses-tu, homme simple, déployer les sublimes vertus des âmes généreuses, et transmettre aux générations à venir cet exemple honorable, comme une preuve éternelle de ce que pouvait un élève de l'innocente Nature." Ibid., 247, 248.

129. "Toutes les infirmités qui affligent l'humanité ont trouvé de nouveaux secours. . . . On a tenté de redresser ceux qui avaient les jambes ou l'épine du dos cambrées; on a réussi sur quelques personnes. Pereire a perfectionné, ou plutôt trouvé l'art de faire parler les malheureux nés sourds et par conséquent muets." Paul-Philippe Gudin de la Brenellerie, *Aux Mânes de Louis XV, et des grands hommes qui ont vécu sous son règne, ou Essai sur les progrès des Arts et de l'Esprit humain, sous le règne de Louis XV* (Paris: Aux Deux-Ponts, à l'imprimerie ducale, 1776), 1:280–81. La Mettrie celebrates Amman's work with deaf-mutes in similar terms in *L'Homme machine,* 77.

130. Thomas Beddoes, cited in Roy Porter, "Medical Science and Human Science in the Enlightenment, in *Inventing Human Science: Eighteenth-Century Domains,* ed. Christopher Fox, Roy Porter, and Robert Wokler (Berkeley: University of California Press, 1995), 63.

131. David B. Morris, "The Marquis de Sade and the Discourses of Pain: Literature and Medicine at the Revolution," in *The Languages of Psyche: Mind and Body in Enlightenment Thought,* ed. G. S. Rousseau (Berkeley: University of California Press, 1990), 297–98.

132. On Pinel's contributions to psychiatry, see Dora B. Weiner, "Mind and Body in the Clinic: Philippe Pinel, Alexander Crichton, Dominique Esquirol, and the Birth of Psychiatry," in *The Languages of Psyche: Mind and Body in Enlightenment Thought,* ed. G. S. Rousseau (Berkeley: University of California Press, 1990), 331–402, esp. 331–64, 391–95. See also Jan Goldstein, *Console and Classify: The French Psychiatric Profession in the Nineteenth Century* (Cambridge: Cambridge University Press, 1987).

133. Morris, "Marquis de Sade," 318, 298. For more on Cabanis and his ideas, see Martin S. Staum, *Cabanis: Enlightenment and Medical Philosophy in the French Revolution* (Princeton: Princeton University Press, 1980). These scientists were not the first to seek evidence of correlations between brain states and cognitive events; almost a hundred years earlier François de la Peyronie had done operations on brain-damaged patients to pinpoint the place in the brain where the reciprocal actions between the mind and body take place. See John Yolton, *Locke and French Materialism* (Oxford: Oxford University Press, 1991), 102–3.

134. Jean Itard, *The Wild Boy of Aveyron (Rapports et mémoires sur le sauvage de l'Aveyron),* trans. George and Muriel Humphrey (New York: Century, 1932), xxiii. "Eclairées du flambeau de l'analyse, et se prêtant l'une à l'autre un mutuel appui, ces deux sciences [la médecine et la philosophie] ont de nos jours dépouillé leurs vieilles erreurs, et fait des progrès immenses." Jean Itard, *De l'éducation,* in Gineste, *Victor de l'Aveyron,* 281.

135. "Quelles sont maintenant les circonstances qui ont amené l'enfant de l'Aveyron à cet état d'idiotisme? . . . en excluant de cet état une complication avec l'épilepsie, ou un vice rachitique, ces causes se réduisent à trois points principaux: 1e une vive frayeur éprouvée par la mère pendant la grossesse ou l'enfantement; 2e une frayeur ou des convulsions survenues durant l'enfance par des affections vermineuses; 3e le travail pénible et orageux de la première ou deuxième dentition. Rien ne peut déterminer laquelle de ces trois causes a pu agir sur l'enfant de l'Aveyron, et porter une atteinte funeste à ces facultés morales, mais . . . on peut conjecturer que des parents inhumains ou réduits à l'état de disette ont abandonné cet enfant comme incapable de culture." Phillipe Pinel, "Rapport fait à la Société des Observateurs de l'Homme sur l'enfant connu sous le nom du Sauvage de l'Aveyron," in *Aux Origines de l'anthropologie française: Les Mémoires de la Société des Observateurs de l'Homme en l'an VIII,* ed. Jean Copans and Jean Jamin (Paris: Editions Le Sycomore, 1978), 113. (This report was read before the *Société des Observateurs de l'Homme* on 29 December 1800.)

136. Candland, *Feral Children,* 17.

137. Itard, *Wild Boy,* 50. "[L]a médecine moderne . . . de toutes les sciences naturelles, peut coopérer le plus puissamment au perfectionnement de l'espèce humaine, en appréciant les anomalies organiques et intellectuelles de chaque individu, et déterminant par-là ce que l'éducation doit faire pour lui, ce que la société peut en attendre." Itard, *De l'éducation,* 321.

138. "[L]es espérances des philosophes commencent à se réaliser. . . . En très-peu de temps le citoyen Itard a obtenu des succès qui tiennent du prodige; je les ai vérifiés par moi-même." Joseph-Marie Degérando, "Présentation du rapport de J.M.G. Itard à la

Société des Observateurs de l'homme," 20 October 1801, in Gineste, *Victor de l'Aveyron,* 327.

139. Itard, *Wild Boy,* 99. "J'ai dû m'arrêter . . . et me résigner à voir, comme dans maintes autres circonstances, mes espérances s'évanouir, comme tant d'autres, devant un obstacle imprévu." Itard, *Rapport fait à son excellence le Ministre de l'Intérieur, sur les nouveaux développements et l'état actuel du sauvage de l'Aveyron* (1806), reprinted in Gineste, *Victor de l'Aveyron,* 443.

140. Report of 19 November 1806, to the Ministre de l'Intérieur, in Gineste, *Victor de l'Aveyron,* 396–97.

141. John F. Gaynor, "The 'Failure' of J. M. G. Itard," *Journal of Special Education* 7, no. 4 (winter 1973): 439–45.

142. Gineste, *Victor de l'Aveyron,* 107.

143. "Les bornes qui séparent la raison de la folie, le bien et le mal de notre existence morale sont, en quelque sorte, plantées très au hasard et d'une manière arbitraire, ici par le médecin, là par le moraliste et sujettes à varier." Jean Itard, "Vésanies" (1802), reprinted in Gineste, *Victor de l'Aveyron,* 339.

144. "[O]n retrouve l'homme tout entier dans l'aliéné." Itard, "Vésanies," in Gineste, *Victor de l'Aveyron,* 338.

145. Praise of Itard the experimentalist is in Gaynor, "'Failure,'" 445.

146. As L. J. Delasiauve declared in his 1865 article on Itard: "On s'attaque trop à l'intelligence. Chez l'idiot, l'éducation veut être toute action, toute pratique. Jeux multipliés, travaux divers, exercices variés, à chaque heure, à chaque minute, en des mains successives et habiles, il doit être à l'oeuvre. [. . .] Le sauvage de l'Aveyron, ainsi cultivé, se fût certainement manifesté par plus de surfaces." "Le Sauvage de l'Aveyron," *Journal de médecine mentale* 5 (1865): 211.

147. Antonie Luyendijk-Elshout surveys a number of these methods in "Of Masks and Mills: The Enlightened Doctor and His Frightened Patient," in *The Languages of Psyche: Mind and Body in Enlightenment Thought,* ed. G. S. Rousseau (Berkeley: University of California Press, 1990), 186–230.

148. These claims are drawn from the work of Abbé Sans, professor of experimental physics at the Université de Perpignan and author of *Guérison de la paralysie* (1772). Cited in Barbara Maria Stafford, *Body Criticism: Imaging the Unseen in Enlightenment Art and Medicine* (Cambridge: MIT Press, 1991), 459.

149. F. J. Gall and G. Spurzheim, *Anatomie et physiologie du système nerveux en général et du cerveau en particulier* (Paris: F. Schoell, 1810–19), 2:35.

150. George W. Stocking, "French Anthropology in 1800," *Isis* 55, no. 2 (1964): 150.

151. Huet, *Monstrous Imagination,* 102.

152. "Le sauvage de l'Aveyron a été ce que, d'après sa nature infirme, il devait être. Certaines virtualités n'existaient pas." Delasiauve, "Le Sauvage de l'Aveyron," 210.

153. Dennis Todd, *Imagining Monsters: Miscreations of the Self in Eighteenth-Century England* (Chicago: University of Chicago Press, 1995), 156.

154. In a letter of 18 February 1755, Friedrich Melchior Grimm cited the story of Leblanc as "un trait bien humiliant pour la pauvre humanité et qui prouve bien que l'état de pure nature serait le despotisme des passions." *Correspondance littéraire, philosophique et critique de Grimm, Diderot, Raynal, Meister, etc.,* ed. Maurice Tourneux (Paris: Garnier, 1877), 2:223.

155. I am grateful to Richard Nash for this list of conceptual categories.

156. See above for discussion of the notable exceptions to this negative attitude, e.g., Mme Hecquet's *Histoire d'une jeune fille sauvage trouvée dans les bois à l'âge de dix ans* (1755), and Buffon, *L'Histoire naturelle.*

157. The priests' admonition against climbing trees is in [M. A. M. N], "Lettre écrite de Châlons," 2983; on her performances of wildness at court, see Charles, duc de Luynes, *Mémoires,* in *La Cour de Louis XV, racontée jour par jour (1753–1754)* (Paris: Henri Vivien, 1864–65), 13:72.

158. Letter from Bonnaterre to the prefect of Aveyron (2 September 1800), cited in Gineste, *Victor de l'Aveyron,* 145–46.

159. Schiebinger, *Nature's Body,* 106.

160. H. Howard, "A New Humorous Song on the Cherokee Chiefs" (broadside, 1762) cited in Hoxie Neale Fairchild, *The Noble Savage: A Study in Romantic Naturalism* (New York: Columbia University Press, 1928), 73.

CHAPTER TWO

1. George Sidney Brett, *A History of Psychology* (London: G. Allen, 1912–21), 2:291. On the many versions of Pygmalion produced by eighteenth-century writers, see J. L. Carr's remarkable study, "Pygmalion and the *Philosophes:* The Animated Statue in Eighteenth-Century France," *Journal of the Warburg and Courtault Institutes* 23, nos. 3–4 (1960): 239–55, and Suzanne L. Pucci, "Metaphor and Metamorphosis in Diderot's *Le Rêve de d'Alembert:* Pygmalion Materialized," *Symposium* (winter 1981–82): 325–40.

2. Walter Moser's excellent article "Experiment and Fiction" was key in conceptualizing this chapter. Moser argues that the fictional experiment should be considered an "epistemic strategy" of the 1750s, given its prevalence in this period: "Around 1750, philosophical . . . and pre-scientific . . . discourse had a choice between two alternatives: either adopt the biblical myth of the origin, or make up an as-if account in which, however, the awareness of its fictional status is inscribed" (70). But whereas Moser claims that this strategy prevailed until the 1790s, when scientific authors rejected it as incompatible with the "serious and useful status" of science, I show that it was challenged much earlier by Scottish critics in particular. Moser, "Experiment and Fiction," in *Literature and Science as Modes of Expresssion,* ed. Frederick Amrine (Boston: Kluwer, 1989), 61–80.

3. I have chosen the term *sensationist philosophy* to describe what is in French referred to as *la philosophie sensualiste,* because of the unintended connotations borne by the adjective *sensualist* in English. For a cogent summary of how associationism and sensationism are co-dependent veins of eighteenth-century thought, see Karl Figlio, "Theories of Perception and the Physiology of Man in the Late Eighteenth Century," *History of Science* 12 (1975): 177–212.

4. Typical of conjectural historians was the Scottish moral philosopher James Dunbar, who envisioned a man just brought to consciousness when the first society was formed. "The scene now opens to the intellectual eye. He marks the relations, and dependences of things; and learns to contemplate the world and himself. Constituted in such circumstances, what more natural to a mind, somewhat elevated above the common life, than this soliloquy: 'Where am I! Whence my original! What my destiny!—Is all around me discord, confusion, chaos! Or is there not some principle of union, consistency, and order?—Am I accountable to my superior? Connected with any great system of being?'" Dunbar, *Essays on the History of Mankind in Rude and Cultivated Ages*

(London: W. Strahan, T. Cadell, 1781), 228–29. On legal discourse, see J. J. Burlamaqui, *The Principles of Natural and Politic Law,* trans. Thomas Nugent, 6th ed. (Philadelphia: H. C. Carey and I. Lea, 1823), 1:27–28. For examples of this trope in libertine literature, see M. Deslandes, *Pigmalion, ou la statue animée* (London: Samuel Harding, 1724), wherein a statue, on awakening, laments that the "science of pleasure" has not yet been perfected and ridicules her lover's invitation to marriage as an unnecessary accessory, suitable only for "madmen and imbeciles" (121).

5. G. J. Barker-Benfield, *The Culture of Sensibility: Sex and Society in Eighteenth-Century Britain* (Chicago: University of Chicago Press, 1992), 3. This "hankering" is cited from Henry Halliwell, *Melapronea: or, A Discourse of the Polity and Kingdom of Darkness* (1681), 77–78.

6. This confluence of medical, literary, and scientific discourse has received much critical attention of late. Prominent English-language titles include Anne C. Vila, *Enlightenment and Pathology: Sensibility in the Literature and Medicine of Eighteenth-Century France* (Baltimore: Johns Hopkins University Press, 1998); Barker-Benfield, *Culture of Sensibility* ; Barbara M. Benedict, *Framing Feeling: Sentiment and Style in English Prose Fiction, 1745–1800* (New York: AMS, 1994); Markman Ellis, *The Politics of Sensibility: Race, Gender, and Commerce in the Sentimental Novel* (New York: Cambridge University Press, 1996); Jerome McGann, *The Poetics of Sensibility: A Revolution in Literary Style* (Oxford: Clarendon, 1996); John O'Neal, *The Authority of Experience: Sensationist Theory in the French Enlightenment* (University Park: Pennsylvania State University Press, 1996); Adela Pinch, *Strange Fits of Passion: Epistemologies of Emotion, Hume to Austen* (Stanford: Stanford University Press, 1996); and Ann Jessie Van Sant, *Eighteenth-Century Sensibility and the Novel: The Senses in Social Context* (Cambridge: Cambridge University Press, 1993).

7. Barbara Benedict, "Reading Faces: Physiognomy and Epistemology in Late Eighteenth-Century Sentimental Novels," *Studies in Philology* 92, no. 3 (summer 1995): 325–26.

8. See Locke,"Of Simple Ideas of Sense" (bk. 2, chap. 3) and "Of the Association of Ideas" (bk. 2, chap. 33), in *An Essay Concerning Human Understanding,* ed. Alexander Campbell Fraser (1690; reprint, New York: Dover, 1959).

9. Barker-Benfield, *Culture of Sensibility,* 4.

10. Albrecht von Haller, *A Dissertation on the Sensible and Irritable Parts of Animals* (1732). For more on Haller's innovations, see Figlio, "Theories of Perception," or Vila, *Enlightenment,* 25–26, 42.

11. As Figlio points out, however, this physiological analysis is limited; Haller pointedly rejected any discretely circumscribed area of sensibility in the brain. "The *medulla oblongota, corpus striatum, thalamus* and *pons* were one continuous medullary mass, whose sensibility revealed the presence of the soul. From this medullary system arose all the nerves, endowed with sensibility by the continuity of the medullary matter." Figlio, "Theories of Perception," 188.

12. Antonie Luyendijk-Elshout, "Of Masks and Mills: The Enlightened Doctor and His Frightened Patient," in *The Languages of Psyche: Mind and Body in Enlightenment Thought,* ed. G. S. Rousseau (Berkeley: University of California Press, 1990), 186–230, esp. 208.

13. Cited in J. H. Teacher, *Catalogue of the Anatomical Preparations of Dr. William Hunter* (Glasgow, 1970), lxiv.

14. Consider Gudin de la Brenellerie, who called for more research on babies' capacity to live in water and lamented the hypocritical opposition to such a useful project: "La vie des hommes est cependant si précieuse, qu'il n'y a peut-être aucun Roi en Europe aussi hardi pour ordonner qu'on tentât cette expérience, sur une demi-douzaine d'enfans: eux qui font massacrer les hommes par milliers pour satisfaire un caprice politique." In *Aux mânes de Louis XV, et des grands hommes qui ont vécu sous son règne, ou Essai sur les progrès des Arts et de l'Esprit humain, sous le règne de Louis XV* (Paris: Aux Deux-Ponts, à l'imprimerie ducale, 1776), 1: 91–92.

15. To remedy this state of affairs, the *Encyclopédie* article "Anatomy" included a long list of blood-curdling experiments to be tried on condemned—but still living—criminals, including blood transfusions, leg amputation, and heart and brain dissections. Others advocated experiments in human breeding. If zoologists could create sturdier beasts of burden through cross-breeding, why couldn't enlightened men improve their own race through selective breeding? On breeding experiments, see Anne Carol, *Histoire de l'eugénisme en France: Les médecins et la procréation XIXe–XXe siècle* (Paris: Editions du Seuil, 1995), 19–20. The complaint was still resonant at the end of the nineteenth century. After discussing eighteenth- and nineteenth-century researches into blood pressure, Austin Flint complained that little was yet known about the phenomenon in 1888: "Physiologists have only an approximative idea of the arterial pressure in the human subject, derived from experiments on the inferior animals." Flint, *A Text-Book of Human Physiology,* 4th ed. (London: H. K. Lewis, 1888), 73.

16. Condillac imagined the scenario of two lost children, wandering in the desert after the deluge, to conceptualize how the first language came into being in his *Essai sur l'origine des connaissances humaines,* pt. 2, sec. 1. See also Adam Smith, who imagined a similar story in his "Considerations concerning the First Formation of Languages, and the Different Genius of Original and Compounded Languages" (1761), in *The Early Writings of Adam Smith,* ed. Ralph Lindgren (New York: Augustus Kelly, 1967), 225.

17. Not all virtual experiments presupposed a positive result. J. Formey's *Anti-Emile* (1763) suggested that a group of children should be relegated to isolation for several generations, hypothesizing that they would never learn anything and would gradually perish, thus proving mankind's inability to survive without the beneficial effects of culture. Cited in Robert R. Palmer, *Catholics and Unbelievers in Eighteenth-Century France* (Princeton: Princeton University Press, 1939), 169.

18. Le Chevalier de Mérian, "Histoire du problème de Molyneux" (1772), ed. Alain Grosrichard, in "Une expérience psychologique au 18e siècle; suivie de Histoire du problème de Molyneux par le chevalier de Mérian," *Cahiers pour l'analyse* 1–2 (1966): 102–24; esp. 120.

19. "J'ai tâché de remonter aussi haut qu'il m'étoit possible dans la mécanique de nos idées." Charles Bonnet, *Essai analytique sur les facultés de l'âme,* in *Oeuvres d'histoire naturelle et de philosophie* (Neuchâtel: Samuel Faulche, 1782), 6:407.

20. But given their preoccupation with style, one might well argue with Geoffrey Bremner that these writers studied nature as aestheticians rather than as scientists. Bremner, "Buffon and the Casting out of Fear," *Studies on Voltaire and the Eighteenth Century* 205 (1982): 82.

21. Porter, "Medical Science and Human Science in the Enlightenment," in *Inventing Human Science: Eighteenth-Century Domains,* ed. Christopher Fox, Roy Porter, and Robert Wokler (Berkeley: University of California Press, 1995), 72.

22. One might usefully see this evolution running alongside the shift in eighteenth-century medicine, from the iatromechanical speculation of the early 1700s to the more biologically grounded clinical knowledge that emerged after 1740. See Theodore M. Brown, "The Changing Self-Concept of the Eighteenth-Century London Physician," *Eighteenth-Century Life* 7, n.s. 2 (January 1982): 31–40.

23. Georges Louis Leclerc, comte de Buffon, *Natural History, General and Particular, by the Count Buffon,* trans. William Smellie (London: T. Cadell and W. Davies, 1812), 3:286. "[D]es matières actives desquelles dépendent le jeu de toutes les parties et l'action de tous les membres," Buffon, *De l'homme,* ed. Michèle Duchet (Paris: F. Maspero, 1971), 207. All the citations to Buffon in this chapter refer to these editions.

24. This reflection on the link between tactile sensitivity and intelligence leads to a cultural critique: the European habit of swaddling children could well be impeding the intellect of future citizens and should be abandoned. Buffon, *De l'homme,* 213.

25. "Si la chose étoit moins importante, on auroit raison de nous blâmer; mais elle est peut-être, plus que toute autre digne, de nous occuper: et ne sait-on pas qu'on doit faire des efforts toutes les fois qu'on veut atteindre à quelque grand objet?" Buffon, *De l'homme,* 214.

26. Although based on a theological premise, Buffon's tale is strikingly free of theological implications, though it is heavily loaded with other cultural references. His Adamic figure discovers mortal life in the highly stylized apparatus of a pastoral *locus amoenus* that English readers quickly recognized as a pastiche of Milton's *Paradise Lost.* The similarity between Buffon's Adamic narrative and Adam's monologue in *Paradise Lost* was rarely noted by French readers, but Goldsmith ironically remarked in his *Animated Nature,* "All that I can say to obviate the imputation of plagiarism is, that the one treats the subject more as a poet, the other more as a philosopher." Oliver Goldsmith, *A History of the Earth and Animated Nature* (Philadelphia: John Grigg, 1830), 1:230.

27. See the cover illustration of Duchet's edition of Buffon, *De l'homme.*

28. Buffon, *Natural History,* 3:295–96. "[L]a lumière, la voute celeste, la verdure de la terre, le cristal des eaux, tout m'occupoit, m'animoit, et me donnoit un sentiment inexprimable de plaisir. . . . Le chant des oiseaux, le murmure des airs, formoient un concert dont la douce impression me remuoit jusqu'au fonds de l'âme." *De l'homme,* 215.

29. Buffon, *Natural History,* 3:300."Quelle saveur! quelle nouveauté de sensation! Jusque-là je n'avois eu que des plaisirs; le goût me donna le sentiment de la volupté." *De l'homme,* 217.

30. Buffon, *Natural History,* 3:301. "Je portai ma main sur ce nouvel être: quel saisissement! ce n'étoit pas moi; mais c'étoit plus que moi, mieux que moi. . . . Je la sentis s'animer sous ma main, je la vis prendre de la pensée dans mes yeux; les siens firent couler dans mes veines une nouvelle source de vie: j'aurois voulu lui donner tout mon être: cette volonté acheva mon existence, je sentis naître un sixième sens." *De l'homme,* 218.

31. Duchet, "L'Anthropologie de Buffon," in Buffon, *De l'homme,* ed Michèle Duchet (Paris: François Maspero, 1971), 9–10.

32. Buffon, *Natural History,* 3:301. "Dès cet instant, l'astre du jour sur la fin de sa course éteignit son flambeau; je m'aperçus à peine que je perdois le sens de la vue, j'existois trop pour craindre de cesser de l'être." *De l'homme,* 218.

33. See Aram Vartanian's wonderful essay for more on these issues: "La Mettrie, Diderot, and Sexology in the Age of Enlightenment," in *Essays on the Age of Enlightenment in Honor of Ira O. Wade,* ed. Jean Macary (Geneva: Librairie Droz, 1977), 347–67.

34. Margaret C. Jacob, "The Materialist World of Pornography," in *The Invention of Pornography: Obscenity and the Origins of Modernity, 1500–1800,* ed. Lynn Hunt (New York: Zone, 1993), 177.

35. Buffon, *Natural History,* 3:140. "[U]ne sage retenue qui fait la décence du style . . . avec cette indifférence philosophique qui détruit tout sentiment dans l'expression, et ne laisse aux mots que leur simple signification." *De l'homme,* 76. Apparently this strategy was ineffectual; Lester Crocker reports that much of the popularity of *L'Histoire naturelle* was due to the detailed descriptions of genitalia and sexual functioning such as those found in this passage. Crocker, *An Age of Crisis: Man and World in Eighteenth-Century French Thought* (Baltimore: Johns Hopkins University Press, 1959), 102–6.

36. *The Charters and Statutes of the Royal Society of London for Improving Natural Knowledge* (London, 1728), chap. 5, para. 4.

37. Buffon, *De l'homme,* 219–22.

38. Although dismissed by some of his *confrères* in the scientific establishment (especially Réaumur), Buffon's work enjoyed much popular success until the revolutionary era, when it was castigated for its "aristocratic" style and his authority was tainted by association with literature. For more on the reception history of Buffon's *Histoire naturelle,* see Londa Schiebinger, *The Mind Has No Sex? Women in the Origins of Modern Science* (Cambridge: Harvard University Press, 1989), 153–54.

39. Thomas L. Hankins, *Science and the Enlightenment* (Cambridge: Cambridge University Press, 1985), 21.

40. Condillac had already helped disseminate Locke's ideas to the French in his *Essai sur l'origine des connaissances humaines* (Essay on the origin of human knowledge, 1746).

41. O'Neal, *Authority of Experience,* 58. One must remember, however, that the physiological grounding for this work is minimal. Figlio notes that Condillac, like other "historians of the intellect," "tended to follow Locke both in concentrating upon the introspective analysis of mind and in avoiding inquiry into the physical causes of ideas. Nonetheless, a presumption of causal mechanism remained strong enough in their occasional speculations to spawn physiological analogies corresponding to their philosophical models." Figlio, "Theories of Perception," 192.

42. L. Rosenfeld, "Condillac's Influence on French Scientific Thought," in *The Triumph of Culture: Eighteenth-Century Perspectives,* ed. P. Fritz and D. Williams (Toronto: University of Toronto Press, 1972), 163.

43. *Virtual witnessing* connotes the linguistic devices that create naturalistic images in the reader's mind, such as circumstantial details, modest admissions of failure, a self-professed "naked way of writing," and advice on the practical strategies of variation and repetition as means of ensuring reliability. Steven Shapin and Simon Schaffer, *Leviathan and the Air-Pump: Hobbes, Boyle, and the Experimental Life* (Princeton: Princeton University Press, 1985), 56–66.

44. "[N]ous imaginâmes une statue organisée intérieurement comme nous, et animée d'un esprit privé de toute espèce d'idées. Nous supposâmes encore que l'extérieur tout de marbre ne lui permettoit l'usage d'aucun de ses sens, et nous nous réservâmes la liberté de les ouvrir à notre choix, aux différentes impressions dont ils sont susceptibles." Abbé Etienne Bonnot de Condillac, *Traité des sensations* (Paris: Fayard, 1984), 11. Con-

dillac, *Condillac's Treatise on the Sensations,* trans. Geraldine Carr (Los Angeles: USC School of Philosophy, 1930), xxx–xxxi. All citations from this work refer to these editions.

45. "J'avertis donc qu'il est très important de se mettre exactement à la place de la statue que nous allons observer. Il faut commencer d'exister avec elle, n'avoir qu'un seul sens, quand elle n'en a qu'un; n'acquérir que les idées qu'elle acquiert, ne contracter que les habitudes qu'elle contracte: en un mot, il faut n'être que ce qu'elle est." This advice stands out immediately; it is published ahead of the *Traité* in the "Avis important au lecteur." Condillac, *Traité des sensations,* 9; Condillac, *Condillac's Treatise on the Sensations,* xxxvii.

46. Shapin and Schaffer, *Leviathan and the Air Pump,* 24–25.

47. Condillac, *Treatise,* xxxvii. "Je crois que les lecteurs, qui se mettront exactement à sa place, n'auront pas de peine à entendre cet ouvrage; les autres m'opposeront des difficultés sans nombre." *Traité,* 9.

48. Condillac, *Treatise,* 55. "Ne donnant de sensibilité qu'à l'intérieur de la bouche de notre statue, je ne saurois lui faire prendre aucune nourriture: mais je suppose que l'air lui apporte à mon gré toutes sortes de saveurs." *Traité,* 69.

49. This conventional setting replicates Buffon's. Evoking the excitement of her first vision, the statue exclaims: "Des tapis de verdure, des bosquets de fleurs, des massifs de bois où le soleil pénètre à peine, des eaux qui coulent lentement ou qui se précipitent avec violence, embellissent ce paysage, que paroît animer une lumière qui répand sur lui mille couleurs différentes." Condillac, *Traité,* 261.

50. "Ces scènes de la nature ont la particularité d'être *purement naturelles,* au sens où toute trace d'influence d'humaine en aura été soigneusement effacée." Yves Citton, "Fragile euphorie: La statue de Condillac et les impasses de l'individu," *Studies on Voltaire and the Eighteenth Century* 323 (1994): 282 (emphasis added). Further references appear in the text.

51. Condillac, *Treatise,* 57. "Il faudrait se mettre tout-à-fait à sa place." *Traité,* 71. See also p. 16: "Que les philosophes à qui il paroît si évident que tout est matériel, se mettent pour un moment à sa place."

52. Cited in Robert G. Weynant, introduction to Condillac, *An Essay on the Origin of Human Knowledge,* trans. Thomas Nugent (Gainesville, Fla.: Scholars' Facsimiles and Reprints, 1971), xi.

53. See Condillac, *Traité,* 45–46.

54. Figlio, "Theories of Perception," 193.

55. In every reference but the chapter headings (which posit a male identity), the subject is called *la statue*—a feminine noun requiring feminine adjectives and verb endings. The *Traité* itself is conceived in a feminine triangle, Citton argues, composed by the woman to whom the book is dedicated (Mme de Vassé), the woman by whom it was inspired (Mlle Ferrand), and the subject who realizes their hopes *(la statue).*

56. See pt. 2, chap. 5: "Comment un homme borné au toucher découvre son corps et apprend qu'il y a quelque chose hors de lui," in Condillac, *Traité,* 101–12. The subheadings demonstrate the mixing of genders; for example: "Sensation par laquelle l'âme découvre qu'elle a un corps," "Son étonnement de n'être pas tout ce qu'elle touche," "Comment elle a appris à toucher," *Traité,* 103, 105, 107.

57. See pt. 4, chapter 7: "D'un homme trouvé dans les forêts de Lithuanie," in ibid.,

253–55. Listed in Linnaeus's *Systema naturae* as *Juvenis Ursinus Lithuanus,* this boy was reportedly discovered in the 1690s in the forests of Lithuania, living the company of bears. Mute, quadrupedal, and seemingly idiot, he gave little evidence of perfectibility.

58. Condillac, *Treatise,* 234. "Instruite par l'expérience, j'examine, je délibère avant d'agir. Je n'obéis plus aveuglément à mes passions, je leur résiste, je me conduis d'après mes lumières, je suis libre." *Traité,* 263.

59. As O'Neal notes, "Notwithstanding their sometimes eloquent arguments for freedom, the sensationists in their preoccupation with the very early stages of cognition tend to underscore human passivity." *Authority of Experience,* 215.

60. Condillac's primary work of political science is *Le Commerce et le gouvernement considéré relativement l'un à l'autre* (1776), which is in truth more a work of economics than political science as such. Condillac argues—*contre* the Physiocrats—that commerce and industry are just as productive as agriculture and that a liberal, laissez-faire economic policy will bring the nation the best chance for prosperity. As Paul Janet notes, Condillac's political vision is derivative of Montesquieu; he too holds up a moderate monarchy as the ideal form of government. See Janet, *Histoire de la science politique dans ses rapports avec la morale,* 5th ed. (Paris: Librairie Félix Alcan, 1925), 2:482–85.

61. "Un peuple est un corps artificiel; c'est au magistrat . . . d'entretenir l'harmonie et la force dans tous les membres. Il est le machiniste qui doit rétablir les ressorts, et remonter toute la machine aussi souvent que les circonstances le demandent. . . . Pour conduire le peuple, il faut établir une discipline qui entretienne un équilibre parfait entre tous les ordres, et qui par-là fasse trouver l'intérêt de chaque citoyen dans l'intérêt de la société. Il faut que les citoyens . . . se conforment nécessairement aux vues d'un système général." Condillac, *Traité des systèmes,* in *Oeuvres philosophiques,* ed. Georges LeRoy (Paris: Presses Universitaires de France, 1947–51), 1:208.

62. Although Condillac's influence on the liberal Idéologues of the Directory is often cited, one must be careful to consider the nature of that influence. It was not for his political ideas that Condillac was useful, but rather for the extreme rigor of his methods, his attention to logic and language, and his demand that one "go back to origins" in analyzing intellectual phenomena. The Idéologues' desire to facilitate the "gradual perfection of the individual and the species" called for a more active populace than Condillac allowed. This would be a major point of contention with later political thinkers, such as August Comte, as well. On this issue, see O'Neal, *Authority of Experience,* 225–44, and Gérard Buis, "Le projet de régénération sociale dans les oeuvres de jeunesse d'A. Comte," in *Régénération et reconstruction sociale entre 1780 et 1848* (Paris: Vrin, 1978), 133–48.

63. For details of Bonnet's early career as an experimentalist, see Lorin Anderson, *Charles Bonnet and the Order of the Known* (Dordrecht, The Netherlands: Reidel, 1982), 4–5.

64. Bonnet, *Essai analytique,* xxv.

65. "J'ai étudié ce qui se passe dans l'organe [le cerveau], lorsqu'il transmet à l'Ame l'impression des Objets. J'ai tâché de découvrir les rapports qui lient les fibres sensibles, et les résultats de ces rapports." Ibid., 6:viii. All citations from the *Essai* refer to this edition; all translations are mine.

66. Ibid., 6:6, Vila, *Enlightenment and Pathology,* 31. For more on Bonnet's relation to rival theories of consciousness, see Vila, 30–42; O'Neal, *Authority of Experience,* 62–82; and Anderson, *Charles Bonnet,* 16–33.

67. "La valeur physique et morale de notre Automate dépendra donc de sa constitution originelle et de la manière dont nous aurons su jouer de cette Machine. . . . Déjà les mouvements vitaux s'opèrent dans la Statue; les liqueurs y circulent et portent à toutes les parties la nourriture qui leur est nécessaire." Bonnet, *Essai analytique,* 6:11.

68. "[L]es corpuscules infiniment petits qui émanent de la rose, forment autour d'elle une atmosphère odiferante. Ils sont introduits par l'air dans l'intérieur du Nez. Ils agissent sur les fibres nerveuses qui le tapissent. Cette action est le résultat des rapports qui sont entre ces corpuscules et ces fibres." Ibid., 6:19.

69. "La Liberté est donc, en général, la Faculté par laquelle l'Ame exécute la Volonté. Ainsi, la Liberté est subordonnée à la Volonté, comme la Volonté l'est à la Faculté de sentir; cette Faculté l'est à l'action des Organes; cette action à celle des Objets. . . . La Liberté est donc en soi indéterminée. C'est une simple Force, un simple pouvoir d'agir ou de mouvoir. La Volonté détermine cette Force à s'appliquer à tel ou tel Organe, à telles ou telles fibres." Ibid., 6:85–86.

70. Vila, *Enlightenment and Pathology,* 32–33.

71. "Ce que j'ai exposé sur l'odorat peut s'appliquer facilement aux autres Sens. J'ai tâché de remonter aussi haut qu'il m'étoit possible dans la méchanique de nos idées." Bonnet, *Essai analytique,* 6:407.

72. Jacob Robert Kantor, *The Scientific Evolution of Psychology* (Chicago: Principia, 1963–69), 2:190.

73. "Le langage met donc en valeur toutes les fibres du Cerveau. Le Cerveau de l'Hottentot n'est pas, sans doute, moins bien organisé que celui de l'Anglois; mais quelle différence dans l'emploi des fibres!" Bonnet, *Essai analytique,* 6:405.

74. Bonnet, *Contemplation de la nature,* in *Oeuvres d'histoire naturelle et de philosophie* (Neuchâtel: Samuel Faulche, 1781), 4:122.

75. "Le nombre des conséquences justes que différents esprits tirent du même principe ne pourrait-il pas servir de fondement à la construction d'un *Psychomètre*? Et ne peut-on pas présumer qu'un jour on mesurera les esprits comme on mesure les corps?" Bonnet, cited in Jean Rostand, *Un grand biologiste: Charles Bonnet, expérimenteur et théoricien* (Paris: Université de Paris, "Palais de la Découverte," 1966), 32–33.

76. Nearly fifty years after the *Traité des sensations* was published, the eminent Idéologue Pierre Jean Georges Cabanis praised Condillac's "perfect method" all the while rejecting his static, universalist conclusions. Revealing the shift toward a more positivistic approach to human science, Cabanis declared that it is no longer sufficed to consider the mind in abstraction; physiological and physical factors must be weighed as well. Physical factors are crucial not only because they have great impact on the mind, but because they may be altered and thus the mind may be improved at will. See Cabanis, "Rapport du physique et du moral, I," in *Oeuvres philosophiques de Cabanis,* ed. Claude Lehec and Jean Cazeneuve (Paris: Presses Universitaires de France, 1956), 1:141, 143–44.

77. "Were such a man as *Adam,* created in the full vigour of understanding, without experience, he would never be able to infer motion in the second ball from the motion and impulse of the first. . . . no inference from cause to effect amounts to a demonstration. . . . It would have been necessary, therefore, for *Adam* (if he was not inspired) to have had *experience* of the effect which followed upon the impulse of these two balls." Hume, *An Abstract of a Treatise of Human Nature,* ed. J. M. Keynes and P. Sraffa (Cambridge: Cambridge University Press, 1938), 13, 14.

78. Hume, *Abstract,* 6.

79. Stewart, cited in Edward Tagart, *Locke's Writings and Philosophy Historically Considered, Vindicated from the Charge of Contributing to the Scepticism of Hume* (1855; reprint, New York: Garland, 1984), 143–44 (emphasis in original).

80. "It is not . . . to be supposed, that man ever existed apart from the qualities and operations of his own nature, or that any one operation and quality existed without the others. . . . It may no doubt be convenient, we may again repeat, in speculation, or in assigning the origin and in deriving the progress of any attainment, to consider the attainment itself abstractly, or apart from the faculty or power by which it is made; and we must not deny ourselves the use of such abstractions, in treating of any other subject. But there is a caution to be observed in the use of abstractions, . . . That they be not mistaken for realities, nor obtruded for historical facts." Adam Ferguson, *Principles of Moral and Political Science* (Edinburgh: Printed for A. Strahan and T. Cadell, London, and W. Creech, Edinburgh, 1792), 1:195–96.

81. Voltaire, Condillac, and Diderot are just a few of the philosophes who used the phenomenon of blind or deaf-mute people regaining their senses as a departure for speculation on the role of the senses in human cognition. See Carr, "Pygmalion and the *Philosophes,*" 250–51.

82. Adam Ferguson, *An Essay on the History of Civil Society,* ed. Duncan Forbes (Edinburgh: Edinburgh University Press, 1966), 4.

83. Ibid.

84. Shapin and Schaffer, *Leviathan and the Air-Pump,* 25.

85. Ibid., 56–66.

86. For more on this ambivalence about the truth value of experimental results, see Rose-Mary Sargent, *The Diffident Naturalist: Robert Boyle and the Philosophy of Experiment* (Chicago: University of Chicago Press, 1995), 159–204.

87. "[L'expérience] cherche à pénétrer [la nature] plus profondément, à lui dérober ce qu'elle cache; à créer en quelque manière, par la différente combinaison des corps, de nouveaux phénomènes pour les étudier: enfin elle ne se borne pas à écouter la Nature, mais elle l'interroge et la presse." Diderot et al., "Expérimental," *Encyclopédie,* 6:298.

88. Moser, "Experiment and Fiction," 77. For more on the judicial metaphor in period science, see Robert Kargon, "The Testimony of Nature: Boyle, Hooke and Experimental Philosophy," *Albion* 3 (1971): 72–80.

89. "Descartes, & Bacon lui-même, malgré toutes les obligations que leur a la Philosophie, lui auroient peut-être été encore plus utiles, s'ils eussent été plus physiciens de pratique & moins de théorie; mais le plaisir oisif de la méditation & de la conjecture même, entraîne les grands esprits." Diderot et al.,"Expérimental," *Encyclopédie,* 6:299.

90. Moser, "Experiment and Fiction," 65.

91. Ibid., 72.

92. The most famous figures associated with this school are Adam Ferguson, James Dunbar, John Millar, and Adam Smith. For more on this issue, see H.-M. Höpfl, "From Savage to Scotsman: Conjectural History in the Scottish Enlightenment," *Journal of British Studies* 7 (1978): 19–40.

93. Francis Jeffrey, article on John Millar in *The Edinburgh Review* (1803): 157. Christopher Fox has illustrated this denigration of the eighteenth-century "gaze" and preference for the more scientific "systematic and illuminated record" of nineteenth-century natural history. For more on the visual rhetoric associated with these traditions,

and the so-called birth of the observer, see Christopher Fox, introduction to *Inventing Human Science,* 11–13.

94. Roger Emerson charts a decline in Scottish fascination with French sources from the 1740s (when Montesquieu and Buffon were at the height of their influence) to the 1770s, when French travel accounts (of Prévost, Lafitau, and Charlevoix) enjoyed more popularity than abstract French philosophy. See "American Indians, Frenchmen, and Scots Philosophers," *Studies in Eighteenth-Century Culture* 9 (1979): 222–26; 225.

95. Höpfl, "From Savage to Scotsman," 27.

96. Ibid., 26–40. Note that it is his articulation of laws such as these that enabled Vico to use the term *science* in his major work, *New Science* (1725; rev. 1730 and 1744).

97. Mary Poovey, *A History of the Modern Fact: Problems of Knowledge in the Sciences of Wealth and Society* (Chicago: University of Chicago Press, 1998), 221. Further references appear in the text.

98. John Millar, *Observations concerning the Distinction of Ranks in Society* (Edinburgh, 1771), cited in Poovey, *History,* 223.

99. For a masterful analysis of these issues in a slightly earlier period, consult Steven Shapin, *A Social History of Truth: Civility and Science in Seventeenth-Century England* (Chicago: University of Chicago Press, 1994).

100. Andrew Skinner, "Natural History in the Age of Adam Smith," *Political Studies* 15, no. 1 (1967): 46 (emphasis added).

101. David Hume, *Treatise of Human Nature* (1739; reprint, Buffalo: Prometheus, 1992), 402.

102. Christopher Lawrence, "The Nervous System and Society in the Scottish Enlightenment," in *Natural Order: Historical Studies of Scientific Culture,* ed. Barry Barnes and Steven Shapin (Beverly Hills: Sage, 1979), 19–40. Explaining Hume's conservatism, Henry D. Aiken points out that Hume's notion of legitimacy in politics was primarily a matter of tradition and custom, not rights. "There is no single criterion: original contract, long possession, present possession, succession, and continuously operating laws, all contribute to the title of sovereignty. . . . Like Burke, Hume tends to believe that the fact that a people accepts without protest an existing authority is evidence that the rule of the latter is not unduly oppressive. . . . Whatever his shortcomings, and they are many, few philosophers have been less inclined to confuse what is with what ought to be." Aiken, introduction to *Hume's Moral and Political Philosophy,* ed. H. D. Aiken (New York: Hafner/Macmillan, 1948), xlix–l.

103. Charles-Georges LeRoy declared in 1781 that all efforts by missionaries to civilize savage babies have ended in failure, because "la force du sang l'a toujours emporté sur l'éducation," and thus cast a pessimistic prognosis of mankind's potential perfectibility: "L'histoire nous apprend que le genre humain, après plusieurs siècles de lumière, a plus d'une fois été replongé dans l'ignorance et la barbarie, par la pente invisible qu'ont les hommes en général vers la paresse, et vers les idées matérielles et grossières." In LeRoy, *Lettres philosophiques sur l'intelligence et la perfectibilité des animaux, avec quelques lettres sur l'homme* (Lettres posthumes sur l'homme: Lettre 15), ed. Elizabeth Anderson (Oxford: Voltaire Foundation, 1994), in *Studies on Voltaire and the Eighteenth Century* 316 (1994): 209.

104. G. S. Rousseau, "Nerves, Spirits, and Fibres: Towards Defining the Origins of Sensibility," *Blue Guitar* 2 (1976): 143.

105. John Arthur Passmore, *The Perfectibility of Man,* 2d ed. (New York: Scribner Sons, 1970) 165.

106. Richardson's Lovelace held that women's spirits were "naturally soft" and claimed that one must take special care in talking to women because, "like so many musical instruments, touch but a single wire, and the dear souls are sensible all over." Samuel Richardson, *Clarissa* (1747–48), cited in Barker-Benfield, *Culture of Sensibility,* 27.

107. For more on English writers who posited connections between women's behavior and their nervous system, see Barker-Benfield, *Culture of Sensibility,* 26–36.

108. Lieselotte Steinbrügge, *The Moral Sex: Woman's Nature in the French Enlightenment,* trans. Pamela W. Selwyn (Oxford: Oxford University Press, 1995), 37.

109. "[L]a difficulté de se dérober à la tyrannie des sensations l'attachant continuellement aux causes immédiates qui les produisent, ne lui permettent point de s'élever à la hauteur convenable pour les embrasser toutes d'une seule vue." Pierre Roussel, *Système physique et moral de la femme, ou tableau philosophique de la constitution, de l'état organique, du tempérament, des moeurs, & des fonctions propres au sexe* (Paris: Vincent, 1775), 30.

110. "Leurs organes délicats se ressentiroient davantage les inconvénients inévitables qu'elle [une étude sérieuse] entraîne!" Ibid., 103.

111. "Leurs sens mobiles parcourent tous les objets & en emportent l'image. . . . Le monde réel ne leur suffit pas; elles aiment à se créer un monde imaginaire; elles l'habitent & l'embelissent." Antoine Thomas, *Essai sur le caractère, les moeurs et l'esprit des femmes dans les différents siècles* (Paris: Moutard, 1772), 84. Richardson cited women's putatively superior powers of imagination to defend their writing skills in his novel *Clarissa* (1747–48). Speaking through the heroine, he argued that "the pen, next to the needle," was the most proper employment for women, "best adapted to their geniuses," because "[t]he gentleness of their minds, the delicacy of their sentiments . . . and the liveliness of their imaginations qualify them . . . for this employment." Cited in Barker-Benfield, *Culture of Sensibility,* 170–71.

112. Steinbrügge, *Moral Sex,* 39. As evidence of the downside of Thomas's theory, Steinbrügge notes his comment that "[l]es spectres, les enchantemens, les prodiges, tout ce qui sort des loix ordinaires de la nature, sont leurs ouvrages & leurs délices. Leur ame s'exalte & leur esprit est toujours plus près de l'enthousiasme." Thomas, *Essai sur le caractère,* 84.

113. For other views on this debate, consult Mary D. Sheriff, *The Exceptional Woman: Elisabeth Vigée-Lebrun and the Cultural Politics of Art* (Chicago: University of Chicago Press, 1996), 33–38, 64–69; Schiebinger, *The Mind Has No Sex?* 188–213; and Ludmila Jordanova, *Sexual Visions: Images of Gender in Science and Medicine between the Eighteenth and Twentieth Centuries* (Madison: University of Wisconsin Press, 1989).

114. Michèle LeDoeuff, *The Philosophical Imagination,* trans. Colin Gordon (Stanford: Stanford University Press, 1989), 138–70.

115. Madelyn Gutwirth, *The Twilight of the Goddesses: Women and Representation in the French Revolutionary Era* (New Brunswick, N.J.: Rutgers University Press, 1992), 146.

116. Vila, *Enlightenment and Pathology,* 244. Further references appear in the text.

117. Vila notes that Roussel's restrictive vision of women's intellectual capabilities had an immense impact on medicine well into the next century (ibid., 254).

118. On Hartley's debt to Locke and Haller, see Figlio, "Theories of Perception," 196–99.

119. This idea was shared by Hartley's editor and great disciple Joseph Priestley. On the relation between the two philosophers, see Martin Fitzpatrick, "Joseph Priestley and the Millennium," in *Science, Medicine and Dissent: Joseph Priestley (1733–1804),* ed. R. G. W. Anderson and Christopher Lawrence (London: Wellcome Trust/Science Museum, 1987), 29–37.

120. David Hartley, *Observations on Man, his Frame, his Duty, and his Expectations* (New York: Garland, 1971), 1:81.

121. "If Beings of the same Nature, but whose Affections and Passions are, at present, in different Proportions to each other, be exposed for an indefinite Time to the same Impressions and Associations, all their particular Differences will, at last, be overruled, and they will become perfectly similar, or even equal. They may also be made perfectly similar, in a finite Time, by a proper Adjustment of the Impressions and Associations." Ibid, 1:81–82.

122. Claude Adrien Helvétius, *A Treatise on Man; His Intellectual Faculties and His Education,* trans. W. Hooper (1810; reprint, New York: Burt Franklin, 1967), 1:97. "[L]a supériorité de l'esprit, n'est le produit ni du tempérament, ni de la plus ou moins grande finesse des sens, ni d'une qualité occulte, mais l'effet de la cause très-connue de l'éducation." Helvétius, *De l'homme,* ed. Geneviève and Jacques Moutaux (Paris: Fayard, 1989), 1:142–43.

123. "Des faits sans nombre prouvent que par-tout les hommes sont essentiellement les mêmes . . . en tous les Pays leurs organes sont à peu près les mêmes, qu'ils en font à peu près le même usage. . . . Rien n'indique donc, comme on le répète sans cesse, que ce soit à la différence des latitudes qu'on doive attribuer l'inégalité des Esprits." Helvétius, *De l'homme,* 1:302.

124. "Ou aucun individu de l'espèce humaine n'a de véritables droits, ou tous ont les mêmes." Marie-Jean-Antoine-Nicolas de Caritat, marquis de Condorcet, *Sur l'admission des femmes au droit de Cité,* in *Oeuvres de Condorcet,* ed. A. Condorcet O'Connor and M. F. Arago (Paris: Firmin Didot Frères, 1847; reprint, Stuttgart: Friedrich Frommann Verlag, 1968), 10:122. Note that Condorcet's reasoning presaged Olympe de Gouges' argument in *Déclaration des droits de la femme et de la citoyenne* (1791). For more on the parallels between the two authors, see Dominique Godineau, *Citoyennes tricoteuses: Les femmes du peuple à Paris pendant la Révolution française* (Aix-en-Provence: Editions Alinea, 1988), 271–72.

125. "Pourquoi des êtres exposés à des grossesses, et à des indispositions passagères, ne pourroient-ils exercer des droits dont on n'a jamais imaginé de priver les gens qui ont la goutte tous les hivers, et qui s'enrhument aisément?" Condorcet, *Sur l'admission des femmes,* 10:122.

126. That women should think differently than men was quite logical, as J. Salwyn Shapiro points out; "[r]eceiving a different education and living under different laws, women naturally did not have the same sense of justice and fairness as did men." Shapiro, *Condorcet and the Rise of Liberalism in France* (New York: Harcourt, Brace, 1934), 191.

127. "De plus, l'espèce de contrainte où les opinions relatives aux moeurs tiennent l'âme et l'esprit des femmes presque dès l'enfance, et surtout depuis le moment où le génie commence à se développer, doit nuire à ses progrès dans presque tous les genres." Condorcet, *Lettres d'un bourgeois de New-Haven* in *Oeuvres,* 9:19.

128. Gutwirth, *Twilight of the Goddessses,* 203. "[E]xcepté une classe peu nombreuse

d'hommes très-éclairés, l'égalité est entière entre les femmes et le reste des hommes." Condorcet, *Sur l'admission des femmes,* 10:123.

129. Helvétius, *Treatise on Man,* 2:406–7 (emphasis added). "L'esprit et les talens ne sont jamais dans les hommes que le produit de leurs désirs, et de leur position particulière. La science de l'éducation se réduit peut-être à placer les hommes dans une position qui les force à l'acquisition des talens et des vertus désirés en eux." *De l'homme,* 2:882.

130. Helvétius, *Treatise on Man,* 2:421. "Ce que peut une excellente éducation, c'est de multiplier le nombre des gens de génie dans une Nation; c'est d'inoculer, si je l'ose dire, le bon sens au reste des citoyens." *De l'homme* 2:900.

131. Helvétius, *Treatise on Man,* 2:447. "Qu'on leve ces obstacles qu'une stupidité religieuse ou tyrannique met au progrès de la morale, c'est alors qu'on pourra se flatter de porter la science de l'éducation au degré de perfection dont elle est susceptible." *De l'homme,* 2:923–24.

132. Ibid., 2:441. "Que l'Eglise Catholique se rassure donc et croie qu'en un siècle aussi superstitieux, ses Ministres conserveront toujours assez de puissance pour s'opposer efficacement à toute réforme utile." *De l'homme,* 2:916.

133. Passmore, *Perfectibility of Man,* 173.

134. Ibid. Passmore is citing Tocqueville's *Ancien régime et la révolution* (bk. 3, chap. 1).

CHAPTER THREE

1. For a good synthesis of these changing attitudes and practices in education, see Georges Snyder, *La Pédagogie en France aux XVIIe et XVIIIe siècle* (Paris: Presses Universitaires de France, 1965) and Philippe Ariès, *L'Enfant et la vie familiale sous l'Ancien Régime* (Paris: Seuil, 1973).

2. "La nature ne nous a pas fait méchants: c'est la mauvaise éducation, le mauvais exemple, la mauvaise législation qui nous corrompent," Denis Diderot, letter to Sophie Volland, cited in Snyder, *La Pédagogie,* 282.

3. As Alexis de Tocqueville remarked in *L'Ancien régime et la révolution* (1856): "Dans l'éloignement presque infini où ils vivaient de la pratique, aucune expérience ne venait tempérer les ardeurs de leur naturel; rien ne les avertissait des obstacles que les faits existants pouvaient apporter aux réformes mêmes les plus désirables; ils n'avaient nulle idée des périls qui accompagnent toujours les révolutions les plus nécessaires." In *De la démocratie en Amérique, Souvenirs, L'Ancien régime et la révolution,* ed. Jean-Claude Lamberti and Françoise Mélonio (Paris: Robert Laffont, 1986), 1036–37. See also Norman Hampson, "The Enlightenment in France," in *The Enlightenment in National Context,* ed. Roy Porter and Mikulás Teich (Cambridge: Cambridge University Press, 1981), 41–53. Keith Baker has argued, however, that many of the philosophes (especially "reforming administrators" such as Turgot) had close ties to the monarchy. Baker usefully delineates the overlapping professional and social spheres in which the philosophes circulated in *Condorcet: From Natural Philosophy to Social Mathematics* (Chicago: University of Chicago Press, 1975), 18. However, it remains that the authors discussed here were never in any positions of official influence or bureaucratic power.

4. Benjamin Martin, *The Young Gentleman's and Lady's Philosophy, in a Continued Survey of the Works of Nature and Art; By Way of a Dialogue,* 2d ed. (London: W. Owen, 1772), 1:306–7.

5. Jean-Jacques Rousseau, *Emile,* trans. Barbara Foxley (London: J. M. Dent, 1938), 115. "Plus nous nous éloignons de l'état de nature, plus nous perdons de nos gout naturels." Jean-Jacques Rousseau, *Emile ou de l'éducation,* in *Oeuvres complètes,* ed. Bernard Gagnebin and Marcel Raymond (Paris: Gallimard, 1969),4:407. All citations from *Emile* refer to these editions, unless otherwise noted.

6. "Elever Emile signifie faire un homme qui conserve ses habitudes 'naturelles' jusque dans la vie sociale." Note by Burgelin in *Emile,* 4:282 n. 3.

7. Rousseau's concern with the clash of private interest and general good runs throughout *Le Contrat social* (written during the same years as *Emile*), as when the author writes: "[l]oin que l'intérest [*sic*] particulier s'allie au bien général, ils s'excluent l'un l'autre dans l'ordre naturel des choses, et les lois sociales sont un joug que chacun veut bien imposer aux autres, mais non pas s'en charger lui même," *Le Contrat social (1e version),* in *Oeuvres complètes,* ed. Bernard Gagnebin and Marcel Raymond (Paris: Gallimard, 1969), 3:284. Rousseau praises the strong state intervention practiced by great leaders of antiquity, such as Lycurgus, Moses, and Numa, who realized that "Celui qui ose entreprendre d'instituer un peuple doit se sentir en état de changer, pour ainsi dire, la nature humaine; de transformer chaque individu, qui par lui-même est un tout parfait et solitaire, en partie d'un plus grand" (3:381). The theme was already a preoccupation a decade earlier, as we see in *Le Discours sur l'origine de l'inégalité,* where pre-social man gradually loses his bestial freedoms in becoming socialized and civilized. For a cogent summary of this theme in Rousseau's works, see Robert Wokler, "Rousseau's Perfectibilian Libertarianism," in *The Idea of Freedom: Essays in Honour of Isaiah Berlin,* ed. Alan Ryan (Oxford: Oxford University Press, 1979), 233–52.

8. Locke's work was immensely popular: by the end of the eighteenth century *Some Thoughts* had been reprinted at least twenty-one times; it was translated into French almost immediately on publication and reprinted at least sixteen times. For more details, see J. L. Axtell, ed., *The Educational Writings of John Locke* (Cambridge: Cambridge University Press, 1968), 98–104. *Emile* was not the first eighteenth-century novel to fictionalize an experimental education, however. *Martinus Scriblerus* and *Tristram Shandy* evince a similar zeal for enriching their sons' minds. Satirizing "false tastes in learning," the protagonist of *Memoirs of Martinus Scriblerus* (1741) is raised on butter and honey, since his parents believe that if beef is fed to the young it spoils their understanding. See Alexander Pope, *Works,* ed. Whitwell Elwin and William Courthope (New York: Gordian, 1967), 10:291–92. As for Laurence Sterne's *Tristram Shandy* (1759–67), his father believes the best way to enrich the child's mind is with auxiliary verbs and a multitude of incoming ideas! See *Tristram Shandy,* ed. Wilbur L. Cross (New York: J. F. Taylor, 1904), bk. 5, chap. 42, 326.

9. Rousseau reflects on these issues in *Les Confessions,* describing how his sojourn in Venice had made him see the pernicious effects of a bad government and had reignited his life-long goal of writing a book called *Les Institutions politiques:* "J'avois vu que tout tenoit radicalement à la politique, et que, de quelque façon qu'on s'y prit, aucun peuple ne seroit jamais que ce que la nature de son Gouvernement le feroit être" *Confessions,* in *Oeuvres complètes,* ed. Bernard Gagnebin, Marcel Raymond, and Robert Osmont (Paris: Gallimard, 1959), 1:404.

10. John Locke, *Some Thoughts Concerning Education,* ed. John W. and Jean S. Yolton (Oxford: Clarendon, 1989), 265. Further references appear in the text.

11. My translation, which I prefer because it retains Rousseau's metaphor of social

degeneration, to Foxley's translation: "God makes all things good; man meddles with them and they become evil" (*Emile,* 5). "Tout est bien, sortant des mains de l'auteur des choses: tout dégenére entre les mains de l'homme" (*Emile,* 4:245).

12. *Emile,* 16. "Voulez-vous donc qu'il garde sa forme originelle? Conservez-le dès l'instant qu'il vient au monde. Sitôt qu'il naît, emparez-vous de lui, ne le quittez plus qu'il ne soit homme." *Emile,* 4:261.

13. Yves Touchefeu, "Le Sauvage et le citoyen: Le Mythe des origines dans le système de Rousseau," in *Primitivisme et mythes des origines dans la France des lumières,* ed. Chantal Grell and Christian Michel (Paris: Presses de l'Université de Paris–Sorbonne, 1989), 177–91.

14. On these debates see Robert R. Palmer, *Catholics and Unbelievers in Eighteenth-Century France* (Princeton: Princeton University Press, 1939), 194–95.

15. In an earlier version the tutor did not call his pupil by name until book 4. For more on the evolution of Emile's character, see John S. Spink, introduction to *Emile, Première Version (Manuscrit Favre),* in *Oeuvres complètes,* 4:lxxix.

16. Here too the sense of touch is crucial: "Il veut tout toucher, tout manier; ne vous opposez point à cette inquiétude; elle lui suggère un apprentissage très nécessaire, c'est ainsi qu'il apprend à sentir la chaleur, le froid, la dureté, la molesse, la pesanteur, la légéreté des corps, à juger de leur grandeur, de leur figure et de toutes leurs qualités sensibles en regardant, palpant, écoutant, surtout en comparant la vüe au toucher, en estimant à l'oeil la sensation qu'ils feroient sous ses doigts." *Emile,* 4:284.

17. Passmore declared Locke a great "Enlightener," stating that "Locke has opened up, in principle, the possibility of perfecting men by the application of readily intelligible, humanly controllable mechanisms . . . according to which men can be morally improved to an unlimited degree." John Arthur Passmore, *The Perfectibility of Man,* 2d ed. (New York: Scribner Sons, 1970), 163.

18. *Emile,* 14. "Observez la nature, et suivez la route qu'elle vous trace." *Emile,* 4:259.

19. According to Pierre Burgelin, the tutor's conduct toward Emile represents an exemplary friendship, analogous to the somewhat pedagogical relationship between the lovers Julie and Saint Preux. Burgelin, *La Philosophie de l'existence de Rousseau* (Paris: Presses Universitaires de France, 1952), 504. Claude Habib also stresses the give-and-take between tutor and pupil and describes the teacher as a feminized love object in Habib, "L'Intelligence du sexuel: Rousseau," *Littérature* 60 (December 1985): 39. The dark side of Rousseauian pedagogy has a strong critic in Josué Harari, who rebuts such soft-hearted analyses by foregrounding the tutor's techniques of surveillance and "spying" on his pupil and evokes a relationship based on inequality and a will to control. Harari, *Scenarios of the Imaginary: Theorizing the French Enlightenment* (Ithaca: Cornell University Press, 1987), 102–32.

20. Locke argues that by raising children with a strong hand, the relationship between parent and child will necessarily be based on "fear and awe" in early years, but later it will change to "love and friendship." *Some Thoughts,* 110.

21. For an exhaustive summary of Rousseau's impact in Europe, see Gilbert Py, *Rousseau et les éducateurs: Etude sur la fortune et les idées pédagogiques de Jean-Jacques Rousseau en France et en Europe au XVIIIe siècle* (Oxford: Voltaire Foundation, 1997), in *Studies on Voltaire and the Eighteenth Century* 356 (1997); on Rousseau in England, see Alan Richardson, *Literature, Education, and Romanticism: Reading as Social Practice,*

1780–1832 (Cambridge: Cambridge University Press, 1994), and on women's responses to Rousseau, see Mary Seidman Trouille, *Sexual Politics in the Enlightenment: Women Writers Read Rousseau* (Albany: State University of New York Press, 1997).

22. On toys, Locke writes, "They should make them themselves, or at least endeavour it; and set themselves about it: Till then they should have none; and till then they will want none of any great artifice." *Some Thoughts,* 192.

23. *Emile,* 139. "Je veux que nous fassions nous-mémes toutes nos machines. . . . J'aime mieux que nos instrumens ne soient point si parfaits et si justes, et que nous ayons des idées plus nettes de ce qu'ils doivent être et des opérations qui doivent en résulter. . . . Tant d'instrumens inventés pour nous guider dans nos expériences et suppléer à la justesse des sens en font négliger l'exercice." *Emile,* 4:441–42.

24. Tom explains a series of physical principles in Lecture 1, "Of Matter and Motion," through reference to objects such as a top, a marble shot upon the ice (a body in motion will always move in a straight line), a cricket ball and a fives-ball (the relative swiftness of two objects, deduced from distanced moved), and a hoop (a body at rest cannot give itself motion). See Tom Telescope [Newbery], *The Newtonian System of Philosophy Adapted to the Capacities of Young Gentlemen and Ladies* (London: Printed for J. Newbery, 1761), 5–8. For more on experimental science for children, see Barbara Maria Stafford, *Artful Science: Enlightenment, Entertainment, and the Eclipse of Visual Education* (Cambridge: MIT Press, 1994), 47–70. On the moral lessons contained in Newbery's work see James A. Secord, "Newton in the Nursery: Tom Telescope and the Philosophy of Tops and Balls, 1761–1838," *History of Science* 23 (1985): 127–51.

25. *Emile,* 139. "Pour ma prémiére leçon de statique, au lieu d'aller chercher des balances, je met un bâton en travers sur le dos d'une chaise, je mesure la longueur des deux parties du bâton en équilibre; j'ajoûte de part et d'autre des poids tantôt égaux tantôt inégaux, et le tirant ou le poussant autant qu'il est necessaire, je trouve enfin que l'équilibre resulte d'une proportion réciproque entre la quantité des poids et la longueur des leviers. Voila déja mon petit physicien capable de rectifier des balances avant que d'en avoir vû." *Emile,* 4:442.

But figure 14 supplies numerous details that clash with the narrative of *Emile.* Tutor and child appear dressed in the elegant garb of the urban aristocracy: buckled shoes, stockings, breeches, and waistcoat, and the interior resembles an upper-class milieu furnished in the Louis XVI style. Why did illustrators take such freedoms with Rousseau's ideas? The reasons probably have more to do with the conventions of book illustration than any desire to subvert Rousseauian pedagogy. Many painter-engravers worked both as book illustrators and as designers of costume plates for the fashion industry, which was achieving much success in this period by catering to an increasingly wealthy and numerous audience of upwardly mobile merchants, bankers, tradesmen, and lawyers. Preoccupied with personal wealth and social status, this group, which sought to adorn their homes and bodies with stylish accoutrements, was also the main public for illustrated books, which were themselves luxury goods. For more on this commodity-driven market economy, see Neil McKendrick, John Brewer, and J. H. Plumb, eds., *The Birth of a Consumer Society: The Commercialization of Eighteenth-Century England* (Bloomington: Indiana University Press, 1982).

26. Newbery writes that the little gentry was conducted to the Marquis de Setstar's home "that they might have the use of proper instruments." *Newtonian System of Philosophy,* 4.

27. On Martin's career as an instrument-maker, see John Millburn, *Benjamin Martin: Author, Instrument-Maker, and 'Country Showman'* (Leiden: Noordhoff International, 1976).

28. Martin, *Young Gentleman and Lady's Philosophy,* 1:403.

29. *Emile,* 137. "Ma foi, Messieurs, si j'avois quelque autre talent pour vivre, je ne me glorifierois guére de celui-ci. . . . [I]l ne faut pas se presser d'étaler étourdiment ce qu'on sait; j'ai toujours soin de conserver mes meilleurs tours pour l'occasion, et après celui-ci j'en ai d'autres encore pour arrêter de jeunes indiscrets. . . . Je fais payer mes tours et non mes leçons. . . . . Que de suites mortifiantes attire le prémier mouvement de vanité!" (4:439–40).

30. Stafford, *Artful Science,* 79. On the dubious morality assumed of such traveling showmen as Martin, see also Simon Schaffer, "The Consuming Flame: Electrical Showmen and Tory Mystics in the World of Goods," in *Consumption and the World of Goods,* ed. John Brewer and Roy Porter (London: Routledge, 1993), 489–526.

31. On the Académie des Science's response to the popularity of Mesmer, Marat, and their forms of pseudo-science, see Baker, *Condorcet,* 76–77. On Mesmer and Cagliostro, see Robert Darnton, *Mesmerism and the End of the Enlightenment in France* (Cambridge: Harvard University Press, 1968), and W. R. H. Trowbridge, *Cagliostro* (New Hyde Park, N.Y.: University Books, 1910).

32. Henri Decremps, *Les Petites aventures de Jérôme Sharp, professeur de physique amusante; Ouvrage contenant autant de tours ingénieux que de leçons utiles, avec quelques petits portraits à la manière noire,* ed. Jean-Marc Drouin (Geneva: Editions Champion-Slatkine, 1989), 177–82.

33. *Emile,* 131, 139. "[Q]u'il n'apprenne pas la science, qu'il l'invente. Si jamais vous subsituez dans son esprit l'autorite a la raison, il ne raisonera [sic] plus; il ne sera plus que le jouet de l'opinion des autres" (4:430). "L'air scientifique tue la science" (4:441). Rousseau wielded a mighty influence with critics of the Académie such as Bernardin de Saint-Pierre and Brissot; for more on these disputes, see Roger Hahn, *Anatomy of a Scientific Institution: The Paris Academy of Sciences, 1666–1803* (Berkeley: University of California Press, 1971), 152–55, 183, 212–13.

34. *Emile,* 97. "N'exercez donc pas seulement les forces, exercez tous les sens qui les dirigent, tirez de chacun d'eux tout le parti possible, puis vérifiez l'impression de l'un par l'autre. Mesurez, comptez, pesez, comparez. N'employer la force qu'après avoir estimé la resistance." *Emile,* 4:380.

35. Such advice would be familiar to readers of Montaigne as well; Montaigne cites writers of antiquity such as Seneca and Plutarch in advising that children avoid eating meat, be exposed to cold and wet weather, and take part in much physical activity (bk. 1, chap. 26), and wear loose-fitting clothing (bk. 1, chap. 36). See Michel de Montaigne, *Essais,* in *Oeuvres complètes,* ed. Maurice Rat (Paris: Gallimard, 1962).

36. Indeed, Rousseau was vehemently against habits of any kind, and declared: "La seule habitude qu'on doit laisser prendre à l'enfant est de n'en contracter aucune." *Emile,* 4:282.

37. "Un enfant supportera des changemens que ne supporteroit pas un homme: les fibres du prémier, molles et fléxibles, prennent sans effort le pli qu'on leur donne; celles de l'homme, plus endurcies, ne changent plus qu'avec violence le pli qu'elles ont receu." *Emile,* 4:260. This doctrine of "fibres" relates to brain physiology in Bonnet, whereas the *Dictionnaire de Trévoux* defines *fibres* as "de petits filets ou filaments, dont les mem-

branes et les muscles sont entretissus." On the use of baths for health, see John Arbuthnot, *An Essay Concerning the Effects of Air on Human Bodies* (London, 1751). See notes by Pierre Burgelin in *Emile,* 4:1310.

38. On firearms, Rousseau writes: "S'agit-il d'exercer Emile au bruit d'une arme à feu? Je brule d'abord une amorce dans un pistolet. Cette flame brusque et passagère, cette espéce d'éclair le réjoüit; je repéte la même chose avec plus de poudre: peu à peu j'ajoûte au pistolet une petite charge sans bourre, puis une plus grande. Enfin je l'accoutume aux coups de fusil, aux boetes, aux canons, aux détonations les plus terribles." *Emile,* 4:284.

39. See my discussion of "the electrified boy" in the introduction. In an effort to judge the power of the human will over the physiological effects of vision, Newton reportedly poked brass plates and bodkins between his eyeball and bone. Cited in Simon Schaffer, "Self Evidence," *Critical Inquiry* 18 (1992): 329. Other dangerous self-experimentation includes Lazzaro Spallanzani's work on digestion, wherein he swallowed various tubes and bags of samples in spite of the danger to his alimentary canal. Cited in Thomas L. Hankins, *Science and the Enlightenment* (Cambridge: Cambridge University Press, 1985), 123.

40. Suart Strickland, "The Ideology of Self-Knowledge and the Practice of Self-Experimentation," *Eighteenth-Century Studies* 31, no. 4 (summer 1998): 453–71.

41. *Emile,* 158. "Travailler est donc un devoir indispensable à l'homme social. . . . Or de toutes les conditions qui peuvent fournir la subsistance à l'homme, celle qui le rapproche le plus de l'état de Nature est le travail des mains." *Emile,* 4:470.

42. Although Locke introduced some remarkable innovations, such as encouraging training in manual trades, his program ultimately reinforces the status quo enjoyed by the middle and upper classes. Among the manual trades he recommends are ironwork, perfuming, engraving, working with precious stones, or optical glasses, but above all woodwork, gardening, or "*Husbandry* in general," which is cited as most useful and healthful for a "Country-Gentleman" (*Some Thoughts,* secs. 202, 204, 209). The results to be gained by learning such trades have no apparent connection with politics, nor do they inspire empathy for the working poor. Locke does recommend that children be taught civility toward servants and compassion toward the poor, however, in *Some Thoughts* sec. 117.

43. *Emile,* 401."Allez voir . . . ce jeune homme à l'attelier, et vous verrez s'il méprise la condition du pauvre!" *Emile,* 4:807.

44. *Emile,* 316. "Le Peuple ne s'ennuye guéres, sa vie est active; si ses amusemens ne sont pas variés ils sont rares; beaucoup de jours de fatigue lui font gouter avec délices quelques jours de fêtes." *Emile,* 4:685.

45. For an overview of Rousseau's innovations, see Burgelin, "Introduction à *Emile ou de l'éducation,*" in *Emile,* 4:lxxxviii–cxix.

46. Rousseau is widely cited for encouraging breast-feeding, condemning swaddling clothes, recognizing tears as a language, and conceiving the principle of an education that would not "force nature" but rather conform to the "four ages" of the child's progress toward maturity (infancy, sensation, reason, and sentiment). Although Rousseau has the great merit of popularizing these ideas, it remains true that many of his ideas were taken from earlier sources, especially Locke, Buffon, and Fénelon. For more on the parallels between Rousseau and Buffon, consult Otis Fellows, "Buffon and Rousseau: Aspects of a Relationship," *PMLA* 75, no. 1 (March 1960): 194–96; Charles W. Hendel,

Jean-Jacques Rousseau, Moralist (London: Oxford University Press, 1934), esp. vol. 2; and Jean Starobinski, "Rousseau et Buffon," in *Jean-Jacques Rousseau et son oeuvre: Problèmes et recherches* (Paris: Klincksieck, 1964), 135–46. On Rousseau's debt to Locke and earlier writers, see Peter D. Jimack, *La genèse et la rédaction de l'Emile de J.-J. Rousseau* (Geneva: Institut et Musée Voltaire, 1960), in *Studies on Voltaire and the Eighteenth Century* 13 (1960).

47. Harari, *Scenarios of the Imaginary,* 106.

48. *Emile,* 136. "[C]ette petite scéne étoit arrangée et que le bâteleur étoit instruit du rolle [*sic*] qu'il avoit à faire." *Emile,* 4:1420.

49. *Emile,* 64. "Jeunes maîtres, pensez, je vous prie, à cet exemple, et souvenez-vous qu'en toute chose vos leçons doivent être plus en actions qu'en discours." *Emile,* 4:333.

50. *Emile,* 138. "Tout le détail de cet exemple importe plus qu'il ne semble. Que de leçons dans une seule!" *Emile,* 4:440.

51. *Emile,* 238. "La seule génération des corps vivans et organisés est l'abîme de l'esprit humain; la barriére insurmontable que la nature a mise entre les différentes espéces, afin qu'elles ne se confondissent pas, montre ses intentions avec la derniére évidence. Elle ne s'est pas contentée d'établir l'ordre; elle a pris des mesures certaines pour que rien ne pût le troubler." *Emile,* 4:580.

52. *Emile,* 237. "Je suis comme un homme qui verroit pour la prémiére fois une montre ouverte. . . . Je ne sais, diroit-il, à quoi le tout est bon, mais je vois que chaque piéce est faite pour les autres, j'admire l'ouvrier dans le détail de son ouvrage, et je suis bien sûr que tous ces rouages ne marchent ainsi de concert que pour une fin commune qu'il m'est impossible d'appercevoir." *Emile,* 4:578.

53. Scientific endeavors, Rousseau claims, are often motivated less by a disinterested search for knowledge than by petty vices and perversions: "L'Astronomie est née de la superstition . . . la Géométrie, de l'avarice; la Physique, d'une vaine curiosité; toutes, et la Morale même, de l'orgueil humain. Les Sciences et les Arts doivent donc leur naissance à nos vices." Addressing the "Philosophes illustres" of his day, Rousseau inquires, "Revenez donc sur l'importance de vos productions; et si les travaux des plus éclairés de nos savans et de nos meilleurs Citoyens nous procurent si peu d'utilité, dites-nous ce que nous devons penser de cette Foule d'Ecrivains obscurs et de Lettrés oisifs, qui dévorent en pure perte la substance de l'Etat." Rousseau, *Discours sur les sciences et les arts* in *Oeuvres complètes,* ed. Bernard Gagnebin and Marcel Raymond (Paris: Gallimard, 1959), 3:17, 3:19. For more on Rousseau and science, see Catherine Chevalley, "Should Science Provide an Image of the World?" in *Scientists and Their Responsibility,* ed. William R. Shea and Beat Sitter (Canton, Mass.: Watson, 1989), 159–70, esp. 164.

54. "Peuples, sachez donc une fois que la nature a voulu vous préserver de la science, comme une mere arrache une arme dangereuse des mains de son enfant; que tous les secrets qu'elle vous cache sont autant de maux dont elle vous garantit." Rousseau, *Discours sur les sciences et les arts,* 3:15. This sense of scientific hubris weighed heavily on Rousseau's thought and should remind us that Rousseau was not as confident about man's progress as were the other philosophes. Whereas many of his contemporaries construed *perfectibilité* to mean progress, Rousseau understood the concept to mean openness to change—for good or bad. As Chevalley concludes: "The essence of man is to be free, which does not entail that mankind behaves rationally; freedom therefore calls for stronger protection and more stability than those that science can provide." Chevalley, "Should Science Provide an Image of the World?" 165.

55. On this point I disagree with Graeme Garrard, who claims that Rousseau regarded education "as a means of preventing, not disseminating enlightenment and preserving, not dispelling, ignorance." Garrard, "Rousseau, Maistre, and the Counter-Enlightenment," *History of Political Thought* 15, no. 1 (spring 1994): 97–120, esp. 118.

56. The "juvenile" label is from Chevalley, "Should Science Provide an Image of the World?" 163. See Rousseau, *Discours sur les sciences et les arts,* 4:54. Describing the maelstrom incited by the publication of *Emile,* Rousseau defended his work as "le meilleur de mes écrits, ainsi que le plus important" and declared, with characteristic bravura, that he awaited the government's repression "trop heureux, quelque persecution qui dut m'attendre d'être appelé à l'honneur de souffrir pour la vérité." *Confessions,* 1:573, 1:579.

57. *Emile,* 261. "Quoi! toujours des témoignages humains? Toujours des hommes qui me raportent ce que d'autres hommes ont rapporté! Que d'hommes entre Dieu et moi! Voyons toutefois; éxaminons, comparons, vérifions." *Emile,* 4:610. For more on the theological debates provoked by *Emile* and its condemnation by the Catholic church, see Py, *Rousseau et les éducateurs,* 22–25.

58. *Emile,* 259. "Si l'on n'eut écouté que ce que Dieu dit au coeur des hommes, il n'y auroit jamais eu qu'une religion sur la terre." *Emile,* 4:608. Elsewhere Rousseau argued that "Sitôt que les h[ommes] vivent en société il leur faut une Religion qui les maintienne. Jamais peuple n'a subsisté ni ne subsistera sans Religion et si on ne lui en donnoit point, de lui-même il s'en feroit une ou seroit bientôt détruit." "[De la religion civile]," in *Oeuvres complètes,* ed. Bernard Gagnebin and Marcel Raymond (Paris: Gallimard, 1959), 3:336.

59. Regarding nonbelievers, the vicar counsels: "Fuyez ceux qui sous prétexte d'expliquer la nature sément dans les coeurs des hommes de désolantes doctrines et dont le scepticisme apparent est cent fois plus affirmatif et plus dogmatique que le ton décidé de leurs adversaires. . . . Jamais, disent-ils, la vérité n'est nuisible aux hommes: je le crois comme eux, et c'est à mon avis une grande preuve que ce qu'ils enseignent n'est pas la vérité." *Emile,* 4:632.

60. *Emile,* 3, 1. "Il me suffit que par-tout où naîtront des hommes, on puisse en faire ce que je propose; et qu'ayant fait d'eux ce que je propose, on ait fait ce qu'il y a de meilleur et pour eux-mêmes et pour autrui" (*Emile,* 4:243); "une bonne mere qui sait penser" (4:241).

61. *Emile,* 150. "[Q]uand [*sic*] au véritable [Emile], un enfant si différent des autres ne serviroit d'exemple à rien." *Emile,* 4:459.

62. *Emile,* 172, 181. "Comme le mugissement de la mer précéde de loin la tempête, cette orageuse révolution s'annonce par le murmure des passions naissantes: une fermentation sourde avertit de l'approche du danger" (*Emile* 4:489–450). "Peu-à-peu le sang s'enflamme, les esprits s'élaborent . . . le sang fermente et s'agite; une surabondance de vie cherche à s'étendre au dehors. L'oeil s'anime et parcourt les autres" (4:502).

63. *Emile,* 409. "Il ne dépend pas de nous d'avoir ou de n'avoir pas des passions, mais il dépend de nous de régner sur elles." *Emile,* 4:819.

64. As Yolton and Yolton have pointed out, in this respect Locke was a traditionalist. In *Some Thoughts* he preaches responsibility to civil society above all. Rather than seeking ways to nourish the child's individuality, he sought means by which parents might integrate children into society more effectively and teach them to regulate their whims into rational action, by directing their curiosity to utility, for instance, or learning to

overcome vain fears. John W. Yolton and Jean S. Yolton, introduction to Locke, *Some Thoughts Concerning Education,* ed. J. W. and J. S. Yolton (Oxford: Clarendon, 1989), 27.

65. Allan Bloom, "The Education of Democratic Man: *Emile,*" *Daedalus* 107 (summer 1978): 135–53, esp. 138; James Hamilton, "Literature and the *Natural Man* in Rousseau's *Emile,*" in *Literature and History in the Age of Ideas: Essays on the French Enlightenment Presented to George R. Havens,* ed. Charles G. S. Williams (Columbus: Ohio State University Press, 1975), 195–206, esp. 200.

66. This theme has been noted by many critics; see for instance, Pat Rogers, *Robinson Crusoe* (London: George Allen & Unwin, 1979), 73–91, and Jean-Pascal LeGoff, "Emile entre l'enfant de nature et le citoyen," in *Primitivisme et mythes des origines,* ed. Chantal Grell and Christian Michel (Paris: Presses de l'Université de Paris–Sorbonne, 1989), 165–75.

67. Rogers, *Robinson Crusoe,* 90.

68. For more on the socioeconomic significance of *Robinson Crusoe,* see Maximilian Novak, *Economics and the Fiction of Daniel Defoe* (Berkeley: University of California Press, 1962), 32–67; Rogers, *Robinson Crusoe,* 77–82; and Peter Earle, *The World of Defoe* (London: Weidenfeld and Nicholson,1976), 107–201.

69. Daniel Defoe, *Robinson Crusoe,* ed. Angus Ross (New York: Penguin, 1965), 126; further references appear in the text. See also the description of the arduous labor of grinding tools (98–99) and the "inexpressible labour" needed to build walls (92).

70. Ian Watt, "'Robinson Crusoe' as a Myth," *EIC* 1 (1951): 173. On *Crusoe* pornography, see Alastair Fowler, *A History of English Literature* (Cambridge: Harvard University Press, 1987), 191.

71. The beginning and the ending of the novel, Rousseau writes, are mere "fatras." "Ce roman débarrassé de tout son fatras, commençant au naufrage de Robinson près de son Isle, et finissant à l'arrivée du vaisseau qui vient l'en tirer sera tout à la fois l'amusement et l'instruction d'Emile." *Emile,* 4:455.

72. Harari, *Scenarios of the Imaginary,* 114–15.

73. *Emile,* 193. "[A] mesure que ses desirs s'allument, choisissez des tableaux propres à les réprimer." *Emile,* 4:518.

74. *Emile,* 179. "[U]n voile de tristesse qui amortit l'imagination et réprime la curiosité." *Emile,* 4:499.

75. Sideshows of this period commonly displayed wax models of syphillis victims and masturbators. The "museums of morality" built on this interest by displaying bodies that bore the most visible horrors of vice: chancres and running sores, ulcerated noses and penises, and unseeing eyes. For a contemporary description of one of these museums, see J. F. Bertrand, *Tableaux historiques et moraux* (Paris, 1799). Also relevant are George Mosse, *Nationalism and Sexuality: Respectability and Abnormal Sexuality in Modern Europe* (New York: Howard Fertig, 1985), 33–60, and Eric Jameson, *The Natural History of Quackery* (Springfield, Ill.: Charles C. Thomas, 1961), 97–99.

76. *Emile,* 321. For an overview of critical writings on Rousseau's sexual politics, see Mary Trouille, "The Failings of Rousseau's Ideals of Domesticity and Sensibility," *Eighteenth-Century Studies* 24, no. 4 (summer 1991): 451–55; Joel Schwartz, *The Sexual Politics of Jean-Jacques Rousseau* (Chicago: University of Chicago Press, 1984).

77. *Emile,* 321. "En tout ce qui ne tient pas au séxe la femme est homme." *Emile,* 4:692.

78. *Emile,* 331. "[E]lle attend le moment d'être sa poupée elle-même." *Emile,* 4:707.

79. *Emile,* 331, 332. "[P]resque toutes les petites filles apprennent avec répugnance à lire et écrire; quant à tenir l'aiguille, c'est ce qu'elles apprennent toujours volontiers"; "Il y en a bien peu qui ne fassent plus d'abus que d'usage de cette fatale science." *Emile,* 4:707, 708.

80. "Female animals are without this sense of shame, but what of that? Are their desires as boundless as those of women, which are curbed by shame? The desires of the animals are the result of necessity, and when need is satisfied, the desire ceases. . . . Their seasons of complaisance are short and soon over. Impulse and restraint are alike the work of nature. But what would take the place of this negative instinct in women if you rob them of their modesty?" *Emile,* 322.

81. *Emile,* 324. "Le mâle n'est mâle qu'en certains instans, la femelle est femelle toute sa vie ou du moins toute sa jeunesse; tout la rappelle sans cesse à son séxe." *Emile,* 4:697.

82. As Mme de Staël declared in 1788: "C'est l'éloquence de Rousseau qui ranima le sentiment maternel, dans une certaine classe de la société; il fit connoître aux mères ce devoir et ce bonheur; il leur inspira le desir de ne céder à personne les premières caresses de leurs enfans. . . . Qui, des mères ou des enfans, doit le plus de reconnoissance à Rousseau? Ah! ce sont les mères sans doute." Staël, *Lettres sur les ouvrages et le caractère de J-J. Rousseau* (n.p., 1788), 56–57. Women's periodicals give further evidence of this vogue. In her study of *Le Journal des dames,* Nina Rattner Gelbart reveals the wide appeal of Rousseau's ideas among well-to-do bourgeois readers: "For over a decade, Rousseau's ideas had been working a revolution in female psychology, and by the 1770's many women, especially mothers, had come to see him as their champion rather than their foe." See Gelbart, "*Le Journal des dames* and Its Female Editors: Censorship and Feminism in the Old Regime Press," in *Press and Politics in Eighteenth-Century France,* ed. Jack R. Censer and Jeremy Popkin (Berkeley: University of California Press, 1987), 59.

83. As a young woman, Sophie is said to overcome gourmandise—this "low kind of self-indulgence." *Emile,* 358.

84. As Jean-Claude Bonnet has argued, " Si le système de la cuisine est plat chez Rousseau ce n'est pas le fait d'une pauvreté affectée: le jeu culinaire complexe des assaisonnements, des saveurs vives et relevées corrompt le goût. Voilà, entre autres choses, en quoi la cuisine des riches est 'déstructrice.'" Bonnet, "Le système de la cuisine et du repas chez Rousseau," *Poétique* 22 (1975): 258–59.

85. *Emile,* 323. "Loin de rougir de leur foiblesse elles en font gloire . . . elles auroient honte d'être fortes." *Emile,* 4:696.

86. "[L]e corps désirable, au dix-huitième siècle, n'est jamais le corps 'naturel.'" Philippe Roger, "L'Imaginaire libertin et le corps 'spectaculeux,'" in *Le Corps-spectacle,* ed. France Borel, spec. ed. of *Revue de l'Université de Bruxelles* 3–4 (1987): 57.

87. *Emile,* 356–57. "Sa parure est très modeste en apparence et très coquete en effet; elle n'etale point ses charmes, elle les couvre, mais en les couvrant elle sait les faire imaginer. . . . Tant qu'on reste auprès d'elle les yeux et le coeur errent sur toute sa personne sans qu'on puisse les en détacher, et l'on diroit que tout cet ajustement si simple n'est mis à sa place que pour en être ôté piéce à piéce par l'imagination." *Emile,* 4:747.

88. *Emile,* 13–14. "Mais que les méres daignent nourrir leurs enfans, les moeurs vont se réformer d'elles-mêmes, les sentimens de la nature se réveiller dans tous les coeurs, l'Etat va se repeupler; ce prémier point, ce point seul va tout réunir. . . . Le tracas des enfans qu'on croit importun devient agréable; il rend le pére et la mére plus nécessaires,

plus chers l'un à l'autre, il resserre entre eux le lien conjugal. . . . Ainsi de ce seul abus corrigé resulteroit bientôt une réforme générale; bientot la nature auroit repris tous ses droits." *Emile,* 4:258.

89. Madelyn Gutwirth, *The Twilight of the Goddesses: Women and Representation in the French Revolutionary Era* (New Brunswick, N.J.: Rutgers University Press, 1992), 120.

90. Mona Ozouf, "'Public Opinion' at the End of the Old Regime," in *The Rise and Fall of the French Revolution,* ed. T. C. W. Blanning (Chicago: University of Chicago Press, 1996), 105.

91. *Emile,* 438. "La vie patriarcale et champêtre, la prémiére vie de l'homme, la plus paisible, la plus naturelle, et la plus douce à qui n'a pas le coeur corrompu." *Emile,* 4: 859. This language is reproduced almost word for word from the patriarchal model in *Le Contrat social,* 3:352. It also resonates with the description of Clarens in *La Nouvelle Héloïse,* where Saint-Preux describes the communal workings in the vineyard: "L'objet de l'utilité publique et privée le rend intéressant; et puis, c'est la premiere vocation de l'homme, il rapelle à l'esprit une idée agréable, et au coeur tous les charmes de l'âge d'or. . . . La simplicité de la vie pastorale et champêtre a toujours quelque chose qui touche." Jean-Jacques Rousseau, *La Nouvelle Héloïse,* in *Oeuvres complètes,* ed. Bernard Gagnebin and Marcel Raymond (Paris: Gallimard, 1959), 2:603. On links between *Emile* and the utopia of *La Nouvelle Héloïse,* see John S. Spink, "La Phase naturaliste dans la préparation de l'*Emile,* ou Wolmar éducateur," in *Jean-Jacques Rousseau et son oeuvre: Problèmes et recherches* (Paris: Klincksieck, 1964), 171–81; and James F. Jones Jr., *La Nouvelle Héloïse: Rousseau and Utopia* (Geneva: Librairie Droz, 1978).

92. *Emile,* 438. "Je m'attendris en songeant combien de leur simple retraite Emile et Sophie peuvent répandre de bienfaits autour d'eux, combien ils peuvent vivifier la campagne et ranimer le zéle eteint de l'infortuné villageois. Je crois voir le peuple se multiplier, les champs se fertiliser, la terre prendre une nouvelle parure, la multitude et l'abondance transformer les travaux en fêtes. . . . On traitte l'age d'or de chimére, et c'en sera toujours une pour quiconque a le coeur et le goût gatés. . . . Que faudroit-il donc pour le faire renaitre? Une seule chose . . . ce seroit de l'aimer." *Emile,* 4:859.

93. Critics have often accused Rousseau and other utopian writers of sacrificing the individual to the totality, a vice avoided in *Emile* because, as Jean-Michel Racault has argued, Rousseau posits the relationship not as an antagonism but rather as an idyllic communion through which both emerge enriched. See Racault, *L'Utopie narrative en France et en Angleterre 1675–1761* (Oxford: Voltaire Foundation, 1991), 778, in *Studies on Voltaire and the Eighteenth Century* 280 (1991). See also Tzvetan Todorov, who sees a "veritable revolution" in sociopolitical thought brought about by Rousseau's formulation of "a new concept of man as a being who *needs others.*" In Todorov, "Living Alone Together," *New Literary History* 27, no. 1 (winter 1996): 1–14, esp. 2. But Rousseau portrays the countryside in such exaggeratedly rosy hues—this in an age prone to famine, joblessness, and widespread misery among the rural populations—that he remains open to charges of callousness. In this he was not unlike other well-off *hommes de lettres* who promoted enlightened ideas such as crop rotation while remaining blind to the suffering of people on their own land. (Witness Voltaire, who trumpeted any number of progressive ideas about politics and religion, but who declared: "Il me paraît essentiel qu'il y ait des gueux ignorans.") For more on the philosophes' conflicted attitudes toward the peasantry, see André J. Bourde, *Agronomie et agronomes en France au XVIIIe siècle* (Paris: S.E.V.P.E.N., 1967), 2:1055–67.

94. Sadly, however, the sweetness and mutual benevolence assumed in Rousseau's utopia would prove singularly difficult to maintain in a world threatened by dystopian realities. Paul H. Meyer argues that Rousseau did not expect his utopian visions to serve any practical purpose but rather to provide a *morale provisioire* for the "regenerated individual" living in the world more or less as it is. Meyer, "The Individual and Society in Rousseau's *Emile*," *Modern Language Quarterly* 19 (1958): 99–114.

95. Jean-Jacques Rousseau, *Oeuvres complètes*, ed. Pierre Alexandre Du Peyrou, 29 vols. (London, 1780–82). For more on *Emile et Sophie*, see Thomas M. Kavanagh, *Writing the Truth: Authority and Desire in Rousseau* (Berkeley: University of California Press, 1987); and *Yale French Studies* (1997), a special issue dedicated to sociability in the seventeenth and eighteenth centuries.

96. "[J]e ne vous suis plus rien. Un autre a souillé votre lit." Jean-Jacques Rousseau, *Emile et Sophie ou les Solitaires*, in *Oeuvres complètes*, ed. Bernard Gagnebin and Marcel Raymond (Paris: Gallimard, 1959), 4:890. My translation. It is unfortunate that modern English translations do not include this text, for it holds great interest and serves as a cautionary corrective to *Emile*.

97. For more on this issue of female agency in Rousseau and his critic, Mary Wollstonecraft, see Moira Gatens, "Rousseau and Wollstonecraft: Nature vs. Reason," *Women and Philosophy*, ed. Janna L. Thompson, supplement to *Australasian Journal of Philosophy* 64 (June 1986): 1–9.

98. Reaffirming the appeal of *Emile* as a middle-class idyll, a reviewer presented the scene of Sophie's guilty avowal as the high point of *Emilius and Sophia:* "[T]here is nothing in nature more terrific than this, nor is there any thing more pathetic." Significantly, this author held up *Emilius and Sophia* as "the only thing really worthy of Rousseau, in the whole collection of novelties." Article IV, Review of *Collection complète des Oeuvres de J. James Rousseau*, in *A New Review* (July 1782): 17, 23.

99. "[L]e délicieux charme de l'innocence est évanoui" (*Emile et Sophie*, 4:902); "Oui, tous nos liens sont rompus, ils le sont par elle. En violant ses engagemens elle m'affranchit des miens. Elle ne m'est plus rien, ne l'a-t-elle pas dit encore? Elle n'est plus ma femme . . . je ne la reverrai jamais. Je suis libre" (4:903).

100. Bloom, "Education of Democratic Man," 146–47.

101. Garrard, "Rousseau, Maistre, and the Counter-Enlightenment," 105.

102. Garrard makes a strong case for Rousseau as a counter-Enlightenment figure in "Rousseau, Maistre, and the Counter-Enlightenment." See also Richard A. Lebrun, introduction to Joseph de Maistre, *Against Rousseau: On the State of Nature and On the Sovereignty of the People*, ed. and trans. Richard A. Lebrun (Montreal: McGill–Queen's University Press, 1996), ix–xxx.

103. Although *Crusoe*'s readers today are impressed by the strong vein of religious reflection and the hero's ultimate conversion to active Christianity, the novel's first readers complained that the author was attempting to inculcate unworthy and dangerous—as well as insincere—religious attitudes. For a survey of the book's early reception, see Charles Eaton Burch, "British Criticism of Defoe as a Novelist, 1719–1860," *Englische Studien* 68 (1933): 178–98.

104. Kirkby's theological beliefs grew out of his training as an Anglican clergyman. He rose to the position of rector before the church's use of ecclesiastical revenues cast him into disfavor. Forced into penury, he accepted a position as tutor to the young Edward Gibbon, who later wrote in his *Memoirs* of liking and respecting Kirkby and admired his

knowledge of languages and education. Gibbon considered *Automathes* a poor performance, however, and a plagiarism of the *History of Autonous* (1736). Two editions of *Automathes* came out, in 1745 and 1747. Kirkby wrote no other fiction; his other works deal with theological controversies, mathematics, and grammar (*The Dictionary of National Biography,* ed. Leslie Stephen and Sidney Lee [London: Oxford University Press, 1937–], 11:207). Few critics have addressed *Automathes,* apart from Maximilian Novak, who like Gibbon argues that Kirkby copied sections from *Autonous* but that Kirkby's novel was ultimately better received by the public. It is also interesting to note, as Novak points out, how similar *Automathes* is to the plot and rhetoric of Defoe's "Mere Nature Delineated" (analyzed in chapter 1). See Novak, "The Wild Man Comes to Tea," in *The Wild Man Within,* ed. Edward Dudley and Maximilian E. Novak (Pittsburgh: University of Pittsburgh Press, 1972), 208–10.

105. John Kirkby, *The Capacity and Extent of Human Understanding Exemplified in the Extraordinary Case of Automathes* (1745; reprint, New York: Garland, 1974), 284. All citations from *Automathes* refer to this edition.

106. The spiritual autobiography vogue grew out of the habit of diary keeping, a widespread phenomenon in late seventeenth- and early eighteenth-century England. Pious individuals typically recorded almost everything in their day; since they considered worldly events to be hieroglyphic and often cryptic, all details were useful in the search for clues to God's plan and pattern. On the generic conventions of spiritual autobiographies, see J. Paul Hunter, *Before Novels: The Cultural Contexts of Eighteenth-Century English Fiction* (New York: Norton, 1990), 306–8; on Defoe's adoption of this genre in *Crusoe,* see Hunter, *The Reluctant Pilgrim: Defoe's Emblematic Method and Quest for Form in Robinson Crusoe* (Baltimore: Johns Hopkins University Press, 1966); and G. A. Starr, *Defoe and Spiritual Autobiography* (Princeton: Princeton University Press, 1965).

107. Defoe, *Crusoe,* 103–7.

108. For more on the themes of scientific learning and religious awakening in *Crusoe,* see Ilse Vickers, *Defoe and the New Sciences* (Cambridge: Cambridge University Press, 1996), 112–22.

109. Rogers, *Robinson Crusoe,* 54. See textual analysis in Starr, *Defoe,* 81–125, and Hunter, *Reluctant Pilgrim,* 88, 185.

110. Providence books, writes Hunter, were extremely popular in the late seventeenth century, when Christianity perceived itself to be under severe attack from 'Atheists'—that is, deists, freethinkers, some scientists, and untraditional thinkers of many kinds. Such works "drew specific thematic conclusions and tried to persuade readers that God was still (as in biblical times) directly involved in human events." Hunter, *Before Novels,* 217.

111. Compare this dogmatic organization to Crusoe's nascent colony, where although the citizens are all perfectly subjected to his rule, they are nevertheless allowed the liberty of conscience (Defoe, *Crusoe,* 240–41).

112. The popularity of *L'Elève* is evidenced by the fifteen French editions published between 1763 and 1806 and the translations into English (*The Man of Nature,* trans. James Burne, 1773) and German (1765, 1794) listed in Philip Babcock Gove, *The Imaginary Voyage in Prose Fiction* (London: Holland, 1941), 350–52. It was even attributed to Rousseau in one edition (Geneva: Les Frères Cramer, 1768).

113. For more on this distinction and its importance to the debates elicited by *Emile*

on public vs. private education, see Jean Bloch, "Gaspard Guillard de Beaurieu's 'L'Elève de la nature' and Rousseau's 'Emile.'" *French Studies* 26 (1972): 276–84.

114. Perhaps this was due to the author's interest in and affection for children. Children were quite possibly the primary audience for *L'Elève,* since Beaurieu was best known for his juvenile literature on science. According to the *Grande Encyclopédie* entry on Beaurieu, the author—who was apparently something of an oddball ("fort bizarre dans sa tenue et dans ses propos")—wrote "surtout pour l'enfance et la jeunesse. Ses travaux en ce genre ont joui même d'une vogue," *La Grande Encyclopédie: Inventaire raisonné des sciences, des lettres et des arts* (Paris: H. Lamirault, n.d.), 5:1063.

115. This edition also contains a new third section, "Les Plaisirs champêtres," detailing the joys of colonial living on Isle de la Paix.

116. The king, torn between his desire to please a courtier and his humanitarian impulses, resolved to imprison the offending party's newborn son with the provision that he be deported to a desert island later in life.

117. "Une expérience semblable à celle que je voulois faire pouvoit être fort utile." Beaurieu, *L'Elève de la nature* (Lille: C.G.J. Lehoucq, 1778), 2:118. All citations from *L'Elève* refer to this edition.

118. "Une très-grande cage de bois exactement fermée de toutes parts; une petite boîte de carton, une mouche, quelques poignées de paille, une pierre, de la viande, du pain, des fruits et de l'eau, qui me venoient, je ne savois comment, par quelque chose." Ibid., 1:2.

119. "[I]l étoit ordonné que je ne visse ni n'entendisse jamais personne jusqu'au jour où l'on devoit me rendre tout-à-fait à la société." Ibid., 1:4.

120. Beaurieu justifies this odd detail with the great curiosity of some readers: "Pour ne rien laisser d'inconnu à ceux de mes Lecteurs qui veulent être instruits de tout, et qui prouvent par-là qu'ils lisent avec réflexion, je crois devoir les avertir que j'avois des *lieux à l'Angloise,* mais sans siége, c'étoit une pierre taillée en évier, placée au fond de ma cage, et inclinée en dehors, de manière que rien ne pouvoit y rester." Ibid., 1:4.

121. "Nouveau phénomene qui me fait faire deux découvertes; il me donne une idée, du moins confuse, des loix du mouvement, et une sensation très-claire des plaisirs du bain." Ibid., 1:11–12.

122. The rabbit dissection recalls the English physician William Harvey's famous vivisection of a pregnant doe. "[J]e pris une pierre tranchante et d'une main mal assurée j'ouvris le cadavre . . . il palpitoit presqu'encore; je vis un coeur, un estomac, des intestins, je vis un édifice admirablement soutenu par des os mobiles, artistement emboités, et revêtu d'une chair qui, en même-temps qu'elle est assez compacte pour former par elle même un tissu solide, est assez molle, et sur-tout assez entremêlée de muscles pour se prêter à tous les mouvemens que font les os qu'elle couvre" (ibid., 1:192). This dissection combines scientific detail with an extremely sentimental narrative style. The pupil punishes himself for having killed her and vows never to eat meat again (1:188–89). (He later recants, but vows never to let his carniverous habits make him cruel or ferocious [2:49]).

123. In his other works, Beaurieu popularized natural history for children and amateurs: *Abrégé de l'histoire des insectes, dédié aux jeunes personnes* (1764), and *Cours d'histoire naturelle* (1770)—which was reprinted three times.

124. "Un voile que je tremblois de déchirer, me cachoit quelque chose qui me paroissoit être une masse de chair informe, inégale. J'y regarde de plus près, et à travers ce voile qui étoit d'une texture délicate et claire, et fort tendue, je crus appercevoir des têtes, des yeux. Ma pierre me tombe des mains, je la reprends, et pour avoir moins de peine à vaincre ma répugnance, j'ouvre vite. . . . Quel spectacle! Six petits lapins à naître et déjà vivans, trépignent, ouvrent hideusement la bouche, et me reprochent avec horreur, d'avoir osé pénétrer dans l'asyle sacré où la Nature les avoit mis en les tirant du néant; ils respirent, je rejette la malheureuse hase et ses petits dans le buisson. . . . Je fuis vers ma grotte en pleurant, en criant, en faisant des imprécations contre moi-même." Beaurieu, *L'Elève,* 1:192–93.

125. There was increasing sensitivity to vivisection in scientific milieus from the 1750s on. Already in 1746 a student at the University of Halle had prefaced his report of a vivisection with the following confession: "Recently I have cut up a dog alive, a murderous deed. . . . Bring an action against me wherever you want: just listen what I observed on this occasion." Johann August Unzer, cited in Andreas-Holger Maehle and Ulrich Tröhler, "Animal Experimentation from Antiquity to the End of the Eighteenth Century: Attitudes and Arguments," in *Vivisection in Historical Perspective,* ed. Nicolaas A. Rupke (London: Croon Helm, 1987), 28–47.

126. Martin, *Young Gentleman's and Lady's Philosophy,* 1:394–97.

127. Barbara Benedict, "The 'Curious' Attitude in 18th-Century Britain: Observing and Owning," *Eighteenth-Century Life* 14 (November 1990): 59–98.

128. "Je serre les mains de ma charmante compagne, je tombe sur son sein, je m'éveille en sursaut, j'ouvre les yeux et je vois que je suis seul." *L'Elève,* 1:95.

129. "Je respirois autour des bois une odeur délicieuse, une odeur de fécondité. Je voyois quelques fleurs encore fermées, se hâter de s'épanouir, prendre des couleurs plus vives et plus fraîches. Deux tourterelles déjà vues, vinrent recommencer le charmant badinage." Ibid., 1:122.

130. See Londa L. Schiebinger, *Nature's Body: Gender in the Making of Modern Science* (Boston: Beacon, 1993), 23–39.

131. For more on the Physiocrats' model society—which is closely replicated here—see André Bourde, *Agronomie et Agronomes en France au XVIIIe siècle* (Paris: S.E.V.P.E.N., 1967), 2:987–1073, or Baker, *Condorcet,* 291–92.

132. The final recourse to an island has the same function as the intial choice of a cage: it is a negative, isolating environment designed to protect the initiate rather than to change the world. For more on the island topoi in *Emile* and other eighteenth-century texts, see LeGoff, "Emile entre l'enfant de nature et le citoyen," 165–75. For a broader analysis of the island consult Gillian Beer, "Discourses of the Island," in *Literature and Science as Modes of Expression,* ed. Frederick Amrine (Dordrecht, The Netherlands: Kluwer, 1989), 1–27.

133. "[S]acrileges et perturbateurs du repos public." *L'Elève,* 2:216. For more on the Terror's apprehension toward history, as symbolized in libraries, consult Gutwirth, *Twilight of the Goddessses,* 214.

134. "Moi-même, pour donner l'exemple, je brûlerai solemnellement ma plume." *L'Elève,* 2:216.

135. During the revolution, Beaurieu aligned himself with such liberals as Lacépède and Abbé Grégoire and proposed a school that would propagate the "new order of

things" among all classes of society. See *Dictionnaire de biographie française* (Paris: Letouzey et Ané, 1933), 5:1179.

136. For more on criticism of *Crusoe,* see Burch, "British Criticism of Defoe."

137. For the numbers of editions, confiscations, and book orders associated with individual titles, see Robert Darnton, *The Corpus of Clandestine Literature in France, 1769–1789* (New York: Norton, 1995), 57 on *L'Elève,* 58 on *Emile,* and 92 on *Imirce.*

138. Some claim that he was "unmethodical and argumentative, obsessed with a veritable persecution mania"; others report that he was "a caustic and belligerent type" who provoked his teachers and suffered bizarre punishments as a result. See *Dictionnaire des lettres françaises,* ed. Georges Grente (Paris: Arthème Fayard, 1960), 407, and *La Grande Encyclopédie: Inventaire raisonné des sciences, des lettres et des arts* (Paris: H. Lamirault, n.d.) 15:29. Dulaurens played many roles: he was a defrocked priest and cleric, adventurer and impenitent scholar, novelist, pornographer, and sentimentalist.

139. H. Duthilloeul, *Galerie douaisienne, ou Biographie des hommes remarquables de la ville de Douai* (Douai: Adam D'Aubers, 1844), 204–5.

140. Three of Dulaurens's works figure on Darnton's list of clandestine "Bestsellers" of 1769–89, including the first and fifth most popular works of the category "Irreligious, Ribaldry, and Pornography." Dulaurens is cited for *L'Arretin ou la Débauche de l'esprit* (1763), an imitation of the pornographic classic *Aretino's Postures,* and *La Chandelle d'Arras* (1765), a heroic-comic poem. Compare this prominence with that of Rousseau, whose writings appear only once on Darnton's list, as number one in "Collected Works" for his *Oeuvres.*

141. The English translation appeared in *Favorite Tales, Translated from the French* (1787). According to Darnton, *Imirce* was sold by twenty-four major dealers, listed in one out of six catalogues of forbidden books, and was confiscated in four out of ten police inventories.

142. Peter Cryle, *Geometry in the Boudoir: Configurations of French Erotic Narrative* (Ithaca: Cornell University Press, 1994), 8, 271.

143. English translations are taken, when possible, from *Imirce: or, the Child of Nature. A Free Translation from the French of the Abbé Laurent* in *Favorite Tales, Translated from the French* (London: G. G. J. and J. Robinson, 1787).

144. Rivara claims that the details function as "un moyen supposé de garantir la vérité du bilan" in her preface to *Imirce ou la Fille de la nature,* ed. Rivara (Saint-Etienne: Publications de l'Université de Saint-Etienne, 1993), 25. All French citations from *Imirce* refer to this edition.

145. Number 150 of "The 150 Criminal Passions" in *Les 120 Journées* (part 3) is described in terms very reminiscent of *Imirce.* Sade writes: "Il l'attache nue et sans secours au moment où elle vient d'accoucher; il attache son enfant vis-à-vis d'elle, qui crie, et qu'elle ne peut secourir. Il faut qu'elle le voie ainsi mourir. Ensuite de cela il fouette à tour de bras la mère sur le con en dirigeant ses coups dans le vagin. C'est lui qui ordinairement est le père de l'enfant." Donatien-Alphonse-François, marquis de Sade, *Les 120 Journées de Sodome précédé de "La Machine en tête" par Bernard Noël* (Paris: P.O.L. Editeur, 1992), 474–75.

146. *Wright of Derby,* ed. J. E. Egerton (London: Tate Gallery, 1990), 58–61; David Solkin, "ReWrighting Shaftsbury: The Air Pump and the Limits of Commercial Humanism," in *Painting and the Politics of Culture,* ed. John Barrell (Oxford: Oxford

University Press, 1992), 73–99; David Fraser, "Joseph Wright of Derby and the Lunar Society: An Essay on the Artist's Connections with Science and Industry," in *Wright of Derby,* ed. J. E. Egerton (London: Tate Gallery, 1990), 15–24.

147. *Critical Observations on the Pictures, which are now exhibited in the Great Room, Spring-Garden, Charing-Cross, by the Society of Artists of Great Britain* (London, 1768), cited by Solkin, "ReWrighting Shaftesbury," 97.

148. For more on opposition to Boyle's respiration experiments and animal experimentation in general, see Maehle and Tröhler, "Animal Experimentation," 22–30.

149. Martin, *Young Gentleman's and Lady's Philosophy,* 1:307. On Martin, see also Solkin, "ReWrighting Shaftesbury," 96–97, and William Schupbach, "A Select Iconography of Animal Experiments," in *Vivisection in Historical Perspective,* ed. Nicolaas A. Rupke (London: Croom Helm, 1987), 340–60, esp. 342–47. On Tom Telescope, see Secord, "Newton in the Nursery," 137.

150. Among the many Enlightenment writers intrigued with this "virtual experiment," one could cite Montesquieu (in "Mes Pensées"), La Mettrie (in *L'Homme machine*), and Jauffret. Cited in Georges Hervé, "Le premier programme de l'anthropologie," *Revue scientifique* (1909): 520–28. The motif also organizes Marivaux, *La Dispute* (1744). Jean-Michel Racault discusses these texts, rather schematically, in "Le motif de 'L'Enfant de la nature' dans la littérature du XVIIIe siècle, ou la recréation expérimentale de l'origine," in *Primitivisme et mythes des origines dans la France des Lumières,* ed. Chantal Grell and Christian Michel (Paris: Presses de l'Université de Paris-Sorbonne, 1989): 101–17.

151. "Nous nous entendions déjà; nous avions peu de mots, aussi avions-nous peu d'idées. Nos paroles sortaient du gosier, et nos termes tenaient assez du cri disgracieux de certains animaux." Dulaurens, *Imirce,* 71.

152. This discourse of primitivism was widely identified with sexual freedom in eighteenth-century Europe, especially after travelers' tales brought back images of the South Sea islands as a sexual haven. Texts such as Bougainville's *Voyage autour du monde* (1771) and Diderot's fictional *Supplément au voyage de Bougainville* (1796) provoked heated debates on the "natural" function of human sexuality in social groups. For more on myths of Tahiti as a sexual paradise, see Julia Douthwaite, *Exotic Women: Literary Heroines and Cultural Strategies in Ancien Régime France* (Philadelphia: University of Pennsylvania Press, 1992), 140–83.

153. "Nous ne cessions de nous toucher, de nous examiner; nos coeurs purs comme le jour et nos mains innocentes ne trouvaient point déshonnêtes ces caresses naturelles." *Imirce,* 72.

154. Cryle (*Geometry in the Boudoir,* 76) cites the tendency for characters to arrive on the scene at age fifteen; Marcel Hénaff claims that Sade's "character never has a childhood." Hénaff, *Sade: L'Invention du corps libertin* (Paris: Presses Universitaires de France, 1978), 53.

155. "Ma gorge avait crû sous ses yeux. Cet objet le captivait; il la caressait sans cesse: je me fâchais quelquefois; ses grands ongles me blessaient; Emilor apprit insensiblement à la toucher moins rudement; j'en fus aise." *Imirce,* 72.

156. "Nous nous accouplâmes sans le savoir. La douleur légère de cette opération fut payée par une ivresses délectable: mon amant me devint plus cher, et je sentis que le plaisir était préférable au pain, au panier, et au maître de la cave." Ibid.

157. Fowler, *History of English Literature,* 191.

158. Margaret Jacob, "The Materialist World of Pornography," in *The Invention of Pornography: Obscenity and the Origins of Modernity, 1500–1800* (New York: Zone, 1993), 157–202, esp. 165.

159. After receiving the mirror, she affects headaches on days when her complexion is flawed, thus aping a "woman of fashion" though "still too provincial" to understand why. *Imirce,* 91.

160. "Aristus perceived I was pretty, fancied my mind equal to my person, fell in love with me, and took me from his cellar." Ibid., 93.

161. My translation. "[Elles] se laissaient chiffonner aussi naturellement que je faisais dans ma prison." Ibid. "On les enferme à cause que les curés ne leur ont pas permis de coucher avec ces soldats; nous les méprisons, nous les traitons de coquines. A ce compte, je suis donc une coquine dans ta cave?" Ibid., 94.

162. John Locke, *An Essay Concerning Human Understanding,* ed. Alexander Fraser (1690; reprint, New York: Dover, 1959), 1:31.

163. "Nous ne pouvons pas faire une cave comme lui, vivons dans la sienne, caressons-nous, et mangeons son pain." *Imirce,* 73.

164. Donatien-Alphonse-François, marquis de Sade, *Français, encore un effort* (Paris: Pauvert, 1965), 81.

165. In this regard, one might compare *Imirce* to the many other fictions in which a Rousseauian "natural man" comically exposes the follies of contemporary society, notably Frances Brooke's popular novel, *The Fool of Quality; or the History of Henry Earl of Moreland* (1765) or Miltenberg's *The Man of Nature or Nature and Love* (1797).

166. According to Raymond Trousson, "Le roman libertin se fonde sur un art de convaincre, il privilégie la dialectique, l'art du séducteur consistant à amener l'autre à reconnaître la loi du plaisir." Trousson, preface to *Romans libertins du XVIIIe siècle* (Paris: Editions Robert Laffont, 1993), x.

167. Hampson, "Enlightenment in France," 45.

168. Owen Bradley, *A Modern Maistre: The Social and Political Thought of Joseph de Maistre* (Lincoln: University of Nebraska Press, 1999), 141–42.

CHAPTER FOUR

1. On the history of *Emile*'s reception and censorship in France, see Gilbert Py's remarkably thorough study, *Rousseau et les éducateurs: Etude sur la fortune des idées pédagogiques de Jean-Jacques Rousseau en France et en Europe au XVIIIe siècle* (Oxford: Voltaire Foundation, 1997), 17–74, in *Studies in Voltaire and the Eighteenth Century* 356 (1997); and André Ravier, *L'Education de l'homme nouveau* (Issoudun: Editions SPES, 1941), vol. 1. On Rousseau's later years in exile, consult Matthew Josephson, *Jean-Jacques Rousseau* (New York: Harcourt, Brace, 1931), 359–491.

2. For German and Swiss examples, see Py, *Rousseau et les éducateurs,* 130–31, 163–69, and passim. On the Tighe family, see William Tighe, *William Tighe's Statistical Observations relative to the County of Kilkenny made in the years 1800 & 1801* (Kilkenny: Grangesilvia, 1998), xi–xiiii. On the Fitzgerald family, see Stella Tillyard, *Citizen Lord: The Life of Edward Fitzgerald, Irish Revolutionary* (New York: Farrar, Straus and Giroux, 1997), 13–21, and Emily, Duchess of Leinster, *Correspondence of Emily, Duchess of Leinster (1713–1814),* ed. Brian Fitzgerald (Dublin: Stationery Office, 1949), which includes several letters discussing the relative merits and dangers of applying *Emile* to child-rearing, e.g., letters 236, 248, and 342. On Mirabeau's plan to raise his baby daughter à

la Emile, see Roger Barny, *Prélude idéologique à la révolution française: Le Rousseauisme avant 1789* (Paris: Les Belles Lettres, 1985), 17–21.

3. Cited in Edward Duffy, *Rousseau in England: The Context for Shelley's Critique of Enlightenment* (Berkeley: University of California Press, 1979), 17. For the negative response of English intellectuals, see Py, *Rousseau et les éducateurs,* 33–36.

4. This figure comes to us from Jacques Pons, *L'Education en Angleterre entre 1750 et 1800, aperçu sur l'influence pédagogique de Jean-Jacques Rousseau en Angleterre* (Paris, 1919).

5. To give a sense of the urgency and personal concern: on 4 October 1763, the prince wrote to Rousseau describing his four-month-old daughter (letter 2955); Rousseau responded on 17 October (letter 2976); the prince wrote back on 21 October (2983) asking for advice on protecting her from spoiling and noting her suffering from teething pains; Rousseau responded 10 November (3017). Clearly Rousseau was committed to his role as parent's assistant, and in the 10 November letter he gives a lengthy list of instructions to the prince on the choice and conduct of the baby's nurse. His main advice, here as elsewhere, is "ne gâtez rien" (don't spoil anything), and a warning against the temptation to abandon the difficult task of childrearing (as noted in letter 3066, dated 15 December). For more examples of this correspondence, see letters 3092, 3116, 3128, 3220, and 3222 in Jean-Jacques Rousseau, *Correspondance complète de Jean-Jacques Rousseau,* ed. Ralph A. Leigh (Oxford: Voltaire Foundation, 1973), vols. 18 and 19.

6. "Tant pis, monsieur, pour vous et pour votre fils, tant pis." Cited by François and Pierre Richard, introduction to Jean-Jacques Rousseau, *Emile ou de l'éducation* (Paris: Garnier, n.d.), xxxviii.

7. "Vous dites très bien qu'il est impossible de faire un Emile. Mais je ne puis croire que vous preniez le Livre qui porte ce nom pour un vrai traitté d'Education. C'est un ouvrage assez philosophique Sur ce principe avancé par l'Auteur dans d'autres écrits *que l'homme est naturellement bon.*" Letter to Philibert Cramer, 13 October 1764, in Rousseau, *Correspondance complète,* 21:248.

8. "S'il est vrai que vous ayés adopté le plan que j'ai taché de tracer dans l'Emile, j'admire votre Courage; Car vous avés trop de lumieres pour ne pas voir que, dans un pareil systeme, il faut tout ou rien." Letter to Abbé Jean Maydieu, 18 February 1770, in ibid., 37:309. For more on Rousseau's ideas on the applicability of *Emile,* see Aubrey Rosenberg, "Rousseau's *Emile:* The Nature and Purpose of Education," in *The Educational Legacy of Romanticism,* ed. John Willinsky (Waterloo, Ontario: Wilifred Laurier University Press, 1990), 11–32.

9. For Rousseau's impact on French schemes for national education, see Jean Bloch, *Rousseauism and Education in Eighteenth-Century France* (Oxford: Voltaire Foundation, 1995), in *Studies in Voltaire and the Eighteenth Century* 325 (1995), and Py, *Rousseau et les éducateurs.* Madame de Genlis comments caustically on the woeful effects of parental neglect inspired by *Emile* ("j'ai vu des enfants entièrement livrés à eux-mêmes . . . montrant d'ailleurs une grossièreté rustique, une indocilité, et une inéptie qui me causaient un véritable étonnonement"). Most surprising to her, however, is that people justified such sloth by citing an author who prescribes constant surveillance and involvement on the part of the tutor. In Genlis, *Adèle et Théodore ou Lettres sur l'éducation* (Paris: Chez Maradan, 1804), 1:389–90. David Williams lists a number of tragic examples of child abuse caused by Rousseauian doctrine in his *Lectures on Education read to*

a society for promoting reasonable and human improvements in the discipline and instruction of youth (London, 1787), 61, 111, 151, 165.

10. For more on Edgeworth's many mechanical inventions and his contribution to the Lunar Society, see Robert E. Schofield, *The Lunar Society of Birmingham: A Social History of Provincial Science and Industry in Eighteenth-Century England* (Oxford: Clarendon, 1963), chaps. 3, 8, and 13.

11. Marilyn Butler, *Maria Edgeworth: A Literary Biography* (Oxford: Clarendon, 1972); Peter Rowland, *The Life and Times of Thomas Day, 1748–1789, English Philanthropist and Author: Virtue Almost Personified* (Lampeter, Wales: Edwin Mellen, 1996); George Warren Gignilliat Jr., *The Author of "Sandford and Merton": A Life of Thomas Day, Esq.* (New York: Columbia University Press, 1932).

12. Edgeworth was twenty-three years old when he launched this project. Richard Lovell Edgeworth and Maria Edgeworth, *Memoirs of Richard Lovell Edgeworth, Esq. Begun by Himself, and Concluded by his Daughter, Maria Edgeworth,* 2d ed. (London: Printed for R. Hunter and Baldwin, Cradock, and Joy, 1821), 1:172–73. All citations from Edgeworth's memoirs refer to this edition.

13. Butler, *Maria Edgeworth,* 43–44.

14. Jacques Voisine, *J.J. Rousseau en Angleterre à l'époque romantique: Les écrits autobiographiques et la légende* (Paris: Didier, 1956), 46.

15. In manuscript notes of 1778, Edgeworth remarks that starting at age three, his children were made to dress themselves and make their beds, or they would receive no breakfast. Cited in Butler, *Maria Edgeworth,* 50. As Butler remarks, these were uncommon tasks for a young child in an age of servants and elaborate clothes.

16. Cited in ibid., 99.

17. Letter from Thomas Day to Paul Elers (maternal grandfather of Richard Edgeworth Jr.), cited in Rowland, *Life and Times of Thomas Day,* 272.

18. Letter from Richard Lovell Edgeworth to Thomas Day, 8 July 1784, cited in ibid., 273.

19. Letter from Richard Lovell Edgeworth to Mrs. Powys, [1796], cited in Butler, *Maria Edgeworth,* 107.

20. John Timbs describes Richard Edgeworth Jr. as a headstrong "*child of nature* [who] grew up perfectly ungovernable, and never could or would apply to anything; so that there remained no alternative but to allow him to follow his own inclination of going to sea!" Timbs, "A Child of Nature," in *A Century of Anecdote, from 1760 to 1860* (London: Frederick Warne, [1865?]), 337.

21. Jane Austen, *Persuasion,* ed. D. W. Harding (1818; reprint, Harmondsworth, U.K.: Penguin, 1965), 76–77. I am grateful to Rowland for this connection to Austen.

22. See Anna Seward, *Memoirs of the Life of Dr. Darwin, Chiefly During his Residence at Lichfield, with Anecdotes of his Friends, and Criticisms on his Writings* (London: J. Johnson, 1804).

23. Rowland, *Life and Times of Thomas Day;* Gignilliat, *Author of "Sandford and Merton."*

24. Edgeworth, *Memoirs,* 1:221. My account of Day's project is drawn largely from Edgeworth's detailed description in *Memoirs,* 1:209–13, 220–40; 332–35; 2:92–97.

25. For (rather amusing) examples of Day's poor social skills and details of his unsuccessful courtship of Margaret Edgeworth, Honora Sneyd, and Elizabeth Sneyd, see

Rowland, *Life and Times of Thomas Day,* 10–18, 28–51. Monsieur de la Souche is the would-be husband of Molière's parodic *Ecole des femmes* (1662).

26. Strict legal conditions were stipulated for this arrangement: for example, within one year after his adoption, Day was obliged to give up one of the girls to a tradeswoman with one hundred pounds to bind her as an apprentice. See Gignilliat, *Author of "Sandford and Merton,"* 55–57.

27. Ibid., 65.

28. Rowland, *Life and Times of Thomas Day,* 27.

29. Such testimony comes not only from Anna Seward's vituperative memoirs but also from one Reverend R. G. Robinson, cited in Mary Alden Hopkins, *Dr. Johnson's Lichfield* (New York: Hastings House, 1952), 148. See Seward, *Memoirs of the Life of Dr. Darwin,* 39–40.

30. In *Emile* Rousseau gives methods of gradually accustoming a child to the sound of firearms. Jean-Jacques Rousseau, *Emile,* trans. Barbara Foxley (London: Dent, 1938), 31. Citing the practices of savages in their sports, Rousseau discusses how to accustom oneself to burns and claims one should not be a slave to pain (95).

31. Letter from Thomas Day to Richard Lovell Edgeworth, cited in James Keir, *An Account of the Life and Writings of Thomas Day, Esq.* (London: 1791; reprint, New York: Garland, 1970), 29.

32. Thomas Day, *The History of Sandford and Merton* (Philadelphia: W. P. Hazard, 1850), 305–6.

33. James Keir had already mentioned the phenomenon—without names—in his biography (Keir, *Account of the Life and Writings of Thomas Day,* 27–29), but Seward's account insulted Sabrina and her sons much more, because they were unaware of Keir's work and because Seward spoke so disrespectfully of Sabrina. See Rowland, *Life and Times of Thomas Day,* 356–57. Already in 1789 Seward had publicized her animosity toward Day in a letter to the editor of the *General Evening Post* in which she wrote that despite "his first rate abilities," Day was "a splenetic, capricious, yet bountiful misanthropist" who was "generally slovenly, even to squalidness." Cited in Rowland, 338.

34. Frances Burney, French Notebook II [1804] (Manuscript in the Berg Collection, New York Public Library.) This text is of doubtful validity, however. Burney calls the girls Sabrina and Juliana and claims that Juliana eloped with a merchant and that Sabrina eloped with one William Bicknell. I thank Betty Rizzo for telling me about this document.

35. Letter from Maria Edgeworth to her step-mother Frances Edgeworth, cited in Rowland, *Life and Times of Thomas Day,* 357.

36. Gita May, *Madame Roland and the Age of Revolution* (New York: Columbia University Press, 1970); Madeleine Clemenceau-Jacquemaire, *The Life of Madame Roland,* trans. Laurence Vail (London: Longmans, Green, 1930); Mary Seidman Trouille, *Sexual Politics in the Enlightenment: Women Writers Read Rousseau* (Albany: SUNY Press, 1997).

37. Roland was twenty-one years old when her mother died. I thank Lesley Walker for clarifying this point for me.

38. See, e.g., her letter to Sophie (21 March 1776) in Marie Jeanne Phlipon (Manon) Roland de la Platière, *Lettres de Madame Roland,* ed. Claude Perroud, n.s. (Paris: Imprimerie Nationale, 1913), 1:392; her letters to M. Roland (13 January 1787 and 1 December 1787) in *Lettres de Madame Roland,* ed. Perroud (Paris: Imprimerie Nationale,

1900–1902), 1:662, 716–19; and her letter to M. de Fenille (21 March 1789) in *Lettres,* 2:48.

39. She left a detailed account of her problems with breastfeeding and the remedies that helped her through this difficult time in Roland, *Avis à ma fille en âge et dans le cas de devenir mère,* in *Oeuvres de M. J. Ph. Roland,* ed. L.-A. Champagneux (Paris: Bidault, 1800), 1:300–344.

40. "[J]'en ai conclu que la fable d'Eve n'était pas si bête et que la gourmandise était véritablement un péché originel. Vous autres, philosophes, qui n'y croyez guère, qui nous dites que tous les vices sont nés dans la société, par le développement des passions qu'elle excite et par l'opposition des intérêts, apprenez-moi pourquoi cet enfant de six semaines, dont l'imagination ne peut rien dire encore, dont les sens paisibles et réglés ne doivent avoir d'autre maître que le besoin, passe déjà les bornes de celui-ci?" Letter to M. Roland (18 November 1781) in Roland, *Lettres,* 1:57–58.

41. At sixteen, Roland was already studying Buffon, Nollet, Réaumur, and Bonnet. She followed public courses on botany and natural history by Jussieu and Daubenton at the Jardin du Roi in the months following her marriage in 1780 and there met a young botanist, Louis Bosc d'Antic, who would be her lifelong friend. See May, *Madame Roland,* 102–4. The subject of inoculation was apparently a thorny issue for Mme Roland. When Eudora was six and a half, Roland wrote to Bosc asking him "to find some good reasons which would decide her" to opt for inoculation, but in vain. See the letter to Bosc (6 April 1788), Roland, *Lettres,* 2:7.

42. On Roland's paradoxical attitude toward other prominent women of her time, and her espousal of Rousseau's "antifeminist" ideas, see May, *De Jean-Jacques Rousseau à Madame Roland: Essai sur la sensibilité préromantique et révolutionnaire* (Geneva: Droz, 1964), 179–90; and Trouille, *Sexual Politics in the Enlightenment,* 163–92.

43. For a description of their routine, see the letter of September 1787 to M. Roland in Roland, *Lettres,* 1:685.

44. "Eudora lit bien, commence à ne plus connaître d'autres joujoux que l'aiguille, s'amuse à faire des figures de géométrie . . . n'a peur de rien." Letter to M. Bosc (10 November 1786) in ibid., 1:640.

45. "Eudora est forte et roide en proportion; je l'emporte toujours, mais toujours aussi mon coeur saigne de la victoire." Letter to M. Roland (May 1786[?]). "Notre grande affaire, c'est l'obéissance; il y a eu des crises; j'ai prononcé une privation, on a crié à tue-tête." Letter to M. Roland (1 December 1787) in ibid., 1:609, 718.

46. "Si la nature ne l'a pas fait naître pour les belles connaissances, ne pressons pas l'instruction, formons le caractère de préférence à tout, et que le reste vienne par inspiration, non par contrainte." Ibid., 1:718

47. "Enseignez-moi à vaincre, à diriger un caractère indocile, une trempe insouciante, sur qui les douces caresses, de même que les privations et la fermeté, n'ont presque aucun empire. Voilà mon tourment de tous les jours. L'éducation, cette tâche si chère pour une mère à l'égard d'un enfant qu'elle aime, semble être la plus rude des épreuves qui m'aient été réservées." Letter to M. Lavater (7 July 1788) in ibid., 2:22.

48. "[I]l faudrait être tout entière à cet être-là, sans aucun partage, et il faut convenir qu'il n'est guère de situations en ce monde où l'on puisse se concentrer ainsi et se dévouer uniquement à une éducation." Letter to M. Roland (30 November 1791) in ibid., 2:392.

49. "[I]l ne faut pas se le dissimuler, ta fille . . . n'a pas une idée, pas un grain de

mémoire; elle a l'air de sortir de nourrice et de ne promettre aucun esprit. Elle m'a joliment brodé un sac à ouvrage et elle travaille un peu à l'aiguille; d'ailleurs, aucun goût n'est né chez elle." Letter to M. Roland (9 September 1791) in ibid., 2:377.

50. "[J]e l'ai nourrie, je l'ai élevée avec l'enthousiasme et les sollicitudes de la maternité . . . mais jamais son âme stagnante et son esprit sans ressort ne donneront à mon coeur les douces jouissances qu'il s'était promises." Manon Roland, *Mémoires de Madame Roland,* ed. Paul de Roux (Paris: Mercure de France, 1966, 1986), 42.

51. Cited in Clemenceau-Jacquemaire, *Life of Madame Roland,* 317, 344n. 133. It must be noted that these claims were voiced by Public Prosecutor Fouquier-Tinville, who then compelled the girl to agree.

52. Clemenceau-Jacquemaire criticizes Roland's high intellectual expectations: "In no way did Eudora resemble that young Manon Phlipon who at seven gave lessons to her priest, astonished the painter Guibal by reciting the Athanasian Creed, and, by her promise of extraordinary wit, made herself the talk of the entire Ile de la Cité Notre-Dame." *Life of Madame Roland,* 160.

53. In the chapter on servants, Edgeworth writes: "Madame Roland, in one of her letters to De Bosc, says, that her little daughter Eudora had learned to swear; 'and yet,' continues she, 'I leave her but one half hour a day with servants. Admirez la disposition!' Madame Roland could not have been much accustomed to attend to education." Maria and Richard Lovell Edgeworth, *Practical Education* (London: J. Johnson, 1798), 1:126. In the chapter titled "Female Accomplishments, Masters, and Governesses," however, Edgeworth cites approvingly the maxims on female education of the "celebrated Madame Roland" (2:526–28).

54. Such is the claim of Trouille in *Sexual Politics in the Enlightenment,* 174.

55. "Me voilà comme les femmes qui n'ont pas nourri leurs enfants . . . je voudrais que [l'enfant] eût encore besoin de lait, et en avoir à lui donner." Marie-Jeanne Roland, *Mémoires de Madame Roland,* 3d ed., ed. Berville and Barrière (Paris: Baudouin, 1827), 1:295.

56. See letters such as "A la personne chargée du soin de ma fille" in *Mémoires de Madame Roland,* 2:310–12. On Roland's image as an exemplary mother and the important theme of mother-daughter love in Roland's *Memoirs,* see the interesting analysis in Lesley Heins Walker, *Politics, Pleasure, and Domesticity in the Writings of Madame Roland* (Ph.D. diss., University of Minnesota, 1996).

57. Indeed, Pierre Fauchery has labeled *Adèle et Théodore* "l'apothéose du roman d'éducation" in his monumental study, *La Destinée féminine dans le roman européen du XVIIIe siècle (1713–1807)* (Paris: Librairie Armand Colin, 1972), 406.

58. On Mme de Genlis's efforts to improve education for the poor, see her *Discours sur l'éducation publique du peuple* (Paris, 1791) and *Projet d'une Ecole rurale pour l'éducation des filles* (Paris, 1801), and Gabriel de Broglie's indispensable biography, *Madame de Genlis* (Paris: Perrin, 1985), 139–40.

59. There are many accounts of Genlis's work as governess to the d'Orléans family that depict her teachings as a positive experience with lasting value. See, e.g., Louis Philippe, *Mémoires de Louis-Philippe, duc d'Orléans* (Paris: Plon, 1973–74), the memoirs of la duchesse de Gontaut, and other contemporary sources cited in Broglie, *Madame de Genlis,* 131–32. Genlis herself left voluminous records of her teachings in *Leçons d'une gouvernante à ses Elèves, ou fragment d'un journal qui a été fait pour l'éducation de M. d'Orléans,* 2 vols. (Paris: Onfroy, 1791), and in her *Mémoires inédits sur le XVIIIe siècle et la Ré-*

volution française, 10 vols. (Paris: L'advocat, 1825–28). Some notes of discord do emerge, however, in the fact that Genlis's second daughter Pulchérie and her adopted daughter Paméla both resisted the training (Broglie, *Madame de Genlis,* 134, 142–45). Note also the comment reported by Maria Edgeworth after a conversation with the dowager duchesse d'Orléans, widow of Philippe Egalité, in 1820: she "spoke of Mme de Genlis in a true Christian spirit of forgiveness, but in a whisper, and with a shake of her head, allowed 'qu'elle m'avait causé bien des chagrins.'" Letter to Mrs. Ruxton (July 1820) in *Maria Edgeworth in France and Switzerland: Selections from the Edgeworth Family Letters,* ed. Chistina Colvin. (Oxford: Clarendon, 1979), 187.

60. For an account of the daily routine at Bellechasse, where Genlis undertook her innovative method with the d'Orléans children, see Alice M. Laborde, *L'Oeuvre de Madame de Genlis* (Paris: Editions A.-G. Nizet, 1966), 68–69.

61. In January 1780, Buffon wrote Genlis a surprisingly gushy letter praising the many virtues of her work and declaring her an "angel" for her formative influence on children. "Je ne suis plus amant de la nature, je la quitte pour Vous, Madame, qui faites plus et méritez mieux. Elle ne sait que former des corps, et vous créez des âmes." For more on Buffon's relation to Genlis, and on her *Théâtre à l'usage des jeunes personnes,* see Broglie, *Madame de Genlis,* 105–7.

62. For more on this doubling, see Bernard Grosperrin, "Un manuel d'éducation noble: *Adèle et Théodore* de Madame de Genlis," *Cahiers d'histoire* 19 (1974): 343–52.

63. As Genlis notes in the preface to the 1801 edition, "j'ai employé vingt-deux ans d'expériences, et j'ai mis tous mes soins à perfectionner dans cette nouvelle édition celui de mes ouvrages que le public en général a toujours paru préférer à mes autres productions, et celui que je crois aussi le plus utile, car je n'y propose rien que je n'aie exécuté avec succès pour mes enfans ou pour mes élèves." [Stéphanie Félicité Ducrest de Saint-Aubin, comtesse de] Genlis, *Adèle et Théodore, ou Lettres sur l'éducation,* 4th ed., 4 vols. (Paris: Chez Maradan, An X [1801]), 1:xxxiv–xxxv. All French citations refer to this edition unless otherwise indicated. Notes throughout her text reiterate the method's success with Genlis's many pupils (e.g., 1:80, 93, 85, 2:51–2) and stress the novel's truth value by announcing Mme d'Almane's resemblance to the author (3:332) and Mme d'Ostalis's resemblance to Caroline, her eldest daughter (2:350–1).

64. Published in 1782, the novel was already in its second edition the same year; six more editions appeared by 1827, as well as translations into English and Dutch. For the "key" to this roman à clef, consult the *Intermédiaire des chercheurs et curieux* (1874).

65. See, e.g., Trouille, *Sexual Politics in the Enlightenment,* 246–55.

66. The unrealistic nature of this education concerns the mother as well as the pupils. On the exemplary learning and leisure demanded of the mother, see the plaint by the vicomtesse de Limours, who challenges the baronne: "[I]l est nécessaire à votre plan que les mères soient en état de diriger les maîtres: où les trouverez-vous ces mères? Quelle est la femme qui, comme vous, a passé sa vie à cultiver ses talens, à s'instruire, afin de pouvoir être utile à ses enfans?" (*Adèle,* 1:99). The baronne does not answer this query. The huge intellectual burden on the children was also a major point of contention, as Genlis's critics pointed out in *Le Mercure de France* (2 April 1782): "Par quel secret Mme de Genlis vient-elle à bout de donner à ses élèves une aussi prodigieuse multitude de connaissances et de si bonnes qualités?" (62).

67. This complete devotion to the child, which strikes modern readers as excessive to the point of pathology, is also found in other period works on pedagogy such as

Mme d'Epinay's *Lettres à mon fils: Essais sur l'éducation et morceaux choisis* (1757). On the "symbiotic" nature of these relationships, see Elisabeth Badinter, *Emilie, Emilie: L'Ambition féminine au XVIIIe siècle* (Paris: Flammarion, 1983), 365–70.

68. These vignettes include the *cours de vertu expérimentale* testing Adèle's ability to keep a secret (*Adèle et Théodore,* 2:56–70) and the *cours d'expérience artificielle* whereby Adèle regrets spending her money on frivolities instead of giving it to a poor woman (3:2–14). Note also that the mother produced empathy and charity in her child by exposing her to "scenes" of poverty and distress (3:366).

69. Genlis, *Adelaide and Theodore, or Letters on Education: Containing All the Principles relative to three different Plans of Education; to that of Princes, and to those of young Persons of both Sexes,* 3 vols. (London: C. Bathhurst and T. Cadell, 1783), 3:131. All English citations from Genlis's work refer to this edition, unless otherwise noted. "Ah! Cette imprudence, je n'y retomberai plus!" *Adèle,* 4:95.

70. *Adelaide,* 3:30, 1:15. "[J]'ai suivi vos conseils, et j'ai retrouvé tout mon bonheur"; "Dans toutes nos disputes, vous avez toujours fini par avoir raison, et moi par avouer mes torts: je vois que nous conserverons cette habitude. Oui, ma chère amie, vous avez encore raison." *Adèle,* 3:311, 1:21.

71. *Adelaide,* 3:128. "[V]ous ne pouvez vous enorgueillir des qualités et des talens que vous possédez, sans oublier que c'est à moi que vous les devez." *Adèle,* 4:89.

72. *Adelaide,* 3:262. "Quel intérêt n'avez-vous pas à le corriger de ses défauts, et à former autant qu'il sera possible et son caractère et son esprit!" *Adèle,* 4:350.

73. *Adelaide,* 1:82, 2:61. "Rousseau a dit fort éloquemment que l'homme naît essentiellement bon, et qu'entièrement livré à lui-même, il le seroit toujours, &c. Je crois cette idée fausse"; "L'homme est né bon . . . mais aussi la réflexion le refroidit, le change et le rend personnel; il est inconséquent, parce qu'il n'est qu'un être imparfait et borné, et c'est la religion seule qui lui peut donner le goût constant de la vertu." *Adèle,* 1:148, 2:269–70.

74. *Adelaide,* 1:137. "[Q]uand on a su forcer à la soumission un esprit naturellement impérieux, il ne faut plus l'abandonner à lui-même un seul instant; car, si vous perdez de vue l'enfant que vous avez dompté, soyez sûre qu'il se dédommagera, à la première occasion, de la contrainte que vous lui imposez. . . . Ainsi, ne le quittez donc que pour le remettre en des mains aussi sûres que les vôtres; ayez toujours les yeux sur lui jusqu'à le temps, la raison, et l'habitude aient absolument changé son caractère." *Adèle,* 1:251.

75. References to Rousseau run throughout the novel; see, e.g., her comparison of Rousseau and Locke (*Adelaide,* 1:52), her disagreement on breastfeeding (1:91), a list of authors from whom Rousseau borrowed ideas in *Emile* (1:111), and punishment for hitting a servant (2:107).

76. On Genlis's edition of *Emile,* see Arnold H. Rowbotham, "Mme de Genlis and Jean-Jacques Rousseau," *Modern Language Quarterly* 3 (1942): 363–77. On her enmity toward the philosophes and theirs toward her, see Broglie, *Madame de Genlis,* 117–23. On her plans to create éditions épurées of various philosophical works (of Voltaire, Helvétius, Raynal, and the entire *Encyclopédie*), see Broglie, 432–37.

77. As Laborde cogently points out, "Les philosophes ont fait faillite dans la mesure où ils n'ont pu changer la nature humaine. Ils ont cru qu'en démolissant les entraves imposées par la morale sociale on améliorerait la condition de l'homme. Mais, après leur suppression, on a été forcé d'en imaginer de nouvelles afin d'éviter le chaos." *L'Oeuvre de Mme de Genlis,* 169.

78. For an interesting and original analysis of Rousseau's concept of censorship as a necessary evil in civil society, consult Dennis Porter, "Jean-Jacques Rousseau: Policing the Aesthetic from the Left," in *The Administration of Aesthetics: Censorship, Political Criticism, and the Public Sphere,* ed. Richard Burt (Minneapolis: University of Minnesota Press, 1994), 106–22.

79. Py concludes his otherwise dependable summary of Genlis's novel with this highly debatable declaration: "La nature est donc le milieu éducatif par excellence pour mener à bien cette formation, dont le but est de conduire à la régénération de l'espèce, conformément au mythe de l'innocence mis à la mode par 'l'éloquence' de Rousseau." Py, *Rousseau et les éducateurs,* 155–56.

80. *Adelaide,* 3:277. "[J]e vous jure la même soumission, la même obéissance que vous m'avez vue jusqu'ici. Vous prendre pour modèle, vous imiter, s'il est possible, suivre tous vos conseils, vous consacrer ma vie, voilà les plus chers désirs de mon coeur; tout votre bonheur, je le sais, dépend de ma conduite." *Adèle,* 4:377.

81. This vision of maternal rectitude emerges strikingly in one of the many interpolated tales in *Adèle et Théodore:* the "Histoire de la Duchesse de C***." After relating the (true) story of a woman who suffered innumerable indignities and tortures at the hands of a tyrannical husband, culminating in a live burial, the baronne dismisses the duchess as a case of self-inflicted suffering. She should have listened to in her mother! ("[T]ous ses malheurs venoient uniquement d'avoir manqué de confiance en sa mère," 3:190).

82. Rousseau, *Emile,* 7. "Les bonnes institutions sociales sont celles qui savent le mieux dénaturer l'homme, lui ôter son existence absolue pour lui en donner une relative, et transporter le *moi* dans l'unité commune; en sorte que chaque particulier ne se croye plus un, mais partie de l'unité, et ne soit plus sensible que dans le tout." *Emile,* in *Oeuvres complètes,* ed. Bernard Gagnebin and Marcel Raymond (Paris: Gallimard, 1959), 4:249.

83. This issue of holding all authority in the mother's hands provoked a good deal of antagonism from Genlis's critics. In *Adèle et Théodore* as at Bellechasse with the d'Orléans family, Genlis refused to delegate religious instruction to priests and instead taught such classes as she saw fit. Her high-handed authoritarianism elicited a storm of outrage not only from her Catholic critics but also from the Abbé Guyot, who was originally hired to teach religion and who quit Bellechasse in 1786. See Broglie, *Madame de Genlis,* 134–35, 139.

84. Indeed, Maria Edgeworth has been much criticized for her indifference to her countrymen's trauma. As one source notes, "Bodies lay bloating in the sun for days in the bogs and hillsides, though the visiting novelist Maria Edgeworth noted in her diaries only the handsome uniforms and appearance of the government troops." Thomas Bartlett, Kevin Dawson, and Dáire Keogh, *Rebellion: A Television History of 1798* (Dublin: Gill and Macmillan, 1998), 140. Edgeworth Sr. would be best described as a "moderate" loyalist-unionist. He was an active Volunteer reformer in the 1780s but spoke against the Volunteers' marching to Parliament in 1784. He opposed heavy-handed repression in the later 1790s but mustered a yeomanry unit (in which he included local Catholics). The only tenuous connection between Edgeworth and the radical cause is that the family home at Edgeworthstown was spared by the rebels in 1798, leading to dark rumors of complicity. But such rumors were typical loyalist paranoia at the time, according to Jim Smyth, whom I thank for these valuable insights into Richard Edgeworth's politics.

85. For more on the Edgeworths' domestic situation during Maria's childhood, consult Butler, *Maria Edgeworth,* 36–77.

86. Cited in *The Life and Letters of Maria Edgeworth,* ed. Augustus J. C. Hare (Boston: Houghton, Mifflin, 1895), 1:12–13.

87. Samuel Taylor Coleridge, cited in Butler, *Maria Edgeworth,* 51.

88. Carolyn Gonda debunks such images of Maria Edgeworth in *Reading Daughters' Fictions, 1709–1834: Novels and Society from Manley to Edgeworth* (Cambridge: Cambridge University Press, 1996), 204–15, 233–38.

89. Seamus Deane, *A Short History of Irish Literature* (1986; reprint, Notre Dame, Ind.: University of Notre Dame Press, 1994), 94. For a more extensive discussion of the historical significance of *Castle Rackrent* and *The Absentee,* see W. J. McCormack, *Ascendancy and Tradition in Anglo-Irish Literary History from 1789 to 1939* (Oxford: Clarendon, 1985), 97–168.

90. As Marilyn Butler points out, Edgeworth did not do this work for nought; she incorporated the ideas of *Adèle et Théodore* in the voices of Julie and Caroline (in *Letters for Literary Ladies,* 1795) and in the plot of *Leonora* (1806) (Butler, *Maria Edgeworth,* 148–49). The parallels between the interests, life experience, and writings of Genlis and Edgeworth are striking; indeed, John Ruskin called Genlis "the French Miss Edgeworth" (cited in Broglie, *Madame de Genlis,* 479).

91. Cited in Butler, *Maria Edgeworth,* 65.

92. Brian Simon, *Studies in the History of Education, 1780–1870* (London: Lawrence and Wishart, 1960), 89; Alice Paterson, *The Edgeworths: A Study of Later Eighteenth-Century Education* (London: W. B. Clive, 1914), 33.

93. The need for a children's room will ring true to anyone who lives with children: "[M]ost well ordered families allow their horses and their dogs to have houses to themselves; cannot one room be allotted to the children of the family? If they are to learn chemistry, mineralogy, botany, or mechanics; if they are to take sufficient bodily exercise without tormenting the whole family with noise, a room should be provided for them." Maria and Richard Lovell Edgeworth, *Practical Education,* 2 vols. (London: J. Johnson, 1798), 1:29. See also chapter 1, "Toys," and chapter 12, "Books." All citations from *Practical Education* refer to this edition unless otherwise noted.

94. Ibid., 2:502. See chapter 19, "On Public and Private Education," 2:499–518.

95. Edgeworth and Edgeworth, *Practical Education,* 2:723. This message was clearly well received by members of the Fitzgerald family, noted above for their great interest in Rousseauian pedagogy. In a letter of 17 July 1780, Lady Sarah Napier wrote to her niece Sophia Fitzgerald: "May I recommend to your Studdy [*sic*] an *Irish book of Education*—this will be held in great contempt by English people who think us *too savage to educate* & I will own this book is a little Irish, for it is called *Practical Education* & it is *impracticable.* But I advise you to buy it tho Dear—it is so very useful to resort to, on a thousand occasions, & it is *high* time to studdy it for Lucy as I find Miss Edgeworth the very sensible author begins in the Nurses arms & she is quite right.—pray don't neglect buying it." Letter in the Lennox-Fitzgerald-Campbell papers, National Library of Ireland, mss. 35,004 (6). I thank Kevin Whelan for his help in locating these letters, which are not only fascinating as a record of women's history, but also illustrate very well the impact of progressive thinking among the Anglo-Irish intelligentsia.

96. In the "Advertisement" to the 1801 edition, the Edgeworths responded to the two main charges made against the first edition, writing, "The Authors continue to pre-

serve the silence upon this subject [religion], which they before thought prudent; but they disavow in explicit terms the design of laying down a system of Education founded upon morality exclusive of Religion." *Essays on Practical Education,* 3d ed., (London: 1811), 1:xii.

97. Alan Richardson, *Literature, Education, and Romanticism: Reading as Social Practice* (Cambridge: Cambridge University Press, 1994), 54.

98. See chapter 1, on toys, where even the infant is an active intellect exploring his environment (*Practical Education,* 1:19), and chapter 2, on tasks, which declares that children's play is a valuable "occupation" and lists several examples of eminent scientists who made important discoveries "at play" (1:52). Or consider the following advice: "Children should have empty shelves in their cabinets, to be filled in with their own collection; they will then know how to direct their researches, and how to dispense of their treasures" (1:34).

99. On this evolution in attitudes toward science and scientists in the 1790s, see Simon Schaffer, "Self Evidence," *Critical Inquiry* 18 (winter 1992): 327–62. On the changing status of chemistry and chemists, in particular, see Wilda C. Anderson, *Between the Library and the Laboratory: The Language of Chemistry in Eighteenth-Century France* (Baltimore: John Hopkins University Press, 1984).

100. Maria's sister Anna married the famous experimentalist in pneumatics in 1794. Beddoes is cited throughout *Practical Education,* especially in chapter 1, on "rational toys." See Schofield, *Lunar Society of Birmingham,* for Edgeworth's involvement in contemporary science and technology.

101. "A Paris on lit votre livre sur l'éducation—à Genève on l'avale—à Paris on admire vos principes—à Genève on les suit," Abbé Morellet to Maria Edgeworth, 1802. Cited in Butler, *Maria Edgeworth,* 190. Edgeworth cites numerous admirers met during her sojourn in Paris in *The Life and Letters of Maria Edgeworth,* 1:104–41. On the British reception of *Practical Education* see Butler, *Maria Edgeworth,* 172–74.

102. Little has been written on Edgeworth's impact on her female readers, apart from brief comments on her American influence in Nina Baym, *Woman's Fiction: A Guide to Novels by and about Women in America, 1820–1870* (Ithaca: Cornell University Press, 1978), 29; and Josephine Donovan, *New England Local Color Literature: A Women's Tradition* (New York: Ungar, 1983), 11–24. This subject calls for investigation, as does her influence on women writers more generally. Edgeworth's correspondence, which includes letters to and from mothers who were applying her work to real-life childrearing, offers an excellent place to begin.

103. Myers writes: "[I]rreproachably moral and instructive, Edgeworthian feminism provided a readily imitated paradigm for women authors and readers." "Socializing Rosamond: Educational Ideology and Fictional Form," *Children's Literature Association Quarterly* 14, no. 2 (summer 1989): 53.

104. Maria Edgeworth, *Letters for Literary Ladies, to which is added An Essay on the Noble Science of Self-Justification,* ed. Claire Connolly (1795; reprint, London: J. M. Dent, 1993), 29. Edgeworth is ambivalent on the issue of women's equality, however, and in the "Advertisement" to the second edition (1798) she expresses her desire "to assert more strongly the female right to literature" (xxvii).

105. Seamus Deane, *Strange Country: Modernity and Nationhood in Irish Writing since 1790* (Oxford: Clarendon, 1997), 31.

106. On gender-neutral language, Edgeworth writes: "No intelligent preceptress

will, it is hoped, find any difficulty in the application of the observations she may meet with in the chapters on imagination, sympathy and sensibility, vanity and temper. The masculine pronoun *he* has been used for grammatical convenience, not at all because we agree with the prejudiced and uncourteous grammarian, who asserts, 'that the masculine is the more worthy gender.'" *Practical Education,* 2:552. On the chid's freedom, see Myers, "Socializing Rosamond," 55. On paternalism, see Colin B. Atkinson and Jo Atkinson, "Maria Edgeworth, *Belinda,* and Women's Rights," *Eire-Ireland* 19, no. 4 (1984): 115. David Roberts defines the paternalist outlook: "The doctrine that everyone in a well-ordered society has definite duties is as necessary to any definition of paternalism as the belief in an authoritarian, hierarchical, organic, and pluralistic society. These four assumptions, joined with the doctrine of duties, form the core of the paternalist social outlook." *Paternalism in Early Victorian England* (New Brunswick, N.J.: Rutgers University Press, 1979), 6.

107. As Genlis writes, "[O]n doit éviter d'enflammer l'imagination des femmes et d'exalter leurs têtes; elles sont nées pour une vie monotone et dépendante. Il leur faut de la raison, de la douceur, de la sensibilité, des ressources contre le désoeuvrement et l'ennui. . . . Le génie est pour elles un don inutile et dangereux; il leur sort de leur état, ou ne peut servir qu'à leur en faire connoître les désagrémens." *Adèle,* 1:45.

108. See Rousseau, *Emile,* trans. Foxley, 330–31 (on dolls), 350 (on cunning). Rousseau's discussion of dolls was notorious among progressive thinkers: both Germaine de Staël and Mary Wollstonecraft responded to it in their works. The chapters explicitly addressed to women are "On Temper," "On Female Accomplishments," and "Prudence and Economy"; for more on female education the reader is referred to Edgeworth's *Letters for Literary Ladies* (*Practical Education,* 1:viii). All but eight chapters (six by Edgeworth Sr. and two inspired by others: Thomas Beddoes and Lovell Edgeworth) were authored solely by Maria—as inspired by notes left by her stepmother Honora. For details on authorship, see *Practical Education,* 1:ix–x.

109. "Nature herself has decreed that woman, both for herself and her children, should be at the mercy of man's judgment. . . . A woman's honour does not depend on her conduct alone, but on her reputation" (Rousseau, *Emile,* 328).

110. Genlis, *Adelaide,* 3:275. "M. et madame d'Almane ne parlent jamais aux indifférens de ce qui se passe dans l'intérieur de leur famille." *Adèle,* 4:372.

111. Maria Edgeworth, *The Absentee,* ed. W. J. McCormack and Kim Walker (Oxford: Oxford University Press, 1988), 133.

112. Emile Faguet, cited in Broglie, *Madame de Genlis,* 140.

CHAPTER FIVE

1. As Ronald Paulson has pointed out, this concept of progress was central to the doctrine of the Physiocrats in France as well as their colleagues in Scotland. Adam Smith writes in *The Wealth of Nations* (1776) that "[t]he encrustations of convention have to be removed for nature to carry on its normal growth. Whether for a plant or a human body, the process of healthy development involves cropping, removing swaddling bonds or corsets, and allowing an organic fulfillment." Cited in Paulson, *Representations of Revolution (1789–1820)* (New Haven: Yale University Press, 1983), 48. The scholarship on the idea progress in the eighteenth century is of course vast. For the principal treatments, see Ferdinand Brunetière, "La formation de l'idée de progrès au

XVIIIe siècle," *Etudes critiques sur l'histoire de la littérature française,* 5th ser. (Paris, 1893), 183–250; J. B. Bury, *The Idea of Progress: An Enquiry into Its Origins and Growth* (London: Macmillan, 1920); Jules Delaville, *Essai sur l'histoire de l'idée de progrès jusqu'à la fin du XVIIIe siècle* (Paris, 1910); Robert Flint, *Historical Philosophy in France and French Belgium and Switzerland* (New York, 1894); Lois Whitney, *Primitivism and the Idea of Progress: English Popular Literature in the Eighteenth Century* (Baltimore: Johns Hopkins University Press, 1934); Morris Ginsburg, *The Idea of Progress: A Revaluation* (Cambridge: Harvard University Press, 1956); R. V. Sampson, *Progress in the Age of Reason* (London: Heinemann, 1956).

2. Daniel Gordon, *Citizens without Sovereignty: Equality and Sociability in French Thought, 1670–1789* (Princeton: Princeton University Press, 1994), 229.

3. Madelyn Gutwirth's rich analysis of textual and visual materials produced before and during the revolution has been immensely helpful in writing this chapter. *The Twilight of the Goddesses: Women and Representation in the French Revolutionary Era* (New Brunswick, N.J.: Rutgers University Press, 1992).

4. Lynn Hunt, *Politics, Culture, and Class in the French Revolution* (Berkeley: University of California Press, 1984), 87–119, 119.

5. On conspiracy theories in revolutionary writings, see François Furet, *Interpreting the French Revolution,* trans. Elborg Forster (Cambridge: Cambridge University Press, and Paris: Editions de la Maison des Sciences de l'Homme, 1981), 46–72; and Hunt, *Politics, Culture, and Class,* 37–48.

6. "Counterrevolutionary" authors did not necessarily counter every aspect of the revolution. Whereas Burke, Maistre, and Barruel did adopt an uncompromising attitude as regards the supreme importance of the church and the monarchy in the life of the French state, many émigré journalists evinced a more accommodating approach. As Simon Burrows has explained, émigré journalists eschewed the traditional absolutist and legitimist theories and instead criticized the revolution because it was not truly "popular" and did not enjoy widespread support. "On one level , this was pragmatic—they hoped to undermine the revolution's main claim to legitimacy and to promote foreign political or military intervention by convincing their readers that support for royalism was widespread. On another level, it indicates the extent to which revolutionary political culture had penetrated. The émigré journalists were suggesting that political power must be based on popular consent. They differed from the revolutionaries only about which side enjoyed that consent." Burrows, "The Image of the Republic in the Press of the London Emigrés, 1792–1802," in *The French Emigrés in Europe and the Struggle Against Revolution, 1789–1814,* ed. Kirsty Carpenter and Philip Mansel (London: Macmillan, 1999), 184–96, esp. 186.

7. Furet, *Interpreting,* 58.

8. "[Son allumette] N'est pas plus grosse qu'un fétu; / Que toujours molle et toujours croche, / Il n'a de v. . . que dans la poche." *Les Amours de Charlot et Toinette,* cited in Robert Darnton, *The Literary Underground of the Old Regime* (Cambridge: Harvard University Press, 1982), 200–201. See Darnton, 167–208 for more on the circulation of such materials in this period and the serious effect they had on public opinion. Of course, as we shall see below, materials that ridiculed the king's impotence often painted an equally derisory portrait of the queen—as a scheming manipulator, nymphomaniac, or lesbian, among other things.

9. "A l'instant de cette lecture je vis un autre univers et je devins un autre homme." Jean-Jacques Rousseau, *Les Confessions,* in *Oeuvres complètes,* ed. Bernard Gagnebin and Marcel Raymond (Paris: Gallimard, 1959), 1:351.

10. "Je ne trouvai plus rien de grand et de beau que d'être libre et vertueux, au dessus de la fortune et de l'opinion, et de se suffire à soi-même." Ibid., 1:356.

11. Carol Blum, *Rousseau and the Republic of Virtue* (Ithaca: Cornell University Press, 1986), 43.

12. For more on the important metaphors of revolutionary "energy," consult Michel Delon, *L'idée d'énergie au tournant des lumières (1770–1820)* (Paris: Presses Universitaires de France, 1988).

13. Jean-Jacques Rousseau, *Emile,* trans. Barbara Foxley, 437. "La liberté n'est dans aucune forme de gouvernement, elle est dans le coeur de l'homme libre, il la porte par tout avec lui." Rousseau, *Emile ou de l'éducation,* in *Oeuvres complètes,* ed. Bernard Gagnebin and Marcel Raymond (Paris: Gallimard, 1959), 4:857.

14. "C'est l'éducation qui doit donner aux ames la force nationale, et diriger tellement leurs opinions et leurs gouts, qu'elles soient patriotes par inclination, par passion, par nécessité." Jean-Jacques Rousseau, *Considérations sur le gouvernement de Pologne,* in *Oeuvres complètes,* ed. Bernard Gagnebin and Marcel Raymond (Paris: Gallimard, 1959), 3:966.

15. Rousseau's concern for a patriotic education that would strengthen ties between the individual and the state was shared by many contemporaries. Already in 1750, Charles [Pinot] Duclos declared: "On trouve parmi nous beaucoup d'instruction et peu d'éducation. On y forme des savants, des artistes de toute espèce. . . . Mais on ne s'est pas encore avisé de former des hommes, c'est-à-dire de les élever respectivement les uns pour les autres . . . de façon qu'ils fussent accoutumés à chercher leurs avantages personnels dans le plan du bien général, et que, dans quelque profession que ce fût, ils commençassent par être des patriotes." In Duclos, *Considérations sur les moeurs de ce siècle,* ed. F. C. Green (Cambridge: Cambridge University Press, 1946), 20. Keith Baker has argued that this demand for a patriotic education was common to the work of many philosophes, including Abbé Coyer, D'Alembert, Dupont, and Helvétius. See Baker, *Condorcet: From Natural Philosophy to Social Mathematics* (Chicago: University of Chicago Press, 1975), 286–93.

16. Nancy Armstrong, *Desire and Domestic Fiction: A Political History of the Novel* (New York: Oxford University Press, 19), 31–32.

17. As Rousseau declares at the beginning of *Le Contrat social:* "Je veux chercher si dans l'ordre civil il peut y avoir quelque regle d'administration légitime et sûre, en prenant les hommes tels qu'ils sont, et les loix telles qu'elles peuvent être." *Le Contrat social,* in *Oeuvres complètes,* ed. Bernard Gagnebin and Marcel Raymond (Paris: Gallimard, 1959), 3:351.

18. Paul Janet, *Histoire de la science politique dans ses rapports avec la morale,* 5th ed. (Paris: Librairie Félix Alcan, 1925), 2:453–54.

19. The literature on Rousseau's influence, especially through his *Contrat social,* on the revolutionary leaders is vast. Representative works include E. Champion, *Rousseau et la Révolution française* (Paris, 1909); Alfred Cobban, *Rousseau and the Modern State* (London, 1964); Joan McDonald, *Rousseau and the French Revolution 1762–1791* (London: Athlone, 1965); Nathalie-Barbara Robisco, *Jean-Jacques Rousseau et la Révolution française: Une esthétique de la politique 1792–1799* (Paris: Honoré Champion, 1998); and

James Swenson, *On Jean-Jacques Rousseau: Considered as One of the First Authors of the Revolution* (Stanford: Stanford University Press, 2000), 159–228.

20. Mona Ozouf, "'Public Opinion' at the End of the Old Regime," in *The Rise and Fall of the French Revolution,* ed. T. C. W. Blanning (Chicago: University of Chicago Press, 1996), 105.

21. Particularly useful are Antoine de Baecque, "L'Homme nouveau est arrivé: La 'Régénération' du français en 1789," *Dix-huitième siècle* 20 (1988): 193–208; Mona Ozouf, *L'Homme régénéré: Essais sur la révolution française* (Paris: Gallimard, 1989); and Nina Rattner Gelbart, "The French Revolution as Medical Event: The Journalistic Gaze," *History of European Ideas* 10 (1989): 417–27.

22. Conversely, the concept of degeneration was often associated with bad maternal practices such as wet-nursing. Many people believed that women transmitted their moral traits through their milk to their nurslings. And since wet-nurses, like servants, were believed to be contaminated with vices such as superstition, laziness, and disorderly passions, the children raised on their milk necessarily embodied those bad habits of thought.

23. M. Riballier (with the collaboration of Mlle Cosson), *De l'éducation physique et morale des femmes avec une notice alphabétique de celles qui se sont distinguées* (Brussels, 1779), 17. Cited in Gutwirth, *Twilight of the Goddesses,* 150.

24. "Il est devenu de bon ton d'être nourrice. Les mères ont paru plus intéressantes." Madame de Miremont, *Traité de l'éducation des femmes,* 2:505, cited in Laurent Versini, *Laclos et la tradition* (Paris: Kincksieck, 1968), 545.

25. On Marie-Antoinette in antimonarchical pamphlets, see Chantal Thomas, "L'héroïne du crime—Marie-Antoinette dans les pamphlets," in *La Carmagnole des muses,* ed. Jean-Claude Bonnet (Paris: Armand Colin, 1988); and Lynn Hunt, "The Many Bodies of Marie Antoinette: Political Pornography and the Problem of the Feminine in the French Revolution," in *Eroticism and the Body Politic,* ed. L. Hunt (Baltimore: Johns Hopkins University Press, 1991), 108–30.

26. On agricultural reform and natural history as loci of regeneration discourse, see E. C. Spary, *Utopia's Garden: French Natural History from Old Regime to Revolution* (Chicago: University of Chicago Press, 2000), 99–154.

27. Cited in Ozouf, *L'Homme régénéré,* 128.

28. In Sébastien Mercier's eulogy for 1789 (what he calls *l'Année régénératrice*), he writes, "Que d'événemens inattendus renferme cette Année! Dans l'espace de quelques mois, on a réparé les malheurs & les fautes de plusieurs siècles; l'homme a recouvré sa dignité première . . . un Roi Citoyen & honnête a préféré son Peuple à sa Cour; & en voulant la régénération de la France, il a su élever son ame à la hauteur de sa puissance." *Annales politiques* (31 December 1789), in *Histoire de France à travers les journaux du temps passé: La Révolution française, 1789–1799,* ed. André Rossel (Paris: A l'Enseigne de l'Arbre verdoyant, 1988), 57.

29. "Qu'est-ce qu'une révolution? C'est une crise par laquelle le peuple, vieilli dans les maux, reprend la vigueur de la jeunesse, en sortant des bras de la mort." *Catéchisme d'un peuple libre* (London: 1789), 7–8, reprinted in *Jean-Jacques Rousseau dans la Révolution française, 1789–1801* (Paris: Editions d'histoire sociale, 1977).

30. This episode is reported in Ernest F. Henderson, *Symbol and Satire in the French Revolution* (New York: G. P. Putnam's Sons, 1912), 276.

31. "Français, vous avec reconquis votre liberté, cette liberté dont les premiers

Francs, vos ancêtres, étaient jaloux; vous allez redevenir comme eux, forts et sains, comme eux vous laisserez croître votre barbe, et vous arborerez la chevelure longue qu'ils avaient en honneur. . . . Adieu les coiffeurs, coiffeuses et les marchands de mode, vous vous couvrirez de toile ou de bure." Le Tellier, *Le Triomphe des Parisiens* (Paris, July 1789), cited in de Baeque, "L'Homme nouveau," 199.

32. At the level of national stereotypes, the British had long regarded well-born Frenchmen as subtle, effeminate, intellectually devious fops, preoccupied with high fashion, fine cuisine, and superficial etiquette. For more on this discourse, see Linda Colley, *Britons: Forging the Nation, 1707–1837* (New Haven: Yale University Press, 1992), 5–6, 33–36, and passim. See also Gillray's caricature of Jack English exchanging insults with Monsieur the Frenchman in his engraving "Politeness" (1779), reproduced in *The French Revolution (version anglaise),* ed. David Bindman (Vizille: Musée de la Révolution Française, 1990), 64.

33. For more on artistic representations of fraternity and the emotional bonds it cemented among men, see Thomas Crow, *Emulation: Making Artists for Revolutionary France* (New Haven: Yale University Press, 1995).

34. Philippe Pinel, *Gazette de Santé* 46 (1789): 181–82. Cited in Gelbart, "French Revolution as Medical Event," 419.

35. Philippe Pinel, "Coup d'oeil d'un médecin," *Esprit des journaux* (February 1790): 365–68. Cited in Gelbart, "French Revolution as Medical Event," 420.

36. As an article in *La Bouche de fer* (17 March 1791) stated, à propos of a new "cercle fédératif de patriotes," "l'on ne saurait trop encourager ces associations régénératrices: le moyen le plus doux et le plus sûr de nous faire aimer les loix, est de nous engager à les former nous-mêmes en société." In *Histoire de France à travers les journaux,* 100.

37. Mona Ozouf sketches the folk genealogy of maypoles and the social tensions elicited by the state-sponsored planting of liberty trees in *La Fête révolutionnaire, 1789–1799* (Paris: Gallimard, 1976), 294–316. See also Hunt, *Politics, Culture, and Class,* 59–60.

38. De Baeque, "L'Homme nouveau," 203–6.

39. As Godineau reports, "L'orateur de la section de la République s'écrie: 'Que le sang de Marat devienne une semence d'intrépides républicains.' Le lendemain, les Citoyennes Républicaines Révolutionnaires jurent à la Convention de 'peupler la terre de la Liberté d'autant de Marats qu'elles pourront en posséder.'" Dominique Godineau, *Citoyennes tricoteuses: Les femmes du peuple à Paris pendant la Révolution française* (Aix-en-Provence: Editions Alinea, 1988),150–51.

40. J. Guilhaumou, "Description d'un événement discursif: La mort de Marat à Paris (le 13–16 juillet 1793)," in *La Mort de Marat,* ed. J.-C. Bonnet (Paris: Flammarion, 1986), cited in Godineau, *Citoyennes tricoteuses,* 150.

41. Gutwirth, *Twilight of the Goddesses,* 294.

42. Ibid., 290.

43. "De ces effrayantes femelles / Les intarissables mamelles / Comme de publiques gamelles, / Offrent à boire à tout passant; / Et la liqueur qui coule, / Et dont l'abominable foule / Avec avidité se saoule, / Ce n'est pas du lait, mais du sang." Jacques-René Hébert, *Le Père Duchesne,* no. 280. Translated by Gutwirth and cited in *Twilight of the Goddesses,* 342.

44. Although there were about fifty women's or mixed popular societies and political clubs in the years 1789–93, virtually all over France, by October 1793, such associ-

ations were being denounced from many quarters. On 30 October 1793, the Committee of General Security voted to outlaw women's societies. For more on this history, see Godineau, *Citoyennes tricoteuses,* 333–54.

45. Simon Schama, *Citizens: A Chronicle of the French Revolution* (New York: Knopf, 1989), 644.

46. Ozouf, *La Fête révolutionnaire,* 184.

47. Lajer-Burcharth describes this festival in the larger context of David's attempts to control the body as an "active agent in the process of signification" in *Necklines: The Art of Jacques-Louis David after the Terror* (New Haven: Yale University Press, 1999), 162–63.

48. "O femmes! la liberté attaquée par tous les tyrans, pour être défendue a besoin d'un peuple de héros. C'est à vous à l'enfanter. Que toutes les vertus guerrières et généreuses coulent avec le lait maternel dans le coeur des nourrissons de France!" Hérault de Séchelles, as quoted by Charles-Aimé Dauban, *La Démagogie en 1793 à Paris ou Histoire jour par jour de l'année 1793 accompagnée de documents contemporains rares ou inédits* (Paris: 1868), 321–22.

49. Gutwirth, *Twilight of the Goddesses,* 365.

50. Ozouf, *La Fête révolutionnaire,* 184.

51. On the religious overtones of American revolutionary discourse, see Alan Heimert, *Religion and the American Mind: From the Great Awakening to the Revolution* (Cambridge: Harvard University Press, 1966), 239ff.

52. "Voici donc le jour de la colère, de la justice et de la vengeance! . . . Le cri de la convocation, comme l'éclat d'un tonnerre vengeur, appellera de l'obscurité des Provinces les coupables et les innocents, tous se rassembleront sur les marches de son trône. . . . Alors le livre formidable de la Vérité s'ouvrira; tout y est gravé." *Le Dies Irae,* 1789, cited in de Baecque, "L'Homme nouveau," 205.

53. Joseph Priestley, *Letters to the Right Honourable Edmund Burke occasioned by his Reflections on the Revolution in France,* 2d ed. (Birmingham: Thomas Pearson, 1791), 154. For more on this vein of millenarian thinking, see Martin Fitzpatrick, "Joseph Priestley and the Millennium," in *Science, Medicine and Dissent: Joseph Priestley (1733–1804),* ed. R. G. W. Anderson and Christopher Lawrence (London: Wellcome Trust/Science Museum, 1987), 29–37; and Jack Fruchtman Jr., *The Apocalyptic Politics of Richard Price and Joseph Priestley: A Study in Late Eighteenth-Century English Republic Millennialism* (Philadelphia: American Philosophical Society, 1983), 81–104.

54. One deputy who tried to keep revolutionary reforms in line with the gospel of Jesus Christ was A.-A. Lamourette, who rose from obscurity to become the constitutional bishop of Lyon. For more on his works, see Ozouf, *L'Homme régénéré,* 129–30.

55. On the romantic poets' involvement in revolutionary politics, see E. P. Thompson, *The Romantics: England in a Revolutionary Age* (New York: Norton, 1997); Marilyn Butler, *Romantics, Rebels, and Reactionaries: English Literature and Its Background* (New York: Oxford University Press, 1981), 11–93; Seamus Deane, *The French Revolution and Enlightenment in England, 1789–1832* (Cambridge: Harvard University Press, 1988), 59–71 (on Coleridge); and Paulson, *Representations,* 248–85 (on Wordsworth).

56. William Wordsworth, *The Prelude. or Growth of a Poet's Mind,* XI:108–9, in *Poetical Works* (1850 ed.), ed. Thomas Hutcheon (New York: Oxford University Press, 1990), 570. Further references appear in the text.

57. Proverbs 26:11.

58. For a detailed analysis of this image and Blake's millenarian motifs, see Paulson, *Representations,* 88–110. See also David Bindman, *William Blake: His Art and Times* (New York: Thames and Hudson, 1982).

59. Klaus Herding, "Visual Codes in the Graphic Art of the French Revolution," in *French Caricature and the French Revolution, 1789–1799* (Los Angeles: Grunwald Center for the Graphic Arts, 1988), 83–100, esp. 97.

60. His passivity is especially striking if one compares this image to the engraving of "Liberty Triumphant Destroying Abusive Powers" from *Révolutions de France et de Brabant* 6 (1790; reproduced in Gutwirth, *Twilight of the Goddesses,* 261). In the earlier image, a woman symbolizing Liberty directs a cluster of lightning bolts that she holds in her hand to strike down and destroy the same emblems of nobility, monarchy, and the clergy as we find in Perée's image. Unlike Perée's regenerated man, Liberty controls the lightning bolts, and she uses this natural energy to free the French nation from its one-time masters.

61. A further case in point is the report on the regenerated world by the Chorus of Spirits in act 4 of Percy Bysshe Shelley's *Prometheus Unbound* (1820). When the Spirits first look, they notice no changes; they are more subtle than the Spirits can imagine. Hence these exalting lines: "We come from the mind / Of humankind, / Which was late so dusk, and obscene, and blind; / Now 'tis an ocean / Of clear emotion, / A Heaven of serene and mighty motion." Shelley, *Prometheus Unbound,* in *Romanticism: An Anthology,* ed. Duncan Wu (Oxford: Blackwell, 1994), 931. This may say something about the difference between the trope of regeneration in the 1790s and after Waterloo. I thank a reviewer at the University of Chicago Press for this insight.

62. "Nous ne sommes point des sauvages, arrivant nus des bords de l'Oréonoque pour former une société. Nous sommes une nation vieille." Mirabeau, "Discours sur la sanction royale aux décrets des 4 et 11 août" (18 September 1789), in *Orateurs de la Révolution française,* ed. François Furet and Ran Halévi (Paris: Gallimard, 1989), 1:687.

63. In the *Discours sur l'inégalité,* it is the Caraïbes who enjoy this precious equilibrium. I thank Sue Lanser for alerting me to this Rousseauian allusion in Mirabeau.

64. Gregory Dart, *Rousseau, Robespierre, and English Romanticism* (Cambridge: Cambridge University Press, 1999), 103.

65. "Cultiver . . . dans chaque génération, les facultés physiques, intellectuelles et morales, et par-là, contribuer à ce perfectionnement général et graduel de l'espèce humaine, . . . Tel doit être encore l'objet de l'instruction." Marie-Jean-Antoine-Nicolas de Caritat, marquis de Condorcet, "Rapport et projet de décret sur l'organisation générale de l'instruction publique (présentés à l'Assemblée nationale, au nom du Comité d'Instruction Publique, les 20–21 avril 1792)," in Condorcet, *Oeuvres* (1847–89; reprint, Stuttgart: Friedrich Frommann Verlag, 1968), 7:450.

66. "Plus [les lois] auront respecté les droits de l'indépendance personnelle et de l'égalité naturelle, plus elles rendront facile et terrible la tyrannie que la ruse exerce sur l'ignorance, en la rendant à la fois son instrument et sa victime." Condorcet, *Sur l'instruction publique: Premier mémoire,* in *Oeuvres* (1847–89; reprint, Stuttgart: Friedrich Frommann Verlag, 1968), 7:226. See Keith Baker, *Condorcet: From Natural Philosophy to Social Mathematics* (Chicago: University of Chicago Press, 1975), 334–35.

67. This scheme may not be as far-fetched as it appears, argue Michalina Vaughan and Margaret Scotford Archer; rather, it substitutes a concern—based on Enlighten-

ment concepts of individual rights—to attempt to curb state control for concern with individual autonomy. See Vaughan and Archer, *Social Conflict and Educational Change in England and France, 1789–1848* (Cambridge: Cambridge University Press, 1971), 161–71.

68. Dart, *Rousseau,* 105.

69. Baker, *Condorcet,* 334.

70. "Visiblement Condorcet manquait de sens pratique," wrote Albert Duruy in his *L'Instruction publique et la révolution* (Paris: Librairie Hachette, 1882), 83.

71. Although the Directory did not fulfill the promise of primary education, it did make significant reforms in secondary education, creating *Ecoles centrales* and a number of key institutions that took on even greater importance under Napoleon's reign, e.g., the Ecole Polytechnique, the Conservatoire des Arts et Métiers, and the Institut—all of which built on Condorcet's ideas. For more on educational reforms during the Directory, see Martyn Lyons, *France under the Directory* (Cambridge: Cambridge University Press, 1975), 90–95.

72. Joseph de Maistre, *Considerations on France,* trans. Richard A. Lebrun (Cambridge: Cambridge University Press, 1994), 29. Maistre characterizes Condorcet as "ce philosophe si cher à la révolution, qui employa sa vie à préparer le malheur de la perfection présente, léguant bénignement la génération à nos neveux. Il n'y a qu'un moyen de comprimer les fléaux de la guerre, c'est de comprimer les désordres qui amènent cette terrible purification." Josephe, comte de Maistre, *Considérations sur la France* (Lyon: Chez Rusand, 1829), 48.

73. "[S]on erreur propre, c'est de croire qu'on n'a qu'à vouloir et que tout est désormais pour le mieux, qu'en changeant les institutions on va changer les mobiles du coeur humain, que chaque citoyen deviendra insensiblement un philosophe raisonnable et rationnel." Charles Augustin Sainte-Beuve, "Condorcet," in *La Littérature française: des origines à 1870* (Paris: La Renaissance du livre, 1926), 7:13.

74. After being assassinated by a royalist, Lepeletier (also written as Lepelletier or Lepelletier de Saint-Fargeau) became one of the "martyrs of the Revolution" along with Marat and Barras. According to Duruy, it is only because of his martyr status that such a radical scheme for pedagogical reform was even entertained by the Convention, which had much more serious concerns—of national defense and financial insolvency—at this crucial juncture. Duruy, *L'Instruction publique et la révolution,* 93–95.

75. "[C]onsidérant à quel point l'espèce humaine est dégradée par le vice de notre ancien systême social, je me suis convaincu de la nécessité d'opérer une entière régénération, &, si je peux m'exprimer ainsi, de créer un nouveau peuple." Louis-Michel Lepeletier, "Plan d'éducation nationale (juillet 1793)," in *Une éducation pour la démocratie: Textes et projects de l'époque révolutionnaire,* ed. Bronislaw Baczko (Paris: Garnier, 1982), 348.

76. Ibid., 351, 354.

77. Notebook of Antoine Louis Léon de Saint-Just, cited in Robert Darnton, "What was Revolutionary about the French Revolution?" *New York Review of Books* 32, 21–22 (January 19, 1989): 4.

78. Dart, *Rousseau,* 109.

79. "Le peuple français a dépassé les autres peuples; cependant le régime détestable dont nous secouons les lambeaux, nous tient encore à grande distance de la nature; il reste un intervalle énorme entre ce que nous sommes et ce que nous pourrions être.

Hâtons-nous de combler cet intervalle; reconstituons la nature humaine en lui donnant une nouvelle trempe." Abbé Grégoire, *Rapport sur l'ouverture d'un concours pour les livres élémentaires de la première éducation* (Séance du 3 pluviôse an II, Convention Nationale), in Grégoire, *Oeuvres de l'Abbé Grégoire* (Paris: EDHIS Editions d'Histoire Sociale, 1977), 2:187.

80. "Acte du Directoire exécutif," *Journal de Paris* (9 November 1795), cited in *Histoire de France à travers les journaux,* 271.

81. "Le ministre de la police générale de la République, aux membres du bureau central de la commune de Paris," *Moniteur* (11 January 1795), cited in *Histoire de France à travers les journaux,* 275.

82. J. J. Leuliete, "On a trop usé, ou plutôt trop abusé des moyens violens; ayons recours à une douce séduction; créons de nouveaux amis de la liberté . . . et le passé n'excitera plus nos regrets. Nous verrons renaître ces jours si chers à notre mémoire, et le présent, quelque pénible qu'il soit, sera du moins adouci par l'idée d'un agréable avenir." *Orateur plébéien* (26 March 1796), cited in *Histoire de France à travers les journaux,* 277.

83. Fouché (Minister of the Police), "De ce moment un nouvel ordre de choses commence. Le gouvernement fut oppresseur parce qu'il fut faible; celui qui lui succede s'impose le devoir d'être fort pour remplir celui d'être juste," *Moniteur* (11 November 1799), cited in *Histoire de France à travers les journaux,* 318.

84. François Furet, *Revolutionary France, 1770–1880* trans. Antonia Nevill (Oxford: Blackwell, 1988), 163.

85. "Une république de trente millions d'hommes! Avec nos moeurs, nos vices! Où en est la possibilité? C'est une chimère dont les Français sont engoués, mais qui passera comme tant d'autres." Napoléon's comments at Montebello, cited in Furet, *La Révolution de Turgot à Jules Ferry 1770–1880* (Paris: Hachette, 1988), 194, and Furet, *Revolutionary France,* 189.

86. Maistre, *Considerations,* 56–57. "Ouvrez les yeux, et vous verrez qu'elle ne *vit* pas. Quel appareil immense! quelle multiplicité de ressorts et de rouages! quel fracas de pièces qui se heurtent! quelle énorme quantité d'hommes employés à réparer les dommages! . . . tout est factice, tout est violent, tout annonce qu'un tel ordre de choses ne peut durer." Maistre, *Considérations,* 101–2. On the symbolic opposition of organic versus mechanical forces, and the pejorative connotations of the latter in romantic writing, see M. H. Abrams, *The Mirror and the Lamp: Romantic Theory and the Critical Tradition* (New York: Oxford, 1953), 156–83, 204.

87. Vaughan and Archer, *Social Change,* 179. This verdict on revolutionary pedagogical reforms has been a point of contention for centuries, however. For more on these debates, see H. C. Reading, *Education and the French Revolution* (Cambridge: Cambridge University Press, 1969), 210–46.

88. "Malheur à cette créature qui se complaît en elle-même. . . . Elle sera bientôt la malheureuse victime de son orgueil." *Les destinées de la France* (1790), cited in de Baecque, "L'homme nouveau," 202.

89. Edmund Burke, *Reflections on the Revolution in France,* in *The Writings and Speeches of Edmund Burke,* ed. L. G. Mitchell and William B. Todd (Oxford: Clarendon, 1989), 3:128.

90. Maistre, *Considerations,* "On nous cite l'Amérique: je ne connois rien de si im-

patientant que les louanges décernées à cet enfant au maillot: laissez-le grandir." Maistre, *Considérations,* 60.

91. The reference to Medea comes from Ovid, *Metamorphoses,* bk. 7, and Hobbes's reference, which Burke is recalling, in *Leviathan,* chap. 30. We must recall, however, that the "dangerous French ideas" Burke condemned were less French than one might think. Like many other British writers, Burke couched his interpretation of the revolution in references to English politics. As L. G. Mitchell has shown, Burke's reaction astounded his contemporaries, who knew him as an enthusiastic supporter of the American rebels. See Mitchell, introduction to *The Writings and Speeches of Edmund Burke,* ed. L. G. Mitchell and William B. Todd (Oxford: Clarendon, 1989), 3:28–36; 34.

92. Paine's readership alone is amazing. Part 1 of *The Rights of Man* (1791) sold 50,000 copies in its first year, considerably more than Burke's *Reflections* (which sold 19,000). Part 1 was reprinted with Part 2 in 1792, and together they sold 200,000 copies between 1791 and 1793. Because his tracts were priced so cheaply, they were widely read in lower-class circles; and these figures give some notion of Paine's influence. Figures on readership are drawn from Marilyn Butler, "Tom Paine," in *Burke, Paine, Godwin, and the Revolution Controversy,* ed. Marilyn Butler (Cambridge: Cambridge University Press, 1984), 108.

93. Tom Paine, *The Rights of Man,* in *Burke, Paine, Godwin, and the Revolution Controversy,* ed. Marilyn Butler (Cambridge: Cambridge University Press, 1984), 111.

94. On the Jacobin groups in Britain, see Gary Kelly, *The English Jacobin Novel, 1780–1805* (Oxford: Clarendon, 1976); Marilyn Butler, *Romantics, Rebels and Reactionaries: English Literature and Its Background, 1760–1830* (Oxford: Oxford University Press, 1981); Deane, *French Revolution,* 10–11, 31.

95. John Courtney, *Philosophical Reflections on the Late Revolution in France and Conduct of the Dissenters in England, in a Letter to the Rev. Dr. Priestley* (London, 1790), 17–18. Cited in Deane, *French Revolution,* 31.

96. "Trait remarquable de la femme d'un membre d'un comité révolutionnaire, qui est accouchée d'un monstre dans la posture d'un guillotiné." In *Courier républicain* (15 February 1795), reprinted in *Histoire de France à travers les journaux,* 259.

97. *Le Journal de Paris* (10 October 1797), advertisement promising the possibility of treating "les égarements d'esprit, dûs à la Révolution, par des bains médicaux." Cited in Nicolas Wagner, "Fête et dissolution sociale: A Propos de quelques notices du *Journal de Paris* (1797)," in *Les Fêtes de la Révolution: Colloque de Clermont-Ferrand (juin 1974),* ed. Jean Ehrard and Paul Viallaneix (Paris: Société des Etudes Robespierristes, 1977), 525–36, esp. 527.

98. It is surprising that this book was so widely read as to warrant the multiple editions and translations it enjoyed, given its rambling and paranoid style, its repetition, its irrational leaps of logic, and its sheer heft. On Barruel's influence in the 1790s, see Paulson, *Representations of Revolution,* 223–24, 240–40; or Burrows, "Image of the Republic," 195n. 34, where we find a long list of émigré journal articles that "endorse Barruel's conspiracy theories and accuse the *philosophes* of preparing revolution by undermining religion and morality" (189).

99. "Qu'est-ce donc ces hommes sortis, pour ainsi dire, tout à coup des entrailles de la terre, avec leurs dogmes & leurs foudres, avec tous leurs projets, tous leurs moyens & toute la résolution de leur férocité? Qu'est-ce cette secte dévorante? D'où viennent tout

à la fois & cet essaim d'adeptes, & ces systèmes & ce délire de rage contre tous les autels & tous les trônes, contre toutes les institutions religieuses & civiles de nos ancêtres?" Abbé Augustin de Barruel, *Mémoires pour servir à l'histoire du jacobinisme,* 4 vols. (London: Chez Ph. Le Boussonnier, 1797), 1:iv.

100. J. M. Roberts, *Mythology of the Secret Societies* (London, 1972), 10; cited in Paulson, *Representations,* 223.

101. Paulson, *Representations,* 223–224.

102. [T. J. Mathias], *Pursuits of Literature: A Satirical Poem in Four Dialogues, with Notes,* 7th ed. (Philadelphia: H. Maxwell for A. Dickins, 1800), 421–22.

103. As Simpson notes, these antagonisms between French theory and English common sense are still operative today. See David Simpson, *Romanticism, Nationalism, and the Revolt against Theory* (Chicago: University of Chicago Press, 1993), chaps. 2 and 3. See also Linda Colley, *Britons: Forging the Nation, 1707–1837* (New Haven: Yale University Press, 1992), 5–6, 152–66.

104. For more on English sentimentalism in painting and borrowings from French models such as Greuze and Chardin, see E. D. H. Johnson, *Paintings of the British Social Scene from Hogarth to Sickert* (New York: Rizzoli, 1986), 80–128.

105. David Denby, *Sentimental Narrative and the Social Order in France, 1760–1820* (Cambridge: Cambridge University Press, 1994), 77, 80.

106. For an interpretation of the colonial subtext in *Belinda,* see Susan C. Greenfield, "'Abroad and at Home': Sexual Ambiguity, Miscegenation, and Colonial Boundaries in Edgeworth's *Belinda,*" *PMLA* 112, no. 2 (March 1997): 214–28.

107. Lady Delacour uses French expressions about twenty times more frequently than the other characters, and it is at her house that the reader notes "several volumes of French plays and novels." Maria Edgeworth, *Belinda,* ed. Eiléan Ní Chuilleanáin (1801; reprint, London: J. M. Dent, 1993), 162. All citations refer to this edition.

108. One might note that the antiheroine Harriet Freke is another character whose French abilities are underlined, as in her exclamation "I hate slavery! *Vive la liberté!*" in the chapter titled "Rights of Woman" (216). Another incident of negative Francophilia: in "Mlle Panache" Edgeworth tells of a woman who loses her suitor after he discovers her reading not only an immoral French novel, but the *second* volume at that! Cited in Alan Richardson, *Literature, Education, and Romanticism: Reading as Social Practice* (Cambridge: Cambridge University Press, 1994),186–87.

109. Edgeworth, *Belinda,* 95. "La Femme comme il y en a peu" first appeared in the collection *Nouveaux contes moraux,* published in 1765. More than fifteen English editions of the *Moral Tales* and *New Moral Tales* were published in the period 1764–1895. "La Femme comme il y en a peu" recounts how a young wife saves her family from ruin by taking financial control away from her foolish gambling husband, by selling off unnecessary luxuries, and by steering her husband away from Paris to their country estate, where he learns to appreciate agriculture and takes an active role in his children's education.

110. For more on Thomas Percival's activities, see Schofield, *Lunar Society of Birmingham,* 195, 307. In her Irish novels as well, Edgeworth's choice of names was extremely relevant. See W. J. McCormack, *Ascendancy and Tradition in Anglo-Irish Literary History from 1789 to 1939* (Oxford: Clarendon, 1985), 150.

111. As we saw in chapter 4, Day was a close family friend of the Edgeworths; Maria even spent some school vacations at his home. But she disagreed with him on women's

education and created semi-parodic images of him here as well as in other works, notably in *Letters for Literary Ladies* and the short story "Forester." For more on Edgeworth's literary representation of Day, see Anne K. Chandler, *Pedagogic Fantasies: Rousseau, Maleness, and Domesticity in the Fiction of Thomas Day, Maria Edgeworth, and Mary Wollstonecraft* (Ph.D. diss., Duke University, 1995), 129–43, esp. 142.

112. Norman Bryson, *Word and Image: French Painting of the Ancien Régime* (Cambridge: Cambridge University Press, 1981), 181.

113. See Carolyn Gonda, *Reading Daughters' Fictions, 1709–1834: Novels and Society from Manley to Edgeworth* (Cambridge: Cambridge University Press, 1996), 216–19.

114. Until very recently the novel had been almost entirely forgotten, even among the legions of scholars who have studied the Gothic. *Secresy* does not figure in any of the bibliographies of the many historians of the Gothic period, such as Summers, Varma, Thompson, or Kiely. It had never been reedited until 1974. Signs of recent interest include Julia Wright's article, "'I am ill fitted': Conflicts of Genre in Eliza Fenwick's *Secresy*," in *Romanticism, History, and the Possibilities of Genre: Re-Forming Literature, 1789–1837,* ed. Tilottama Rajan and Julia M. Wright (Cambridge: Cambridge University Press, 1998), 149–75, and Nicola Watson's comments in *Revolution and the Form of the British Novel, 1789–1825: Intercepted Letters, Interrupted Seductions* (Oxford: Clarendon, 1994), 39–44. Mystery shrouds the novelist's early life as well, apart from glimpses of an appalling domestic situation (wife of a drunkard, then single mother of two), and perhaps Fenwick's most noted experience, her friendship with Mary Wollstonecraft. The reprints include: *Secresy: Or, the Ruin on the Rock,* ed. Gina Luria (New York: Garland, 1974); *Secresy or, the Ruin on the Rock,* ed. Janet Todd (London: Pandora, 1989); *Secresy; or, The Ruin on the Rock,* ed. Isobel Grundy (Petersborough, Ont.: Broadview, 1994, 1996). Fenwick's juvenile literature includes *Visits to the Juvenile Library; or, Knowledge proved to be the source of happiness* (1805; reissued in 1977); and *The Life of Carlo, the famous dog of Drury Lane Theatre* (1804, 1809).

115. Isobel Grundy, introduction to *Secresy,* ed. Grundy, 9. All citations to *Secresy* refer to this edition.

116. Review of *Secresy; or the Ruin on the Rock,* in *British Critic* 6 (1795): 545 and in *Monthly Magazine* 18 (September 1795): 351.

117. Fenwick was a good friend indeed; she cared for mother and baby when Wollstonecraft gave birth in 1797 and nursed the newborn in the days following Wollstonecraft's death. The best account of Fenwick's life and works is Isobel Grundy's introduction to the Broadview edition, 7–35.

118. Terry Castle, "Sublimely Bad," review of *Secresy; or, The Ruin on the Rock, London Review of Books* 17, no. 4 (February 23, 1995): 18.

119. Much recent work has explored this motif and uncovered fascinating tales of gendered warfare, such as the duchesse de C——'s battle with her husband in Genlis's *Adèle et Théodore,* Emily St. Aubert's struggle with the evil Montoni in Ann Radcliffe's *Mysteries of Udolpho* (1794), or Father Anthony's persecution of the twin heroines in Sophia Lee's *The Recess* (1783–85). Of course, one could also cite female-authored novels that celebrated women who receive decent educations thanks to the intervention of ideal father figures (in the person of Fanny Price in Jane Austen's *Mansfield Park,* 1814, and Monimia in Charlotte Smith's *Old Manor House,* 1794). The term "female Gothic" was coined by Ellen Moers in *Literary Women* (Garden City: Doubleday, 1976). More recent work on Radcliffe and other late eighteenth-century English women writers includes

Claudia Johnson, *Equivocal Beings: Politics, Gender, and Sentimentality in the 1790s: Wollstonecraft, Radcliffe, Burney, Austen* (Chicago: University of Chicago Press, 1995); Anne Williams, *Art of Darkness* (Chicago: University of Chicago Press, 1995); Kay Mussell, *Women's Gothic and Romantic Fiction* (Westport, Conn.: Greenwood, 1981); Juliann Fleenor, ed., *The Female Gothic* (Montreal: Eden, 1983); and Kate Ellis, *The Contested Castle: Gothic Novels and the Subversion of Domestic Ideology* (Urbana: University of Illinois Press, 1989).

120. As her lover exclaims: "Oh, she is Nature's genuine child! . . . soft as her lover's bounding wishes can desire: yet stedfast [*sic*], aspiring, brave enough to lead an army in the field." Fenwick, *Secresy*, 154–55.

121. The language of both novels reflects the villains' view of other people as so many experimental subjects. Writing to Merteuil, Laclos's vicomte de Valmont declares that "conquérir est notre destin; il faut le suivre," and claims to set up "le plus grand projet qu'[il ait] jamais formé" at the beginning of the novel. See Choderlos de Laclos, *Les Liaisons dangereuses*, ed. René Pomeau (Paris: Garnier-Flammarion, 1964), 24.

122. Compare this to Burke's description of Rousseau: "That acute, though eccentric, observer had perceived, that to strike and interest the public, the marvellous must be produced . . . that is, the marvellous in life, in manners, in characters, and in extraordinary situations, giving rise to new and unlooked-for strokes in politics and morals." Burke, *Reflections*, 283–84.

123. When Sibella lies on her deathbed, Valmont sends "his stewart with forgiveness, blessings, and an earnest request that Sibella would make her own disposition of her fortune, by which he has resolved most faithfully to abide" (357).

124. Jacques Blondel, "On Metaphysical Prisons," *Durham University Journal* 32 (March 1971): 135.

125. Compare Caroline's stirring defense of Sibella to Wollstonecraft's description of women's frustrations. Caroline writes that Sibella "would rather think herself born to navigate ships and build edifices, than to come into a world for no other purpose, than to twist her hair into ringlets, learn to be feeble, and to find her feet too hallowed to tread on the ground beneath her" (93). Wollstonecraft queries: "How many women thus waste life away the prey of discontent, who might have practised as physicians, regulated a farm, managed a shop, and stood erect, supported by their own industry, instead of hanging their heads surcharged with the dew of sensibility?" Mary Wollstonecraft, *A Vindication of the Rights of Woman*, ed. Candace Ward (Mineola, N.Y.: Dover), 153.

126. On the Gothic convention of "generic guilt," see Blondel, "Metaphysical Prisons," 135.

127. For more on the status of women in eighteenth-century family law, consult Leonore Davidoff and Catherine Hall, *Family Fortunes: Men and Women of the English Middle Class, 1780–1850* (Chicago: University of Chicago Press, 1987); *English Family Life, 1576–1716: An Anthology from Diaries*, ed. Ralph Houlbrooke (London: Basil Blackwell, 1988); Roy Porter, *English Society in the Eighteenth Century* (London: Penguin, 1982), 22–34, 128–29; and Armstrong, *Desire and Domestic Fiction*, 28–58, 164ff.

128. Evelina is heroine of Frances Burney's *Evelina: or The History of a Young Lady's Entrance into the World* (1778); Monimia is the heroine of Charlotte Smith's *The Old Manor House* (1792); Fanny Price is the heroine of Jane Austen's *Mansfield Park* (1814), and Jane Eyre is heroine of Charlotte Brontë's novel by the same name (1847). A great deal has been written on this corpus in English literature; among the principal works of

criticism (all of which contain excellent bibliographies), one might cite Janet Todd, *The Sign of Angellica: Women, Writing and Fiction, 1660–1800* (New York: Columbia University Press, 1989); Johnson, *Equivocal Beings*; Mary Poovey, *The Proper Lady and the Woman Writer: Ideology as Style in the Works of Mary Wollstonecraft, Mary Shelley, and Jane Austen* (Chicago: University of Chicago Press, 1984); Moers, *Literary Women*, and Sandra Gilbert and Susan Gubar, *The Madwoman in the Attic: The Woman Writer and the Nineteenth-Century Literary Imagination* (New Haven: Yale University Press, 1979).

129. Colley, *Britons*, 256.

130. Ibid., 275.

131. It is important to note the particular political atmosphere in which these books were written. The decade and a half immediately following the publication of Wollstonecraft's *Vindication* (1792) witnessed one of the most reactionary periods in British history. As Alan Richardson explains: "In place of Macaulay's and Wollstonecraft's assertions of women's 'rights'—a now suspect term—and their radical program of equal education, writers like Reeve, Gisborne, More, and West developed a position on female education allowing for a certain measure of social reform while upholding traditional class and gender hieararchies, reasserting the separation of male and female spheres, re-emphasizing 'negative' virtues (especially modesty), and advocating much greater attention to religious and moral discipline." Richardson, *Literature, Education, and Romanticism*, 178–79.

132. Emma Spary, "Political, Natural, and Bodily Economies," in *Cultures of Natural History*, ed. N. Jardine, J. A. Secord, and E. C. Spary (Cambridge: Cambridge University Press, 1996), 178–96, esp. 194.

133. Gelbart, "French Revolution as Medical Event," 424; Matthew Ramsey, *Professional and Popular Medicine in France, 1779–1830: The Social World of Medicine* (Cambridge: Cambridge University Press, 1988), 74. For examples of quack practitioners who flourished in this situation and the chaotic years that followed, see Ramsey, 80–105 and passim.

134. Trent Mitchell surveys the debates over itinerant lecturing in "The Politics of Experiment in the Eighteenth Century: The Pursuit of Audience and the Manipulation of Consensus in the Debate over Lightning Rods," *Eighteenth-Century Studies* 31, no. 3 (1998): 307–31, esp. 319.

135. J. L. Heilbron, *Electricity in the 17th and 18th Centuries: A Study of Early Modern Physics* (Berkeley: University of California Press, 1979), 78–83.

136. Martyn Lyons, *France under the Directory* (Cambridge: Cambridge University Press, 1975), 122–23.

137. Ibid., 120–21.

138. On the distribution of Condorcet's work by the Directory's Committee of Public Education, see ibid., 118. On the imagery of longing and rootlessness that marks this period, see my analysis of the émigré motifs in *Pauliska*, below.

139. Adam Walker, *Analysis of a course of lectures on natural and experimental philosophy* (Manchester, for the author, 177?), 20–26. Cited in Simon Schaffer, "Priestley and the Politics of Spirit," in *Science, Medicine, and Dissent: Joseph Priestley (1733–1804)* (London: Wellcome Trust/Science Museum, 1987), 39–53, esp. 42.

140. For more on these figures, see Roy Porter, *Doctor of Society: Thomas Beddoes and the Sick Trade in Late-Enlightenment England* (London: Routledge, 1992), esp. 37–57; David Knight, *Humphry Davy: Science and Power* (Oxford: Blackwell, 1992); and

Jan Golinski, *Science as Public Culture: Chemistry and Enlightenment in Britain, 1760–1820* (Cambridge: Cambridge University Press, 1992), 153–235. In the last decades of the ancien régime, many scientists collaborated on state-sponsored projects, however, justifying the image of the scientist as civil servant that we see in texts such as Condorcet's 1786 declaration: "There is no more need to tell princes that they have an interest in protecting the sciences, or the public that scientists have a right to their gratitude." Condorcet, in *Histoire de l'Académie royale des sciences. Avec les mémoires de mathématiques et de physique . . . tirés des registres de cette académie (1699–1790),* 92 vols. (Paris: 1702–97); année 1783 (1786), 34. Napoleon would put great trust in the sciences as a means to strengthen the manufacturing power of France, as well. But during the late 1790s, there was a strong vein of anxiety about science.

141. A. Temple Patterson, *Radical Leicester: A History of Leicester, 1780–1850* (Leicester: Leicester University Press, 1954), 68–73. Cited by Schaffer, "Priestley and the Politics," 42.

142. Mathias, *Pursuits of Literature,* 333–34.

143. For more on the changing moral connotations of experimentalism in the 1780s, see Marie-Hélène Huet, *Mourning Glory: The Will of the French Revolution* (Philadelphia: University of Pennsylvania Press, 1997), 9–31.

144. Burke, *Reflections on the Revolution in France and on the Proceedings in Certain Societies in London Relative to that Event,* ed. Conor Cruise O'Brien (London: Penguin, 1968), 277.

145. The novel's pornographic character is unsurprising since its author, Jacques Antoine Réveroni Saint-Cyr, was a career army officer. On Réveroni's life and career, see Michel Delon, preface and chronology to *Pauliska ou la perversité moderne: Mémoires récents d'une Polonaise,* ed. Michel Delon (Paris: Editions Desjonquères, 1991), 7–24. All citations from *Pauliska* refer to this edition.

146. After two centuries of obscurity, three editions of *Pauliska* have been published recently: ed. Béatrice Didier (Paris: Desforges, 1976); ed. Delon; and ed. Antoine de Baecque (Paris: Rivages poche, 2001). See also Michel Foucault, "Un si cruel savoir," *Critique* 18, no. 182 (June 1962): 597–611, and Annie LeBrun, *Les Châteaux de la subversion* (Paris: J. J. Pauvert, 1982), 277–78.

147. On the conventions of the émigré novel, see Malcolm Cook, "The Emigré Novel," in *The French Emigrés in Europe and the Struggle against Revolution, 1789–1814,* ed. Kirsty Carpenter and Philip Mansel (London: Macmillan, 1999), 151–64.

148. "Puissent les tableaux qu'ils présentent arrêter ces torrents de maximes perverses, de systèmes absurdes qui . . . ébranlent aujourd'hui chez presque tous les peuples les fondements de la morale et de la société!" Réveroni, *Pauliska,* 29.

149. The connection to *La Nouvelle Héloïse* is even stronger when one compares the language and illustrations of the two scenes, which are practically identical; see Claude Labrosse, *Lire au XVIIIe siècle: La Nouvelle Héloïse et ses lecteurs* (Lyon: Presses Universitaires de Lyon, 1985), 55–59, 226. This scene of vampirish tendencies also presages the much gorier scene in *Juliette* in which Saint-Fond bites off his victim's skin and nipple and sucks her blood as a twisted form of foreplay to murder, exclaiming, "The executioner must fuck his victim . . . protocol demands it." Donatien-Alphonse-François, marquis de Sade, *Juliette,* trans. Austryn Wainhouse (New York: Grove Weidenfeld, 1968), 336.

150. "Dois-je convenir que cet état était presque délicieux"; "Je me trouvai alors dans un état d'ivresse dont le souvenir me couvre encore de rougeur. . . . Je balbutiai l'accent du désir et ne m'entendis plus." *Pauliska,* 60, 66.

151. Klossowski, "Nature as Destructive Principle," in Donatien-Alphonse-François, marquis de Sade, *The 120 Days of Sodom and Other Writings,* trans. Austryn Wainhouse and Richard Seaver (New York: Grove Weidenfeld, 1966), 71 (emphasis added).

152. Donatien-Alphonse-François, marquis de Sade, *The Complete Justine,* trans. Richard Seaver and Austryn Wainhouse (New York: Grove, 1965), 551–52. "Jamais, dit Rodin, l'anatomie ne sera à son dernier degré de perfection, que l'examen des vaisseaux ne soit fait sur un enfant de quatorze ou quinze ans, expiré d'une mort cruelle." Sade, *Justine ou les malheurs de la vertu* (Paris: Jean-Jacques Pauvert, 1955), 1:176.

153. Révéroni, *Pauliska,* 58; Sade, *Complete Justine,* 640–44; *Justine,* 2:150–55.

154. Sade, *Juliette,* 340. "[C]elui qui veut connaître toute la force, toute la magie des plaisirs de la lubricité, doit se bien convaincre que ce n'est qu'en recevant ou produisant sur le système nerval le plus grand ébranlement possible, qu'il réussira à se procurer une ivresse telle qu'il la faut pour jouir; car le plaisir n'est que le choc des atomes voluptueux, ou émanés d'objets voluptueux, embrasant les particules électriques qui circulent dans la concavité de nos nerfs; il faut donc, pour que le plaisir soit complet, que le choc soit le plus violent possible." Sade, *Histoire de Juliette,* in *Oeuvres* (Paris: Gallimard, 1998), 3:482. For more on this pseudoscientific subtext in Sade, see Jean Deprun, "Sade et la philosophie biologique de son temps," in *Le Marquis de Sade* (Paris: Librairie Armand Colin, 1968), 189–205; and David Morris, "The Marquis de Sade and the Discourses of Pain: Literature and Medicine at the Revolution," in *The Languages of Psyche: Mind and Body in Enlightenment Thought,* ed. G. S. Rousseau (Berkeley: University of California Press, 1990), 291–330.

155. Sade, *Juliette,* 1058. "Parce que la cruauté n'est, elle-même, qu'une des branches de la sensibilité, dis je." *Histoire de Juliette,* 3:1138–39.

156. "La liberté, comme un météore ardent, brille, circule, embrase toutes les nations . . . elle enfante des phénomènes brillants: bientôt elle produit mille éclairs, gronde, forme la foudre, et ne s'annonce sur la terre que par les commotions, les orages, et la destruction." Révéroni, *Pauliska,* 82.

157. M. Thébenien, "Personne n'est ce qu'il était en 1789, ou ce que, dans le bilan de sa vie, il s'attendait à être en 1796. . . . Nous sommes tous des ci-devant; les uns des ci-devant riches, les autres des ci-devant pauvres: les uns des ci-devant nobles, les autres des ci-devant roturiers. . . . La raison en est qu'actuellement nous sommes tous déplacés." Thébenien, review of *De la situation intérieure de la République,* cited in *Le Journal de Paris* (4 March 1797). Cited in Wagner, "Fête et dissolution sociale," 528.

158. See Sade, *Complete Justine,* 667–68; *Justine,* 2:196–97. Although exhausting, the wheel in *Justine* plays a relatively anodyne role, symbolizing the "dreadful chain gang" that imprisons a group of young women to the dastardly counterfeiter Roland (670). But a wheel also plays a role in some of Sade's more gruesome torture scenes, as in *Les 120 Journées de Sodome,* where a girl is strapped to a wheel, "qui tourne sans cesse en effleurant un cercle garni de lames de rasoir où la malheureuse s'égratine et se coupe en tous les sens à chaque tour, mais comme elle n'est qu'effleurée, elle tourne au moins deux heures avant que de mourir," *Les 120 Journées,* 519. See also *L'Histoire de Juliette,*

where there is a "une roue fatale" that operates in much the same way (*Juliette,* 3:505–6, and illustration 3:507).

159. "Cette expérience, qui est le comble de la folie, n'en est pas moins actuellement en vogue et a été transportée de Berlin à Paris." Réveroni, *Pauliska,* 187.

160. On the function of these so-called pleasure machines in Sade's works, see Lucienne Frappier-Mazur, *Writing the Orgy: Power and Parody in Sade* (Philadelphia: University of Pennsylvania Press, 1996), 30–32.

161. The "magnetico-electric bed" is featured, along with other titillating gadgets, in E. L. J. Toulotte, *Le Dominicain ou les crimes de l'intolérance et les effets du célibat religieux* (Paris: Pigoreau, 1803); the other machines are mentioned in Frappier-Mazur, *Writing the Orgy,* 29–32, 209. See also Henri Lafon, "Machines à plaisir dans le roman français du XVIIIe siècle," *Revue des sciences humaines* (1982).

162. For a historical view of eighteenth-century methods of creating light through electricity, see Heilbron, *Electricity,* 229–33, 281–84.

163. "Bientôt, ses yeux étincellent . . . ses membres se crispent, ses cheveux se dressent et soulevent sa perruque" [et il crie] 'je viens d'acquérir cinquante ans d'existence.'" Réveroni , *Pauliska,* 190.

164. This verbiage may not be quite so empty as it seems; as Paul Ilie notes, Juliette's hopes for "les macérations où je vais, pour expier mes crimes" offer a rather explicit suggestion of the heroine's "fantasy-laden concern with physical torment." Ilie, "Polymorphosis in Sade," *Symposium* 38, no. 1 (spring 1984): 3–12, esp. 5.

165. Sade, *120 Days of Sodom,* 209. Describing Curval's pleasure as blameworthy yet "very easily understood," Sade writes: "Par un raffinement de cruauté atroce, et pourtant bien aisé à comprendre, la classe de l'infortune était celle sur laquelle il aimait le plus à lancer les effets de sa perfide rage." *Les 120 Journées de Sodome précédé de 'La Machine en tête' par Bernard Noël* (Paris: La Collection P.O.L., 1992), 26.

166. Sade, *120 Days of Sodom,* 603, 604. "Il fout une chèvre en levrette pendant qu'on le fouette; il fait un enfant à cette chèvre, qu'il encule à son tour quoique ce soit un monstre." *Les 120 Journées,* 457.

167. Sade, *120 Days of Sodom,* 655. "Il lui fait dans le même jour l'opération de la pierre, du trépan, de la fistule à l'oeil, de celle à l'anus. On a bien soin de les manquer toutes, puis on l'abandonne ainsi sans secours jusqu'à la mort." *Les 120 Journées,* 507.

168. Critics of the 1790s interpreted *Justine*'s great success as a symptom of the degenerate age that saw its publication. According to an apocryphal story circulating among émigré writers of the 1790s, the leaders of the Terror were so fond of *Justine* that they would reread favorite passages when they were weary of their grisly tasks, and come away from Sade's novel with their revolutionary fervor restored. Charles de Villers, "Lettre sur le roman intitulé *Justine, ou les malheurs de la nature,*" *Le Spectateur du nord* 4 (1797): 407–14. Cited in Françoise de Laugaa-Trautt, *Lectures de Sade* (Paris: Armand Colin, 1973), 73–78.

169. For an excellent argument on *Juliette*'s political significance for Sade, who during the revolution "went through extraordinary personal vicissitudes" including constant death threats, imprisonment, and daily denunciations, see Frappier-Mazur, *Writing the Orgy,* 122–29.

170. Sade, *Juliette,* 774–75. "Tourmentez donc, anéantissez, détruisez, massacrez, brûlez, pulvérisez, fondez, variez enfin sous cent mille formes toutes les productions des

trois règnes, vous n'aurez jamais fait que les servir. . . . Comment osons-nous penser que la nature puisse imprimer dans nous des mouvements qui la contrarient? Ah! croyons qu'elle a bien su mettre à l'abri de nos coups, ce qui réellement pourrait la troubler et lui nuire. . . . Ne nous inquiétons nullement du reste: il est entièrement à notre disposition: tout ce qui se trouve à notre portée, nous appartient; troublons-le, détruisons-le, changeons-le, sans crainte de lui nuire." *Histoire de Juliette,* 3:878–79.

171. Such was the opinion of a contemporary reviewer, M. Laya, in *Les Veillées des Muses* 10 (1798), cited in Révéroni, *Pauliska,* 213–20. For more on Sade's allusions to freemasonry in *Juliette,* see Frappier-Mazur, *Writing the Orgy,* 52–57.

EPILOGUE

1. Roland Barthes, "Image, raison, déraison," in *Univers de l'Encyclopédie,* ed. Roland Barthes, Robert Mauzi, and Jean-Pierre Seguin (Paris: Les Libraires Associés, 1964), 15.

2. The tangled social, political, and scientific reasons why eighteenth-century audiences and scientists were so fascinated by monsters and took such pains to describe and explain their physical particularities are more complex than I can explain in this short epilogue. Along with the sources noted in this chapter, two recent books have made major contributions to the field. For more on the scientific and novelistic discourse on monsters in Diderot's work, see Andrew Curran, *Sublime Disorder: Physical Monstrosity in Diderot's Universe* (Oxford: Voltaire Foundation, 2001), in *Studies on Voltaire and the Eighteenth Century* 1 (2001). On the curiosity value of such creatures, consult Barbara M. Benedict, *Curiosity: A Cultural History of Early Modern Inquiry* (Chicago: University of Chicago Press, 2001).

3. Accounts written in 1818 of Mme Gobert, the "French Female Hercules," claimed that "[s]he has an infant which now sucks at her breast, about eleven months old, that lifts with very little exertion, a quarter of a hundred weight." Cited in Thomas Frost, *The Old Showmen and the Old London Fairs* (London: Chatto and Windus, 1881), 246. The "Windsor Fairy" was advertised in 1792 with a note stating: "The above Lady's mother is with her, and will attend at any Lady or Gentleman's house, if required." Cited in Frost, 205.

4. Dennis Todd, *Imagining Monsters: Miscreations of the Self in Eighteenth-Century England* (Chicago: University of Chicago Press, 1995), 157.

5. Authenticity was a real concern, since cases of trumped-up, man-made monsters were well-known in eighteenth-century France and Britain. Abbé Prévost writes of peasants deforming their young into sideshow attractions as a fairly common practice among the poor in the 1760s, and the success of the Princess Caraboo hoax in 1817 embarrassed even the most sophisticated viewers and demonstrated how easy it was to dupe the eye with the trappings of exoticism. Prévost's last novel, *Le Monde moral* (1760), recounts the experience of a peasant boy whose body was mutilated by his parents in the hopes of creating a profitable sideshow attraction. Prévost describes the parents as "à l'exemple de quantité d'autres misérables, que les lois ont laissés jusqu'à présent sans punition, avaient entrepris de se tirer de la pauvreté." Abbé Prévost, *Le Monde moral, ou mémoires pour servir à l'histoire du coeur humain* in *Oeuvres de Prévost,* ed. Robert Favre and Jean Sgard (Grenoble: Presses Universitaires de Grenoble, 1984), 6:302. Margaret Russet relates details of Princess Caraboo—a working-class Devonshire woman who

convinced the English gentry that she was a displaced Oriental princess—in "The 'Caraboo' Hoax: Romantic Woman as Mirror and Mirage," *Discourse* 17, no. 2 (winter 1994–95): 26–47.

6. On albino exhibits, see Robert M. Isherwood, *Farce and Fantasy: Popular Entertainment in Eighteenth-Century Paris* (New York: Oxford University Press, 1986), 233; and R. Blanchard, "Sur un cas inédit de négresse-pie au 18e siècle," *Zoologische Annalen* 1 (1901): 41–46.

7. M. Le Romain, "Nègres blancs (Hist. Nat.)," in *Encyclopédie,* ed. Denis Diderot et al. (Neuchâtel: Samuel Faulche, 1765), 11:79.

8. Georges Louis Leclerc, comte de Buffon, *Natural History, General and Particular, by the Count Buffon,* trans. William Smellie (London: T. Cadell and W. Davies, 1812), 3:422. "La nature aussi parfaite qu'elle peut l'être a fait les hommes blancs, et la nature altérée autant qu'il est possible les rend encore blancs; mais le blanc naturel, ou blanc de l'espèce, est fort différent du blanc individuel ou accidentel," Buffon, *De l'homme,* ed. Michèle Duchet (Paris: F. Maspero, 1971), 304.

9. P. L. Moreau de Maupertuis, *Vénus physique* in *Oeuvres* (Lyon, 1768; reprint, Hildesheim: Georg Olms Verlagsbuchhandlung, 1965), 2:115.

10. "[N]ous ne voyons que trop souvent . . . des races de louches, de boiteux, de goutteux, de phthisiques: et malheureusement il ne faut pas pour leur établissement une longue suite de générations. Mais la sage Nature, par le dégoût qu'elle a inspiré pour ces défauts, n'a pas voulu qu'ils se perpétuassent; chaque pere, chaque mere [*sic*] fait de son mieux pour les éteindre." Ibid., 2:111.

11. Buffon met Geneviève in April 1777 and gave her a thorough examination, which he transcribes in *L'Histoire naturelle.* He writes that her breasts are "grosses, rondes, très fermes, et bien placées" in *Oeuvres complètes de Buffon avec les Supplémens, augmentées de la classification de G. Cuvier, et accompagnées de 700 vignettes gravées sur acier, représentant au moins 900 animaux* (Paris: P. Duménil, 1836), 4:252. Further references appear in the text. Unfortunately, Smellie's translation does not mention either Marie Sabina or Geneviève, nor does it include their portraits.

12. George Edwards, *Gleanings of Natural History* (London: Printed for the Author, at the Royal College of Physicians, 1758), 1:5.

13. On the conventions of eighteenth-century botanical illustration, see Charlotte Klonk, *Science and the Perception of Nature: British Landscape Art in the Late Eighteenth and Early Nineteenth Centuries* (New Haven: Yale University Press, 1996), 49–52.

14. See, e.g., Charles Bonnet, who concludes his opus of natural history by declaring: "Tout ce que j'ai exposé dans cet Ouvrage sur la Génération des animaux s'applique naturellement à celle des Végétaux. Rien ne prouve mieux l'analogie de ces deux classes d'Etres organisés, que la belle découverte du *sexe* des Plantes." Charles Bonnet, *Oeuvres d'histoire naturelle et de philosophie* (Neuchâtel: Samuel Faulche,1779), 3:542–43.

15. It is unclear why Edwards included this image at the forefront of his book. The magnified view of the skin deformity recalls period medical texts, which routinely featured images of physical anomalies, effects of illness, and birth defects. But Edwards's text is not concerned with diagnosing or healing human defects, nor does the illustration serve a clinical function. Rather, this image was chosen for its decorative interest as a collector's item. Let us recall that Edwards was best known as author of a *Natural History of Birds* (1745–51) and as a highly esteemed bird painter. His watercolors were highly valued for their decorative value and were even reproduced on luxury products

produced by the Chelsea porcelain factory. Given this background, it seems most likely that Edwards chose the hand for its aesthetic interest and the family's celebrity value. For more on Edwards's career in art, see Lionel Lambourne and Jean Hamilton, *British Watercolours in the Victoria and Albert Museum. An Illustrated Summary of the National Collection* (London: Sotheby Parke Bernet, 1990), 120.

16. Oliver Goldsmith, *The Citizen of the World* (London: Dent. 1891), 1:124.

17. Like an animated statue, Shelley's creature retains few ideas from this time apart from a relentless hunger and thirst, saying: "It is with considerable difficulty that I remember the original aera of my being: all the events of that period appear confused and indistinct." Mary Shelley, *Frankenstein,* ed. J. Paul Hunter (New York: Norton, 1996), 68. All citations from *Frankenstein* are from this edition unless otherwise noted.

18. The creature's anguished laments to God-Frankenstein that run throughout this novel echo Milton's Adam, of course, but they also recall the pitiful plea of Marie-Angélique Leblanc in *Histoire d'une jeune fille sauvage* and other tales of wild men. Compare *Frankenstein*'s Miltonian epigraph, "Did I request thee, Maker, from my clay / To mould me man? Did I solicit thee / From darkness to promote me?" and the monster's many pleas, such as "Remember, that I am thy creature: I ought to be thy Adam" (*Frankenstein,* 3, 66), to the impassioned conclusion of the *Histoire:* "For what purpose . . . has God brought me from among wild beasts and made me a Christian? not surely, afterwards, to abandon, and suffer me to perish for hunger, that is impossible" (Hecquet, *The History of a Savage Girl, Caught Wild in the Woods of Champagne* (London: R. Dursley, T. Davidson, et al. [1760], 59–60). On *Frankenstein*'s similarity to other contemporary tales of wild men and its lasting impact on the British imaginary, consult Louis James's remarkable essay, "Frankenstein's Monster in Two Traditions," in *Frankenstein: Creation and Monstrosity,* ed. Stephen Bann (London: Reaktion, 1994), 77–94.

19. But as the critics Samuel Vasbinder and Sue Schopf have argued, Shelley's philosophy also borrows from the work of the English philosopher David Hartley. Like Hartley's scheme, the creature's development goes beyond sequential awakening to organize experience into distinct stages of moral development. His self-awareness replicates Hartley's categories by running from (1) sensations, (2) imagination, (3) ambition, (4) self-interest, (5) sympathy, and 6) theopathy to finally arrive at (7) the moral sense. Samuel Holmes Vasbinder, *Scientific Attitudes in Mary Shelley's Frankenstein* (Ann Arbor: University of Michigan Research Press, 1984), 40–41; and Sue Weaver Schopf, "'Of what a strange nature is knowledge!': Hartleian Psychology and the Creature's Arrested Moral Sense in Mary Shelley's *Frankenstein,*" *Romanticism Past and Present* 5 (1981): 33–52.

20. Whether Shelley took theoretical assumptions out of Rousseau's work by herself or with the help of her husband Percy, similarities abound. Huet argues that Percy alone read Rousseau and influenced the passages of *Frankenstein* that are in his wake; Marie Hélène Huet, *Monstrous Imagination* (Cambridge: Harvard University Press, 1993), 148–57. As Lawrence Lipking has commented, "with wretched literal-mindedness, *Frankenstein* tests each of Rousseau's first principles by fleshing them out and turning them into a story." Lipking, "*Frankenstein,* the True Story; or, Rousseau Judges Jean-Jacques," in Shelley, *Frankenstein,* ed. Hunter, 323. See also David Marshall's fine work documenting that ideas from Rousseau's other works (such as the *Discours sur l'inégalité* and the *Essai sur l'origine des langues*) were incorporated in Shelley's novel. Marshall,

The Surprising Effects of Sympathy: Marivaux, Diderot, Rousseau, and Mary Shelley (Chicago: University of Chicago Press, 1988), 178–227.

21. This was one of the criteria demanded by Bacon and Boyle; we see Frankenstein complying when he mentions: "I was encouraged to hope my present attempts would at least lay the foundations of future success," 31.

22. For the text of the 1831 additions and revisions, see Shelley, *Frankenstein or, the Modern Prometheus,* ed. James Rieger (Chicago: University of Chicago Press, 1974), 222–59. For an analysis of these changes, see Anne K. Mellor, *Mary Shelley: Her Life, Her Fiction, Her Monsters* (New York: Methuen, 1988), chap. 9, or Mary Poovey, *The Proper Lady and the Woman Writer: Ideology as Style in the Works of Mary Wollstonecraft, Mary Shelley, and Jane Austen* (Chicago: University of Chicago Press, 1984), 133–42.

23. Tim Marshall, *Murdering to Dissect: Grave-Robbing, Frankenstein, and the Anatomy Literature* (Manchester: Manchester University Press, 1995).

24. On Darwin's influence on the Shelleys, see Mellor, *Mary Shelley,* 95–103; and Carl Grabo, *A Newton among Poets* (Chapel Hill: University of North Carolina Press, 1930).

25. Golinski, "Humphry Davy and the Lever of Experiment," in *Experimental Inquiries: Historical, Philosophical, and Social Studies of Experimentation in Science,* ed. H. E. LeGrand (Dordrecht: Kluwer, 1990), 99–136. For more on Davy's influence on Shelley, see Mellor, *Mary Shelley,* 89–95.

26. Sir Humphry Davy, *The Collected Works of Sir Humphry Davy* (London: Smith, Edler, 1839–40), 2:319.

27. John Robison, introduction to Joseph Black, *Lectures on the Elements of Chemistry* (Edinburgh, 1803), vol. 1.

28. On Haller's reliance on vivisection, see Anne C. Vila, *Enlightenment and Pathology: Sensibility in the Literature and Medicine of Eighteenth-Century France* (Baltimore: Johns Hopkins University Press, 1998), 13–28.

29. Shelley, *Frankenstein,* ed. Hunter, 28; *Frankenstein,* ed. Rieger, 239.

30. Marilyn Butler, "*Frankenstein* and Radical Science," in Shelley, *Frankenstein,* ed. Hunter, 302–13.

31. William Lawrence, *Lectures on Comparative Anatomy, Physiology, Zoology, and the Natural History of Man,* 9th ed. (London: Bohn, 1848), 313–14.

32. Lawrence, cited in D. J. Cunningham, "Anniversary Address: Anthropology in the Eighteenth Century," *Journal of the Royal Anthropological Institute* 38 (1908): 30.

33. Judith Halberstam, *Skin Show: Gothic Horror and the Technology of Monsters* (Durham, N.C.: Duke University Press, 1995), 47.

34. See chap. 5 of Mikhail Bakhtin, *Rabelais and His World,* trans. Hélène Iswolsky (Cambridge: MIT Press, 1968).

35. Walter Stephens, *Giants in Those Days: Folklore, Ancient History, and Nationalism* (Lincoln: University of Nebraska Press, 1989), 32.

36. See Ronald Paulson, *Representations of Revolution, 1789–1820* (New Haven: Yale University Press, 1983); and Fred Botting, *Making Monstrous: Frankenstein, Criticism, Theory* (Manchester, U.K.: Manchester University Press, 1991).

37. See Marshall, *Surprising Effects of Sympathy,* for an analysis of the broader implications of sympathy—as a philosophical or anthropological concept—in *Frankenstein* and other texts of the period.

38. Teratology is the branch of biology dealing with monsters or malformations; it is

usually associated with the work of Etienne Geoffroy Saint-Hilaire and his son Isidore (who coined the term in 1830). See Huet, *Monstrous Imagination,* 108–23.

39. "L'augmentation extrême du volume de leurs organes semble user en eux les principes de la vie, et la plupart périssent comme épuisés, après avoir achevé leur énorme et rapide croissance." Isidore Geoffroy Saint-Hilaire, *Histoire générale et particulière des anomalies de l'organisation* (Paris: J-B. Baillière, 1832), 1:184–85.

40. Mellor, *Mary Shelley,* 101.

41. Edward J. Wood, *Giants and Dwarfs* (London: Richard Bentley, 1868), 152–56.

42. The story may have originated in advertisements for the Irish Giant, which conflated his excessive growth with his visit to Cloyne. Consider the report from the *Dublin Journal* (1752): "There is now in this city one Cornelius Magrath, a boy of 15 years 11 months old, of a most gigantick stature . . . he is grown to the monstrous size he is of within these twelve months. He was a month at the Bishop of Cloyn's who took great care of him." Cited in A. A. Luce, *The Life of George Berkeley, Bishop of Cloyne* (London: Thomas Nelson and Sons, 1949), 187.

43. Thomas Campbell, *Philosophical Survey of the South of Ireland in a Series of Letters to John Watkinson, M.D.* (Dublin: W. Whitestone et al., 1778), 187.

44. "L'expérience réussit complètement, j'entends pour le philosophe; car le pauvre Macgrath, déjà accablé au sortir de l'enfance de toutes les infirmités de la vieillesse, mourut à 20 ans, victime d'un essai que l'intention louable qui l'a dicté ne saurait faire pardonner entièrement à son auteur." Isidore Geoffroy Saint-Hilaire, *Histoire générale et particulière des anomalies,* 1:185.

45. "Hélas! oui, la science peut être impie! ainsi ces sublimes connaissances données à l'homme pour le bonheur de l'humanité, sont plus coupables que la plus coupable ignorance, quand elles peuvent inspirer à celui qui les possède la pensée de faire le malheur d'un seul individu, fût-ce même pour le bien de tous les autres." Michel Masson, *Les Enfants célèbres ou histoire des enfants de tous les siècles et de tous les pays qui se sont immortalisés par le malheur, la piété, le courage, le génie, le savoir, et les talents,* 6th ed. (Paris: Didier, 1859), 106.

46. "Ce temps horrible, qu'il faut considérer comme un phénomène monstrueux que rien de régulier n'explique ni ne produit." Germaine de Staël, cited in P. E. Charvet, *A Literary History of France,* vol. 4, *The Nineteenth Century, 1789–1870.* (London: Ernest Benn, 1967), 9.

INDEX

Page numbers in italics refer to illustrations.

CPSIA information can be obtained
at www.ICGtesting.com
Printed in the USA
LVHW081254120122
708413LV00020B/154

9 780226 160566